All Write

A Student Handbook for WRITING and LEARNING

Written and Compiled by

Dave Kemper, Patrick Sebranek, and Verne Meyer

Illustrated by

Chris Krenzke and Mary Ross

WRITE SOURCE®

GREAT SOURCE EDUCATION GROUP
a Houghton Mifflin Company
Wilmington, Massachusetts

Acknowledgements

We're grateful to many people who helped bring *All Write* to life. First, we must thank all the teachers and students from across the country who contributed writing models and ideas. Also, thanks to the following consultants who helped make this book a reality.

Anita Alcozer	Linda Gonzales	Judith O'Loughlin
Nancy Alexander	Noelle Jaddaoui	Patricia Payne
Jackie Basralian	Amy Kargauer	Carolyn Pompeo
Joan Burns	Raquel Mercado	Judith Ruhana
Lyda Enríquez	Kitty Okano	Evadney Smith

In addition, we want to thank our Write Source/Great Source team for all their help: Laura Bachman, Diane Barnhart, Colleen Belmont, Sherry Gordon, Lois Krenzke, Ellen Leitheusser, Mildred Pearson, Randy VanderMey, and Sandy Wagner.

Technology Connection for *All Write*

Visit our Web site for additional student models, writing prompts, multimedia reports, information about submitting your writing, and more.

The Write Source Web site. . . . . **<thewritesource.com>**

Using the Handbook

The *All Write* handbook contains a great deal of information that will help you improve your writing and learning skills. With practice, you will be able to find this information quickly and easily using the guides explained below.

The **Table of Contents** (starting on the next page) lists the five major sections in the handbook and the chapters found in each section. Use the table of contents when you're looking for a general topic.

The **Index** in the back of the handbook (starting on page 502) lists, in alphabetical order, all of the specific topics discussed in *All Write.* Use the index when you are looking for a specific piece of information.

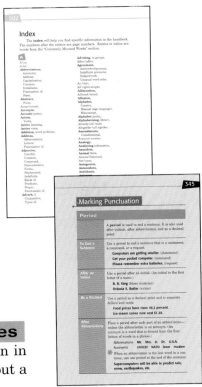

The **Color Coding** used for the *Proofreader's Guide* (the pages are yellow) makes this important section easy to find. These pages contain rules for spelling, grammar, punctuation, capitalization, and so on.

The **Special Page References** in the book itself tell you where to turn in the handbook for more information about a specific topic. Example:

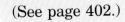

(See page 402.)

If, at first, you're not sure how to find something in the handbook, ask your teacher for help.

Table
of
Contents

The Process of Writing

The Forms of Writing

The Tools of Learning

Proofreader's Guide

Student Almanac

The Process of Writing

Meeting Your Language Needs 1

Learning About the Writing Process 2

All About Writing 3
One Writer's Process 11
Traits of Effective Writing 17
Writing with a Computer 23
Developing a Portfolio 27
Publishing Your Writing 31

Using the Writing Process 34

Choosing a Subject 35
Gathering Details 43
Writing and Revising 51
Group Advising 57
Editing and Proofreading 61

Basic Elements of Writing 64

Writing Basic Sentences 65
Combining Sentences 73
Writing Paragraphs 77
Writing Essays 89

The Art of Writing 104

Writing with Style 105
Writing Techniques and Terms 113

The Forms of Writing

Personal Writing — 124

Journal Writing — 125
Writing Personal Narratives — 129
Writing Friendly Letters — 137

Subject Writing — 142

Biographical Writing — 143
Writing About Literature — 149
Writing Explanations — 155
News Writing — 161

Creative Writing — 168

Writing Poems — 169
Story Writing — 179

Report Writing — 186

Writing Observation Reports — 187
Writing Summaries — 191
Writing Classroom Reports — 195

Workplace Writing — 208

Writing in the Workplace — 209
Writing Business Letters — 211
Writing E-Mail and Proposals — 217

The Tools of Learning

Searching to Learn   222

    Types of Information   223
    Using the Internet   227
    Using the Library   233

Thinking to Learn   242

    Thinking and Writing   243
    Thinking Clearly   251
    Thinking Creatively   257

Reading to Learn   260

    Study-Reading Skills   261
    Reading Symbols and Charts   277
    Improving Your Vocabulary   285
    Understanding Literature   301

Learning to Learn   306

    Viewing Skills   307
    Classroom Skills   313
    Group Skills   319
    Speaking and Listening Skills 323
    Taking Tests   331
    Planning Skills   339

Proofreader's Guide

Marking Punctuation — 345

Editing for Mechanics — 362

Capitalization — 362
Plurals — 367
Abbreviations — 369
Numbers — 371

Improving Your Spelling — 372

Commonly Misused Words — 379

Understanding Idioms — 395

Understanding Sentences — 402

Parts of a Sentence — 402
Types of Sentences — 406
Kinds of Sentences — 407

The Parts of Speech — 408

Nouns — 409
Pronouns — 413
Verbs — 417
Adjectives — 427
Adverbs — 430
Interjections — 431
Prepositions — 432
Conjunctions — 433

Student Almanac

Language 435

Manual Alphabet 435
Language Families 436
Manuscript Alphabet 438
Cursive Alphabet 439
Traffic Signs 440

Science 441

Animal Facts 441
Periodic Table of the Elements 442
The Metric System 443
American to Metric Table 444
Conversion Table 445
Our Solar System 446
Additional Units of Measure 448

Mathematics 449

Math Symbols and Tables 449
Word Problems 451
Math Terms 454

Computers 459

Computer Keyboard 460
Computer Terms 462

Geography 465

Using Maps 465
World Maps 467
Index to World Maps 477
World Time Zones 480

Government 481

Branches of Government 481
President's Cabinet 482
Individual Rights
and Responsibilities 483
U.S. Presidents and Vice Presidents 484
The U.S. Constitution 486

History 489

Historical Time Line 489

Credits 501

Index 502

Meeting Your Language Needs

Every student comes to school with different language skills. You may be an experienced learner in English while some of your classmates may be newer to the language. Then again, you may be somewhat new yourself.

The **All Write** student handbook will help you develop all of your writing and learning skills—whether you are an old pro with the language, or eager to become one. Once you get to know this handbook, it will become a very valuable school resource.

How Will *All Write* Help You

Writing Skills Writing is covered in a variety of ways, so you are sure to find the help you need. You will really like the writing samples written by students just like you.

Study-Reading Skills If you are having trouble understanding your textbooks, the reading strategies covered in your handbook will be sure to help.

Classroom Skills Taking notes, taking tests, working in groups, listening, organizing your time—all of these valuable skills are covered in *All Write*.

Editing and Language Skills The "Proofreader's Guide" gives you helpful rules for spelling, grammar, punctuation, capitalization, and sentences.

And That's Not All

If that's not enough, turn to "Student Almanac" in the back of the handbook. The tables, lists, and charts in this section cover everything from science to government. This information truly makes *All Write* an all-school handbook!

All Write will help you become a better student now and in the future. It is a guide to your own writing and learning.

Learning
About the
Writing
Process

All About Writing

One Writer's Process

Traits of Effective Writing

Writing with a Computer

Developing a Portfolio

Publishing Your Writing

All About Writing

Writing is one of the most important skills that you can develop as a student. It can help you in so many ways. For example, writing can help you become . . .

- **an active learner** (someone who really gets involved in his or her school work),
- **a clear thinker** (someone who knows how to make decisions or solve problems), and
- **a good communicator** (someone who knows how to express his or her ideas).

In fact, writing is so important that you need to learn many things about it. In addition, you need to write as often as you can. To become a good writer, you must practice!

What's Ahead

All of the chapters in "The Process of Writing" will help you learn about writing . . . and encourage you to write regularly. This chapter, for example, provides key background information and introduces you to the writing process.

- **How to Become a Good Writer**
- **The Steps in the Writing Process**
- **The Writing Process in Action**
- **A Basic Writing Guide**

How to Become a Good Writer

"Writing helps me think and understand better."
—Kevin Williams, student writer

Write Every Day Write in a journal, write letters, write stories, take notes, and so on. (Each of these forms is listed in the handbook index.) As you become better as a writer, you will begin to see how important it is to write every day.

  Practice is especially important if English is your second language.

Write About Important Things In a journal, write about your thoughts and memories. Also write about things you see, hear, or read. In your notebooks, write about the different subjects you are studying. (See page 318.) For writing assignments, try to write about subjects that really interest you.

Write Freely . . . and Write More Carefully In most cases, you should write as freely as you can in a journal or notebook, with little concern about making mistakes. The purpose of this type of writing is to explore your thoughts and feelings about different things that are important to you.

For writing assignments, however, you should work with more care. The purpose of this type of writing is to share information clearly and effectively. Be sure to follow the steps in the writing process for your assignments. (See the next page.)

Write to Learn Always try your best to learn something new when you write. For example, when you write in a journal, try to explore *all* of your thoughts and feelings about a subject.

And when you are working on a writing assignment, try to make your writing as interesting and informative as you can make it. If you approach writing in this way, you will begin to appreciate it as a powerful learning tool.

The Steps in the Writing Process

Experienced writers use the writing process to help them do their best work. (*Process* means "the steps or actions it takes to do something.") The steps in the writing process are described below.

PREWRITING At the start of the writing process, a writer chooses a subject to write about. A subject can be a person, a place, a thing, an event, a strong feeling, and so on. Next, a writer collects details about the subject and plans how to use these details in the writing.

WRITING A writer then does the actual writing, using the planning as a general guide. This writing is called the first draft.

REVISING After reviewing the writing, a writer will change any parts that are not clear and complete.

EDITING A writer then checks the revised writing for spelling, punctuation, and grammar errors and prepares a neat final copy for publication.

PUBLISHING This is the final step in the writing process. It simply means sharing a finished piece of writing. Forms of publishing for student writers include reading the work out loud, posting it in your class or on-line, submitting it to a school magazine, etc.

Points to Remember . . .

- **A writer may repeat some of the steps of the writing process.** For example, a writer may decide to gather more details about the subject after doing some of the writing.
- **Each writer works a little differently.** Some writers do a lot of their early work (prewriting) in their heads, while others need to put everything on paper. Some writers find it helps to talk about their writing in these early stages.
- **Even the best writers use the writing process.** It takes a lot of planning, writing, and rewriting to create good stories, essays, and reports.

The Writing Process in Action

"Writing and rewriting is a constant search for what one is trying to say."

—John Updike

These two pages provide a closer look at the writing process. Use this information as a general writing guide. *Remember:* The writing process will help you do your best writing.

PREWRITING Choosing a Subject

1. Think of possible subjects to write about. If you need help, use one of the selecting activities listed on pages 35-39 in this handbook. You could also study the list of writing ideas on page 40.

2. Choose a subject that really interests you, and make sure that it meets the requirements for your assignment.

Gathering Details

1. Collect details about your subject using one of the collecting activities listed on pages 43-48. If you already know a lot about your subject, you may not need to do much collecting.

2. You can also collect details by reading or talking about your subject.

3. Think of an interesting way to write about your subject.

4. Decide which details you will include in your writing. Also decide on the best method or way to organize these details. (See page 50 for help.)

WRITING Writing the First Draft

1. Complete the first copy of your writing. This copy is called the *first draft*. Don't worry about making mistakes. Just get all of your ideas on paper.

2. Use your collecting and planning as a general guide. Also feel free to add new ideas as you go along.

3. Keep going until you get all of your ideas on paper. (Remember that your writing should have a beginning, a middle, and an ending.)

REVISING Improving Your Writing

1. Read the first draft. Ask someone else to read it, too.

2. Decide which parts need to be revised or changed. For example, look for parts that seem confusing or out of order.

3. Improve your writing by rewriting, reordering, adding, or cutting different parts.

EDITING Checking for Errors

1. Check your revised writing for capitalization, punctuation, spelling, and grammar errors. (See pages 61-63 for help.)

2. Also ask someone else to check your writing for errors.

3. Prepare a neat final copy of your writing. Check it for any additional errors. This last check is called *proofreading*.

PUBLISHING Sharing Your Work

Share your writing with classmates, friends, and family.

A Basic Writing Guide

On the next three pages, you can find answers to seven very important questions about the writing process.

1. What should I write about

Repeat this line: *I will write about a subject that really interests or excites me.* Say it again. Let this point be your guide each time you start a new writing project. Writing about something that interests you can make all the difference! It's what writing is all about.

> **When you can't think of anything to write about, complete one of the selecting activities listed on pages 35-39.**

"I wrote about Selena's life because it was interesting, and she was my favorite singer."
—Lorena Ibaney, student writer

2. Do I have to gather a lot of details before I write

That depends on the type of writing you are doing. If you are writing about a personal experience (like your first day in a new school), most of the important facts and details will be very clear to you. So you may have to do very little collecting.

But let's say you are writing a classroom report about a specific medical career (veterinary medicine). You would have to gather a lot of information before you could begin writing about this subject.

You can start gathering details by talking to someone about your subject. You can also write down what you already know about it. Then you can go on from there, reading and trying other collecting activities.

> **See pages 43-48 for basic guidelines and strategies to help you gather details for your writing.**

3. Should I say everything I know about my subject ❓

No, you should think of a focus for your writing. A focus can be a special feeling that you have about a subject. It can also be one specific part of a subject that you really want to talk about. For example, in a story about a family member, you could focus on his or her *sense of honor* or *generosity*.

See page 49 for more information about finding a focus.

4. How should I write my first draft ❓

Write your first draft freely and honestly, almost as if you were telling it to someone you know very well. Do your best to be neat and clear; but it's okay to cross out a few words and add ideas in the margins.

Also, don't worry about saying too much or too little about your subject. A first draft is your first look at a writing idea; you will make changes later.

See pages 51-53 for more on writing first drafts.

5. How do I know what changes to make in my first draft ❓

You are the best judge of your own writing. If important details seem to be missing, add them. If a certain part doesn't sound right, change it. It is also necessary to have at least one or two other people review your work. They may catch some important things you didn't see.

When you make changes (revise), look first at the main ideas in your writing; make sure that they are clear and complete. After all of these ideas are in order, look at more specific things.

See pages 54-56 for more information about revising writing.

6. Do I have to find all of the spelling and grammar errors in my writing ?

Let's put it this way: No one expects you to be an expert speller or a master of all of the mechanics and grammar rules. But *everyone* expects you to correct as many errors as you can before you share or publish a piece of writing. Writing that contains a lot of errors is hard to read.

Find as many errors as you can on your own. Then ask a classmate or your teacher to check your work. All professional writers have editors who help them edit and proofread their work.

See pages 61-63 for more information on editing and proofreading.

7. How do I know if my writing is good ?

Here is a quick and simple way to evaluate your writing. If you can answer *yes* to at least three of these questions, you should feel good about your writing.

_____ *Did I select a subject that really interests me?*

_____ *Did I think of a special way to write about this subject (my focus)?*

_____ *Did I make changes in my writing until all of the ideas are clearly stated?*

_____ *Did I ask others to review my writing?*

See page 60 for a response checklist that will help you evaluate your writing.

One Writer's Process

It takes a lot of planning, writing, and revising to develop a good story or report. That is why it is so important to use the writing process to complete writing assignments. If you try to take any shortcuts, your writing will never turn out as good as it could be.

Writing is a lot like home building; certain steps must be followed during the construction. For example, collecting details helps you write first drafts. Revising first drafts helps make your writing clearer, and so on. Each new step adds to the strength of the whole structure.

What's Ahead

This chapter shows you how one student writer, Maria Ostrovskaya, used the writing process to develop one of her writing assignments. As you will see, she did a lot of planning, writing, and revising.

- **Prewriting: Choosing and Gathering**
- **Writing: Writing the First Draft**
- **Revising: Improving Your Writing**
- **Editing: Checking for Errors**
- **Publishing: Sharing Your Work**

PREWRITING Choosing a Subject

For her writing assignment, Maria was asked to introduce her family, including her parents, any brothers or sisters, and any other close relatives. To get started, she simply listed the people she would write about.

Mother's Side
Mother - Natalia Mouzitchkina
Grandmother - Henriatta Repinskaya
Grandfather - Vladimir Mouzitchkin
Great-Grandfather - Nicolus Repinsky

Father's Side
Father - Alexander Ostrovsky
Grandmother - Roxanne Monich

Gathering Details

Maria had to give the following types of information about her subjects: names, ages, jobs, hobbies, plus any other interesting facts. To gather this information, she asked her parents for help. She also made a collection sheet to keep her facts organized. Here is part of this sheet:

My Family	Natalia Mouzitchkina (mother)	Alexander Ostrovsky (father)	Henriatta Repinskaya (grandmother)
Date of Birth	Feb. 27, 1960	Aug. 14, 1957	Nov. 6, 1937
Job	artist	surgeon, sells medicine and medical equipment	journalist, works for radio

WRITING Writing the First Draft

After Maria collected enough information, she freely wrote her first draft. (She knew she could make changes later on.) Maria decided to tell about her family in the following order: her parents, her grandparents on her mother's side, and then her grandparent on her father's side. Here is the beginning part of her first draft.

In the opening paragraph, the writer introduces her subject.

I am lucky to have such a wonderful family. They have always treat me like a special person. Now that I live in United States I dont get to see most of them. I live across the world from them. Writing about my family is good. It keeps my family close to my heart.

She continues by giving details about each family member.

I will start by telling about my mother. Her name is Natalia Mouzitchkina. She was born in the year of 1960. Her berthday is on February 27. She is an artist. My mother loves to sing and have a very good voise. Her hobbies are to go on trips and to bake foods on fire. She is a very understanding mom. She is the best person in the whole world!

REVISING Improving Your Writing

Next, Maria carefully reviewed her first draft. She also read her first draft out loud to a partner. The partner's questions and comments helped Maria decide what to change.

The writer adds an article (the), crosses out unnecessary words, and combines two sentences.

I am lucky to have such a wonderful family. They have always treat me like a special person. Now that I live in the United States I dont get to see most of them. ~~I live across the world from them.~~ Writing about my family ~~is good. It~~ keeps ~~my family~~ them close to my heart.

I will start by telling about my mother. Her name is Natalia Mouzitchkina. She was born in ~~the year of~~ 1960 in Moscow, Russia. Her berthday is on February

The writer changes two sentences and adds an interesting detail.

27. She is an artist. ~~My mother loves to sing and have a very good voise.~~ In her childhood, she sang in some school operas. Her hobbies are to go on trips and to bake ~~foods on~~ food over a fire. She is a very understanding mom. She is the best person in the whole world!

EDITING Checking for Errors

Finally, Maria checked her revised writing for errors. She had another person check it as well. Then she corrected the errors and made a final copy. (She will also proofread her final draft before handing it in.)

The writer corrects a verb-tense error and adds two punctuation marks.

I am lucky to have such a wonderful family. They have always ~~treat~~ _treated_ me like a special person. Now that I live in the United States, I don't get to see most of them. Writing about my family keeps them close to my heart.

I will start by telling about my moher. Her name is Natalia Mouzitchkina. She was born in 1960 in Moscow, Russia. Her ~~berthday~~ _birthday_ is on

Spelling and subject-verb agreement errors are corrected.

February 27. She is an artist. My mother loves to sing and ~~have~~ _has_ a very good ~~voise~~ _voice_. In her childhood, she sang in some school operas. Her hobbies are to go on trips and to bake food over a fire. She is a very understanding mom.

"My mother" is substituted to avoid repeating "she."

~~She~~ _My mother_ is the best person in the whole world!

PUBLISHING Sharing Your Work

Maria produced a neat final copy of her essay to share with her classmates and teachers. She made sure that this copy was as clean and correct as she could make it. (See pages 24-25 for designing tips for final copies.) Here is a portion of Maria's first page.

Maria Ostrovskaya
Ms. Southwell
History
September 25, 2002

From Russia with Love

I am lucky to have such a wonderful family. They have always treated me like a special person. Now that I live in the United States, I don't get to see most of them. Writing about my family keeps them close to my heart.

Points to Remember . . .

Do the necessary prewriting. Maria knew a lot about her subject before she started writing. It helped her to organize her facts in lists before she began writing. Careful prewriting makes the rest of the writing process go more smoothly.

Write with confidence. After listing her facts, Maria was able to write her first draft freely and naturally.

Expect to make changes. Maria knew she would have to make changes to make her writing as clear and complete as possible. Remember: No writer, not even a professional author, ever gets it right the first time.

Traits of Effective Writing

Musical conductors know what it takes to present a powerful symphony. They need talented musicians, a well-crafted musical score, and everyone playing together. It's the same with good writers. They know that an effective piece of writing requires interesting ideas, clear organization, well-chosen words, and so on. Learning about these traits of effective writing—and using them—will help you become a better writer.

Practicing often is the other key to becoming a better writer. Just as musicians practice their skills to perform well, you must practice applying the traits of effective writing to produce your best work.

What's Ahead

The next page in this chapter discusses six traits of effective writing. Writing samples that demonstrate the traits in action will help you understand each trait and begin to use it in your own writing.

- **Traits of Effective Writing**
- **Writing Traits in Action**
- **Checklist for Effective Writing**

Traits of Effective Writing

There are six main traits found in the best essays, stories, and reports. If you write with these traits in mind, you and your readers will be happy with the results.

Stimulating Ideas Good writing is interesting; it holds a reader's attention from start to finish. Writing that contains good ideas shows that a writer knows a lot about his or her subject.

Logical Organization Good writing is well organized. It has a clearly developed beginning, middle, and ending, and each main point is carefully explained with examples and details. In short, good writing is easy to follow.

Engaging Voice In the best writing, you can hear the writer's voice. Voice is the special way a writer expresses ideas and feelings; it reveals the writer's personality. A strong personal voice shows that a writer really cares about his or her work.

Original Word Choice Good writing contains the best words. It includes vivid verbs (*slither, tiptoe, sneak*), specific nouns (*mansion, avocado, convertible*), and colorful modifiers (*awkward, brilliant, hair-raising*).

Effective Sentence Style Effective writing flows smoothly from sentence to sentence. Smooth sentences make writing enjoyable to read. Writers often vary sentence beginnings and lengths to give their writing a pleasing rhythm.

Correct, Accurate Copy Good writing follows the basic standards of punctuation, mechanics, usage, and spelling. It is edited with care to be sure that it is accurate and easy to follow.

Writing Traits in Action

On the next three pages, a writing sample is provided for each of the six traits. Each sample is an example of effective writing.

Stimulating Ideas

In the following passage from "Half-Cuban" by Monique Rubio, the writer shares an interesting story about "being Spanish."

Sometimes it is even a lot of fun being Spanish because I am very fair skinned, so I look American ("white" as Spanish people sometimes say). One incident occurred when I was in a store, and the cashier was talking to her friend in Spanish and saying things like "look at that 'white girl,' she looks like such a snob, I don't like the way she looks." I understood them clearly, but I didn't say anything until I paid for my groceries. Then I said, "Thank you, have a nice day" in Spanish. The two girls looked at each other in shock and turned burning red with embarrassment. After I left the store, I could not stop laughing.

✳ First Rubio sets the scene by describing her appearance. Then she goes on to describe an encounter at a store.

Logical Organization

In this passage from *A Crossing*, Brian Newhouse describes his father, a hard-working farmer, recovering from a heart attack.

By summer he was taking nice slow walks to the bean field; he'd stand there a minute, surveying, then wade into the waist-deep green until he found a stalk of volunteer corn, which he'd gently pull and heave over a couple rows. By fall, he was chopping wood for the stove. Winter found him on the exercise bike with a mason's brick in each hand; he pedaled them in the air in time with his feet. "He is one tough Norwegian," the neighbors said, to which my siblings and I could only add the cliche, "He'll outlive us all." The thing is, we are reasonably sure he will.

✳ Newhouse describes the father's recovery by organizing the passage chronologically (by time)—summer, fall, and winter.

Engaging Voice

In the following sample from *Anne Frank and me*, Nicole Burns (Girl X) describes when French authorities took her family's piano.

And now, for some excitement. On Day Six of our punishment, two representatives of the CGQJ paid us a visit. We were reminded that under the law of 22 July 1941, French authorities are permitted to seize Jewish property and sell it for the "benefit of France." In other words, legalized stealing. Four workmen came and took away our piano.

Dear reader, if you purchase a grand piano and find a small brass plaque on the inside etched with a Jewish name, then you, too, are a thief. Think of Girl X when you play your stolen piano. By the way, her favorite piece is "Für Elise."

✳ Notice how Burns' personality comes through in her writing voice. Ideas like "And now, for some excitement," "Dear reader," and "Think of Girl X . . . " reveal her intelligence and humor in the middle of a very difficult situation.

Original Word Choice

In the following sample from "One Last Time" in *Living Up the Street* by Gary Soto, the author describes his experiences working in the grape fields to earn money for school clothes.

I cut another bunch, then another, fighting the snap and whip of vines. After ten minutes of groping for grapes, my first pan brimmed with bunches. I poured them on the paper tray, which was bordered by a wooden frame that kept the grapes from rolling off, and they spilled like jewels from a pirate's chest. The tray was only half-filled, so I hurried to jump under the vines and begin groping, cutting and tugging at grapes again. I emptied the pan, raked the grapes with my hands to make them look like they filled the tray, and jumped back under the vine on my knees.

✳ See how Soto uses specific verbs—"brimmed," "poured," "raked," and so on. Also note the effective expressions, such as "fighting the snap and whip of vines," and the colorful simile: "and they spilled like jewels from a pirate's chest."

Effective Sentence Style

In *My Dog Skip,* Willie Morris honors his loyal pet. In this particular sample, the writer describes Skip's first night in the Morris household.

I led him into the house and gave him some puppy food in a dish. Then I followed him as he gingerly explored every room in the house. That night he jumped into my bed and stared at me, as if he were looking me over. Then, perhaps because he missed his mother in Missouri, he went to sleep in my arms. I was an only child, and he now was an only dog.

This was the first of our many days and years together. We named him Skipper for the lively way he walked, but he was always just Skip to me.

* Notice how smoothly this passage reads from sentence to sentence. This shows that the writer paid careful attention to the sound, length, and flow of each idea. Morris is very skilled at combining ideas, a key stylistic feature in effective writing.

Correct, Accurate Copy

The sample below comes from *Wilma,* the autobiography of track star Wilma Rudolph. In this passage, Rudolph describes one of her first experiences with defeat. As you will see, she uses punctuation to control the flow of her ideas.

I did think I could wipe them out because, after all, I had won every single race I had ever been in up to that point. So what happens? I got wiped out. It was the absolute worst experience of my life. I did not win a single race I ran in, nor did I qualify for anything. I was totally crushed. The girls from Georgia won everything. It was the first time I had ever tasted defeat in track, and it left me a total wreck.

* See how the well-placed commas and periods draw the reader's attention to each and every detail. Correct punctuation creates an effective pace or flow in the passage, making it clear and easy to read.

Checklist for Effective Writing

How can you tell if something you read or write includes the traits of effective writing? You can use the following checklist.

✔ Stimulating Ideas

The writing . . .

____ presents important and interesting information.

____ has a clear focus or purpose.

____ holds the reader's attention.

✔ Logical Organization

____ includes a clear beginning, middle, and ending.

____ uses specific details to support main ideas.

✔ Engaging Voice

____ shows enthusiasm for the topic.

____ speaks in a pleasing and sincere way.

✔ Original Word Choice

____ contains specific and colorful words.

____ uses a level of language that the audience can relate to.

✔ Effective Sentence Style

____ flows smoothly from sentence to sentence.

____ uses varied sentence beginnings and lengths.

✔ Correct, Accurate Copy

____ follows the basic rules of grammar, punctuation, and spelling.

Writing with a Computer

Today, students still take notes on paper and store their work in notebooks and folders. However, more and more students are doing their writing on laptops and personal computers. Once you know how to keyboard, it's often easier to write a first draft on a computer than by hand.

Computers make it easier to improve or revise your writing, too. For example, you can rearrange or add ideas right on the screen. Then you can print out a clean copy to make another round of revisions. A computer makes editing simple because it allows you to change words or sentences quickly. When everything has been checked for accuracy and correctness, you can print out a final copy for each of your readers.

What's Ahead

This chapter contains tips for those of you just starting to write with computers. It also offers guidelines for experienced users, including a section on graphic design.

- **Designing Your Writing**
- **Elements of Design in Action**
- **Computer Tips**

Designing Your Writing

Good page design makes your writing clear and easy to follow. Remember to focus on content first and then follow the tips below for creating clear, attractive essays, reports, and research papers.

Typography

- **Use an easy-to-read serif font.** (*Serif* type, like this, has tails at the tops and bottoms of the letters.) For most kinds of writing, use a 10- or 12-point type size.

- **Keep titles and headings short.** Follow the rules for capitalizing titles and headings. Write all headings in the same style; for example, use all *-ing* words, short phrases, or so on.

- **Consider using a sans serif font for the title and headings.** (*Sans serif* type, like this, does not have tails.) Use larger type, perhaps 18-point, for your title and 14-point type for any headings. (Use **boldface** for headings if they seem to get lost on the page.) By varying the size and style of your type, you help your readers follow your writing. Avoid fancy, hard-to-read typefaces.

Spacing and Margins

- **Keep one-inch margins on all four sides of each page.**

- **Indent the first line of each paragraph.** Set the tabs at five spaces.

- **Leave only one space after a period** for easier reading.

- **Avoid placing headings, hyphenated words, and new paragraphs** at the bottom of a page. Also avoid *widows* (single words, or a partial word at the bottom of a page or column) and *orphans* (single words or a partial word at the top of a page).

Graphic Devices

- **Create bulleted lists.** Most computer programs allow you to do this quite easily. (See page 25.) Be careful, though, not to use too many lists in your writing.

- **Include charts or other graphics** to add visual appeal. They should not be too small or too large. (You can also put graphics on a separate sheet.)

Elements of Design in Action

These sample pages from a research report highlight several design elements.

Kendall McGinn
Mr. Gilding
Social Studies
Feb. 25, 2002

The title is 18-point sans serif type.

The Return of the Buffalo

At one point in the early twentieth century, it seemed that the American buffalo would continue to exist only in pictures or on the buffalo nickel. Its population of 100 million in 1700 had been reduced to 1,000 by 1889. In recent years, that number has increased to nearly 400,000 (Hodgson 71). The buffalo, once endangered, has returned.

The main text is 12-point serif type.

Before the Europeans came to North America, the native people of the North American plains and the buffalo were one *Pte Oyate*, or Buffalo Nation. The big bull *tantanka* was life itself. These Native Americans followed the herds and used the buffalo for food, clothing, shelter, religious ceremonies, and medicine. A Lakota leader summed up this unity between human and animal: "When the Creator made the buffalo, he put power in them. When you eat the meat, that power goes into you, heals the body and spirit" (qtd. in Hodgson 69).

This heading is 14-point sans serif.

Open Season on Buffalo

During the expansion of occurred, and the European
By the year 1800, it was rep

McGinn 5

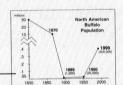

millions
30
20
10
.4
.3
.2
.1
.05

North American Buffalo Population

1870

1999 (400,000)

1889 (1,000)
1950 (25,000)

1800 1850 1900 1950 2000

A graphic adds visual appeal.

The buffalo is "returning" to North America in ever-increasing numbers. Cable Network News owner Ted Turner and actress Jane Fonda raise almost 10,000 buffalo on their Montana and New Mexico ranches. "I guess I've gone buffalo batty," Turner says. Both he and Fonda support the raising of buffalo as an excellent source of low-fat meat and as a way to help save this once endangered species (Hodgson 75).

Buffalo ranchers are, in fact, learning that raising buffalo has many benefits. Raising buffalo is more cost-effective and more environmentally safe than raising cattle. Here are four main benefits:

A bulleted list is used.

- Buffalo don't overeat.
- Their sharp hooves loosen hard soil.
- Buffalo improve grass crops.
- They adapt to any climate.

Buffalo living in Florida seem just as happy as those living in Alaska. In Hawaii, they even survived a hurricane. Hawaiian rancher Bill Mowry recalls how the buffalo "loved every minute of it."

Computer Tips

Learn the language of computers.

When you use computers, you use a whole new vocabulary. The more terms you know, the easier it will be to learn about and use computers. See the list of computer terms beginning on page 462.

Discover your own computer style.

Some writers like to do all their writing on a computer, from first draft to final proofreading. Others like to do a rough draft on the computer and print it out double-spaced. Then they make changes by hand, before keyboarding their revisions. Still others write their first drafts by hand and use the computer for revising. Experiment to find out how the computer works best for you.

Save your work often.

When you use a computer, remember to save your work. Saving your work often will help you avoid losing any of it. Work that you don't save will be lost when the program or the computer shuts down.

Make backup copies of your work.

Even work that has been saved can be destroyed if something happens to the computer. So always save your work onto a backup disk and print out a copy of it.

Proofread your final hard copy.

When you use a computer, you can't trust your spelling to a spell checker. For one thing, a spell checker can't tell if you used the wrong word. You may, for example, have written "it," when you really meant to write "hit." Always do a complete, careful proofreading of your work.

Developing a Portfolio

How can you judge your progress as a writer? The best way is to put together a writing portfolio. A portfolio usually is a collection of your writing completed at different times during the year. With a portfolio, you can compare different pieces to see what kind of improvements you have made.

Your portfolio may include writing that you like very much or writing that simply took a lot of effort to complete. Your teacher may also tell you what types of writing to include. But finally, the choices will be your decision, because you know your writing better than anyone else.

What's Ahead

This chapter will help you better understand how to develop a writing portfolio. It includes helpful explanations, guidelines, and several sample portfolio reflections by different students and professional writers.

- **Types of Portfolios**
- **Planning Your Portfolio**
- **Sample Portfolio Reflections**

Types of Portfolios

There are three types of portfolios you should know about. A personal portfolio contains writing that you like to do on your own: poems, stories, plays, songs, and so on. Showcase or growth portfolios contain writing assigned in school. Portfolios help students . . .

- **preserve** important thoughts, feelings, and experiences,
- **show** their growth as writers,
- **display** important pieces of work,
- **showcase** the whole range of their writing skills, and
- **reflect** upon their own process of becoming writers.

Personal Portfolio

Many professional people, including writers, artists, and designers, keep portfolios. A portfolio, in a way, speaks for the person. It says, "This is who I am; this is what I can do." Keeping a personal portfolio is a way of saving writing that is important to you, writing you want to keep and share with others.

Showcase Portfolio

A showcase portfolio is often presented for evaluation at the end of a grading period. It might include different kinds of writing: a story, a poem, an expository essay, a summary, a research paper. It might show specific skills: planning, organizing, revising, editing, researching, and so on. This portfolio is meant to show your best writing.

Growth Portfolio

A growth portfolio shows the way in which you are changing and growing as a writer. It might include examples of writing done throughout the year (from September to May). Comparing the examples will show you how your skills are developing: writing beginnings and endings, supporting thesis statements, choosing vivid words, writing dialogue, and so on.

Planning Your Portfolio

Putting together an effective portfolio takes time and effort. The following planning ideas should help you.

1 Collect

Whenever you write something, date it and keep it in your general writing folder. When it is time to make decisions about which pieces to place in your portfolio, it will be easy to find and review all your work.

※ Never throw out any of the drafts for a piece of writing that you might want to include in your portfolio.

2 Select

You may want to review your writing when you have three to five finished pieces. As you look at the pieces, try to recall the feelings you had as you wrote each one. *Which one was the hardest? The most satisfying? The one you are most proud of?*

3 Reflect

A collection of writing becomes meaningful when you take time to think and write about each piece. (See page 30.) You may answer questions like these:

- Why did I choose this piece for my portfolio?
- What special problems did I face in this writing?
- What will I do differently next time?
- What have I learned that will make me a better writer?

4 Project

Use your reflections and what you have learned to set personal goals. Try writing them down: *I will write stronger beginnings. I will learn to use commas better. I will try to let my natural speaking voice come through in my writing.* Writing down your goals will help you realize when you've reached them!

Sample Portfolio Reflections

Whenever you reflect on your writing, you come to a better understanding of your progress as a writer. The following reflections will show you some of the things writers think about.

Student Reflections

If I had to write another comparison essay, I think I would do a lot more planning, and I would read some examples that other people wrote. I also would ask someone who had experience with this type of essay to read my writing. I would do a lot of research ahead of time, and of course, I would follow the rubric!

—Yumo Chi

Usually when I write an essay, I have to do a lot of planning and research. However, for my essay on 9/11/01, I just expressed my true feelings in a sincere way. What I learned from writing this essay is that the words and ideas come easy if you have strong feelings about your subject. My essay is a good example of this.

—Silviu Strain

Professional Reflections

When I was writing *Fables,* I was very confused, and no matter how much I wanted to, I couldn't come to any conclusions about my life. That book turned out to be very ordered, and every story had a moral.

—Author and Illustrator Arnold Lobel

The idea for *Homecoming* began when I went to the supermarket one day and had a stray thought. I parked in the parking lot, and, as I was walking down to the supermarket I saw some kids waiting in a car. As I walked through the door the thought struck me: "What if nobody comes back for those kids?"

—Novelist Cynthia Voigt

Publishing Your Writing

One student writer gives this advice about writing: "Make sure YOU like it, because that's what matters." Yes, you are your most important audience. After all, your writing contains your very own thoughts and feelings, so you should feel good about it. You should also be your most demanding audience, making sure that every piece of writing you complete reflects your best efforts.

Your writing is ready for publication once it says exactly what you want it to say—from beginning to end. It must also be as close to error-free as you can make it. Publishing may take many forms: sharing a personal narrative with classmates, putting a story on the bulletin board, placing an article in the school paper, or posting an essay on a Web site.

What's Ahead

This chapter will help you get your writing ready to publish and give you a variety of publishing ideas.

- **Getting Your Writing Ready**
- **Publishing Ideas**

Getting Your Writing Ready

Publishing is the final step in the writing process—sharing your work so that readers can enjoy it. The following tips will help you prepare your writing for this final step.

Work with your writing until you feel good about it from start to finish. If any part (ideas, organization, voice) is not quite right, your writing is not ready to publish.

Ask for feedback from other people throughout the writing process. Answer any questions these readers may have about your ideas. (See pages 57-60.)

Save all your drafts to help you remember the process you went through to write each paper. This will help you if you are asked to write about your work for your portfolio. (See pages 27-30.)

Check for correctness by having someone read your work for language, punctuation, spelling, and other usage or grammar errors. (See page 62.)

Prepare a neat final copy in black or blue pen (on one side of the paper) or on a computer. Avoid fancy, hard-to-read typefaces and keep your margins the same. (See pages 24-25.)

"Once you know what the story is and get it right—as right as you can, anyway—it belongs to anyone who wants to read it."

—Stephen King

Find creative outlets for your writing. There are many different ways to publish your work. (See the next page.)

Follow the publication guidelines if you send your writing out. Newspapers, magazines, and Web sites have special requirements. (See the "Publish It!" page at **<thewritesource.com>**.)

Publishing Ideas

Publishing may be as simple as sharing your essay or story with your classmates, as challenging as entering a local or national writing contest, or as up-to-date as posting your work on the Internet. Explore a number of publishing opportunities, and have fun growing as a writer.

Performing
Sharing with Classmates
Reading to New Audiences
Recording for a Class Project
Performing on Stage

In School
School Newspaper
Literary Magazine
Writing Portfolios
School Handbook

Self-Publishing
Family Newsletters
Greeting Cards
Binding Your Writing
Personal Web Site

Posting
Bulletin Boards
School or Public Library
Hallway Display Cases
Clinic Waiting Rooms
Business Windows

Sending It Out
Local Newspapers
Church Publications
Magazines and Contests
Writers' Conferences

On-Line Options
School Web Sites
Topical Web Sites

Using the Writing Process

Choosing a Subject

Gathering Details

Writing and Revising

Group Advising

Editing and Proofreading

Choosing a Subject

Each writing assignment presents different problems. For one assignment, you may have trouble thinking of a subject. For another assignment, you may not know how to start your writing. For still another one, you may not be sure which changes you should make to improve a first draft.

When you get stuck at any point in the writing process, discuss your problem with a teacher, an aide, or a classmate. Sometimes talking about a writing problem is the best way to solve it. Also make sure to check your handbook for help. This chapter, for example, will be helpful during prewriting when you need to **select a subject.**

What's Ahead

The first part of this chapter provides strategies for selecting subjects. (*Strategies* are activities that help you do something.) The second part shows you how to collect possible writing ideas. And the third part lists different starting points for writing, including sample subjects and writing prompts.

- **Selecting Strategies**
- **Building a File of Writing Ideas**
- **Starting Points for Writing**
- **Forms of Writing**

Selecting Strategies

Many writing assignments are related to a general subject area you are studying. If you were asked to write about "family customs," a general social studies subject, your job would be to select a specific part of that subject to write about.

The two examples below show the difference between a general subject area and a specific subject for writing.

General Subject Area: **Energy**
Specific Writing Subject: **Using Wind Power**

General Subject Area: **Family Customs**
Specific Writing Subject: **Kwanzaa Celebrations**

On these two pages you will find four different strategies to help you select a specific subject for writing.

Clustering

A cluster, or web, begins with a nucleus word. (*Nucleus* means "in the center or middle.") Use the general subject as the nucleus word. Then cluster related words around it, as you see in the model below. Afterward, pick out an idea that you have strong feelings about. This idea may be the writing subject you're looking for.

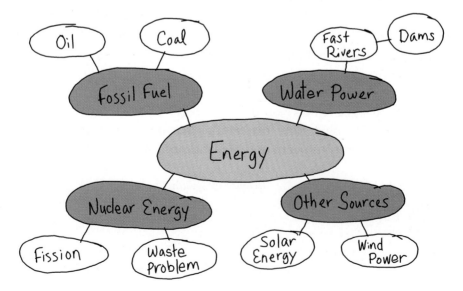

Freewriting

Write quickly for 3 to 5 minutes. Do not stop and think during this time; just write. Begin writing with your general subject in mind: *My family follows many customs.* As you write, you may discover one or two specific subjects that you could use.

Listing

List ideas as they come to mind when you think about your assignment. Keep your list going as long as you can. When you are finished, look for words in your list that you feel would make good writing subjects.

Using the Basics of Life Checklist

The words in this checklist name the categories or groups of things that we need to live a full life.

acceptance	faith	money
agriculture	family	music
animals	food	nationality
art	freedom	neighborhood
books	friends	natural resources
choices	health/medicine	plants
clothing	housing	rules
community	justice	safety
culture	language	science/technology
education	laws	tools
energy	lifestyle	trade/money
environment	love	values
exercise	machines	work/play

Here's how this checklist can help you think of writing subjects:

- Choose one of the categories: **health/medicine.**
- Decide how it relates to your assignment: **Write about tattoos.**
- List possible subjects: **learning about the harmful or negative effects of tattooing, the legal aspects of tattooing, removal of tattoos.**

Building a File of Writing Ideas

"I have a lot of good ideas; this makes writing fun for me."

—Sonia Cadena, student writer

Experienced writers are always collecting writing ideas. You can, too, by following the guidelines listed on these two pages.

Find Writing Ideas Look and listen for interesting sights and sounds. On the way to school, you might see a man in a business suit in-line skating down the street. In the school cafeteria, you might hear someone talk about a fire in his or her apartment. Write down these everyday happenings in a notebook that you carry with you always. These notes can lead to good ideas for stories or reports.

List Experiences Start a personal record or listing of all of the different people, places, and events in your life. Keep adding to the list during the school year. Organize your personal record using the categories or groupings listed below.

- **People I'll Never Forget**
- **Favorite Books, Movies, Music**
- **Best Skills and Talents**
- **Areas of Interest**
- **Important News Events**

- **Great Accomplishments**
- **Biggest Mistakes**
- **Important Beliefs**
- **Dreams and Wishes**
- **Things to Change**
- **Relationships**

Write in a Personal Journal Write about your personal experiences, thoughts, and feelings in a journal. You may want to do this instead of simply listing experiences. (See pages 125-128 for more about journal writing.)

Read Like a Writer Read books, magazines, newspapers, and whatever else you like. Write down interesting names, descriptions, and details. These notes may give you ideas for your own writing.

Draw a Life Map At different points on your map, draw pictures that represent important events in your life. Add numbers or dates to indicate your age or the year. Start with your birth and work right up to the present. Making your map will help you remember many things to write about. Maria Ostrovskaya created the life map below.

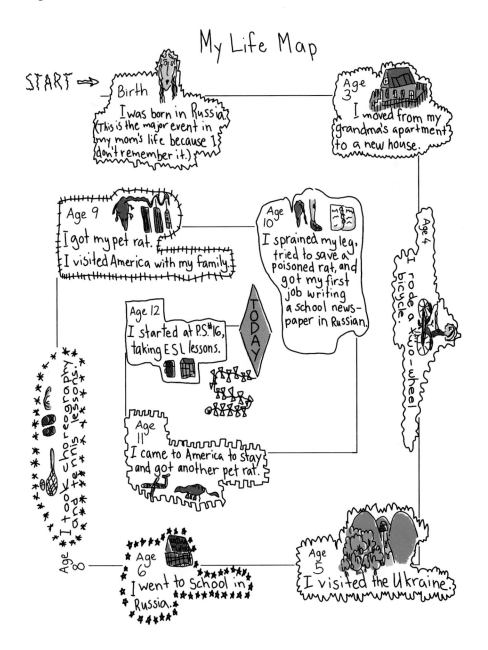

My Life Map

START ⇒

Birth
I was born in Russia.
(This is the major event in my mom's life because I don't remember it.)

Age 3
I moved from my grandma's apartment to a new house.

Age 9
I got my pet rat.
I visited America with my family.

Age 10
I sprained my leg, tried to save a poisoned rat, and got my first job writing a school newspaper in Russian.

Age 12
I started at P.S. #16, taking ESL lessons.

TODAY

Age 4
I rode a two-wheel bicycle.

Age 8
I took choreography and tennis lessons.

Age 11
I came to America to stay and got another pet rat.

Age 6
I went to school in Russia.

Age 5
I visited the Ukraine.

Starting Points for Writing

When you need a subject for a writing assignment, look at the subjects listed below and the prompts listed on the next page.

Sample Subjects

Many general subjects are listed below. They are organized according to the four basic reasons to write.

Describing (telling what a subject looks like, sounds like, does, . . .)

People: a family member, a teacher, a classmate, a neighbor, a friend, someone you wish you were like, a movie character

Places: your bedroom, your kitchen, an attic, a rooftop, an alley, the gym, the library, a river, a park, an old building, a church

Objects or things: a poster, a video game, a book, a photograph, a letter, a stuffed animal, a collection, a hat, a piece of clothing

Narrating (telling about something that happened)

making a mistake, showing your friendship, learning to _____ , moving to a new place, getting hurt, doing something funny, learning a lesson, earning money, losing something (or someone) important

Explaining (giving the steps, the causes, or the kinds of something)

How to . . . make your favorite food, eat a certain type of food, earn extra money, play a game, dress in style, fix something

The causes of . . . thunderstorms, school searches, prejudice, erosion (the wearing away of soil), work strikes, earthquakes, heart attacks, lung cancer, AIDS, success/failure in a school (or anywhere)

Kinds of . . . music, friends, heroes, chores, rules, engineers, exercise, laughter, novels, movie ratings, housing for seniors (places where older people can live and receive care)

Definition of . . . courage, a neighborhood, pollution, news, faith, endurance, school, a team, surviving, love, charity, persistence, family, hate

Persuading (proving your belief or feeling about something)

dieting, dress codes, bicycle helmets, security officers in schools, curfew, grades or testing, something that needs improving, something that seems unfair, something everyone should see or do, gun control, music and movie ratings

Writing Prompts

The prompts or ideas listed on this page will help you think of writing subjects. They will help you the most when you are writing about personal experiences.

Best and Worst

My best day

My worst experience

The hardest thing I've ever done

It could only happen to me!

If only I would have listened!

Once when I was alone . . .

About a week ago . . .

One day I woke up late and . . .

A song that means a lot to me

Whatever happened to my . . .

Quotations

(someone else's words)

"Almost anything in life is easier to get into than out of."

"Other times, other customs." (A *custom* is a way of doing something.)

"Democracy means 'I am as good as you are,' and 'You are as good as I am.' "

"The night is dark, and I am far from home."

"A picture is worth a thousand words."

"The only way to have a friend is to be one."

"He that seeks trouble always finds it."

"It's time for a change."

I was thinking.

Everyone should know . . .

What if I were the teacher?

What do Americans do well?

What are the duties of a good citizen?

I don't understand why . . .

First and Last

My first friend

My last day of _____

My last visit with _____

School, Then and Now

My first days in school

A field trip I'll never forget

What I don't like about my schedule

What my school really needs is . . .

My hardest subject

My best class

People and Places

Someone I admire

Helping a stranger

Learning from a brother or sister

The home I left behind

A river journey

Places to visit

Forms of Writing

This page lists many forms of writing. (Some of them are covered in your handbook.) Thinking about them may give you ideas for writing.

Forms You May Know About

Advertisements	Explanations	Plays
Book Reviews	Family Stories	Poems
Comic Strips	Interviews	Reports
Descriptions	Jokes	Riddles
Dictionaries	Journals	Songs
Directions	Letters	Stories
	News Stories	

Forms That May Be New to You

Anecdotes ● Little stories used to make a point

Autobiographies (personal narratives) ● Writing about yourself

Biographies ● Writing about other people

Dialogues ● Writing down the conversations people have

Editorials ● News stories or letters giving an opinion

E-Mail (electronic mail) ● A message sent between two people using computers

Family Parables ● Family stories that teach something

Myths ● Stories trying to explain natural events

Oral Histories ● Accounts based on recorded or taped conversations

Parodies ● Funny versions of serious writing

Photo Essays ● Essays using pictures and captions to share information (*Captions* are the words under the pictures.)

Profiles ● Detailed reports about individuals

Tall Tales ● Unbelievable stories with characters like Pecos Bill

Travelogues ● Writing that describes places you visit

Web Sites ● Creating theme pages on personal interests or concerns.

Gathering Details

Gathering is also part of prewriting. Gathering deals with all of the collecting and planning you do before you write. First you gather details about your subject. Then you plan how you will use these details in your writing.

Gathering is more important for some writing assignments than it is for others. It may not be that important if you are writing about a personal experience. You will already know a lot about your subject. But it may be very important when you are writing a report or an informational essay because you will need to learn a lot about your subject.

What's Ahead

The first part of this chapter explains strategies, collection sheets, and graphic organizers for gathering details. The second part gives you planning guidelines for getting ready to write.

- **Gathering Strategies**
- **Using Collection Sheets**
- **Using Graphic Organizers**
- **Planning Your Writing**

Gathering Strategies

The strategies listed on these two pages will help you collect ideas and details about a subject. Use two or three strategies if you have a lot to learn about a subject.

Gathering Your Own Thoughts

Listing List things that you already know about the subject and questions you have about it. Keep your list going as long as you can.

Clustering Use your writing subject as the nucleus or key word for your cluster. Then list, circle, and connect words related to the subject. (See page 36 for an example.)

Studying To think carefully about a subject, write answers to two or three of the following questions:

- What do I see or hear when I think of my subject? (Describe it.)

- What other person, place, thing, or idea is my subject like? What is it different from? (Compare it.)

- What parts does my subject have? (Break it down.)

- What are its strengths and weaknesses? (Evaluate it.)

Offbeat Questions To think about your subject in new ways, write and answer offbeat questions. (*Offbeat* means "different or unusual.") Sample questions are listed below.

Writing About a Person
What type of animal is this person like?
What type of weather is this person like?

Writing About a Place
What does this place like to do?
Where would this place like to live?

Writing About an Object or a Thing
What does this object look like upside down?
What places has this object seen?

Writing About an Experience
What colors does this experience make you think of?
What book or movie is this experience like?

Researching

Reading Learn facts and details by reading about your subject. Use nonfiction books, encyclopedias, magazines, and so on. (See pages 261-276 for help.)

Viewing and Listening Watch television programs and videos. Listen to tapes about your subject. (See pages 307-312 for help.)

Surfing Explore the Internet for information about your subject. (See pages 227-232 for help.)

Experiencing Visit or watch your subject in action to learn about it. If your subject involves an activity, participate in it.

Talking to Others

Interviewing Interview an expert about your subject. (In an interview, you ask someone questions about a subject.) You can meet in person for the interview, talk by phone, or send questions to be answered in writing. (See page 164 for help.)

Discussing Talk to your classmates, teacher, or someone else to see what they know about your subject. Take notes to help you remember the important things they say.

Using Collection Sheets

You can use a collection sheet for gathering and organizing ideas. The sample on this page can be used as a guide for reports and other informational writing. The sample on the next page can be used as a guide for story writing. (You can also make up your own collection sheet.)

Gathering Grid

This type of collection sheet is called a **gathering grid.** (A *grid* is a type of chart.) You can use a gathering grid when you are reading and learning facts about a subject for a report or an essay.

The questions down the side will help you decide what to learn about the subject. (See page 200 for a filled-in grid.)

Sample Gathering Grid

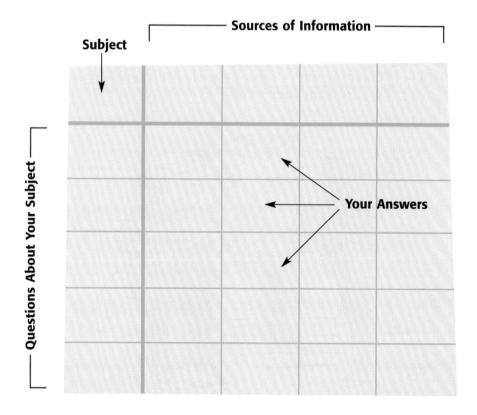

Story Map

A story map can help you plan a fictional (made-up) story. All stories need a setting, characters, a problem, and so on. As you fill in these different parts, your story will begin to take shape. (You don't have to fill in every blank before you start writing. Just complete enough of the map so you have a good idea about the structure of your story.)

Sample Story Map

Title: _____

Setting:

Characters: _____ _____

_____ _____

_____ _____

Problem:

Event 1: _____

Event 2: _____

Event 3: _____

Event 4: _____

Solution:

Using Graphic Organizers

Graphic organizers help you gather and organize details for writing. Clustering is one way to do this. (See pages 36 and 198). This page lists other sample organizers in your handbook.

Line Diagram

To collect and organize details for informational paragraphs and essays (See page 92.)

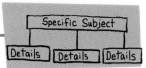

5 W's Chart

To collect the important details (*who? what? when? where?* and *why?*) for narratives, news stories, etc. (See pages 132 and 164.)

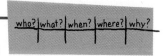

Sensory Chart

To collect ideas for descriptions and observation reports (See page 189.)

Venn Diagram

To collect details for two subjects you are comparing (See page 267.)

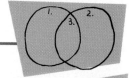

Process List (Cycle Diagram)

To collect details for science reports explaining a process, such as how tadpoles become frogs (See page 269.)

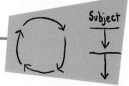

Cause/Effect Organizer

To collect details for paragraphs or essays showing causes and effects, such as the effects of acid rain on the environment (See page 271.)

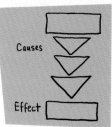

Time Line

To collect details or events chronologically (*according to time*) for essays and reports (See page 273.)

Planning Your Writing

Gathering details helps you learn about your subject. Planning how to use the details helps you get ready to write. The steps that follow will help you with your planning.

1. Review the ideas and details you have collected.

2. Think of an interesting way to write about your subject. The way you write about a subject is called your *focus*. (See below.)

3. Underline or mark the details that support your focus.

4. Organize the details in the best order for your writing.

Finding a Focus

The way you feel about a subject will help you think of a way to write about it *(your focus)*. Let's say you are writing about someone you really like. You could focus on this person's . . .

- appearance and style,
- best quality,
- most important experience, or
- hopes for the future.

Your writing would go on and on, and be hard to follow, if you tried to write about all of these ideas. Instead, you should focus on one (or two) of them.

Samples

Note the focus for each sample assignment below.

Writing Assignment: Report on wildlife
Subject: Peregrine falcon
Focus: Reasons it is endangered

Writing Assignment: Write a book review
Subject: *The Miracle Worker*
Focus: Description of the climax (the most important part)

✳ Some assignments have a built-in focus. If your teacher asks you to write about the funniest thing that ever happened to you, your focus is to share the funny details of that experience.

Organizing the Details

For some assignments, you may know just what you want to say after you think of a focus. In that case, start writing. But for other assignments, you may need to organize your details before you write.

You can organize your details in a list, a cluster, or a brief outline. (See page 96 for help with outlining.) A sample cluster follows. (The numbers in the cluster show the order in which the information will be used.)

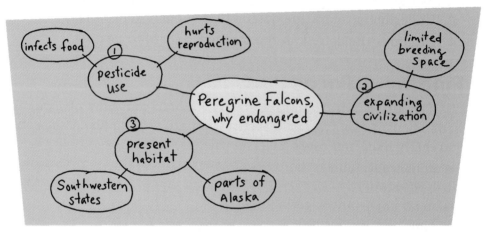

Methods of Organization

The list below shows you different ways to organize details in your writing.

- **Chronological (Time) Order:** Organize details by time. (Use words like *first* and *second*. See page 88 for more time words.)

- **Order of Location:** Organize details by location. (Use words like *above* and *below*. See page 88 for more location words.)

- **Order of Importance:** Organize details from the most important to the least important—or the other way around.

- **Comparison:** Organize details to show how two subjects are alike and different. (See page 88 for comparison words.)

- **Illustration:** Organize your writing so the main idea is stated in the beginning part. Examples, facts, and other details are then added to *illustrate* or support the main idea.

Writing and Revising

Writing the first draft is the second step in the writing process. During this step, you get all of your ideas down on paper. Don't worry about making mistakes. Your goal is to write freely about your subject using your planning as a general guide.

A first draft is your first look at your writing. You will change it in many ways before all of your ideas are clear and complete. When you make changes, you are **revising.** Revising, the third step in the writing process, is very important because it helps you connect the ideas in your writing in the best way.

What's Ahead

This chapter will help you write and revise your first drafts. It includes writing tips, a helpful revising checklist, plus much more.

- **Writing First Drafts**
- **Revising First Drafts**
- **Revising Checklist**
- **More Revising Ideas**

Writing First Drafts

Writing is easier when you know a lot about your subject. So don't start your first draft until you do three things:

1. Gather plenty of details about your subject.

2. Choose an interesting part of the subject to write about.

3. Organize your ideas for writing.

Drafting Tips

Ideas: Use your planning as a guide to connect all the interesting and important ideas you have gathered. Add new ideas as you go along. Note: Don't worry about making mistakes or crossing out words. Your first draft is a developing piece of writing.

Organization: Remember that your writing should have a beginning, a middle, and an ending.

Voice: Write honestly and naturally so the real you comes through in your writing.

Writing the Beginning

If you are writing a personal story, an essay, or a report, you need to plan a beginning paragraph. If you are writing only one paragraph, you need to plan a topic sentence. In either case, your beginning should sound interesting and introduce the focus of your writing. Here are some different ideas for beginnings:

- Begin with interesting or surprising facts about the subject.
- Ask a question.
- Start with a quotation. (Repeat someone else's words.)
- Share a brief story about the subject.

Sample Beginning Paragraph

Interesting facts

Focus statement

There is one bird that can reach the speed of 200 miles an hour when it dives. The United States Air Force Academy has made this bird its official mascot because it is so fast. This bird is the peregrine falcon; and sadly, it is an endangered species.

Developing the Middle Part

In the middle part of your draft, you develop the specific subject, or focus, of your writing. Use the planning and organizing you've done to guide you. Listed below are different ways to develop a subject:

- **Explain:** Support main ideas with examples and reasons.
- **Define:** Make clear the meaning of important terms.
- **Describe:** Share details about some part of the subject.
- **Argue:** Use logic and evidence to prove something is true.

Sample Middle Paragraph

Main idea ——— **The use of pesticides is the main reason the peregrine falcon is an endangered species. Pesticides**

Definition ——— **are chemicals sprayed on plants to kill insects. The falcons are infected when they eat other birds already**

Explanation **infected with pesticides like DDT. A peregrine's ability to reproduce may be upset by these pesticides.**

Writing the Ending

Once you have developed all of your main ideas, you are ready to bring your writing to a close. Use one or more of the following ideas for endings:

- Remind readers about your subject.
- Summarize your main points.
- State the importance of one of your points.
- Say something that will keep readers thinking about the subject.

Sample Ending Paragraph

Restatement of subject — **Steps are being taken to save peregrine falcons. Some scientists are trying to limit the use of chemical sprays. The goal of one group of scientists at Cornell University is to breed more peregrine falcons. More**

Thoughtful final idea — **than 200 falcons have already been bred. Some of these birds must survive, or we will lose one of the fastest birds in the air.**

Revising First Drafts

A first draft never turns out just right. One part may need more specific details. Another part may not be clear enough. To fix or improve these parts, you need to revise your first draft. To learn more about revising, read the questions and answers below.

What Does It Mean to Revise?

Concentrate on the Ideas When you revise, make sure that you have made all of the important points about your subject. Also make sure that your readers can understand all of your ideas.

Organize Your Writing Make sure that all of your ideas are clear and complete.

Wait with Spelling Don't spend a lot of time looking for spelling and other errors. You can do that later.

How Do I Get Started?

Read and Review Read your first draft two or three times. Read it out loud. Think about your writing as you read. Does it follow your plan? Does it say what you wanted it to say?

Share Your Draft Also ask your teacher, a classmate, or someone else to read and react to your draft. Listen carefully to their thoughts about it.

What Should I Look For?

Look for the Strong Parts Put a star (*) next to parts of your draft that you like. You may like your opening paragraph. Or you may like how you explained one of your main ideas. (These parts may not need any changes.)

Look for the Weak Parts Put a check (✔) next to parts that need work. For example, some ideas may be unclear, out of order, or unnecessary. (See the checklist on the next page.)

Revising Checklist

Use this checklist as a guide when you revise a first draft. *Remember:* Wait until all of your ideas are clear and complete before you try correct spelling, punctuation, or grammar errors.

 Does my writing focus on an interesting part of my subject or on a certain feeling I have about it? (See page 49.)

 Does the information in my writing follow a method of organization? (See page 50.)

 Do I need to add any information?

_____ Do I need to add details to make my beginning clearer or more interesting?

_____ Do I need to add ideas to support my subject?

_____ Do I need to make my closing more effective?

 Do I need to cut any information?

_____ Do any of my details not belong?

_____ Do I repeat myself in any parts?

_____ Do I say too much about a certain idea?

 Do I need to rewrite any parts?

_____ Do some sentences sound unclear?

_____ Do I need to reword any explanations?

 Do I need to reorder any parts?

_____ Do any ideas or details seem out of place?

_____ Does the most important point come near the beginning or near the end?

More Revising Ideas

Write with Feeling

Showing a strong interest in your subject will help make your writing more effective. Always use the best words available to express your thoughts and feelings. In the following passage, the writer's concern about her subject is very clear. (She feels it is *tragic* that the peregrine falcon is endangered.)

> At one time, peregrine falcons were common throughout the Rocky Mountain region of the United States. Tragically, not many peregrine falcons are found anywhere in the lower United States today. As of 1978, only 31 pairs were in existence.

Check for Details

Details help make your stories, essays, and reports interesting and colorful. Read the two sets of sentences below. Which set do you find more interesting?

Few Details

> The peregrine falcon is built for hunting. It is a large bird with long wings. It uses its beak and claws to attack its prey.

More Details

> The peregrine falcon is built for hunting. It is a large bird that can grow up to 20 inches in length. The falcon's long, pointed wings can spread to 43 inches in flight. Its hooked beak and razor-sharp claws can slice its prey when it attacks.

Add a Title

The title is another important part of writing. A good title helps introduce your subject and prepares readers for the interesting ideas to follow. Try many different titles before you choose one.

> **Blazing Wings** sounds better than **The Peregrine Falcon**.
>
> **Fast Food** sounds better than **Short Lunch Hours**.

Group Advising

Have you ever had a friend help rearrange your room? Though it's hard to admit, your friend may have had some great ideas: "Move the bookcase over there. And put that poster on the closet door." Your friend's suggestions may have helped you see your room in another way.

The same thing happens when you share a piece of writing that you're still working on. Other people may offer great advice about your writing. **Group advising,** or writing conferences, can help you see your writing through another person's eyes. It is a very important part of the writing process—one that will help you improve as a writer.

What's Ahead

In this chapter you will learn how to work with others in writing conferences. You will learn specific techniques that will take the fear or uncertainty out of sharing your writing.

- **Writing Group Guidelines**
- **Response Checklist**

Writing Group Guidelines

At first, you may choose to conference with only one person: a teacher, a teacher's aide, or a classmate. This person does not expect your work to be perfect. He or she knows that you are still working on your paper.

Later, you will have a chance to help someone else in this way. After a while, you will find that talking to others about writing is much easier than you thought it would be. When you see how much it helps your writing, you will be "sold" on the idea of group advising.

The Author's Role

Select a piece of your writing to share, and make a copy of it for each group member.

GUIDELINES	SAMPLE RESPONSES
Introduce your piece of writing. This is your chance to explain your thinking and writing process. Talk about the *how, what,* and *why* of your paper.	This paper is about Mayan calendars. I got interested in this subject when my uncle . . .
Read your writing out loud. Or ask group members to read it silently.	The ancient Mayan calendar had 365 days, just like ours.
Invite your group members to comment. Listen carefully.	OK, everyone, now it's your turn to talk. I'm listening.
Take notes so you will remember what was said and be able to ask questions.	Did I make it clear that their year started in January?
Answer all questions as best you can. Be open and polite. You don't have to defend your writing; just explain it.	Yes, the Maya actually had two calendars going at the same time.
Ask for help from your group with any writing problems you are having.	What do you think of my title? Does the ending seem right?

The Listener's Role

Listeners should show an interest in the author's writing and treat it with respect.

GUIDELINES	SAMPLE RESPONSES
● **Listen carefully.** Take notes so that you can make helpful comments.	Notes: *Why were the Maya so interested in calendars?*
● **Look for what is good** about the writing. Give some positive comments. Be sincere.	Your explanation of the calendars is very clear.
● **Tell what you think could be improved.** Be polite, but don't be afraid to give an honest opinion.	I think you need a few more details about the Maya themselves.
● **Ask questions** if you are confused about something or want to know more.	What does *zenith* mean?
● **Make helpful suggestions.** Be kind, but also try to help the writer improve his or her work.	I think you should include some drawings.

Helpful Comments

In all your comments, be as specific as you can be. This will help the writer to focus on the sections that need fixing.

Instead of . . .	Try something like . . .
Your writing is boring.	Almost all your sentences begin with "There" or "It."
I can't understand what you're talking about.	The part about religion isn't very clear.
I don't think you've got your facts right.	I think that you've got the Maya and the Aztecs mixed up.

Response Checklist

Use this checklist to guide your responses to writing.

Stimulating Ideas

_____ **Is the subject interesting to readers?**

Logical Organization

_____ **Is the writing well organized?**
Does it have a strong beginning, a complete middle, and a good ending?

_____ **Are all the ideas arranged in the best order?**
(See "Methods of Organization," page 50.)

Engaging Voice

_____ **Does the writing sound natural?**
Does it sound like the writer's true voice?

Original Word Choice and Details

_____ **Does the writing include specific details?**
Hot, still air hung over the dry, cracked creek bed.

_____ **Does the writing give reasons for opinions?**
Does the writing explain *why* something is the way it is?

Effective Sentence Style

_____ **Is the writing easy to follow?**
Is everything clear to you, the reader?

Correct, Accurate Copy

_____ **Is the writing free of errors?**
Are all the verb tenses correct? Are there any sentence fragments?

_____ **Is the writing accurate?**
Does the writing use correct spelling and punctuation?

Editing and Proofreading

Editing and proofreading is the fourth step in the writing process. This is the time to check your writing for errors. You do this *after* you have changed, or revised, your first draft.

When you **edit,** you make sure your sentences and words are clear and correct. When you **proofread,** you check the final copy of your writing for errors. Once your writing has been edited and proofread, it will be ready to share.

It's easy to miss errors when you edit and proofread, so make sure to ask a teacher, a classmate, or a family member for help.

What's Ahead

This chapter includes a helpful checklist that you can use as a guide when you edit and proofread your writing. The checklist covers sentence structure, punctuation, capitalization, usage, and so on. A guide to editing your sentences for style is also included. (See pages 345-433 for more help.)

- **Editing and Proofreading Checklist**
- **Editing for Sentence Style**

Editing and Proofreading Checklist

Sentence Structure
____ Did I write clear and complete sentences?
____ Did I add style to my sentences? (See page 63.)

Punctuation
____ Does each sentence have an end punctuation mark?
____ Did I use apostrophes to show possession *(Pola's purse)* or to mark contractions *(didn't)*?
____ Did I punctuate dialogue correctly *(Luis said, "I want to learn more about computers.")*?

Capitalization
____ Did I start all of my sentences with capital letters?
____ Did I capitalize the names of people and places?

Grammar
____ Did I use correct verb forms? (See pages 421-423.)
____ Do all the subjects and verbs agree in number? Singular subjects go with singular verbs; plural subjects go with plural verbs. (See pages 69-70.)
____ Did I use pronouns correctly in my sentences? (See pages 71-72.)

Usage
____ Did I use specific nouns and verbs and colorful adjectives? (See pages 110-111.)
____ Did I use the correct word (like *to, too,* or *two*)? (See pages 379-394.)

Spelling
____ Did I check for spelling errors? (See pages 372-377.)
____ Did I use a spell checker on my computer?

Editing for Sentence Style

Listed below are two ways to add style to your sentences.

Change Your Sentence Beginnings

If too many of your sentences start with the same word or words, your writing may sound dull. Correct this problem by changing some of your sentence beginnings. The sentences that follow begin with the same words.

> **The old man wiped his eyes with the back of his hand. The old man looked at his wife standing near him. The old man began thinking about the past.**

Replace a Noun with a Pronoun One way to change a sentence beginning is to use a pronoun in place of a noun.

> **He looked at his wife standing near him.** (The pronoun *he* is used in place of the noun phrase *the old man*.)

Start with a Phrase or a Clause Another way to change a sentence beginning is to start with a modifying phrase or clause.

> **As he watched her, the old man began thinking about the past.**

Here is the set of sample sentences from above with some of the beginnings changed: (This writing has more style.)

> **The old man wiped his eyes with the back of his hand. He looked at his wife standing near him. As he watched her, the old man began thinking about the past.**

Combine Short Sentences

Your writing may not sound smooth if you use too many short sentences. Correct this problem by combining some of your sentences.

Four Short Sentences

> **Math is my best class. I love solving word problems. I have a really nice teacher. Her name is Ms. Johnson.**

Two Longer, Smoother Sentences

> **Math is my best class because I love solving word problems. I have a really nice teacher named Ms. Johnson.**

Basic Elements

of Writing

Writing Basic Sentences

Combining Sentences

Writing Paragraphs

Writing Essays

Writing Basic Sentences

Sentences are as important to you, as a communicator and writer, as flour is to a baker or flowers are to a florist. You use sentences to share your ideas in letters, reports, personal stories, e-mail messages, and so on.

To become a good writer, you need to learn as much as you can about sentences. You need to read a lot in order to see how other writers use sentences. You also need to write a lot in order to improve your sentence-writing ability. And, of course, you need to learn the "sentence basics."

What's Ahead

This chapter reviews the basic parts of a sentence, gives examples of different types of sentence errors to avoid, and much more. Turn here (and to pages 402-407) whenever you have a question about writing basic sentences.

- Sentence Review
- Sentence Errors
- Sentence Agreement
- Sentence Problems

Sentence Review

Sentences are groups of words that make complete statements, ask questions, or express strong feelings. As a writer, it's important to use complete, clear sentences so that your readers can follow your thoughts and ideas. Here is an easy-to-follow guide to sentences.

Basic Parts of a Sentence

All sentences have two basic parts—the subject and the predicate.

SUBJECT The subject is the part of a sentence that does something or is talked about. In the sample sentence, *my best friend* is the complete subject, and *friend* is the simple subject. (The simple subject is the subject without the words that modify it.)

My best <u>friend</u> **writes funny stories.**

PREDICATE The predicate is the part of a sentence that says something about the subject. In the sample sentence, *writes funny stories* is the complete predicate, and *writes* is the simple predicate, or verb. (The simple predicate is the verb without the words that modify it or complete the thought.)

My best friend <u>writes</u> **funny stories.**

❋ There are two main types of verbs, action verbs (such as *writes*) and linking verbs (such as *is* and *are*). (See page 417.)

My best friend <u>writes</u> **stories. They** <u>are</u> **funny.**

COMPOUND SUBJECTS AND PREDICATES A sentence may have more than one simple subject or predicate (verb).

<u>Matt</u> and <u>Marisa</u> write news stories.

(The sentence contains two simple subjects, *Matt* and *Marisa*.)

Marisa <u>takes</u> pictures and <u>writes</u> headlines.

(The sentence contains two simple predicates, *takes* and *writes*.)

Basic Sentence Patterns

Sentences in the English language follow these basic patterns:

Subject + Action Verb

S   AV
Guerdy giggles. (Some action verbs, like *giggles*, are intransitive, meaning that they don't need a direct object to express a complete thought. See page 425.)

Subject + Action Verb + Direct Object

S   AV   DO
Kerry tells stories. (Some action verbs, like *tells*, are transitive, meaning that they need a direct object to express a complete thought. See page 424.)

Subject + Action Verb + Indirect Object + Direct Object

S   AV   IO   DO
Kevin gives his friends silly gifts.

Subject + Action Verb + Direct Object + Object Complement

S   AV   DO   OC
The class named Richard the best storyteller.

Subject + Linking Verb + Predicate Noun

S   LV   PN
Christina is a beautiful singer.

Subject + Linking Verb + Predicate Adjective

S   LV   PA
The play director is serious.

In all of the basic patterns above, the subject comes before the verb. There are, however, a few types of sentences in which the verb comes before the subject. Here are three examples:

LV   S   PN
Is Larisa a poet? (A question)

LV   S
There was a meeting. (A sentence beginning with *there*)

AV   S
Here come the kids. (A sentence beginning with *here*)

Sentence Errors

Sentence Fragment A sentence fragment does not express a complete idea. It is missing one or more important parts.

Incorrect: **Hits a lot of home runs.** (There is no *subject*.)

Correct: **Lionel hits a lot of home runs.**
(The subject *Lionel* has been added.)

Incorrect: **Many good pitches** (There is no *subject* and no *verb*.)

Correct: **Ron throws many good pitches.**
(The subject *Ron* and verb *throws* have been added.)

Run-on Sentence A run-on sentence has two sentences joined without punctuation or without a connecting word (*and, but, or*).

Incorrect: **I thought the baseball game would never end our team finally won in the 12th inning.**
(Punctuation is needed.)

Correct: **I thought the baseball game would never end. Our team finally won in the 12th inning.**
(A period has been added after *end*.)

Comma Splice A comma splice is an error made when you join two sentences with a comma instead of a period or semicolon.

Incorrect: **Geraldo and I love movies, we watch them a lot.**
(A comma incorrectly connects two sentences.)

Correct: **Geraldo and I love movies. We watch them a lot.**
(A period is used correctly in place of a comma.)

Rambling Sentence A rambling sentence happens when you put too many little sentences together with the word *and*.

Incorrect: **We went to the video store and rented our favorite movie and we took the movie to Geraldo's house and watched it twice and Geraldo's mom made lunch for us.**

Improved: **We went to the video store and rented our favorite movie. We took the movie to Geraldo's house and watched it twice. Geraldo's mom made lunch for us, too.**

Sentence Agreement

Make sure the parts of your sentence "agree" with one another. If you use a singular subject, use a singular verb. If you use a plural subject, use a plural verb. See the examples below.

One Subject In most basic sentences, one subject is followed by the verb.

Incorrect: **Carmen go to Tucson every summer.**

(*Carmen* is singular; *go* is plural.)

Correct: **Carmen goes to Tucson every summer.**

Incorrect: **Her brothers goes with her.**

(*Brothers* is plural; *goes* is singular.)

Correct: **Her brothers go with her.**

The following chart shows additional sentences with one subject. (The verb agrees with the subject in each sentence.)

SINGULAR SUBJECT	PLURAL SUBJECTS
The player shoots the ball.	The players shoot the balls.
A small dog barks.	Small dogs bark.

Compound Subjects Connected by AND If a sentence contains a compound subject connected by *and*, it needs a plural verb.

Hiro and Sue go to Seattle.

Compound Subjects Connected by OR If a sentence contains a compound subject connected by *or*, the verb must agree with the subject nearer to it.

My brothers or my sister goes to the store.

(The verb is singular because the subject *sister,* closest to the verb, is singular.)

My sister or my brothers go to the store.

(The verb is plural because the subject *brothers,* closest to the verb, is plural.)

Unusual Word Order When the subject is separated from the verb by words or phrases, you must check carefully to see that the subject agrees with the verb.

> **Chen, in addition to two other students, is sick.**
>
> **A group of students is writing a play.**
>
> **Kerry and Patrice, the best players on the team, are helping me.**
>
> **The Ocampos, a large family, are from Peru.**

✳ If you are not sure whether a sentence is in agreement, say the sentence without the words that come between the subject and the verb.

■ When the subject comes after the verb (or part of the verb) in a sentence, you must check carefully to see that the subject agrees with the verb.

> **On the branch sits a bird.**
>
> **On the branch sit two birds.**
>
> **Has your friend seen this movie?**
>
> **Have your friends seen this movie?**

Indefinite Pronouns Use a singular verb with these indefinite pronouns: *each, either, neither, one, everyone, everybody, everything, someone, somebody, something, anybody, anything, anyone, nobody, no one, nothing,* and *another.*

> **Everybody goes to the library tomorrow.**
>
> **Nobody is sick today.**

■ Some indefinite pronouns (*all, any, most, none, some*) can be either singular or plural. You must study the words that come between the subject and verb to decide.

> **Most of the students go to the library.**
> (Because the sentence talks about most of the *students,* a plural noun, use the plural verb *go.*)
>
> **Some of the milk is gone.**
> (Because the sentence talks about some of the *milk,* a singular noun, use the singular verb *is.*)

Sentence Problems

Wordy Sentences Check your sentences for words that only repeat what you've said, but in a different way. (See the words in red below.)

Incorrect: **Chen got up out of bed at 6 a.m. in the morning so he could study and be ready for the test.**

Correct: **Chen got up at 6 a.m. so he could study for the test.**

Double Subjects Do not use a pronoun immediately after the subject. The result is usually a double subject.

Incorrect: **The car it won't start. Sefton he will be late.**

Correct: **The car won't start. Sefton will be late.**

Pronoun-Antecedent Agreement Make sure the pronouns in your sentences agree with their antecedents. (*Antecedents* are the words replaced by the pronouns.)

The students left, but then they came back.

(Since the noun *students* is plural, the plural pronoun *they* is correct.)

Everyone gave his or her opinion.

(Since the pronoun *everyone* is singular, the singular pronouns *his* or *her* are correct.)

Confusing Pronoun Reference When you use a pronoun, be sure the reader knows who or what the pronoun refers to.

Incorrect: **When Carmen tried to balance the book on top of the stack, it fell.** (What does the pronoun *it* refer to—the book or the stack?)

Correct: **The book fell when Carmen tried to balance it on top of the stack.** (The pronoun *it* clearly refers to the book.)

Pronoun Shift Make sure your pronoun agrees in person (*first, second,* or *third*) with the noun it replaces. It is incorrect to shift to another person. (See page 414.)

> *Incorrect:*   **When people are lost, you should ask for directions.**
>   (The second-person pronoun *you* does not agree in person with the noun it replaces. *People* needs a third-person pronoun.)
>
> *Correct:*   **When people are lost, they should ask for directions.**
>   (The third-person pronoun *they* agrees in person with the noun it replaces, *people.*)

Double Negatives Do not use two negative words together, like *never* and *no,* or *not* and *no.*

> *Incorrect:* **I never told no one about it.**
>
> *Correct:* **I told no one about it.** *or* **I never told anyone about it.**

Do not use *hardly, barely,* or *scarcely* with a negative word.

> *Incorrect:* **I did not hardly have no money for the bus.**
>
> *Correct:* **I did not have any money for the bus.**

Confusing OF for HAVE Do not use *of* in a sentence when you really mean *have.* (When *have* is said quickly, it sometimes sounds like *of.*)

> *Incorrect:* **I could of used the money for lunch.**
>
> *Correct:* **I could have used the money for lunch.**

Misplaced Modifiers Make sure that your modifiers are close to the words they describe. Otherwise, the sentence may not say what you mean.

> *Incorrect:* **After completing the assignment, the teacher met with both of us.** (This sentence says that the teacher completed the assignment.)
>
> *Correct:* **After completing the assignment, both of us met with the teacher.**

Combining Sentences

Sentence combining is making one smoother, more detailed sentence from two or more shorter sentences. Sentence combining will be especially helpful when your writing sounds a little choppy. For example, take a look at these sentences:

Ayana loves to prepare Japanese food.
She loves to eat rice balls.
She loves to drink green tea.

These three sentences are fine, but see what happens when they are combined. All of the ideas flow, or fit together, more smoothly.

Ayana loves to prepare Japanese food, eat rice balls, and drink green tea.

What's Ahead

The guidelines in this chapter will help you learn how to combine sentences. Learning this skill will help you write with more style, which in turn will make your essays and reports much more enjoyable to read.

- **Combining with Key Words**
- **Combining with Phrases**
- **Combining with Longer Sentences**

Combining with Key Words

Use a Key Word

Ideas from short sentences can be combined or put together by moving a key word from one sentence to the other. This key word may be an adjective or an adverb.

■ Two Short Sentences:
Eri's paper crane was torn. It was origami.

Combined with an Adjective:
Eri's origami paper crane was torn.

■ Two Short Sentences:
I am going to start my report on Jamaica. I'll start it tomorrow.

Combined with an Adverb:
Tomorrow I am going to start my report on Jamaica.

Use a Series of Words or Phrases

Ideas from short sentences can be combined into one sentence using a series of words or phrases.

■ Three Short Sentences:
In Korea, spring is short.
In Korea, spring is mild.
In Korea, spring is windy.

Combined with a Series of Words:
In Korea, spring is short, mild, and windy.

✳ All of the words or phrases in a series should be **parallel,** or stated in the same way. If you don't do this, your sentence will sound like it's out of balance. (Look at the example below.)

■ Incorrect:
Korean summers are hot, humid, and it rains a lot.
(The modifiers in this series are not parallel.)

Correct:
Korean summers are hot, humid, and rainy.
(The modifiers are now parallel, or stated in the same way.)

Combining with Phrases

Use Phrases

Ideas from short sentences can be put together into one sentence using prepositional or appositive phrases. (See pages 432 and 352.)

■ Two Short Sentences:
Marisol's cat likes to sleep. It likes to sleep on top of her homework.

Combined with a Prepositional Phrase:
Marisol's cat likes to sleep on top of her homework.

■ Two Short Sentences:
Mrs. Yoon makes the best kimchi. Mrs. Yoon is our closest neighbor.

Combined with an Appositive Phrase:
Mrs. Yoon, our closest neighbor, makes the best kimchi.

Use Compound Subjects and Compound Verbs

A compound subject has two or more subjects in one sentence. A compound verb has two or more verbs in one sentence.

■ Two Short Sentences:
Adela danced around the room. Cruz danced around the room, too.

Combined with a Compound Subject:
Adela and Cruz danced around the room.

■ Two Short Sentences:
Yu kicked the soccer ball. Yu tried to make a goal.

Combined with a Compound Verb:
Yu kicked the soccer ball and tried to make a goal.

Combining with Longer Sentences

Use Compound Sentences

A compound sentence joins two or more simple sentences together. The conjunctions *and, but, or, nor, for, so,* and *yet* are used to connect simple sentences. (Place a comma before the conjunction.)

■ Two Simple Sentences:
January and February are the summer months in Chile.
Families vacation during these months.

Combined with "and":
January and February are the summer months in Chile, and families vacation during these months.

■ Two Simple Sentences:
Gai and Pong play takraw.
They serve with their feet instead of their hands.

Combined with "but":
Gai and Pong play takraw, but they serve with their feet instead of their hands.

Use Complex Sentences

A complex sentence joins two ideas connected by words called subordinate conjunctions (*after, when, since, because, before,* etc.) and relative pronouns (*who, whose, which,* and *that*).

■ Two Short Sentences:
Tamaris is wearing a beautiful white dress. She is going to church to celebrate her fifteenth birthday.

Combined with "because":
Tamaris is wearing a beautiful white dress because she is going to church to celebrate her fifteenth birthday.

■ Two Short Sentences:
Japanese writing is called *hirigana, katakana,* and *kanji.* Japanese writing must be learned by all students.

Combined with "which":
Japanese writing, which must be learned by all students, is called *hirigana, katakana,* and *kanji.*

Writing Paragraphs

A **paragraph** is a group of sentences sharing ideas about one subject. The first sentence in a paragraph usually states the subject, and the other sentences give details and facts about it. Here are four reasons to write a paragraph. You can . . .

1. **describe someone or something,**

2. **tell about an event or experience,**

3. **explain or give information about a subject, or**

4. **give your opinion about something.**

What's Ahead

This chapter will help you with all of your paragraph writing. It will also help you learn about key writing skills. For example, you will learn about including details in writing and organizing your ideas in the best way.

- **The Parts of a Paragraph**
- **Types of Paragraphs**
- **Writing Guidelines**
- **Details in Paragraphs**
- **Organizing Your Ideas**

The Parts of a Paragraph

A paragraph has three parts. It usually begins with a **topic sentence.** The sentences in the middle part make up the **body** of a paragraph. The last sentence is called the **closing sentence.**

✳ The first line in a paragraph is indented. (To *indent* means "to begin the first line five spaces in from the margin.")

The End of an Empire

Topic Sentence

The arrival of Hernán Cortés in Mexico in 1519 marked the beginning of the end of the Aztec Empire. When Cortés and his 500 soldiers first entered the Aztec capital city of Tenochtitlán, they were amazed at its beautiful temples and other riches. The Aztec emperor Montezuma II welcomed Cortés as a friend and gave him

Body

many gifts of gold and silver. But the Spaniard proved that he was no friend. He and his soldiers captured the emperor and killed hundreds of his people. Later, the Aztecs drove the Spaniards out of the city, but Montezuma II died in the fighting. Then

Closing Sentence

Cortés and his men attacked and destroyed Tenochtitlán. The Aztec Empire had no chance to survive after that.

A Closer Look at the Parts

The Topic Sentence

The **topic sentence** tells what a paragraph is going to be about. A good topic sentence *(1) names the subject* and *(2) states your feelings about it.* Here is a simple formula for writing good topic sentences:

Formula: **An interesting subject**
+ your specific feeling about it
= a good topic sentence.

Topic Sentence: **The arrival of Hernán Cortés in Mexico in 1519** (interesting subject) **marked the beginning of the end of the Aztec Empire** (specific feeling).

The Body

The sentences in the **body** of a paragraph must give readers all of the information they need to understand the topic.

■ Use a lot of specific details to make your paragraph interesting. The details are shown in red in the sentence that follows:

When Cortés and his 500 soldiers first entered the Aztec capital city of Tenochtitlán, they were amazed at its beautiful temples and other riches.

■ Organize your sentences in the best possible order. There are three main ways to organize your sentences: *chronological (time) order, order of location,* and *order of importance.* (See page 86.)

The Closing Sentence

The **closing sentence** comes after all of the details have been included in the body. This sentence should remind readers about the paragraph topic. The following example reminds us of the topic of the sample paragraph.

Closing Sentence: **The Aztec Empire had no chance to survive after that.**

Types of Paragraphs

You can write four types of paragraphs: *descriptive, narrative, expository,* and *persuasive.* Each one of the types requires a different type of thinking and planning.

Descriptive Paragraph

In a **descriptive paragraph** you give a clear, detailed picture of one person, place, thing, or event.

Jaguar Knight

Topic Sentence	An Aztec warrior could dress like a jaguar knight once he proved himself in battle. On his head, a knight wore a covering that looked like a jaguar's head with its jaws opened very wide. The knight's face fit into this opening. Sometimes a knight would also wear a headdress of big feathers. To protect
Body	his body, a knight wore padded tan clothing painted with black spots to look like a jaguar. On his feet, a jaguar knight wore light sandals, or nothing at all. In one hand, he held a round shield painted with bright Aztec
Closing Sentence	designs, and in the other hand, he held a club or spear. When an Aztec warrior dressed like this, he looked wild and dangerous.

Narrative Paragraph

In a **narrative paragraph,** you share a memorable event or an important experience. (A *narrative* is a retelling of something.) The details in a narrative should answer the 5 W's (*who? what? when? where?* and *why?*) about the event or experience.

This Time You Lose, Cortés

Topic Sentence

One of our class plays about Cortés and the Aztecs came to a surprising ending. During the big moment in the play, Cortés and two of his soldiers were waiting for Montezuma II. Then the Aztec leader entered on a royal chair carried by two Aztec warriors. Montezuma II greeted

Body

Cortés and gave him a cloth bag containing jewels and gold. The two leaders exchanged a few words, and then Cortés suddenly drew his sword as if he were going to kill Montezuma II or one of his warriors. But the sword broke in half as soon as he swung it above his head. Montezuma II looked at

Closing Sentence

the broken weapon and said, "This time you lose, Cortés." The play stopped at that point because everyone kept laughing.

Expository Paragraph

In an **expository paragraph,** you give information. You can explain a subject, give directions, or show how to do something. In expository writing, linking words like *first, second, then,* and *finally* are used to help readers follow the ideas. (See page 88 for more linking words.)

Making Aztec Hot Cocoa

Topic Sentence

Making Aztec hot cocoa is almost as easy as making regular hot cocoa. First pour one cup of milk and two teaspoons of cocoa powder into a pan. Stir this mixture and start warming

Body

it on the stove at medium heat. Then add a little cinnamon, or stir the cocoa with a cinnamon stick. Next, to make your Aztec cocoa truly authentic, stir in a small slice of orange peel. Finally, heat the drink

Closing Sentence

until it is steaming. When you first taste this spicy cocoa, you will understand why it was so popular with the Aztec people.

Persuasive Paragraph

In a **persuasive paragraph,** you give your opinion (or strong feeling) about a subject. In persuasive writing, it's important to include enough facts and details to prove or support your opinion.

Topic Sentence

Body

Closing Sentence

The Aztecs--
the Most Advanced Americans

The Aztec civilization clearly had the most advanced culture in the Americas. Aztec engineers built a city with palaces, temples, and the world's largest pyramid. The Aztecs mined gold, silver, jade, and turquoise for jewelry and carvings. They also wrote books and made colorful paintings. Aztec astronomers created calendars to show people when to plant and harvest crops. They could even predict the coming of comets. If you still don't believe that the Aztecs were the most advanced people of their time, here is one last fact: The Aztecs were the first people to make hot cocoa and other chocolate treats.

Writing Guidelines: Paragraphs

Make sure you understand your assignment before you begin your planning and writing. Then follow the steps listed below.

PREWRITING   Choosing a Subject

■ Select a specific topic that interests you. (Your teacher may give you a general subject area to choose from.)

Gathering Details

■ Collect ideas and details about your topic.
■ Write a topic sentence that states what your paragraph is going to be about. (See page 79 for help.)
■ List ideas and details to include in your paragraph.

WRITING   Writing the First Draft

■ Start your paragraph with the topic sentence. (Make sure to indent the first line.)
■ Follow with sentences that support your topic. Use your list of ideas as a guide.
■ Close with a sentence that reminds readers about your topic.

REVISING   Improving Your Writing

■ Add information if you need to say more about your topic.
■ Rewrite sentences that are not easy to understand.

EDITING   Checking for Errors

■ Check the revised version of your writing for capitalization, punctuation, and spelling errors. Also have someone else check for errors.
■ Then write a neat final copy of your paragraph to share.

Details in Paragraphs

Details are an important part of any paragraph. They are the facts and examples that support or prove your topic sentence. Some of the information you use may be *personal* details—things you know or remember from your own experience. However, you will often go to sources like books, magazines, or experts for the facts you need.

Details from Other Sources

Here are some tips for collecting details from other sources of information:

1. **Ask someone you know.** Parents, neighbors, and teachers may know a lot about your topic.

2. **Talk to an expert.** Ask an expert about your subject by making a phone call, sending a letter, or visiting in person.

3. **Write or call for information.** If you think a museum, a business, or a government office has information you need, send for it. You may also be able to visit these places and gather facts for yourself.

4. **Gather details** from books, magazines, the Internet, and so on.

Personal Details

Details from Your Senses
- These details are things that you see, hear, smell, taste, and touch.

When you first taste this spicy cocoa . . .

Details from Your Memory
- These details are things you remember from past experiences.

The play stopped at that point because . . .

Details from Your Imagination
- These details are things you wonder about, hope for, or wish.

What if Cortés had been defeated by the Aztecs?

Organizing Your Ideas

The sentences in the body of a paragraph must be organized so that readers can follow all of your ideas. Here are three basic ways to organize your sentences:

Chronological Order   Narrative paragraphs should be organized chronologically. (*Chronological* means "according to time.") You can use words like *first* and *second* to help organize your ideas and details according to time. (See page 88 for more *time* words.)

> **Later, the Aztecs drove the Spaniards out of the city, but Montezuma II died in the fighting. Then Cortés and his men attacked and destroyed Tenochtitlán.** (The red words show time.)

✳ You should also use chronological order in paragraphs that explain how to do something.

Order of Location   Descriptive paragraphs are usually organized by location to help readers follow the details. For example, a description may move from left to right or from top to bottom. You can use words like *above* and *below* to move from one part of the description to the next. (See page 88 for more *location* words.)

> **On his head, a knight wore a covering that looked like a jaguar's head with its jaws opened very wide. . . . To protect his body, a knight wore padded tan clothing painted with black spots to look like a jaguar.** (The red words show location.)

Order of Importance   Persuasive paragraphs are usually organized by order of importance. You can arrange your arguments by starting out with the least important point and leading up to the most important, or you can do the opposite. (See page 83 for a persuasive paragraph.)

Organizing Paragraphs in Essays and Reports

When you complete an essay or a report, you will be writing several paragraphs. This means more work, of course. Not only do you have to organize the ideas within each paragraph, but you also have to organize the paragraphs within the longer piece of writing. Here are some tips to follow: (See pages 89-103 and 195-207 for more tips.)

1 **Write each paragraph to stand on its own.** Be sure that every paragraph deals with a main idea and is clear.

2 **Name the subject of your report in the opening paragraph.** Usually, you will begin with some interesting details to get the readers' attention. Then you will tell what your writing is about—the specific subject.

3 **Develop the specific subject in the middle paragraphs, or body.** Each of these paragraphs should add information that further explains the subject of the report. Often, the paragraph that contains the most important information comes right before the final paragraph.

4 **End with a concluding paragraph.** This paragraph is usually a review of the main points of the report. Sometimes it is good to use the last sentence to say why the subject is important.

5 **Use transitions to connect the paragraphs smoothly.** (See page 88.) In the paragraph parts below, the transitions are shown in red.

> **. . . The Aztecs, a very religious people, believed that they could do nothing without the help of their gods.**
>
> **As a result of this belief, several ceremonies and customs developed. Human sacrifices were made to the sky god Tezcatlipoca. . . . Games and sports were not only fun; they were religious ceremonies.**
>
> **Besides these religious interests, the Aztecs wanted their children to go to school. Many children learned to read and write, dance, sing, and play instruments. . . .**

Transition Words

Use the words and phrases in this chart to help you organize your ideas in paragraphs and other forms of writing.

Words that can be used to **show location:**

above	around	between	inside	outside
across	behind	by	into	over
against	below	down	near	throughout
along	beneath	in back of	off	to the right
among	beside	in front of	on top of	under

Words that can be used to **show time:**

about	during	yesterday	until	finally
after	first	meanwhile	next	then
at	second	today	soon	as soon as
before	third	tomorrow	later	when

Words that can be used to **compare things** (show similarities):

likewise	as	in the same way
like	also	similarly

Words that can be used to **contrast things** (show differences):

but	otherwise	on the other hand	although
yet	however	still	even though

Words that can be used to **emphasize a point:**

again	in fact	for this reason

Words that can be used to **add information:**

again	and	for instance	as well
also	besides	next	along with
another	for example	finally	in addition

Words that can be used to **conclude or summarize:**

as a result	finally	in conclusion
therefore	lastly	in summary

Writing Essays

An **essay** is a form of factual writing that is more than one paragraph in length. Some essays are mostly informational and sound a lot like classroom reports. Other essays focus more on the writer's opinion or belief about a subject. Essays like this try to persuade readers to accept a certain point of view.

Writing an essay is really thinking on paper. In one essay you may do a lot of exploring and explaining. In another one you may do more comparing and arguing. Your teachers assign essays because they know it is one of the best ways for you to think clearly and completely about important subjects.

What's Ahead

The first part of this chapter will help you write an informational (expository) essay, while the second part will help you write a persuasive essay. The last part gives special guidelines to help you collect ideas for different types of essays.

- **Sample Informational Essay**
- **Writing Guidelines**
- **Sample Persuasive Essay**
- **Writing Guidelines**
- **Writing About a Person, a Place, an Object, a Definition, an Event, an Explanation, and Writing to Persuade**

Sample Informational Essay

In this essay, Eng Lee shares three important values that guide him. All of his information is based on personal experience. Other informational essays may be based on reading and other forms of research.

My Personal Values

BEGINNING

After a few opening comments, the writer names his specific subject.

Each and every one of us has many personal values. These values are important to us. They are the rules that we live by. There are three main values that guide me.

Getting a good education is my most important value. For the last 20 to 30 years, my family has suffered through a war and lost almost everything. Now education has given me a chance to get some of these things back. I learned about the value of education from my grandfather. He always said that education can take me anywhere, and I believe he is right.

MIDDLE

Each middle paragraph discusses an important value.

Respect for the Hmong culture is my next most important value. I will never forget where I came from, what languages I speak, what food I eat, what my religion is, and so on. I also learned this value from my grandfather. He always told me never to forget who I am, and one day it will help me get my people back together.

Believing in love is my third most important value. I know that someone is and always will be there for me, in bad times or in good times. There will always be someone who cares a lot about me and knows how I feel. I learned this value from my friends, my cousins, and the radio station I listen to.

I will always value education, my culture, and the power of love. These three values may not be important to some other people, but they will guide me forever. They will help me do many good things in life, for myself and for many other people.

ENDING

The closing emphasizes the writer's feeling about his subject.

The Basic Shape of an Essay

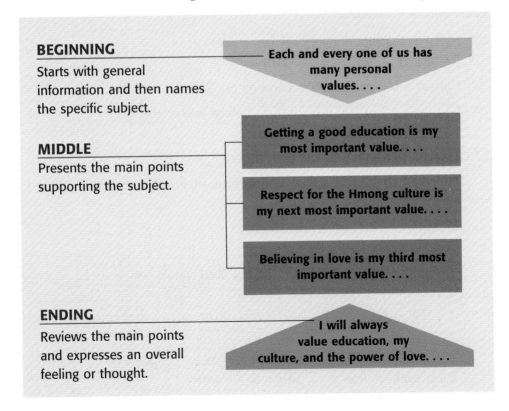

BEGINNING

Starts with general information and then names the specific subject.

Each and every one of us has many personal values. . . .

MIDDLE

Presents the main points supporting the subject.

Getting a good education is my most important value. . . .

Respect for the Hmong culture is my next most important value. . . .

Believing in love is my third most important value. . . .

ENDING

Reviews the main points and expresses an overall feeling or thought.

I will always value education, my culture, and the power of love. . . .

Writing Guidelines: Informational Essay

PREWRITING Choosing a Subject

- In an informational essay, you share important or interesting information about a subject. (See pages 40-41 for ideas.) Your job will be to select a specific subject to write about. Here is an example:

  General subject area: Values

  Specific writing subject: Personal values that guide me

- Discuss possible subjects with your teacher before you choose one for your essay. Make sure to select a subject that interests you and that you know something about.

Gathering Details

- List all of your ideas about the subject.
- Review this list
- Collect additional information as needed.
- Organize all of the information before you write.

Using a Graphic Organizer

The **line diagram** below is one type of graphic organizer that will help you organize your ideas.

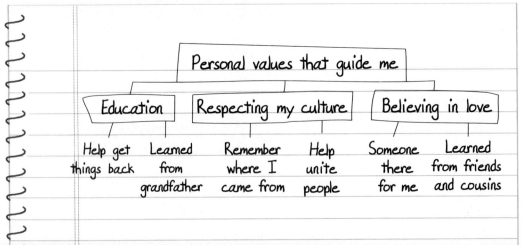

WRITING Writing the First Draft

When you write an informational essay, remember that each of the three parts—the beginning, the middle, and the ending—plays an important role.

BEGINNING The opening paragraph should make general comments about your subject and then state the specific part of the subject that your essay will cover.

MIDDLE The middle paragraphs should include information that supports or explains the subject. Put one main point (and the details that go with it) in each paragraph. (See page 53.)

ENDING The closing paragraph should restate the subject and/or summarize the main points covered in the essay. In addition, you may remind readers why the subject is important.

REVISING Improving Your Writing

Review the first draft of your essay using the checklist below as a guide. Also have a teacher or classmate review your work.

_____ Does the opening paragraph introduce the subject in an interesting way?

_____ Does all of the information in the middle paragraphs support the subject? Is enough information included?

_____ Are the ideas organized in the best way?

_____ Does the title (if one is already written) help identify the subject?

_____ Does the last paragraph bring the essay to an effective close?

Make the necessary changes or improvements in your first draft.

EDITING Checking for Errors

Check your revised writing for spelling, grammar, punctuation, and capitalization errors. Have a teacher or classmate check for errors also.

Sample Persuasive Essay

In this persuasive essay, Stephanie Wood argues against capital punishment. She includes three main points to support her opinion.

BEGINNING

The writer introduces her subject and states her opinion.

MIDDLE

The ideas in the middle paragraphs support the opinion.

ENDING

The writer restates her opinion and her main points.

Capital Punishment Is Wrong!

Capital punishment results in death by execution. It is legal in many states as a punishment for serious crimes, but that does not make it right. Capital punishment should be stopped because it is morally wrong, expensive, and such a slow process.

First of all, there is no moral basis for it. When we use the death penalty, we are following the criminals' example by doing something equally as bad ourselves. We are taking one life for another life. There is also a chance that a mistake will be made, and the wrong person will be put to death. Is this type of revenge worth such a risk?

Another problem with capital punishment is the high cost. For example, the special prison housing is expensive to staff and keep up. States with the death penalty use taxes to pay these expenses. Over the past 13 years, Florida has spent $57 million to carry out 18 executions. If you divide this dollar amount by the number of executions, you come up with a cost of $3.2 million for each execution. That is a great deal of money.

In addition, using the death penalty is a very slow process. At least 97 percent of all death-row prisoners are not executed on time. As a result, the waiting list for executions grows year after year. If the U.S. legal system executed one inmate every day, it would still take 30 years to empty all of the cells on death row. A process this slow does not make sense.

In conclusion, capital punishment should be dropped from our legal system. People should see that it is morally wrong. If not, then common sense should tell them that it doesn't work well since it is so expensive and such a slow process.

Writing Guidelines: Persuasive Essay

PREWRITING Choosing a Subject

■ In a persuasive essay, your goal is to convince readers to accept your opinion about a subject. So it is important to choose a subject that you have strong feelings about. Your teacher may provide writing ideas for you to choose from. If not, review the list of persuasive topics in your handbook (page 40).

■ Discuss possible subjects with your teacher before you select one. This brief chart shows the difference between subjects for an informational essay and a persuasive essay.

Subjects for an Informational Essay	Subjects for a Persuasive Essay
How to practice a new language	Everyone should learn a second language.
History of electric cars	We should switch to electric cars.

Gathering Details

■ List (or cluster) all of your ideas about a specific subject. After reviewing your list, collect additional information as needed—think more about your subject, talk with others, read articles, and so on.

■ Before writing your essay, have at least two or three main points to support your opinion. Here are the three main points in the sample essay:

Subject: Capital punishment is wrong.

Main supporting points: 1. Morally wrong
2. Expensive
3. Slow process

■ Organize your information before you write your first draft. (See the outline on page 96 and the graphic organizer on page 92 for ideas.)

Using an Outline

An **outline** is an organized list of the information you will use in your writing. The details are listed from general to specific. In an outline, if you have a I., you must have at least a II. If you have an A., you must have at least a B., and so on.

Topic Outline

A **topic outline** is an organized list of words and phrases about a subject. You may use a topic outline to organize your ideas for an essay.

Sentence Outline

A **sentence outline** organizes ideas using complete thoughts, which means you can fit in more information. The sentence outline is often used for longer reports and research papers.

Subject: Capital punishment should be stopped.

I. Morally wrong
   A. Makes us act like criminals
   B. Wastes another life
   C. Offers no second chance
II. Expensive
   A. Costs a lot to operate
   B. Uses tax money
      1. $57 million for 18 executions in Florida
      2. $3.2 million for each one
III. Slow process
   A. 97% not executed on time
   B. Huge waiting list

Subject: Capital punishment should be stopped.

I. Capital punishment is morally wrong.
   A. It makes us act like criminals.
   B. It wastes another life for revenge.
   C. It offers no way to correct a mistake.
II. The cost of capital punishment is very high.
   A. Special prison staff and upkeep are expensive.
   B. States with the death penalty use taxes to pay for it.
      1. In the last 13 years, Florida spent $57 million for 18 executions.
      2. Each execution cost $3.2 million.
III. Using this form of punishment is a very slow process.
   A. At least 97% of death-row prisoners are not executed on time.
   B. The waiting list grows year after year.

WRITING   Writing the First Draft

BEGINNING Your opening paragraph should introduce your subject and state your opinion. It may also tell which points you plan to cover in your essay. (See the opening paragraph on page 94.)

MIDDLE Write about each main point in a separate paragraph. Use your outline, list, or other organizer as a guide. In a persuasive essay, the strongest argument is usually presented first, or last.

ENDING The last paragraph should restate your opinion and summarize the main points in your argument. (See the closing on page 94.)

REVISING   Improving Your Writing

Review your first draft using the following checklist as a guide. Also have at least one other person review your work.

_____ Does the opening paragraph give background information and state my opinion?

_____ Do the main points in the middle paragraphs support my opinion?

_____ Are the main points organized so that readers will be able to follow my argument?

_____ Does the title help identify the subject of my essay?

Make the necessary changes or improvements in your essay.

EDITING   Checking for Errors

Check your revised writing for spelling, grammar, punctuation, and capitalization errors. Also have one other person check your writing for errors. Then make a neat final copy to share.

Writing About a Person

When writing about a person, choose someone you know well. That makes it easier to share interesting details about this person. It's important to include many details so readers can picture your subject in their minds. But it's also important to say nothing that will hurt your subject's feelings. The following guidelines will help you collect details for your writing:

Observe ■ Watch the person you plan to write about. Maybe the person moves his or her hands while talking, laughs in a special way, or wears a certain type of hat.

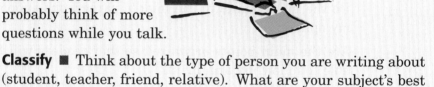

Investigate ■ Plan to talk with your subject. Write down a few questions to ask. Then listen closely to the answers. You will probably think of more questions while you talk.

Classify ■ Think about the type of person you are writing about (student, teacher, friend, relative). What are your subject's best traits?

Remember ■ Share a story that tells something important about your subject.

Compare ■ What other person, place, or thing could your subject be compared to? Is he or she like a sports hero, a roaring lion, a quiet pond, or a personal computer?

Question ■ Ask other people about this person.

Evaluate ■ Ask yourself why this person is important to you.

Writing About a Place

When writing about a place, think of somewhere you have been, or somewhere you have learned about. Your writing should help readers know why this place is important to you. The following guidelines will help you collect ideas for your writing. You may also use the collecting strategies listed in the handbook. (See pages 44-45.)

Observe ■ Study the place you plan to write about. Use photos, postcards, or videos if you can't go there yourself.

Record ■ Write down important details about your subject. Think about the sights, sounds, smells, and colors related to this place.

Question ■ Ask yourself, "If this place could talk, what would it tell me?" Also talk to other people who know about this place.

Identify ■ Consider the type of place you are describing. Is it a public place like a park or a theater? Is it a private place like a room in your home?

Remember ■ Think of a story about this place. It could involve something that happened to you, or it could be a story you heard or read about.

Compare ■ Compare your subject to other places.

Analyze ■ What is the most important thing about this place? When is the best time to go there?

Evaluate ■ Why is this place important to you? How would you feel if this place were no longer there?

When you write about a place, don't try to say everything you know about it. Instead, focus on a few main ideas, presented clearly and colorfully.

Writing About an Object

When writing about an object, tell your readers why it is special to you. (An *object* is something you can see or feel, like a poster or a piece of jewelry.) Use the following guidelines to collect ideas for your writing:

Observe ■ Think about these questions as you study your object: How is the object used? Who uses it? How does it work? What does it look like?

Record ■ Write down details about its color, size, and shape.

Research ■ Learn about the object. Try to find out when it was first made and used. Ask other people about it.

Define ■ What class or category does this object fit into? (See "Writing a Definition" below.)

Remember ■ Think of an interesting story about this object.

Compare ■ Think of similar objects you could compare your subject to. Also consider surprising comparisons. What type of person is the object like? What flavor of ice cream is it like?

Evaluate ■ Why is this object important? Would you or anyone else miss this object if it suddenly disappeared?

✳ An object by itself may not be very interesting. But if you connect it to a person, and to his or her feelings about it, then the object does become interesting to write about.

Writing a Definition

Put the term you are defining *(polar bear)* into a class or category of similar objects or ideas *(large meat-eating animals)*. Then list special characteristics that make this object different from other objects in that class *(lives in the Arctic)*.

Term—*A polar bear . . .*
Class—*is a large meat-eating animal . . .*
Characteristic—*that lives in the Arctic.*

Writing About an Event

When writing about an event, try to make it come alive for your readers by sharing plenty of details. But don't try to say everything. Focus on the important ideas or on one interesting part. The following guidelines will help you collect ideas for your writing:

Observe ■ Study the event carefully. What are the sights, sounds, tastes, and smells of this event? Listen to what people around you are saying.

Remember ■ If you are writing about something that happened to you, list or cluster ideas related to this event. (See page 36 for help.)

List ■ Answer the *who? what? when? where? why?* and *how?* questions for the event.

Search ■ If possible, read about the event. Ask other people what they know about it.

Name ■ What type of event is this? It could be a public event like a city festival, or a private event like a family gathering.

Compare ■ Consider how this event is like (or different from) other events.

Evaluate ■ Decide why the event is important to you. Does it have an interesting background? Did it prove something to you? Has it changed you? Did it affect anyone else?

When you have collected enough information, think of an interesting way to begin your writing. Start with a surprising detail or an important fact about the event to get your readers' attention.

Writing an Explanation

When writing an explanation, you are trying to make something easier to understand. You may be asked to explain how to do or make something. You may need to explain how something works, or how to get from one place to another. The following guidelines will help you collect ideas:

Observe ■ If possible, observe or try out your subject. Pay close attention to the steps and details that will help you write your explanation.

Research ■ If necessary, read and learn about your subject. Find out what makes it different or important.

Ask ■ Talk to people who already understand or know about your subject. Ask them questions about anything you don't understand.

Describe ■ List each step or part needed to follow your explanation. Include all of the important details in your list.

Compare ■ Compare your subject to something easier for your readers to understand. *(Baking bread is like playing basketball. You need to follow certain rules, and timing is important.)*

Analyze ■ What is the most important part or step? What would happen if you leave a part out or skip a step?

Evaluate ■ Why is your subject important? How might it help your readers?

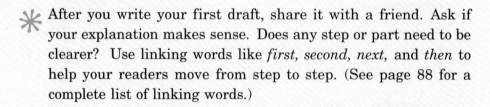

After you write your first draft, share it with a friend. Ask if your explanation makes sense. Does any step or part need to be clearer? Use linking words like *first, second, next,* and *then* to help your readers move from step to step. (See page 88 for a complete list of linking words.)

Writing to Persuade

When writing to persuade, your goal is to get readers to agree with your opinion about something. Here is a sample opinion statement: *Our library should stay open after school.*

To get started, choose a subject that really interests you, one that you have a strong opinion about. Use the guidelines below to collect details to support your opinion.

Reflect ■ How do you feel about the subject? List or write about your reasons for feeling that way.

Investigate ■ Ask other people how they feel about the subject. Understanding how other people feel may help you form a stronger opinion.

Research ■ Read about your subject. Try to find the latest information, and take careful notes.

Show ■ Use facts and examples to support your main point. *(Each day the United States creates enough garbage to cover the state of Rhode Island.)*

Plan ■ Persuasive writing needs to be well organized.

- State your opinion in positive terms. *(Schools should help students learn about different careers.)*
- List your supporting reasons and details under the opinion statement.
- Organize your list so the strongest reason is either first or last. (Saving it for last is probably your best choice.)
- Plan what you want to say in your opening paragraph (or first sentence). Your opening should get your readers interested in your subject, and state your opinion. (See page 94 for more help.)

When you write persuasively, you must prove that your opinion is strong and that it really matters. In order to do this, you really have to care about your subject.

The Art of Writing

Writing with Style

Writing Techniques and Terms

Writing with Style

Your personal style is the way you present yourself to the world. The way that you cut your hair and wear your clothes is part of your style. The things that you like to do and say are also part of your style. Your personal style helps set you apart from everyone else.

Your **writing style** (or voice) is the way you state your ideas on paper. For the most part, your writing style will develop naturally as you continue to write and learn the language. There are, however, some things you can do to help improve your style—as you will see in the pages ahead.

What's Ahead

The first part of this chapter describes the basic elements of style. Then the chapter explains different ways to develop your writing style. The final part talks about using colorful words and knowing what to change in your writing to improve its overall style.

- **Understanding Style**
- **Developing Your Style**
- **Modeling the Masters**
- **Using Strong, Colorful Words**
- **Knowing What to Change**

Understanding Style

Words You show your style in the words that you use. (See pages 110-111.)

In this sample, Tou Moua uses specific words and phrases that show how he feels about his former home. (Some of these words and phrases are highlighted in red.)

> On both sides of the river there were many different kinds of beautiful flowers. When the sun would shine, all of the flowers would sparkle with light. When the wind blew, all the flower petals would float through the village. I was always happy and believed I lived near the sky by God.

Details The details and ideas that you share about a subject also help create your style.

In the following sample, Dimitri Juste includes a lot of specific details about his subject. (Some of the details are shown in red.)

> I woke up feeling great, but I had a strange feeling in my stomach. This was my first day of school. I remember my mom holding my hand. I felt the tight bond between us. As we got closer to the school, her hand slipped away from mine. She said, "Be careful. Have fun." She kissed me good-bye. I felt like my life had ended.

Sentences In addition, you show your style in the way you build sentences. (See pages 73-76.)

In the sample below, Sandra Jerotic connects many of her ideas with *and* or *but* to make her writing flow smoothly.

> We came here on December 1, and I started school on December 8. My English was not good at all, but I tried my best. Students here were strange to me, and I was probably strange to them, too. After a while, my English got better and better. Now I am in sixth grade. I have a lot of friends, and I have very good grades, all A's and B's.

Developing Your Style

Here's how your writing style can be improved:

Read a lot. Read books, magazines, and newspapers. Seeing how other writers express themselves will help you with your own writing.

When you read sentences or words you especially like, write them down in a notebook. Then use these ideas as models for your own writing.

Write every day. Keep a daily journal. Writing every day is one of the best ways to develop your style. (See pages 125-128.)

Look at the world with a writer's eye. Be alert to interesting sights and sounds in your daily life. And keep track of them in a notebook.

Try different forms. Write friendly letters and notes. Write true stories and fictional stories. Write poems and news stories. Writing in different ways helps you express yourself with more style.

Write about subjects that are important to you. You will develop a strong, personal style if you write about subjects that you really care about.

Be yourself. Always try to write sincerely, honestly, and clearly. If you do these three things, your writing will have a natural style.

Listen to your writing. Hearing your writing read out loud makes it easier to know which parts work well . . . and which parts need improvement. If you don't like how your writing sounds, rewrite it.

Write with details. Use details that help readers see, hear, smell, taste, and feel your subject. Also make comparisons, and use other figures of speech. (See page 175.)

Learn the rules for writing. You need to know the basic rules of grammar and sentence structure in order to write with style. (See pages 402-433 for help.)

Modeling the Masters

"The hardest part about writing is finding the correct words to use."

—Waheed Liaquat, student writer

Beginning artists learn a lot about art by studying the work of famous painters. In the same way, you can learn a lot about writing by studying the sentences of some of your favorite authors. When you come across sentences that you really like, practice writing sentences of your own that follow the author's pattern of writing. This process is sometimes called **modeling.** Listed below are basic guidelines you can use for modeling.

Guidelines for Modeling

- Find a sentence or a short passage that you would like to use as a model.
- Think of a subject for your practice writing.
- Follow the pattern of the sentence or passage as you write about your own subject. (You do not have to follow the pattern exactly.)
- Build each sentence one small part at a time. (Don't try to work too quickly.)
- Review your work and change any parts that seem confusing or unclear.
- Save your writing. Share it with a classmate.
- Find other passages to use as models; keep practicing.

Modeling Samples

Modeling Sentences Here is a smooth-reading sentence from the novel *The Cay* by Theodore Taylor: (Notice the modifying phrases beginning with "Stew Cat" and "looking.")

> I stood there on the beach, Stew Cat by my side, looking in the direction of the sounds.

Here is a student sample following this pattern:

> I sat there on the park bench, Sam by my side, thinking about our loss in the soccer match.

Modeling Short Passages Here is a short passage from the novel *The Talking Earth* by Jean Craighead George. (The four sentences in this passage vary in terms of length and word order.)

> Billie Wind eased out of the dugout, testing the depth of the mire (mud). It was only a few inches deep. Beneath the black residue from the swamp was firm sand. She walked swiftly, not even turning around to bid her dugout good-bye.

Here is a student sample following this pattern:

> Julisa rushed into the cafeteria, looking for her best friends. They were in line only ten yards away. In front of these girls were many other hungry classmates. Julisa moved quickly, not even looking at the other students around her.

More Modeling Ideas

- Keep a file of favorite sentences from your classmates' writing. Practice writing sentences like these.
- Rewrite a section of one of your old stories to resemble the style of one of your favorite authors.
- Write new stories in the style of one of your favorite authors.

Using Strong, Colorful Words

Strong, colorful words help make your writing come alive. They give your writing . . . style! The following guidelines will help you choose the best nouns, verbs, and modifiers for your stories, reports, and letters.

 In order to make the best word choices, you need to build your vocabulary. The more words you know, the more words you have to choose from. (See pages 285-300 for help.)

Choosing Specific Nouns

Some nouns are **general** (*car, house, animal*). Other nouns are **specific** (*convertible, mansion, anteater*). Specific nouns give readers clearer, more detailed pictures. As you read down each list in the chart below, the nouns become more specific. The last noun in each list is the type that can make your writing clear and colorful.

person	place	thing	idea
woman	city	food	sickness
athlete	capital	vegetable	virus
Lisa Leslie	Washington, D.C.	cabbage	influenza

Choosing Specific Verbs

Specific **action verbs** tell readers exactly what happened. For example, the specific verbs *chatted* and *argued* say more than the general verb *talked*. The sentence "The customer *argued* with the clerk" is clearer than "The customer *talked* with the clerk."

 Try not to use the "be" verbs (*is, are, was, were*) too often. Many times a stronger action verb can be made from another word in the same sentence.

A "be" verb: Cesar *is* the leader in the election for class president.

A stronger verb: Cesar *leads* the election for class president.

Choosing Words with Feeling

The words you use in your writing should not only be specific, but they should also have the right feeling, or **connotation.** (*Connotation* means "the feeling that a word suggests.")

Let's say you are writing about a serious fire in your apartment building. It would probably not be enough to say that people who lived in this building were *afraid* or *scared*. For this situation, the word with the right connotation is *horrified* (filled with painful dread or fear) or *panicked* (feeling sudden fright).

 You can use a thesaurus to help find the best words for your writing. It will help you pick the word with not only the right meaning but also the right feeling. (See page 287.)

Choosing Effective Modifiers

Adverbs ● Use adverbs to describe the action (the verb) in a sentence. For example, "Takeo laughed at the joke" is okay. But "Takeo laughed *wildly* at the joke" is better because it tells *how* the subject laughed. (See pages 430-431 for more about adverbs.)

Adjectives ● Strong, colorful adjectives can help make the nouns in your writing clearer and more interesting. For example, you may tell your readers that *Black Thunder* is a "water slide," but telling them that it is a *"hair-raising* water slide" says so much more. (See pages 427-429 for more about adjectives.)

 Some adjectives are used so often that they carry very little meaning: *neat, big, pretty, small, cute, fun, bad, nice, good, dumb, great,* and *funny.* Try not to overuse these words in your writing.

Knowing What to Change

How do you know what to change to make your writing more interesting, colorful, and clear? The five points listed below show you things to check for. (See pages 54-56 for more ideas.)

1 Ideas: Your subject is too general or uninteresting.
You may need to think about your subject in a different way. Instead of saying something general like "I like art," try being more specific and creative: "Art is a language we all share."

2 Organization: Your writing lacks focus (a main point).
Maybe your writing covers too many different ideas. You can improve your writing by concentrating on one main point about your subject. (See page 49.)

3 Voice: Your writing doesn't sound like you.
If your writing sounds as though it came out of a textbook, try again. This time, be honest and share your real feelings.

4 Word Choice: Your writing doesn't say enough.
Maybe you need to add more details to support your subject. *Remember:* It's the details you share that make your writing interesting to read. (See pages 44-45 for help.)

5 Sentence Style: Your sentences all sound the same.
If this happens, check your sentence beginnings. You may have started too many of your sentences in the same way, or you may have used too many "be" verbs *(is, are, was, were)*. Then again, you may have repeated a certain word too many times. You can make your writing more interesting by varying your sentence beginnings and changing some of the words you've used.

 Your writing must first be clear and sincere. Add colorful words (or make other stylistic changes) only when you feel they can improve your writing. If you add too many things, your writing will sound flowery or unnatural.

Writing Techniques and Terms

When your teacher discusses a writing assignment, he or she may use important words that are new to you. For example, your teacher may ask you to write a *narrative* that includes plenty of *dialogue*.

You would not be able to complete this assignment unless you knew the meaning of *narrative* and *dialogue*. Nor would you be able to write a *simile* or a *metaphor* unless you knew the meaning of each word. You'll find this chapter very helpful because it explains all of the important words associated with writing—including the four just mentioned above.

What's Ahead

Think of the following pages as your glossary to the vocabulary of writing. Both special writing techniques and general writing terms are included.

- **Writing Techniques**
- **Writing Terms**

Writing Techniques

Writers use different **techniques** to write stories and reports. (*Techniques* are methods or ways of doing something.) Look over the following writing techniques and then experiment with some of them in your own writing.

Allusion A reference to a well-known person, place, thing, or event that the writer assumes the reader will be familiar with.

> **Hector rushed in like Superman and rescued the cat from the burning building.**

Antithesis Antithesis means "exact opposite." In writing, it usually means using opposite ideas in the same thought or sentence.

> **He decided to finish his chores before his chores "finished" him.**

Caricature A description of a character in which his or her features are exaggerated and appear funny or ridiculous.

Dramatic monologue A speech in which a character gives readers a lot of information about himself or herself. The character usually does this by talking, alone, but as if someone else were there.

Exaggeration An overstatement or stretching of the truth used to emphasize a point or paint a clearer picture. (See *hyperbole* and *overstatement*.)

> **I laughed so hard I began to pop the buttons on my shirt.**

Flashback A technique in which a writer interrupts a story to go back and explain an earlier event.

Foreshadowing Hints or clues that a writer uses to suggest what will happen next in a story.

Hyperbole An extreme exaggeration or overstatement that a writer uses for emphasis. (See *exaggeration* and *overstatement*.)

My brother exploded when he saw the damage to his car.

Irony A technique that uses a word or phrase to mean the exact opposite of its normal meaning.

Danielle smiles and laughs all of the time, so we call her Grumpy.

Local color The use of details that are common in a certain place (a *local* area). A story taking place on a seacoast would probably contain details about the water and the life and people near it.

Metaphor A figure of speech that compares two things without using the word *like* or *as*.

The cup of hot tea was the best medicine for my cold.

Overstatement An exaggeration or stretching of the truth. (See *exaggeration* and *hyperbole*.)

We screamed until our eyes bugged out.

Oxymoron A technique in which two words with opposite meanings are put together for a special effect.

jumbo shrimp, old news, small fortune, bittersweet

Paradox A statement that is true but that seems to be saying two opposite things.

The more free time you have, the less you get done.

Parallelism Repeating similar grammatical structures (words, phrases, or sentences) to give writing rhythm.

The doctor took her temperature, checked her heartbeat, and tested her reflexes.

Personification A figure of speech in which a nonhuman thing (an idea, object, or animal) is given human characteristics.

The low clouds bumped into the mountains.

Poetic devices Poets use many of the devices and techniques listed in this chapter. (See pages 175-176 for additional devices.)

Pun A phrase that uses words in a way that gives them a funny effect. The words used in a pun often sound the same but have different meanings.

> **That story about rabbits is a real hare raiser.** (*Hare,* another word for rabbit, is used instead of *hair.* A *hair-raiser* is a scary story.)

Sarcasm The use of praise to make fun of, or "put down," someone or something. The praise is not sincere and is actually intended to mean the opposite thing.

> **"That was a graceful move!" he said, as I tripped over the rug.**

Satire Using sarcasm, irony, or humor to make fun of people's habits or ideas. Satire is often used to raise questions about a current event or political decision. (See *sarcasm* and *irony.*)

Simile A figure of speech that compares two things, using the word *like* or *as.*

> **The dog danced around like loose litter in the wind.**

> **The ice was smooth as glass before the skaters entered the rink.**

Understatement The opposite of *exaggeration.* By using especially calm language, an author can bring special attention to an object or idea.

These hot red peppers may make your mouth tingle a bit.

Writing Terms

This glossary includes **terms** that are often used to describe different parts of the writing process. It also includes terms that explain special ways of stating an idea.

Analogy A comparison of similar objects. An analogy suggests that since the objects are alike in some ways, they will probably be alike in other ways.

> **Pets are like plants. If you give them lots of care and attention, they grow strong and healthy. If you neglect them, they become weak and sickly.**

Anecdote A little story used to illustrate or make a point.

> **Abe Lincoln walked two miles to return several pennies he had overcharged a customer.** (This anecdote shows Lincoln's honesty.)

Argumentation Writing or speaking that uses reasons and logic to make a point.

Arrangement The order in which details are placed in a piece of writing. *Arrangement* is also known as *organization*.

Audience The people who read or hear what has been written.

Balance Arranging words and phrases in a similar way to give them equal importance. Balance gives writing a pleasing flow or rhythm.

> **It was the best of times; it was the worst of times . . .**

Beginning The first or opening part in a piece of writing. In a paragraph, the beginning is the first (topic) sentence. In an essay or a report, the beginning is the first paragraph, including the thesis statement.

Body The main or middle part in a piece of writing. The body comes between the beginning and the ending (closing) and explains the writing's main ideas.

Brainstorming Collecting ideas by talking openly about all the possibilities.

Central idea The main idea or point in a piece of writing, often stated in a thesis statement or topic sentence. (See *thesis statement* and *topic sentence.*)

Cliche A phrase or sentence that has been overused. It is often better to find a new way of saying the same thing. (See *trite.*)

> *Cliche:* **Her face was as red as a beet.**
>
> *Better:* **Her face turned a rosy pink, then a deep red.**

Closing The summary or final part in a piece of writing. In a paragraph, the closing is the last sentence. In an essay or a report, the closing is the final paragraph.

Coherence Putting ideas together in such a way that the reader can easily follow them.

Colloquialism A common word or phrase that is used when people talk to one another. Colloquialisms are usually not used in a formal speech or in most assigned writing.

> **"How's it goin'?" and "What's happenin'?" are colloquialisms for "How are you?"**

Description Writing that uses details to help the readers clearly imagine a certain person, place, thing, or idea.

> **We walked down into a cool ravine, listening to the jay's cheeet-cheeet in the still air.**

Dialogue Written conversation between two or more people.

Diction A writer's choice of words. Diction helps create a formal, proper writing style (for reports and business letters), or an informal, everyday writing style. (See *colloquialism* and *slang.*)

Emphasis Giving great importance to a particular idea in a piece of writing. Emphasis can be achieved by placing the idea in a special position, by repeating a key word or phrase, or by writing more about one idea than about the others.

Essay A piece of factual writing in which ideas on a single topic are presented, explained, argued, or described in an interesting way.

Exposition Writing that explains something.

Extended definition Writing that goes beyond the basic dictionary definition of a term. An extended definition can include personal definitions, similes, metaphors, quotations, and so on.

Figurative language Special comparisons, called *figures of speech,* that make your writing more creative. (See page 175.)

Focus The specific part of a subject that is written about in an essay, a paragraph, or a report.

Form The way a piece of writing is structured or organized.

   Examples: **poem   essay   report   news story**

Freewriting Writing whatever comes to mind about any topic.

Generalization A general statement that gives an overall, general view, rather than focusing on specific details.

Grammar The structure of language. The rules and guidelines that you follow in order to speak and write acceptably.

Idiom Words used in a special way that may be different from their literal meaning. (See pages 395-401.)

Rush-hour traffic moves *at a snail's pace.* (This idiom means "very slowly.")

Teresa was *floating on air* when she finished reading the letter. (This idiom means "feeling very happy.")

Issue A topic that people have different opinions about.

Should calculators be used in math classes?

Jargon The technical language of a particular group, occupation, or field.

Sailing jargon: **jib** **starboard** **stay the course**
tack **port** **lower the boom**

Journal A notebook for writing down thoughts, experiences, information, and writing ideas. (See pages 125-128.)

Juxtaposition Putting two ideas, words, or pictures together to create a new, often ironic meaning.

Oh, the joys of winter blizzards!

(An *ironic statement* uses words to mean the opposite of their usual meaning.)

Limiting the subject Taking a general subject and narrowing it down to a specific topic for a writing or a speaking assignment.

general subject **specific topic**
baseball ➤ **baseball skills** ➤ **hitting skills** ➤ **how to bunt**

Literal The actual or dictionary meaning of a word. Language that is literal means exactly what it appears to mean.

Loaded words Words that make people feel for or against something. Loaded words are often used in persuasive writing such as advertisements.

This new product is very affordable **and** easy-to-use.
Drinking and driving is a deadly combination.

(The red words are loaded words.)

Logic The science of reasoning. Logic uses reasons, facts, and examples to prove or support a point. (See page 253.)

Modifiers Words, phrases, or clauses that describe a subject.

> **The chimpanzee hung lazily by one arm and waved at the giggling children.**
>
> (Without the red modifiers, all we know is that a "chimpanzee hung and waved.")

Narrative Writing that tells about an event or a story.

Objective Writing that gives factual information without adding feelings or opinions. (See *subjective*.)

Personal narrative Writing that shares an event in the writer's life.

Persuasion Writing that is meant to change readers' minds about someone or something. (See *loaded words*.)

Plagiarism Taking someone else's words or ideas and using them as your own.

Point of view The position or angle from which a story is told. (See page 305.)

Process A method of doing something that involves steps or stages.

> **The writing process involves these steps: prewriting, writing the first draft, revising, and editing and proofreading.**

Prose Writing or speaking in the usual sentence form. Prose becomes poetry when it takes on rhyme and rhythm.

Purpose The specific reason that a person has for writing.

> *Examples:* **to narrate**   **to persuade**
> **to explain**   **to describe**

Revision Making changes in a piece of writing to improve its completeness and clarity.

Sensory details Specific details that are usually perceived through the senses. Sensory details help readers to see, feel, smell, taste, and/or hear what is being described.

> **As Derrick spoke, his teeth chattered and his breath made little clouds in the icy cold air.**

Slang Informal words or phrases used by particular groups of people when they talk to each other.

> *Examples:*   **chill out   hang loose   totally awesome**

Spontaneous Writing or speaking that is not planned or thought-out in advance.

Structure The way a piece of writing is organized. (See *form.*)

Style *How* an author writes (his or her choice of words).

Subjective Writing that includes personal feelings, attitudes, and opinions. (See *objective.*)

Summary Writing that presents only the most important ideas in something you have read. (See pages 191-194.)

Supporting details The facts or ideas that are used to make or prove a point, or explain or describe a topic.

Symbol A concrete (or real) object that is used to stand for an idea.

> **The American flag is a symbol of the United States. The stars stand for the 50 states, and the stripes stand for the 13 original U.S. colonies.**

Syntax The order of words in a sentence. The chapter "Writing Basic Sentences" will help you understand the syntax of sentences in English. (See pages 65-72.)

Theme The central idea or main point in a piece of writing.

Examples: **benefits of hard work   peer pressure**
animal rights   a good neighborhood
nonviolent resistance   importance of home
family relationships   quiet times
true friendship   bravery

Thesis statement A statement that gives the main idea or purpose of an essay.

Tone A writer's attitude toward his or her subject.

Examples: **serious   objective   humorous   subjective**

Topic The specific subject of a piece of writing.

Topic sentence The sentence that contains the main idea of a paragraph or a piece of writing. (See *central idea.*)

Eating a healthy breakfast is important.

Transition A word or phrase that connects or ties two ideas together smoothly. (See page 88.)

Examples: **meanwhile   finally   next   then   also**

Trite An expression considered to be an overused and ineffective way of saying something. (See *cliche.*)

Examples: **true blue   red hot   bright as the sun**

Unity A sense of oneness in writing in which each sentence helps to develop the main idea.

Universal A topic or idea that appeals to everyone, not just people of a particular age, race, income, or gender group.

Usage The way in which people use language. (Standard language generally follows the grammar rules; nonstandard language does not.) Most of the writing you do in school will require standard usage.

Personal Writing

Journal Writing

Writing Personal Narratives

Writing Friendly Letters

Journal Writing

There are many good reasons to write in a journal. Four of the most important reasons are listed below. After reading this list, you will begin to see how helpful **journal writing** can be.

Writing to Understand You can write about everything that happens to you (both good and bad). In this way, a journal helps you think about your daily experiences.

Writing to Practice Writing is like any other skill. In order to improve, you need to practice. Writing regularly in a journal is one of the best ways to practice.

Writing to Learn Writing in a journal about the subjects you are studying can help you become a better learner.

Writing to Create If you like to write poems and stories, you can try out different ideas in a journal.

What's Ahead

This chapter will help you learn more about journal writing, including how to get started and how to make discoveries as you write. You will also find information about different types of journals.

- **Getting Started**
- **Types of Journals**

Getting Started

A personal journal is your own special place to write. And it can be whatever you want it to be—a place to practice writing, a place to explore your experiences, and so on. To get started, follow the steps on this page.

1 **Collect the proper tools.** All you need is a notebook and some pens or pencils. You could also use a personal computer.

2 **Choose a regular time to write.** It could be early in the morning, late at night, or sometime in between. Also find a comfortable place to write, a place that is quiet enough for you to concentrate.

3 **Write every day.** Try to write for at least 5 to 10 minutes at a time. Write as freely as you can, and don't worry about how your writing sounds. It's okay to make mistakes in your journal.

✳ Writing in a journal is excellent practice if English is your second language.

4 **Write about things that are important to you.** Here are some ideas to get you started:

- interesting things you see and hear
- personal thoughts and feelings
- daily happenings
- important events
- books you've read
- ideas for stories and poems
- subjects you are studying
- (See pages 40-41 for more ideas.)

5 **Keep track of your writing.** Put the date on the top of the page each time you write. Read through your journal from time to time. Underline ideas that you would like to write more about in the future. Also make comments in the margins. Here are two sample comments: "I could write a story about this idea" or "I want to write more about this event."

Types of Journals

If you find writing in a personal journal helpful, consider keeping other types of journals as well. Four additional types are listed here.

Class Journal In a class journal (also called a *learning log*), you write about subjects you are studying. This kind of writing will help you learn and understand new information. (See page 318 for more about learning logs.)

Dialogue Journal In a dialogue journal, you and a friend, family member, or teacher write to each other. You can write about experiences you've had, books you've read, and ideas you think about. (See the sample on the next page.)

Diary A diary includes daily events in your life. (In a personal journal, you would think and write about these events rather than simply record them.)

Response Journal You may have strong feelings about some of the books you read. You can write about these feelings in a response journal.

Sample Personal Journal Writing

In this entry, Larisa Kurtovic thinks and writes about her new school.

Sept. 10

Today, it was my sixth day at school. Like every day, I had a lot of impressions. Everything is so new to me, that I'm looking forward to every day at school. I had algebra for the first time today. Mr. Jacobson is my teacher. To compare math in the U.S.A. with math in Bosnia, well, math in Bosnia is more serious. Here, there are some simple things, not as we had in Bosnia. But I like Mr. Jacobson, and I think I can be good in algebra class. Then after that, I had my cooking class. That's one of my favorite ones. Most of the things there I know, but it's good to hear them in English. . . .

Dialogue Journal

In this dialogue journal entry, Yong Lee and his teacher talk about *Tracker,* an adventure book by Gary Paulsen.

Nov. 12

Dear Ms. K,

Once I came very close to a deer in a park, and I couldn't believe how beautiful and sad its eyes were. That is what I was thinking when I was reading Tracker. I could picture the deer's beautiful, sad eyes staring at John. I was very happy that John didn't shoot the deer. Now I wonder what his grandma and grandpa will say when there is no meat for dinner.

Sincerely,
Yong

Nov. 16

Dear Yong,

I could picture the deer's eyes, too. Don't you think Gary Paulsen writes great descriptions? When I was reading Tracker, I felt like I was in the forest following the deer.

You have probably finished Tracker by now. How do you feel about the ending?

Sincerely,
Ms. K

Writing Personal Narratives

A **personal narrative** is a true story about some part of the writer's life. Max Lushchan feels his best piece of writing is a personal narrative about coming to this country. He said, "This experience got me interested and pulled me into the writing." Many students (including you, we hope!) find narrative writing interesting.

When you write a personal narrative, you . . .

1. get to relive an important time in your life,

2. learn about yourself through your writing, and

3. establish your special place in the world.
("Hey, listen to me. I have a story to tell.")

What's Ahead

This chapter will help you write personal narratives about the important experiences in your life. You will find student samples, writing guidelines, special tips, and much more.

- **Sample Personal Narrative**
- **Understanding Narratives**
- **Writing Guidelines**
- **Improving Your Narrative**
- **Second Sample: Personal Narrative**

Sample Personal Narrative

In this narrative, Katie Broitman shares an embarrassing experience. After you read this narrative, you will probably think of your own embarrassing experiences to write about.

BEGINNING

The opening paragraph introduces the subject and gives background information.

MIDDLE

The middle part tells the story using specific details.

ENDING

In the last paragraph, the writer shares her feelings about the experience.

Unwanted Solo

I have done a lot of embarrassing things in my life, but the time four years ago when I tried to sing solo in a musical production tops them all. I had gotten a part as a member of the chorus in *Charlie and the Chocolate Factory*.

One day at rehearsal, we were handed copies of "Who Can Make a Rainbow" and were told to memorize it by the next day, which was the first dress rehearsal. When I got home, I memorized this song word for word. I made everyone in my family hear me sing it at least five times.

The next afternoon I went happily to rehearsal. As I stepped into the gym, I took my place on stage just as the piano started. I took a deep breath and began to sing, "Who can make a rainbow, sprinkle it with dew" at the top of my lungs.

Then I realized the piano had stopped, and no one else was singing. I looked around and saw that everyone was staring at me. My teacher sighed and said in an exasperated voice, "You sing only when the chorus comes in."

Then it all hit me. I had been the only person singing along to the solo part. I felt like melting into the stage. My face turned bright red, and I muttered, "Oh." Throughout the rest of the rehearsal, I barely hummed along with the rest of the chorus.

Understanding Narratives

What makes a narrative "personal"?

All forms of personal writing—personal journals, friendly letters, and personal narratives—are alike in two important ways:

- **Subjects for all forms of personal writing come from the writer's own thoughts and experiences.**

- **All three forms are written in a personal style, almost as if the writer were having a conversation with a friend.**

What makes it special?

The personal narrative also has a few special qualities that make it different from a journal entry or a friendly letter. A personal narrative must . . .

- **focus on one specific subject,**

- **include a clear beginning, middle, and ending, and**

- **hold the reader's interest throughout.**

What makes a good subject?

It's enjoyable to write narratives (as well as other personal forms) because you are exploring subjects that interest you, subjects that come from your own experiences. To think of subjects for personal narratives, ask yourself the following questions:

- **Who are the important people in my life?** *(Think about your experiences with them.)*

- **Where have I been?** *(There is a story behind every place you visit.)*

- **What unforgettable things have happened to me?** *(Think of experiences that have changed you in some way.)*

Dear grandma,
You'll never believe what happened...

Writing Guidelines: Personal Narrative

PREWRITING Choosing a Subject

You should find it easy to select a subject for a personal narrative. Think of a memorable experience that happened over a short period of time.

✳ See "What makes a good subject?" on the previous page for help with your subject search.

Gathering Details

The experience you choose to write about may be very clear in your mind. If this is the case, you probably don't need to do any collecting. Just write your first draft.

✳ If you need to collect details, make a list or try doing a cluster. (See page 36.) You could also answer the 5 W's—*Who? What? When? Where?* and *Why?*—to help you remember the basic facts about the experience.

Sample 5 W's Chart

Subject: Embarrassing Time in a Musical

Questions	Answers
Who?	Me, Katie Broitman
What?	Sang out of turn in rehearsal (practice)
When?	Four years ago
Where?	Evanston Recreational Center
Why?	I wasn't listening.

WRITING Writing the First Draft

When writing a first draft, your job is to write down the details about your experience. But don't worry if you miss a few things. You can always add them later when you improve or revise your writing. Here are two different ways to start your first draft:

- Place yourself right in the middle of the action ("My brother and I were watching TV when . . . "). Then write down details as they come to mind until you get to the end of the experience.

- Plan out a beginning that gives background information and helps you focus on your subject. ("I have done a lot of embarrassing things in my life . . . "). Once you complete the beginning part, then continue writing about the experience.

REVISING Improving Your Writing

Review your writing after you finish your first draft. Decide if you have left out any important details or have put things in the wrong order. Also have someone else (classmate, teacher, family member) check your writing to see if any parts are unclear. Then revise your writing as necessary.

A personal narrative is a story, and stories work best when they include a lot of specific details, dialogue, and personal reflections. (See page 134 for examples.)

EDITING Checking for Errors

Check your revised writing for spelling, grammar, punctuation, and capitalization errors. (Have someone else check it as well.) Then write a neat final copy of your narrative to share.

Improving Your Narrative

Adding specific details, dialogue, and reflections can help make your narrative more interesting and enjoyable.

Adding Specific Details

To help readers see (and hear) the action in your narrative, add a lot of specific details. The sentences below from the first sample narrative (page 130) help readers see what is happening.

> **As I stepped into the gym, I took my place on stage just as the piano started. I took a deep breath and began to sing . . . .**
> **Then I realized the piano had stopped, and no one else was singing. I looked around and saw that everyone was staring at me.**

Adding Dialogue

Dialogue helps make your writing come alive for readers. The dialogue below from the second sample narrative (pages 135-136) puts the reader right in the middle of the experience.

> **"What your dad is saying is that his company is transferring him to the United States," my mom clearly explained.**
> **"What!" I stood and exclaimed.**
> **"Anna, sit down. You're the oldest, and you should understand. . . . that's final," my dad said in anger and left.**

Adding Reflections

Reflections help readers understand how you think and feel about your experience. In the following passage from the second sample narrative, the writer reflects upon her situation (red).

> **As I passed the metal detector, it went off because I was wearing a jumper with a metal buckle.** At that time, I wished the police would take me and not let me on the plane.

Second Sample: Personal Narrative

In this narrative, Mae O. Lavente shares an unforgettable experience—the time she left the Philippines for the United States.

Departure

BEGINNING

The writer starts right in the middle of the action.

My brother and I were watching TV when my dad called, "Anna, Patrick, we're going to have a family meeting. Go to the dining room."

My brother's eyes met mine. *Family meeting?* We never had one before. And that gave me a very odd feeling. As soon as we arrived, my dad started, "We've stayed in this country—I mean house—our whole life. And there are times that we have to leave and go on."

I really didn't understand what my dad was saying—country and leave?

MIDDLE

The writer identifies the important details about the experience.

"What your dad is saying is that his company is transferring him to the United States," my mom clearly explained.

"What!" I stood and exclaimed.

"Anna, sit down. You're the oldest, and you should understand. We're all going to leave. Tomorrow we're going to the embassy for the papers and that's final," my dad said in anger and left.

We were approved at the embassy and granted visas, and we were leaving June 10. We spent our last ten days packing up things and selling some of our appliances. We also found someone who would rent our house.

On June 10, my mom woke me up early. She said, "We have to leave early, or we might get caught in traffic."

"Well, I hope we do," I told myself.

MIDDLE
All of the details are organized by time.

We placed all our baggage on top of the van and headed for the airport. I was the last one in the car. As we moved farther along, I could see my home fading away. And in that moment, I felt a part of me would still be there.

We arrived at the airport at 8. As I passed the metal detector, it went off because I was wearing a jumper with a metal buckle. At that time, I wished the police would take me and not let me on the plane. I didn't get bored while waiting for our flight to be called because I was watching the Bulls playing the Supersonics.

"Flight 800 is now boarding. Flight 800 is now boarding," announced the lady. That was our flight.

ENDING
The closing part describes the writer's feelings as she left her country.

We gave the tickets to the flight attendant. We were accompanied by another lady who showed us to our seats. Luckily, I sat beside the window, and watched as I left my country. My body might be going to the U.S. in this journey in my life, but my heart would stay in the Philippines.

Writing Friendly Letters

Some students like to write so they can use their imaginations. Others like to write so they can express their thoughts and feelings. Still others like to write so they can keep in touch with other people.

Student writer Claudia Ramirez would certainly agree with the last reason. She says, "What I like best about writing is that I can write letters to my cousins and family in Mexico and in the United States." Writing a **friendly letter** is one of the best ways to communicate with people you know and care about.

Here are some other good things about friendly letters:

■ Letters usually cost less than phone calls.

■ You can take as long as you want to write them.

■ When you receive one, you can read it again and again.

What's Ahead

This chapter will help you write letters to people you care about. You will find information about the parts of a friendly letter, a sample letter, and writing guidelines.

- **Parts of a Friendly Letter**
- **Sample Friendly Letter**
- **Writing Guidelines**

Parts of a Friendly Letter

1 The **heading** includes your address and the date. Write the heading in the upper right-hand corner, about an inch from the top of the page.

2 The **salutation** is a way of saying hello to the person you are writing to. It usually begins with the word *Dear* and is followed by the person's name. Place a comma after the person's name. Write the salutation at the left-hand margin, two lines below the heading.

3 The **body** of the letter contains the thoughts and ideas you want to share with this person. Begin writing on the second line after the salutation. Keep the paragraphs short for easy reading.

4 The **closing** is a way of saying good-bye. Write your closing two lines below the body of your letter. Capitalize only the first word and follow the closing with a comma. Here are some closings to choose from:

> **Love,**
> **Sincerely,**
> **Yours truly,**
> **Your friend,**
> **Very truly yours,**

5 Write your **signature** two lines below the closing. Your first name is usually enough, unless the person you are writing to doesn't know you very well.

✳ If you are writing to a very close friend or family member, you do not have to follow this form exactly.

Sample Friendly Letter

In this letter, Christina Sung shares her experiences with a friend in another city.

1 756 Dodge Avenue
Evanston, Illinois 60202
June 2, 2002

2 Dear Anna,

I can't believe it's been six months since we moved. Is Kansas City still the same? Have you made any new friends? I have, but I still miss you!

Yesterday our Girl Scout troop went to a television center. We learned about lights, props, and things that television people need. I got to use a camera.

We also got to be on TV. We had to say, "You're watching channel 3, ECTV, Evanston Community Television. Stay tuned!" One person said, "You're watching," the

3 second person said, "channel 3," the third person said, "ECTV," and the rest of us said, "Evanston Community Television. Stay tuned!" Then at the end, we all made monkey faces. It was fun.

My grandmother says hello. She stopped taking English classes. She says she is too busy and doesn't like the way it sounds. But I don't believe her. Sometimes I see her watching TV and trying to say some of the words.

School is fine. I'm doing a lot of writing and reading in English. That keeps me busy. None of my other classes are that hard. As usual, I want to get A's in all of my classes. How is school going for you this year?

4 Your best friend,

5 Christina

Writing Guidelines: Friendly Letter

PREWRITING Choosing a Subject

It should be easy to think of someone to write to: Is there a friend or relative that you miss? Has someone written a letter to you that you should answer? Is your class writing to students in another school?

Gathering Details

List a few ideas that you would like to share in your letter. Here are some ideas:

- **Share a story about something that happened to you.**
- **Describe one of your days in school.**
- **Explain something you are learning.**
- **Describe a family gathering.**
- **Tell about your neighborhood.**
- **Write about a favorite book or movie.**
- **Ask questions that the other person could answer.**

WRITING Writing the First Draft

Getting Started ■ Start by sharing some personal news or asking a few questions. (Look at the first paragraph in the sample.) Continue to write about the ideas on your list until you feel that you have said enough.

Writing Back ■ If you are writing back to a friend, start by answering the questions he or she may have asked. Then add new information about yourself. *Remember:* Writing a friendly letter gives you a chance to think about your own life. In this way, the letter "informs" you as well as the person who receives it.

REVISING Improving Your Writing

Make changes until your letter is clear and complete. You can use the following checklist as a guide.

- Do all of the ideas make sense?
- Have you said enough about each one?
- Did you answer your reader's questions?
- Did you start a new paragraph each time you started a new idea?

EDITING Checking for Errors

Check your revised writing for spelling, grammar, punctuation, and capitalization errors. Also read the letter aloud to see if you have left out any words. (Have a friend or family member check for errors as well.) Then check the form before typing or writing a neat final copy to send. (See page 216 for addressing your envelope.)

 If you finish your letter and then remember something you forgot to say, add a P.S. (postscript) after your signature. (A *postscript* is a note at the end of a letter.)

Sample Postscript

School is fine. I'm doing a lot of writing and reading in English. That keeps me busy. None of my other classes are that hard. As usual, I want to get A's in all of my classes. How is school going for you this year?

Your best friend,

Christina

P.S. Please write soon and tell me all of the things you are doing!

Subject
Writing

Biographical Writing

Writing About Literature

Writing Explanations

News Writing

Biographical Writing

A **biography** is writing about somebody other than yourself. (The word *biography* comes from two Greek words meaning "life writing.") Why should you write a biography? It will help you . . .

save the memories of important people in your life,

discover an interesting world beyond yourself, and

understand your own life better.

You must learn as much as you can about your subject to form an effective biography. You may need to collect ideas from memory, from interviews, from reading, and so on.

What's Ahead

This chapter gives you two biographical writing samples by students like yourself. It also gives easy-to-follow writing guidelines and tips. After reviewing this information, you will be ready to write about a special person—someone that you already know or someone that you would like to learn about.

- **Memory-Based Sample Biographical Writing**
- **Writing Guidelines**
- **Interview-Based Sample Biographical Writing**

Memory-Based Sample Biographical Writing

This biographical writing is by Sefton Reynolds. As you will see, he has strong feelings about his subject, Grandpa Johnson. All of Sefton's ideas show how much he respects his grandfather.

A Grandparent Memory

BEGINNING

The writer establishes the focus of his writing— his special grandfather.

Grandpa Johnson is a very special person to me. The last time I saw him was a year ago on his 60th wedding anniversary in Jamaica. Grandpa speaks only English, not Patois. He can read and write very well. He was born on May 16, 1906, in Jamaica. Soon he will be 96 years old.

I remember that my grandpa always played games with us. One game was "Yankee Doodle." I used to sit on his lap while he sang it, and he would bounce me up and down. He held me so that I wouldn't fall off. I was about six when he did this.

MIDDLE

He shares interesting little stories about his subject.

My father always called him "Barbar" because he used to cut hair. But this wasn't his main job. His main job was growing vegetables and fruits on his farm to sell. Even now, he loves gardening. Grandpa still works very hard, and he does a lot to keep young.

Grandpa enjoys being with his family. He had

13 children, but one died at the age of two. The child died from pneumonia. That was so sad for him to lose a child. He loves children a lot. So now he has 12 children.

MIDDLE
He includes many specific details throughout the writing.

He still plays with his 28 grandchildren and 20 great-grandchildren. Grandpa sometimes tells us jokes, and I always laugh. Anytime a joke is on him, he also laughs. He is always very friendly to me and my sister whenever he visits us.

Grandpa is also a very religious man. He always reads the Bible and then says his prayers. On Sundays, he goes to church meetings. He can't play any musical instrument, but he likes music—especially religious music. He enjoys singing in church.

ENDING
The writer ends by showing the main reason he loves his grandpa.

Grandpa has given me many good memories. He has taught me many good verses from the Bible, like Psalm 23—"The Lord is my Shepherd . . . " Grandpa has also been like a shepherd to me!

 Each paragraph in this writing adds a new piece of information about the subject. Each paragraph begins with a clear topic sentence that is developed with effective details.

Writing Guidelines: Biography

PREWRITING Choosing a Subject

Finding a subject for a biography should be easy. You can probably think of many people to write about.

■ Here are three ways to search for a subject:

1. Think of a person you know better than anyone else does.

2. Think of a person who has had a big influence in your life.

3. Think of an interesting person you have heard about in one of your other classes or from a friend or family member.

■ Make sure to select a subject that truly interests you and would be of interest to your readers.

Gathering Details

Gathering the best details for your writing may or may not be easy for you. It all depends on the subject you choose to write about.

■ Here is a chart that can help you collect details.

KNOWLEDGE LEVEL	EXAMPLES	SOURCES OF INFORMATION
Well-known subject	mother, brother	Search your memory for ideas.
Somewhat-known subject	teacher, grandfather	Search your memory. Watch your subject and take notes. Interview your subject.
Little-known subject	lawyer, bus driver	Interview your subject. Watch your subject and take notes. Interview others. Read any related information.
Famous person	president, actress, athlete	Read magazines, library books, encyclopedias. Listen to radio/TV interviews. Check the Internet.

WRITING Writing the First Draft

When you write a biography, try to make your writing as interesting as possible. To do so, follow these guidelines:

- Review the details you have collected to find the ones that interest you the most.

- Make the most interesting details the focus of your writing; think of the best way to share these details.

- Write the beginning. It should state the focus of your writing. (See page 49 and the models on pages 144 and 148 for help.)

- In the middle part of your writing, use descriptive words that help readers clearly imagine your subject.

REVISING Improving Your Writing

- Here's a reminder of what to keep and what to cut when you are ready to revise your first draft:

KEEP (or Add)	CUT (or Rewrite)
Sentences and paragraphs that are interesting, important, or entertaining	Openings that are unclear or uninteresting
Sentences that relate to your main point or focus	Sentences that include "extra ideas" not related to your main point
Sentences that add supporting examples and details	Sentences that are confusing or lack specific details

- Check your sentences and paragraphs to make sure they follow one another in the best order. If they don't, rearrange them.

EDITING Checking for Errors

- Also check your revised writing for spelling, punctuation, grammar, and capitalization errors. (Have somebody else check it, too.) Then write a neat final copy of your writing to share.

Interview-Based Sample Biographical Writing

Chirayu Patel writes about a person that he did not know before. He gathered his information through an interview.

The Power of the Dream

On November 5, 2001, we went to the North Shore Retirement Hotel for our inter-generational program. I talked to Sylvia Conroe, a resident at the retirement hotel, about her life dreams. Sylvia is now in her 80's, but when she was younger she had dreams of becoming a teacher.

Life was difficult for Sylvia as she grew up. She had to drop out of school when she was 16 and go to work.

Sylvia could not take the money she made from her job and go to school. She had to give all her money to her mother and father to buy food and clothing for her family. Her family was poor, and they depended on her.

Sylvia did not accomplish her dream to become a teacher. However, she did become a secretary in Newark, New Jersey, and she enjoyed it. She also raised a family that gives her great pride.

From this interview, I learned something about my own dreams—that they can be affected by things happening in the world or in my family. I also learned that I have to work hard to achieve my dreams; and, in the future, I may have to change them.

Writing About Literature

Writing a **review** is one way that you can share ideas about literature. In a review, you state an opinion about a novel, play, short story, etc. You then support this opinion with examples from the reading. The subject of a review usually comes from one of the main elements of literature—*plot, characterization, setting,* or *theme.* (See page 150 for definitions.)

Before you can write a good review, you must have a clear understanding of your reading. You also need to "revisit" the parts that you plan to use in your review. Your goal is to share something important or interesting that you learned.

What's Ahead

On the next page, you will find ideas for reviews. After that, you can look over the writing guidelines, read a sample review, and discover another way to write about literature.

- Finding an Idea
- Writing Guidelines
- Sample Focused Review
- Writing a Summary Report

Finding an Idea

This list of ideas for reviews is arranged according to the four main elements of literature: *plot, characterization, setting,* and *theme.* (Also see pages 301-305 for more ideas.)

Plot The action of the story

■ The story includes a number (2, 3, 4, . . .) of important or surprising events.

■ Certain parts of the story are confusing or hard to believe.

■ The climax (the most important event) happens when . . .

■ The ending is surprising . . . predictable . . . unbelievable.

Characterization The people or animals in a story

■ The main character changes from _____ to _____ by the end of the story.

■ Certain forces—people, setting, events, or ideas—make the main character or characters act as they do.

■ A certain character acts believably/unbelievably when . . .

■ _____ is the main character's most important trait.

■ I can identify with the main character when . . .

Setting The time and place of the action

■ The setting helps make the story exciting.

■ The setting has an important effect on the plot or action.

■ The setting (in a historical novel) helped me to understand a certain time in history. Explain.

■ The setting (in a science-fiction story) creates a new and exciting world. Explain.

Theme The author's statement or lesson about life

■ Courage . . . peer pressure . . . growing up . . . happiness . . . greed . . . jealousy . . . is a theme in (title of book).

■ A certain moral, "Don't judge a book by its cover" . . . "Haste makes waste" . . . "Hard work pays off," is developed in (title of the piece of literature).

■ This piece of literature showed me what it is like to be . . .

Writing Guidelines: Review

PREWRITING Choosing a Subject

■ If you are writing a one-paragraph review, choose one of the ideas (subjects) listed on the previous page. If you are writing a longer review, you may want to choose two related ideas. (Also feel free to think of or choose ideas that are not listed.)

■ Talk about possible writing ideas with your teacher or a classmate. Make sure to select a subject that you can support with examples from the reading.

Gathering Details

Use a collection sheet to plan your review. State your subject on the first line. Then list ideas that you will use to explain or develop it. (The collection sheet below lists ideas about *The Miracle Worker,* a play by William Gibson. See page 153 for the review.)

Sample Collection Sheet

Subject: The climax happens when Helen understands that words have meaning.

Main Points
* Helen is deaf, blind, and mute.

* Annie Sullivan tries to help Helen understand.

Example
— She uses sign language all the time.

* Near the end, Annie has Helen fill a pitcher with water.

WRITING Writing the First Draft

■ Pay special attention to the opening part of your review. It should name the title and author of your reading and state the subject (opinion or main idea) of your review. Here is a sample opening sentence for a one-paragraph review:

> **In *The Miracle Worker* by William Gibson, the climax happens when Helen Keller finally understands that words have meaning.**

✳ In a longer review, you would write an opening *paragraph* rather than just an opening sentence.

■ Write the rest of your review, using your collection sheet to help you add ideas.

■ Don't worry about making mistakes. You can correct them later. Just get all of your ideas on paper.

REVISING Improving Your Writing

Use these questions as a guide when you review and revise your first draft.

■ Does the opening name the title and author of my reading—as well as the subject of my review?

■ Do the sentences that follow support or explain the subject?

■ Does the review include examples from the reading?

■ Are the sentences arranged in the best order?

EDITING Checking for Errors

Check your revised review for spelling, grammar, punctuation, and capitalization errors. Have someone else check your work, too. Then write a neat final copy to share.

Titles of novels, plays, and other longer pieces of literature should be underlined or in italics. Titles of short stories and individual poems should be enclosed in quotation marks.

Sample Focused Review

In this sample review, Takashi Kitajima focuses on the climax, or most important event, in the play *The Miracle Worker* by William Gibson. This play is based on the true story of Helen Keller, a young girl who is blind, deaf, and mute, and Annie Sullivan, her teacher. (*Mute* means "unable to speak.")

The Power of Water

BEGINNING

The topic sentence states the subject.

In *The Miracle Worker* by William Gibson, the climax happens when Helen Keller finally understands that words have meaning. Helen is deaf, blind, and mute. Her teacher, Annie Sullivan, tries everything to help Helen understand words.

MIDDLE

Examples from the book help explain the subject.

For example, she uses sign language to spell out each new thing she gives to Helen. But Helen doesn't understand that the signs or spellings mean anything. Annie is very frustrated with Helen's lack of understanding. Then, near the end of the play, Annie has Helen fill a pitcher with water. At the same time, she signs "water" in the palm of Helen's free hand. Helen suddenly looks surprised. She touches the water and quickly signs "water" in her own hand. Then she signs it in Annie's hand and makes a sound like "wah, wah." The miracle has happened.

ENDING

The closing sentence refers back to the subject.

Helen is beginning to understand the meaning of language.

Writing a Summary Report

A **summary report,** which highlights the most important parts of a reading, is another way to write about literature. The following graphic organizer will help you plan and organize a summary report. (Simply answer the questions in your writing.)

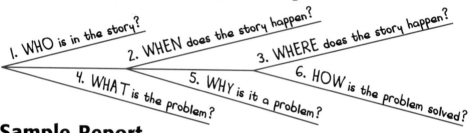

1. WHO is in the story?
2. WHEN does the story happen?
3. WHERE does the story happen?
4. WHAT is the problem?
5. WHY is it a problem?
6. HOW is the problem solved?

Sample Report

Here is a sample summary report written by Ioana Pasca. She reported on *Catherine, Called Birdy* by Karen Cushman.

The numbers show how the writer answers each question from the graphic organizer above.

Arranging a Marriage

① The main character in *Catherine, Called Birdy* by Karen Cushman is Catherine, the 15-year-old daughter of the Lord and Lady of Stonebridge. Other important characters include the members of Catherine's family and her nurse. ②+③ The story takes place in medieval times in a manor in Stonebridge, England. (A *manor* is a big house on a large piece of land.) ④ Catherine's main problem is that her father is trying to arrange her marriage. ⑤ He picks suitors (possible husbands) who are old and rich, but Catherine wants to choose her own husband. ⑥ Finally, she runs away when the richest suitor wants to marry her. When she comes back, she discovers that this suitor has died. She then marries his son, the person she really likes.

Writing Explanations

You probably know things that no one else in your class knows. For example, you may be the only one who knows how to set up an aquarium, make papier-mâché, use the stars to find which way is north, or work the copy machine.

Half the fun of knowing something special is telling someone else about it. And that's what you do in an **explanation.** When you write to explain, you are trying to help readers understand how to do or make something. No matter how easy the explanation may seem, you must always write it carefully to make sure that readers can easily follow your ideas.

What's Ahead

This chapter offers guidelines, writing tips, and models for three kinds of explanations. You'll learn about telling how to make something, explaining how something works, and giving directions to get somewhere.

- Writing Guidelines
- Sample Explanation: How to Make Something
- Sample Explanation: How Something Works
- Sample Explanation: How to Get Somewhere
- Checklist for Writing Explanations

Writing Guidelines: Explanation

PREWRITING Choosing and Collecting

Choose a Subject ■ Pick something that you know about and believe your readers would find interesting. (Sometimes a subject is chosen for you. Shelley Wong's uncle asked her to write down how to get to Shelley's school, so that was her subject. See page 159.)

List the Steps ■ Include every step your readers will need to understand your explanation. (If possible, actually do what you are explaining. Then you will know for sure which steps to include.)

WRITING Writing the First Draft

■ Begin with a topic sentence that tells what your subject is.

■ Write a sentence or two for each step.

■ Use words such as *first, second, next,* and *last* to make your explanation easy to follow.

■ Define any words your readers may not know.

REVISING Improving Your Writing

■ Read your draft. Did you include all of the steps? Did you put in anything that is not needed?

■ Ask a classmate or family member to read your explanation. Does this person have any questions?

■ Make the necessary changes or revisions in your writing.

EDITING Checking for Errors

Check your revised writing for punctuation, grammar, and spelling errors. It is very important to correctly spell the names of ingredients, parts, and places in explanations. A mistake could confuse your readers.

Sample Explanation: How to Make Something

A recipe is one kind of explanation. It tells how to make something to eat. In this sample, Marie Rizkalla explains how to make a special type of salad. (See page 160 for writing tips.)

How to Make Tabouli

BEGINNING

The title and opening sentence tell what the readers will learn.

When my uncle came back from Egypt, he showed me how to make a salad called *tabouli*.

Begin by measuring one cup of bulgur. (*Bulgur* is cracked wheat.) Put the bulgur in a large bowl. Wash it by adding water and then carefully pouring off the water. Add fresh water and let the bulgur soak for two to three hours.

MIDDLE
The steps are carefully written out.

While the bulgur is soaking, dice three spring onions, two tomatoes, three cucumbers, one-half cup fresh parsley, and one-half cup fresh mint leaves. (*Dice* means "to cut into small cubes or pieces.")

Then put three tablespoons of olive oil and three tablespoons of lemon juice in a large salad bowl. When the bulgur is soft, drain off all the water. Put the bulgur and the diced vegetables in the salad bowl. Toss until everything is mixed together well.

ENDING

The ending adds interesting cultural information.

You can eat the tabouli right away or chill it first. People in the Middle East use their fingers to scoop some tabouli onto a lettuce leaf. They roll the leaf around the tabouli and pop it into their mouths.

Sample Explanation: How Something Works

When you explain how something works, you must do two things: (1) Name and explain the parts of your subject. (2) Give the steps in the process in the right order. In this sample, Gabriella Ortiz explains how a French press coffeemaker works. (See page 160 for tips.)

BEGINNING
The opening paragraph introduces the subject in an interesting way.

MIDDLE
The middle names the parts and tells how this machine works.

ENDING
The ending adds a personal touch.

How a French Press Coffeemaker Works

A French press coffeemaker is a non-electrical machine. You can use it to make fresh-brewed coffee or tea just about any-where.

A French press coffeemaker has three main parts: The top holds the filter; the carafe (like a small pitcher) holds the water and the coffee grounds; and the plunger is what you press to make the coffee. That's why it's called a French *press* coffeemaker!

Here's how the French press works: The plunger presses the filter down through boiling water that has been poured into the carafe. Once the filter hits the bottom of the carafe, the flavor of the coffee flows slowly into the water. The longer the coffee filter sits in the water, the stronger the coffee will be.

My dad uses the French press to make coffee. I use it to make tea from herbs. We both like the coffeemaker because it makes a flavorful brew, and it is fun to use.

Sample Explanation: How to Get Somewhere

When you explain how to get somewhere, your directions must be specific. You must give street names, landmarks *(buildings, signs)*, and so on. In this sample, Shelley Wong explains to her uncle, who is visiting from India, how to walk from her family's house to her school. (See page 160 for tips.)

BEGINNING

The topic sentence explains the subject of the directions.

MIDDLE

Each step in the directions is clearly explained.

ENDING

The closing sentence brings the readers to the school.

How to Walk from Our House to My School

It's easy to walk from our house to my school. First, cross the street in front of our house. Turn right and cross the street that is now in front of you. You are on Via de la Escuela, which means *road to the school!* Turn left and walk straight until you reach San Antonio Road. You will see the fire station. Cross San Antonio (at the crosswalk!) and walk straight ahead until you reach Dorinda Road. Cross Dorinda at the crosswalk. Next you will reach Via del Agua. Cross it. You will then come to Yorba Linda Boulevard—a big, busy street. Cross Yorba Linda Boulevard at the crosswalk. Keep walking on Via de la Escuela. You will be walking next to a playground with a fence. Walk until you reach the end of the fence. There you will see a pathway that goes around the side of the school parking lot. Follow that pathway until you reach the main entrance to the school.

Checklist for Writing Explanations

The checklist below will help you write explanations. There are helpful tips to go along with each writing sample in this chapter.

✔ **How to Make Something** (See page 157.)

____ Did I tell what I am making?

____ Did I give the directions, step-by-step?

____ Did I list all the ingredients or parts in exact amounts and measurements?

____ Did I define words that readers need to know?

✔ **How Something Works** (See page 158.)

____ Did I describe what I am explaining?

____ Did I name the parts?

____ Did I put steps of the process in the right order?

____ Did I define special words for my readers?

____ Did I use drawings or diagrams if they will help?

✔ **How to Get Somewhere** (See page 159.)

____ Did I identify the subject of the directions (where the directions will lead someone)?

____ Did I give the street names (or other necessary information) and what to do: *cross, go left, go right,* and so on?

____ Did I use landmarks so readers will know they are in the right place: *a building, a certain tree or large rock, a sign,* etc?

____ Did I draw a map if necessary?

✳ **For other writing samples, refer to . . .**
cookbooks for recipes, science magazines for explanations of processes, and product manuals for explanations of how things work.

News Writing

What's happening? Everyone wants to know the news, and most people have opinions about it . . . especially when the news is about something that affects them.

In **news writing,** both facts and opinions are important; so it is worth knowing which is which. (See pages 253-255.) It is also important to have good listening and writing skills as well as good people skills.

What's Ahead

In this chapter you'll learn how to write both news stories and editorials. To help you do your best, there are samples and guidelines to follow. Here's what you'll find:

- **Sample News Story**
- **Writing Guidelines: News Story**
- **Sample Editorial**
- **Writing Guidelines: Editorial**

Sample News Story

In this news story a student writer reports on an important event at her school. Notice how many details she manages to include in her story.

BEGINNING

The lead paragraph includes the most important details.

MIDDLE

The middle paragraphs give more details and background information.

ENDING

The news story ends with a quotation.

Zambian Choir Is a Hit

A group of 26 boys from Africa came to sing for the Middle and Lower Schools as well as the Upper School on Friday, January 17. The Zambian A Cappella Boys Choir sang as a part of a ceremony in honor of Martin Luther King, Jr. (*A Cappella* means "without any instruments to accompany them.")

The choir is touring the U.S. for a year. The youngest boy is 11 years old, and the oldest is 19. The songs that they sing are original African tunes.

Most of their songs reflect their religious beliefs. Dressed in traditional African vests, the choir looked sharp and seemed very upbeat. They have great voices, a lot of talent, and the ability to connect with their audience.

Everyone enjoyed hearing them sing, and they were fun to be around. It was exciting to have them at our school. After hearing the performance, eighth-grader Zishan Yousuf said, "The Zambian A Cappella Boys Choir was very entertaining in addition to exposing us to a different culture."

Writing Guidelines: News Story

If you saw a headline in a newspaper that said "Kids Rescue Giant Python," you would probably read the story that followed it. Good headlines pull you into the story. The first few sentences in a news story are called the **lead.** That's because they "lead" you into the body, or main part, of the story.

The body of a news story gives details about the subject. *Who were these amazing kids? What led them to rescue a giant snake? When, where, and how did this happen?*

PREWRITING Choosing a Subject

Your first job as a news writer is to find a subject that your readers want to know about. Here's what to look for:

- **Importance** Will this news affect the lives of your readers? *(Are bus fares going up? Is a singing group coming to your school?)*

- **Timeliness** Readers want to know what's happening and what's going to happen. Nobody wants to read old news.

- **Local News** Readers are usually interested in news that is close to home. In general, that means news about their school and their community.

  ✳ If you come from another country, you may know and want to write about local news from your homeland. In most cases, your readers will find these stories very interesting.

- **Human Interest** Readers appreciate stories about people. Would you rather read a story about the path of a hurricane, or a story about a family that got caught in that path?

PREWRITING Gathering Details

■ After you have picked a subject, collect details for your story. You can gather information by interviewing people, watching your subject in action, searching the Internet, and so on.

■ Interviewing is one of the best ways to collect information. (*Interviewing* is talking to people to find out what they have to say about a subject.) Here are some tips for interviews.

Interviewing Tips

● Interview someone who knows about your subject.

● Make a list of questions to ask. (State your questions so they cannot be answered with just a "yes" or "no.")

● Listen carefully as the person answers your questions. (Keep eye contact with the speaker as much as possible.)

● Take brief notes of main ideas. (In addition, you may want to tape-record the interview. But ask the person first.)

● Before you finish the interview, review your notes for follow-up questions, spellings of names and places, dates, and so on.

● Thank the person at the conclusion of the interview.

■ To make sure that you have collected the most important facts and details, you may want to complete a 5 W's chart. The chart below relates to the sample news story (page 162).

Sample 5 W's Chart

Choir Visit				
Who?	What?	When?	Where?	Why?
Zambian Boys Choir	performed a concert	January 17	Middle, Lower, and Upper Schools	part of Martin Luther King, Jr., ceremony

WRITING   Writing the First Draft

- Spend extra time writing the lead paragraph. It should include the most important information in your 5 W's chart. (See the lead paragraph in the sample news story on page 162.)

  ✳ Some writers develop creative leads to get readers interested in the story. Here is a creative lead for the sample story.

  > **Martin Luther King, Jr., would have been proud. On Friday, January 17, we heard 26 African boys sing from their hearts in our school's celebration honoring Dr. King's birthday.**

- After you have written your lead, write the rest of your first draft. Each new paragraph should give more information about your subject. The further you go along in your story, the less important the information should become.

- Include quotations. They help make news stories come alive for readers. (*Quotations* are the exact words from someone you talk to or read about.)

REVISING   Improving Your Writing

Carefully review and revise your first draft. Make sure that you have included all of the important information. (Check your 5 W's chart.) Also make sure that all of your ideas are clearly stated. Ask someone else to review your story as well.

EDITING   Checking for Errors

Double-check each fact. *Is Friday the 17th or the 18th? Did the hockey team raise $200 or $2,000? Did Lita give the award or receive it?* Also make sure that names of people and places are spelled correctly. If your news story is printed in a school or local newspaper, a lot of people will read it, and mistakes will be noticed!

Sample Internet Editorial

An *editorial* usually gives the writer's opinion about a timely news event. (See the note below.) Valerie Keller wrote this editorial for *Kid News International Student News Wire,* a publication on the Internet. Peter Owens, editor and publisher <kidnews.com>.

BEGINNING
The writer gives a fact and states her opinion.

MIDDLE
A new Styrofoam product is described.

ENDING
The writer asks for the readers' support.

Stop Using Styrofoam

Styrofoam fills landfills and takes hundreds of years to decompose. We can no longer ignore the fact that people need to stop using Styrofoam.

There is now a new Styrofoam alternative. It's made of corn syrup and dissolves in water. Except for its beige color, it looks and feels the same as traditional Styrofoam. It is a good alternative to use, and I think that people who absolutely need to use a product like Styrofoam should use this alternative.

Some of the junk in landfills decomposes pretty quickly, but Styrofoam and some other materials don't. In addition, Styrofoam releases harmful CFC's (chlorofluorocarbons) that deplete ozone from the atmosphere. At Eco-Rescue, we fully support the Montreal Protocol, a treaty designed to stop the use of harmful CFC's. Please help us out and stop using Styrofoam. We'd really appreciate the support.

Most editorials try to persuade, but they also do other things. Some editorials may promote something. (*"Does everyone know that we will be collecting canned goods next week?"*) Others may praise someone or something. (*"We thank Ms. Woods for leading our safety patrol."*)

Writing Guidelines: Editorial

PREWRITING Choosing a Subject

- Select a subject that is of real interest to you and your readers. For ideas, think of important events or actions in your school or community. (It may help to brainstorm for ideas.)
- The subject of an editorial is usually stated as an opinion. Try to state your opinion in a positive way: "We can no longer ignore the fact that people need to stop using Styrofoam." (A statement like "Styrofoam does nothing but cause harm" sounds too harsh.)

Gathering Details

Use these questions as a guide:

- **What facts and quotations support my opinion?**
- **What comparisons can I make to support my opinion?**
- **What answers do I have to the opposing argument?**

WRITING Writing the First Draft

In the lead paragraph, give any background information, and then state your opinion. Include your strongest arguments in the main part of your editorial. End with a statement that asks people to support or act on your opinion.

REVISING Improving Your Writing

As you review and revise your first draft, make sure that your main points are clearly stated and in the best order. Also make sure that your information is accurate and up-to-date.

EDITING Checking for Errors

Ask someone to read your editorial out loud. Change any unclear parts. Check your writing for spelling, punctuation, grammar, and capitalization errors. Complete a neat final copy to publish.

Creative
Writing

Writing Poems

Story Writing

Writing Poems

A **poem** is a very personal form of writing in which you share a specific thought, feeling, or experience in a special way. (See pages 170-171 for more details.) In the poem below, student writer Gema Diaz tells . . . in her own special way . . . what life was like for her the first year she arrived in the United States from Bolivia.

EVERYTHING IS NEW FOR ME

A new language, a new city.
New friends, new enemies.
New school, new house.
Weird clothes, weird songs.
A year passed, and look at me.
This is not new anymore,
This is my life!

What's Ahead

The first part of this chapter describes the main features of poetry. Following this, there are guidelines for writing a free-verse poem and much more.

- **What Is Poetry?**
- **Writing Guidelines: Free-Verse Poetry**
- **Special Poetry Techniques**
- **Invented Forms of Poetry**

What Is Poetry?

What makes poetry different from prose? (*Prose* is the regular type of writing you do, using sentences and paragraphs.) Here are some of the differences.

Poetry looks different.

Poems are written in lines and stanzas (groups of lines), and they usually don't take up much space on the page. Here is a one-stanza poem with five lines:

> **MUSIC**
> **Music is like a river**
> **of crystal water**
> **running slowly over a mountain.**
> **Music is like the flowers and fruit trees**
> **in a dreamed paradise.**
> **—Wendy Villegas**

Poetry speaks to the heart and to the mind.

You can like a poem for what it says (that's the mind part), and you can like it for how it makes you feel (that's the heart part). It's the heart part that separates poetry from prose. You can feel the author's suffering in the following poem:

> **IRELAND**
> **I remember the hurt and pain**
> **the shooting, the boom from the bomb**
> **the cries and tears**
> **when will it stop? when will it end?**
> **when will it ever go away?**
> **I see the horror every day**
> **I learn to live with it**
> **it takes some time**
> **but I will survive**
> **in this war-torn country.**
> **—Niall Corrigan**

Poetry says a lot in a few words.

Poets create word pictures using details that describe what they see, hear, smell, taste, and touch. Notice how the sense of sight is stressed in the start of this poem:

> I am a Native American
> I am a weaver, weaving for my ancestors
> I am all the colors of a sand painting.
> —Danilla Wilson

Here are lines from other poems that stress other senses:

> Plip
> Plop
> Splat!
> Water is plunging down
> The rain has come.
> —Shanti Hubbard

> With dainty bites she eats
> Delicious food,
> Then delicately washes herself
> With a long rough tongue.
> —Juliana Perry

> I cry water with a taste of sugar.
> —Karim Yehia

> The spring air
> smells of birth
> and beginning.
> —Audrey Slator

Poetry sounds different.

Poets use many strategies to create special sounds. Here are some of the things you might do to make your poetry sing: (See pages 175-176 for more examples.)

- Repeat words: *I am . . . I am . . .*
- Rhyme words: *ever go away? . . . horror every day*
- Use words that begin with the same letter: *birth and beginning*
- Repeat vowel sounds: *slowly over*
- Repeat consonant sounds: *boom, bomb*
- Use words that sound like what they mean: *plop, splat*

Writing Guidelines: Free-Verse Poetry

Many years ago, most poems had a regular beat or rhythm. Each line had the same number of accented syllables. (See page 176.) These poems often rhymed, too.

Today, most poets write **free-verse poems.** Free verse does not have a regular rhythm, and it does not have to rhyme. Use the guidelines that follow to help you write a free-verse poem.

PREWRITING   Choosing a Subject

You can write a free-verse poem about memories, feelings, dreams, interesting sights, favorite things, and so on. Use one or more of the following strategies to search for a subject:

- **Remember** a special event or experience: *the first day at a new school, a memorable trip, a special meeting.*
- **Look** at the world around you: *What do you see . . . a spider? a stack of unopened mail? a picture? some graffiti?*
- **Describe** something you like or dislike: *a tasty food, a favorite piece of clothing, your worst job.*
- **Think** of a favorite person: *a grandparent, your best friend, a neighbor, etc.*

Gathering Details

Once you've selected a subject, the next step is to gather your thoughts about it. You can do this in a number of ways: listing ideas, writing freely, or clustering. Student writer Juliana Perry used a cluster to collect details about her subject, wild horses.

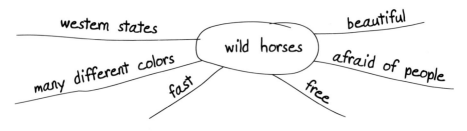

WRITING Writing the First Draft

■ Review the details you have collected. Look for an important idea or a powerful image (mental picture) to use as the central theme of your poem. Juliana Perry focused on two main ideas in her cluster—that wild horses run fast and free. With these ideas in mind, she started the first draft of her poem:

> **Wild horses run along.**
> **They are beautiful.**
> **All different colors**
> **They are so free.**
> **And in a moment**
> **They are gone.**

■ Once you get your first ideas on paper, just keep going until you've said all that you need to say about your subject. Use your cluster (or other notes) as a general guide, but also feel free to add new ideas that come to mind as you write.

✳ Very often, the form or shape of a poem will develop naturally as you add one idea after another.

REVISING Improving Your Poem

After you complete your first draft, carefully review your work. Also make sure to have at least one other person read and react to it. Use the following checklist as your reviewing guide:

■ Are all of the ideas clear and complete?

■ Did I use the best words to describe my subject? (See pages 110-111 for help.)

■ Do all of the words and phrases read effectively? (Think in terms of the meaning *and* the sound of the words.)

■ Does the form of the poem add to its overall effect?

■ Does the title add to the meaning of the poem?

Make the necessary changes in your poem after you review it.

EDITING Checking for Errors

Check your revised poem for capitalization, punctuation, spelling, and grammar errors. Ask someone else to check your work for errors. Then write a final copy of your poem, making all of the corrections. Proofread this copy before sharing it.

✳ In a free-verse poem, you do not have to capitalize the first word in each line. The choice is yours. Use end punctuation marks as you would in regular prose—at the end of complete thoughts. Use other punctuation marks as needed for clarity.

Sample Free-Verse Poem

The final version of Juliana Perry's poem seems to gallop down the page. Notice the specific words that she uses. For example, instead of saying that wild horses are "all different colors," she names specific colors: "white," "buckskin," "dun," etc.

WILD HORSES
Galloping along the plains,
Beautiful,
White,
Buckskin,
Dun,
Chestnut,
Bay, Dappled,
Spotted,
Old and gray,
All colors, quick and sure,
Free and beautiful.
At the slightest sound,
Gone in a flash.

—Juliana Perry

Special Poetry Techniques

Listed below are common techniques that poets use to develop effective poems.

Figures of Speech

Poets uses the following techniques to create word pictures in their poems. These techniques are called **figures of speech.**

A **simile** \\'si-mə-lē\\ makes a comparison using the words "like" or "as."

The snowplow reared up like a stallion.

A **metaphor** \\'me-tə-fōr\\ compares two different things without using a word of comparison, such as "like" or "as."

Peace is a sunrise.

Personification \\pər-sä-nə-fə-'kā-shən\\ describes something non-human as if it had human qualities.

The leaves gossiped among themselves.

Hyperbole \\hī-'pər-bə-lē\\ is an exaggerated statement. Sometimes hyperbole is meant to be funny.

His hands were so dirty the soap ran and hid.

The Sound of Poetry

Poets use the following techniques to make their poems pleasant sounding.

Alliteration \\ə-li-tə-'rā-shən\\ is the repetition of consonant sounds at the beginning of words.

The sun slowly reaches the highest point in its bright, blue home.

—Alejandra Moya

Assonance \\'a-sə-nən(t)s\\ is the repetition of vowel sounds in words.

My stepmom shouted loud as a train.

Consonance \\'kän(t)-sə-nən(t)s\\ is the repetition of consonant sounds anywhere in words, not just at the beginning.

Call me Jack, the wacky one.

(Did you notice the assonance in this line, too?)

End Rhyme \end\ \rīm\ is the use of rhyming words at the end of two or more lines of poetry.

> **The music's pumpin'**
> **I start jumpin'**
> ＿**Maya Liparini**

Internal Rhyme \in-tər-nəl\ \rīm\ is the use of rhyming words within a line of poetry.

> **Hang tight, then make a right**

Onomatopoeia \ä-nə-mä-tə-ˈpē-ə\ is the use of words that sound very much like the noise they name.

> **Swish those skirts, snap those fingers＿**
> **Go ahead, but watch the night go poof.**

Repetition \re-pə-ˈti-shən\ is the technique of repeating a word or phrase for rhythm or emphasis.

> **We feared nothing,**
> **because we had nothing to fear.**
> ＿**Shannon Winston-Dolan**

Rhythm \ˈri-thəm\ is the way a poem flows from one idea to the next. In free-verse poetry, the rhythm seems to follow the poet's natural voice, almost as if he or she were speaking to the reader. In more traditional poetry, a regular rhythm is established. Notice how the accented syllables in the following lines create the poem's regular rhythm.

> **Whose woods these are I think I know.**
> **His house is in the village though.**
> ＿**Robert Frost**

Reading Poetry

A person who knows how poetry is written is going to be a better reader of poetry. Here are some tips to help you fully appreciate the poems you read:

- Read the poem to yourself several times.
- Read the poem aloud; listen to the way it flows.
- Check it for special poetry techniques.
- Copy it into a writing notebook.

Invented Forms of Poetry

Acrostic Poetry To write an acrostic poem, use the letters of a word to begin each new line. Each line should say something about the word. (This poem is about a person named José.)

> **Joker in the back**
> **Oh, so smooth**
> **Sometimes sad—**
> **Eh, get to know me!**

Alphabet Poetry Write a humorous or an imaginative poem using part of the alphabet as your guide.

> **Anthill, quite civilized—**
> **Before**
> **Children poke**
> **Dirty fingers inside.**

Colors Poetry Write a poem about a color, thinking about all the feelings and ideas it brings to mind.

> **ORANGE**
> **Caution! Don't**
> **reach, till Mom says**
> **yes, then O—**
> **pen wide, and shine**

Concrete Poetry Create a poem in which the design and shape help express the meaning and feeling of the poem.

PYTHON AFTER MEETING PIG

Contrast Couplet Write two rhyming lines in which the first line includes two words that are opposites. The second line then comments upon the first.

> **It really doesn't matter if you're young or old.**
> **There's always someone to say: "Do as you're told."**

Five W's Poetry In this form of poetry, each line should answer one of the 5 W's (*who? what? where? when?* and *why?*) about a subject.

I

Love to skate
Along Venice Beach
In the middle of the day
Because people are friendly and get out of your way.

Haiku Haiku is a three-line form of Japanese poetry. In most cases, the first line is five syllables; the second, seven; and the third, five. When writing haiku, focus on some connection between nature and human life.

kite stuck on phone lines
fluttering hard with each gust
angry at the sky
—Randy VanderMey

Limerick A limerick is a humorous five-line verse form. In a limerick, the first, second, and fifth lines rhyme, as do the third and fourth. In addition, the first, second, and fifth lines have three stressed syllables; and the third and fourth have two.

There once were two cats from Kilkenny,
Each thought there was one cat too many.
So they fought, and they "fit,"
And they scratched and they bit,
Till instead of two cats there weren't any.

List Poetry In this form of poetry, just list related words or phrases that express an idea or a feeling.

GROCERY LIST

Ice cream, any flavor,
chocolate syrup, the thicker the better,
those sweet red cherries with the stems,
a can of nuts,
a sprayer full of whipped cream—
medicine for a tummyache.

Story Writing

Storytellers from around the world sometimes begin a **story** by saying, "Once upon a time . . ." This tells the reader that the story takes place in a different world . . . where anything can happen. Frogs turn into people, elephants talk, and pigs can fly.

Other stories are based on reality. The things that happen *could* happen, even though these are made-up stories. Stories can come from real experiences, from your imagination, or from both. Wherever they come from, everybody has a story to tell. And everybody loves a good story.

What's Ahead

In this chapter you will learn how to write a myth. A *myth* is a made-up story that tries to explain something in nature. The sample myth starting on the next page and the guidelines that follow will help you write an effective story. Also included is information about other types of stories.

- **Sample Myth**
- **Writing Guidelines**
- **Short-Story Sampler**
- **Start with a Pattern**

Sample Myth

In this myth, student writer Eng Lee explains why bobcats have short tails. Notice how much dialogue and action he puts into his story. (*Dialogue* is the speaking parts in a story.)

How Bobcats Got Short Tails

BEGINNING

The main character jumps into action in the first sentence.

A long time ago, a big hairy bobcat jumped down the rocky canyon. He was heading down to the oasis, when he saw a snake running like crazy toward him. "What's wrong?" asked Bobcat.

"There's a monster in the oasis!" answered Snake.

"You just don't want me to use the oasis, right?" asked Bobcat.

Snake answered, "No, I just want you to know that there's a monster in the oasis."

Bobcat did not listen to Snake and jumped down the rocks. As Bobcat was jumping, he saw Hawk flying like crazy. Feathers were coming out of his legs and tail. Hawk tried to catch his breath. He screeched, "There's something in the river that bites and looks like a fish!"

MIDDLE

Dialogue moves the story along.

"Are you trying to keep me away from the river?" asked Bobcat.

"No, no, I'm trying to warn you that there's something in the river that bites and looks like a fish," replied Hawk.

Bobcat said, "There's no one that can

MIDDLE

The most exciting event happens near the end after a long buildup.

ENDING

The title is repeated so the readers are sure to "get" the story's meaning.

stop me from going to the oasis to catch me some food." He went on jumping down the canyon. When Bobcat got to the oasis, the water was clear. He drank and swam and went to catch some fish.

Bobcat saw many fish in the deep water. The fish did not swim away from Bobcat. Instead, they were coming straight toward Bobcat. These were not the kind of fish he was looking for. These fish had rows of sharp, jagged teeth. Bobcat tried to get out of the water as quickly as he could, but it was too late. By the time Bobcat got out of the water, his long, beautiful tail was almost gone. The fish had eaten most of it. All that was left was a little stump. Bobcat ran away from the river and never came back.

So that's how bobcats got their short tails. And whenever you see a bobcat standing by the water looking down at the fish, you'll know why. That bobcat is asking the fish to give back the bobcat's tail.

Look for other myths to read in your community or school library. Libraries usually have collections of myths from many different cultures.

Writing Guidelines: Story Writing

PREWRITING Choosing a Subject

Use the following ideas to help you think of a subject for a myth:

- With the help of a partner, list different natural things that you could try to explain: *Why do oceans have waves? Why is the sky blue? Why do squirrels have bushy tails?*

- List different details about human life to explain: *Why does someone go bald? Why does one individual have very big feet while someone else has very little feet?*

- Look at pictures or ads in magazines and newspapers for ideas. An ad showing a fashion model may lead to the following writing idea: *Why do people wear earrings?*

Discuss a few of your ideas with a classmate or teacher before you choose one to write about. Try to picture in your mind a story that explains each one of these ideas.

Gathering Details

Once you select a subject, the next step is to plan the main parts of your story: *the people (characters), a place, a problem,* and *a plot.* Use the following chart as a planning guide or use a story map. (See page 47.)

People	Place	Problem	Plot
• Who are the people (or characters) in your story? • How do they look, dress, walk, talk, think, and so on?	• Where does your story take place? • What does this place look like? • What sounds and smells are in the air?	• What problem does your main character face? (Something scary may be in the main character's way.)	• What's going on? What happens next? • What does the main character do because of his or her problem?

WRITING   Writing the First Draft

In the beginning part of your myth, identify the main character, the setting (place), and the main problem in the story. Then go on from there. (See page 180 for a sample beginning.) A chain of boxes like the ones below can help you plot out your story.

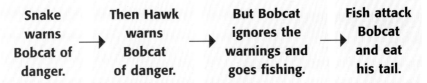

REVISING   Improving Your Writing

Use the following questions as a guide when you review and revise your first draft:

■ Does my story include dialogue? Dialogue makes a story come alive for readers.

> **"What's wrong?" asked Bobcat. "There's a monster in the oasis!" answered Snake. (This is much better than the following: Bobcat asked what was wrong, and Snake said that there was a monster in the oasis.)**

■ Does the main character have a problem to deal with?

■ Is every character, event, and explanation necessary?

■ Does the story make readers want to know what happens next?

■ Does something important happen near the end of the story? Do the last few sentences bring the story to an effective close? (See page 181 for a sample ending.)

EDITING   Checking for Errors

Read your story out loud to a partner. Does it read smoothly and make sense? Choose a title; correct punctuation, grammar, and spelling mistakes; and make a neat final copy to share.

Short-Story Sampler

There are many types of stories to write. Your librarian or teacher can help you find examples of the types of stories described below. You may also have seen movies and TV shows that fit into these different categories.

Scary Story

The goal of a scary story is to scare your readers. To do so, a character must face something frightening: a panther perched on a low tree limb, a dam bursting, wild river rapids.

That night as Carmen was putting her youngest sister to bed, she heard a scratch, scratch, scratch on the window screen. She moved slowly toward the window . . .

Fable

Fables are stories that teach lessons, or morals. Morals are sayings like "The early bird catches the worm," or "Look before you leap." The characters in fables are often animals, just as in myths.

Sook was a young rabbit who liked to take great flying leaps whenever she walked. Her mother warned her to be careful, but Sook did not listen. It was such fun to go flying through the air, never knowing where you might end up. But one day, when Sook had taken a particularly long leap, she landed in a . . .

Urban Fiction

Urban fiction is set in a large city and shows the characters in conflict with their environment. Life is usually seen as being very challenging and difficult.

Most students at Edison Middle School felt that 3:10 p.m. was their favorite time. It signaled the end of another long school day. But Harris Reynolds did not share this feeling. He hated leaving school. It meant that once again he would not be able to take part in his favorite after-school activity—chess.

Mystery

To write a mystery you need a crime, a list of suspects, and a star detective. The goal of a mystery story is to solve the crime.

Mrs. Zolofsky unlocked her desk drawer. The money that the class had collected for its trip was gone. She slowly looked up at the class. We were all suspects.

Science Fiction

A science-fiction story shows life in another time or place (often the future). While things may be different in this new world, they make sense within the context of the story.

When Von looked around, something was different. The cars had no drivers. Furthermore, they seemed to be communicating with one another.

Start with a Pattern

Once upon a time a young man set out in search of riches. On the way, he crossed a river within a deep, deep canyon. Then he guessed the correct name of a two-headed troll who lived in a cave, and plucked a hair from the chin of a fire-breathing dragon. After winning fame and fortune, the young man returned home a hero.

Does this story outline sound familiar? That's because it follows a familiar pattern, the *quest pattern*. Here are three other short-story patterns: (These patterns may give you ideas for your own stories.)

The Choice: Near the end of the story, the main character faces an important decision. Making (or failing to make) this decision is the most important point in the story.

The Reversal: Something happens between two characters near the end of the story. This changes their feelings toward each other.

The Understanding: Different clues lead the main character to some truth or understanding. This discovery comes near the end of the story.

Report
Writing

Writing Observation Reports

Writing Summaries

Writing Classroom Reports

Writing Observation Reports

An **observation report** is a type of descriptive writing. You visit a location (place) and write down all of the things you see, hear, smell, and feel. (In this case, *observation* means "the gathering of information by noting facts and details.")

Writers pay careful attention to everything around them. They seem to see things that other people miss, and they often carry small notebooks to record interesting details. These details give them ideas for their writing. Writing observation reports will help you see the world in the same way that good writers see it.

What's Ahead

The models and guidelines in this chapter will show you how to write an observation report. *Remember:* Always choose words that show readers exactly what you observed.

- **Sample Observation Report**
- **Writing Guidelines**
- **Sample Science Observation Report**

Sample Observation Report

The main idea, or subject, of this report is stated in the first sentence. All of the observations that follow support this idea.

Train Number Seven

BEGINNING

The opening sentence names the subject of the report.

My train ride to school is not very warm and friendly. I ride train number seven on the New York subway system.

When I get on the subway, a voice box says, "This is the local Manhattan number seven train. Stand clear of the closing doors." The rubber edges of the doors bump together, and the subway jerks ahead.

The seat feels cold on my legs. Everything looks and feels a little dirty. The air smells of perfume and sweat. Across from me a homeless man is talking in his sleep. He looks like a bundle of rags.

MIDDLE

The main part of the report shares different observations.

The subway carries many types of people, including students, office workers, and homeless people. At each stop, more and more people get on. Some people read newspapers. Other people just look straight ahead. No one talks. A woman in a fancy suit and high heels sits next to the homeless man. She acts like he isn't there. He never wakes up.

ENDING

The closing sentence refers back to an opening idea.

The train screeches to another stop, and more people get on and off. The voice keeps telling people to "stand clear" of the doors. There are two more stops before my school.

Writing Guidelines: Observation Report

PREWRITING | Choosing a Subject

Choose a place that has interesting sights, sounds, and action—a school lunchroom, a subway, or so one. (See page 41 for other ideas.)

Gathering Details

List details in your notebook as you observe them, or fill in a graphic organizer like the one below. Use all of your senses.

Five Senses Organizer

Sights	Sounds	Smells	Tastes	Textures

WRITING | Writing the First Draft

- Share details in the order you listed them. Here is an example:

  A voice box says, "This is the local Manhattan number seven train." . . . The air smells of perfume and sweat.

- Or organize your observation around a main idea, as you would in a descriptive paragraph. (See page 202.)

REVISING | Improving Your Writing

- Did you include all the important observations?
- Did you use the best descriptive words?
- Did you arrange your details in the best order?

EDITING | Checking for Errors

Check the report's punctuation, spelling, and grammar.

Sample Science Observation Report

In your science class, you may be asked to write an observation report on an experiment or a project. Joey Deigneault observed the feeding behavior of a small freshwater hydra. Here's the summary report he prepared.

BEGINNING

The procedure section tells what was done in the experiment.

MIDDLE

The observation lists what was observed throughout the experiment.

ENDING

The conclusion explains what was learned as a result of the experiment.

Observing a Cnidarian

Procedure: On February 14, I completed a hydra lab. I put a hydra into a petri dish with a small amount of water. I then placed the hydra under a microscope. After I focused on it, I noted its reaction to the touch of a toothpick. I also dropped daphnia (brine shrimp) into the dish, and observed the way the hydra eats. Then I placed the hydra back in its original container.

Observation: The hydra was white. The mouth was located on the top of the body and was surrounded by four tentacles. The hydra attached itself to the bottom of the dish. When I touched it with my toothpick, the hydra launched out its tentacles to protect itself. When I dropped the three daphnia in the dish, the hydra didn't do much until a daphnia swam right by it. Then the hydra launched out a barrage of stinging tentacles at the unsuspecting daphnia. Even though the daphnia was much larger, it didn't try to escape. Perhaps it was paralyzed. The hydra ate two of the three daphnia.

Conclusion: I learned that the hydra is white, and it has four tentacles with stingers. I also learned that the hydra is a very effective predator. Finally, I was able to observe how it feeds.

Writing Summaries

In school you read textbooks, handouts, articles, and so on. If you're like most students, it may be hard for you to understand and remember all of the things you read. If so, you need strategies to help you improve your reading and learning abilities. (A *strategy* is a plan to do something.)

You can use graphic organizers while you read. (See pages 261-276.) You can also take notes or write in a journal about your reading. Another important strategy is **summary writing.** Writing a summary will show you how well you understand what you have read. When you summarize, you find the most important ideas in your reading and state them in clear sentences.

What's Ahead

This chapter will help you write summaries of reading selections. You will find writing guidelines, tips for finding the main idea in a selection, and a sample summary. *Remember:* Summarizing is one of the most important writing skills you will use as a student.

- **Writing Guidelines**
- **Finding the Main Idea**
- **Sample Summary**

Writing Guidelines: Summaries

PREWRITING Choosing a Subject

Your teacher may ask you to summarize a reading selection. You may also decide on your own to summarize something you're reading, in order to understand it better.

Gathering Details

Learn as much as you can about the reading selection.

- Skim the selection to get the general meaning. (*Skim* means "to read quickly.") Then read it carefully.
- List the main points on paper.

WRITING Writing the First Draft

Write your summary, using your own words as much as possible. (See page 194 for a sample.)

- The first sentence should state the main idea of the reading.
- In the next sentences, include just enough important details to support or explain the main idea.
- Arrange your sentences in the best order.
- Add a closing sentence if one seems to be needed.

REVISING Improving Your Writing

As you review your first draft, ask yourself these questions:

- Have I included all of the important information?
- Have I stated my sentences clearly and in the best order?

EDITING Checking for Errors

Check your revised writing for punctuation and capitalization errors. Then write a neat final copy.

Finding the Main Idea

Special features like the title, *italics,* and any **boldfaced** words may help you find the main idea in a reading selection. The activities listed below may help you as well.

Guideline Check ■ Follow all of the steps under "Gathering Details" on page 192.

Important Questions ■ Ask yourself a few important questions: *What do I really want to remember about this reading? What is the biggest or most important idea in the reading? What other ideas are important?*

Sharing Ideas ■ Talk about the reading selection with a classmate. Discuss the main idea and other important points in the reading.

Reading Strategies ■ Use a graphic organizer like a time line or a reading strategy like KWL (**K**now, **W**ant, **L**earn) to help you better understand the important information in a reading selection. (See pages 262-276 for examples.)

These guidelines and tips for writing summaries will also help you write reports, news stories, and book reviews.

Sample Summary

Main Idea

Important Details

> The Panamanian golden frog uses its lungs to hear. It does not have ears on the outside. The lungs are near the surface of the frog's body, and they vibrate when sound waves hit the body. The sound waves move from the lungs to a special inner ear. These frogs also use hand signals to communicate. Scientists need to study more about the golden frog's hearing.

Original Reading Selection

Listening Lungs

DESPITE BEING earless, the Panamanian golden frog appears to respond to sounds made by other members of its species. According to zoologists at The Ohio State University, the unusual frog "hears" through its lungs.

The lungs lie close to the surface of the frog's body and vibrate when sound waves strike the animal's brilliantly colored skin. "In a sense, the frog's lungs act as eardrums," explains Thomas Hetherington, an Ohio State professor who studies the animal.

Although the golden frog does not have the middle and external ears of a typical three-part amphibian ear, it does have an inner ear. Scientists are not sure how sound signals travel between the lungs and the inner ear to enable the frog to hear.

The frog lives along remote mountain streams, where the noise of rushing water makes it difficult to hear other sounds in the environment. Scientists studying Panamanian golden frogs have observed that the frogs regularly communicate using hand signals, waving their forearms at each other. Further studies of this species may provide clues about the evolution of hearing.

— *Dawn Stover*

Writing Classroom Reports

Writing a **classroom report** is a big job. It takes lots of time, and lots of work. But writing a report can be interesting, too. It's a chance to learn about something that you have always wondered about.

Hannah Graff, for example, learned about the Cherokee Nation in social studies class. Then she began to wonder about the Cherokee people of today. What are their lives like now? When she gathered information to write a classroom report, she found out.

What's Ahead

You'll find Hannah's classroom report on the next two pages. Then you can follow step-by-step guidelines for writing your own report. Everything from selecting a subject to preparing the bibliography or works-cited page is covered. The chapter ends with a checklist reviewing the steps in the report-writing process.

- **Sample Report**
- **Writing Guidelines**
- **A Works-Cited Page or Bibliography**
- **Checklist for Writing Reports**

Sample Report

After thinking about her subject and asking questions, Hannah Graff knew that she wanted to learn more about the role of women in the Cherokee Nation. This report was the result.

Wilma Mankiller: Good Times and Bad

"I wept tears that came from deep within the Cherokee part of me. They were tears from my history, from my tribe's past. They were Cherokee tears."
— Wilma P. Mankiller

BEGINNING

After a quotation, the report begins with a main fact about the subject.

Wilma Mankiller was the first woman chief of the Cherokee Nation. She worked to get better education and health care for her people, but her own life has not been easy.

Ms. Mankiller was born in Tahlequah, Oklahoma, in November 1945. She was one of 11 children. Until she was 10, she lived in Mankiller Flats, Oklahoma. Then her family moved to San Francisco. The U.S. government had promised them a better life if they would move. But that better life did not happen.

Although her life was not easy, Ms. Mankiller went to both high school and college. It was at San Francisco State College that she met Hector Hugo Olaya de Bardi. They got married and had two daughters.

MIDDLE

Specific details about the subject's life are shared.

In 1974 Ms. Mankiller and her husband got divorced. Wilma moved back to Oklahoma in 1976 and was determined to help her people. She went to graduate school, but she had more personal problems during that time.

MIDDLE
Each new paragraph flows smoothly from the one before it.

One day Ms. Mankiller was in a car accident. She was not hurt, but the person in the other car died. This person was Wilma's best friend. Later, Ms. Mankiller found out that she had myasthenia gravis, a serious muscle disease.

This was not the only time Ms. Mankiller had faced suffering. In 1960 her brother died of serious burns. In 1971 her father died of kidney disease. Because she had the same disease, Wilma had a kidney transplant in 1990.

Ms. Mankiller did help her people, even though she had these personal struggles. In 1985, she was appointed chief of the Cherokee Nation. She was re-elected in 1987 and 1991. While she was chief, membership in the tribe increased from 55,000 to 156,000.

Wilma Mankiller has won many honors. She is in the Oklahoma Women's Hall of Fame, the International Women's Forum Hall of Fame, and the National Women's Hall of Fame. She also received the Distinguished Leadership Award of the Harvard Foundation.

Alice Walker, an author, said, "Wilma Mankiller is someone I feel I've known in this lifetime and many lifetimes before. I recognize in her the greatest beauty, dignity, and truthfulness."

ENDING
The writer tells what she has learned from her report.

Ms. Mankiller is no longer chief but gives speeches to young women. She overcame great odds to become the first woman chief of the Cherokee Nation. Learning about Wilma Mankiller has inspired me to keep working toward my goals, no matter what.

Writing Guidelines: Classroom Report

To write a good report, there are three things you must do: (1) select an interesting subject; (2) gather information about the subject; and (3) organize the information to make an interesting report.

PREWRITING Choosing a Subject

Choose a subject that you really want to learn about. Also remember that a good report subject must be specific. (The *Cherokee Nation* is too general; the *first Cherokee woman chief* is specific.)

■ You may want to use a web to begin your subject search. Begin the web by writing a general subject area that you want to learn about. (Your teacher may provide you with a list of possible general subjects.) Then think of questions that interest you about the subject.

Sample Web

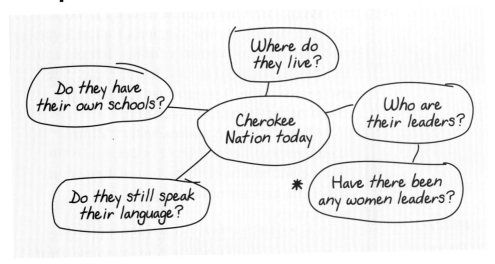

■ Put a star next to your favorite question.

■ Research this question to see if it will lead to a specific subject. (Hannah Graff searched a CD-ROM encyclopedia for the keyword *Cherokee*. There she found out about Wilma Mankiller, the first woman chief of the Cherokee.)

PREWRITING Gathering Details

■ Once you have selected a specific subject, decide what you want to learn about it. Listing research questions about your subject is one way to do this.

> *How did Wilma Mankiller get to be chief?*
> *When did she become chief?*
> *Is she still chief?*
> *What did she do as chief?*
> *What is her family like?*

Try to write questions that cannot be answered "yes" or "no." Questions that begin with *what, why,* and *how* will lead you to more interesting information.

Find Good Sources of Information

- **Look** for books and magazines in a library. (See "Using the Library," pages 233-241.)
- **Search** the Internet and CD-ROM's. (See "Using the Internet" pages 227-232.)
- **Interview** people who know a lot about your topic. (See page 164 for tips.)

Use a Gathering Grid

A gathering grid helps you to organize the information you collect. (See the tips below and the model on the next page.)

- **Write** your topic in the upper left-hand corner of your paper.
- **Copy** your questions on the left side of the grid.
- **Write** your sources across the top. (Sources are books, magazines, the Internet, etc.)
- **Search** your sources and write the answers you find in the columns.

Sample Gathering Grid

Wilma Mankiller	Herstory (book)	Grolier (encyclopedia)	Internet	Kids Discover (magazine)
How did she get to be chief?			See note card ①	"The secret of our success is that we never, never give up." W. Mankiller
When?	1985	Re-elected in 1987 and 1991		
Still chief?			No--did not run in 1995	
What did she do?	Worked for better education, health care	Increased membership, 55,000 to 156,000		
Where does she live?	See note card ②		Oklahoma	
What is her family like?	See note card ③			
What problems has she had?			See note card ④	

Sources of Information

Your Questions

PREWRITING Recording & Checking Information

■ Make a note card if there is not enough room to write all the information on the gathering grid. Number your note cards and write the numbers in the correct spaces on your gathering grid. This way you can match each card to the question it answers.

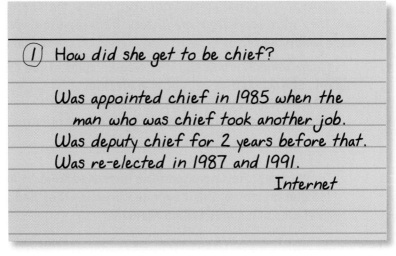

① How did she get to be chief?

Was appointed chief in 1985 when the
man who was chief took another job.
Was deputy chief for 2 years before that.
Was re-elected in 1987 and 1991.
Internet

■ If you think of new questions or ideas, add them to your grid. (Hannah found out that Wilma Mankiller had many problems in her life. So she added a question—and an answer—to her grid.)

■ Review your collecting. Did you answer all your questions? Do you need to find more information?

■ Check with your teacher concerning the accuracy or truthfulness of the information you have collected. Some sources may be more reliable than others.

Collecting Other Types of Information

Here are three ways to collect information that show rather than tell:

1. Make a copy of a photo, map, or chart that you find in one of your sources.

2. Make your own drawing, using information you find.

3. Show an example. (If you are presenting a report on a pet, perhaps you can bring one to your class.)

WRITING Writing the Opening Paragraph

BEGINNING

▪ Start in a way that gets your readers' attention. Hannah started her report with a quotation and an important fact.

> *"I wept tears that came from deep within the Cherokee part of me. They were tears from my history, from my tribe's past. They were Cherokee tears."* —Wilma P. Mankiller

> **Wilma Mankiller was the first woman chief of the Cherokee Nation. She worked to get better education . . .**

Here are three other ways to write your opening sentences:

1. Start with a surprising fact.

> **Recently, the Cherokee tribe increased from 55,000 to 156,000 members. This happened because they had a strong chief. Her name was Wilma Mankiller.**

2. Give an interesting description.

> **Although her own life has not been easy, Wilma Mankiller has helped the Cherokee Nation.**

3. Ask a question.

> **Have you ever wondered if Native Americans had women chiefs?**

▪ Remember to name the specific subject or focus of your report. (At the end of the opening paragraph, Hannah stated that she is going to write about Wilma Mankiller's *life.*)

> **She worked to get better education and health care for her people, but her own life has not been easy.**

WRITING · Writing the Rest of Your Report

MIDDLE

- Develop the main part of your report using your gathering grid as a guide. Here are some ways to organize your ideas:

    Chronological Order ● Put ideas in the order in which they happened. (Most of Hannah's report is organized this way.)

    Order of Importance ● Put ideas in the order of importance. Usually, this means putting the most important idea first. But you can also save the most important idea for last.

    Main Ideas ● Group facts by main ideas. (Hannah could have put all the facts about Wilma Mankiller's family in one paragraph, all the facts about her health in another paragraph, and so on.)

- Use quotations. Readers like to "hear" people talking. (Hannah used quotations from Wilma Mankiller and from Alice Walker.)

- Include brief stories about the subject. Readers find stories very interesting. (Here is a brief story from the sample report.)

> **One day Ms. Mankiller was in a car accident. She was not hurt, but the person in the other car died. This person was Wilma's best friend.**

ENDING

- Write a closing paragraph. This paragraph should summarize the main points you make in your report. In the *last* sentence, you may want to give readers more to think about. Here are two ways to write the final sentence:

    1. Tell one last interesting fact about the subject.

    > **Wilma Mankiller has written a book called *Mankiller: A Chief and Her People*.**

    2. Tell your opinion or feeling.

    > **Learning about Wilma Mankiller has inspired me to keep working toward my goals, no matter what.**

REVISING Improving Your Writing

There are many things to think about when you review and revise a first draft of a report. Use the following checklist as your guide:

BEGINNING Does your opening paragraph get your readers' attention and identify your specific subject?

MIDDLE Does each paragraph include important information about the subject?

Are all of these paragraphs arranged in the best order?

Does any information need to be added, cut, or made clearer?

ENDING Does the closing paragraph summarize the main points in the report?

Does the last sentence tell something interesting about the subject?

OTHER PARTS Are all charts or drawings clear and complete?

Does the title help introduce the subject of the report?

Does it say something interesting about the subject?

 Have at least one other person review your first draft. Ask him or her if any parts seem unclear, incomplete, or out of order.

EDITING Checking for Errors

■ Check the revised copy of your report for punctuation, spelling, capitalization, and grammar errors. Also have your teacher or a classmate check for errors. It's important that all names, dates, and facts are accurate.

■ If you are expected to include a bibliography or works-cited page, make sure that you follow the guidelines on the next page.

■ Use blue or black ink if you are writing your final copy. Write on only one side of the paper, and number each page in the upper right-hand corner, starting with page 2.

Giving Credit for Information

If you are asked to give credit in your writing to the authors whose ideas or words you have used, follow the guidelines your teacher gives you.

Citing Your Source in Your Writing

To give credit in the body of your report, place (in parentheses) the author's last name and the page number(s) on which you found the information. This reference is placed at the end of the last sentence or idea taken from that author. The sample reference below tells the reader that this information was originally found on the on-line *Encarta Encyclopedia*. The parenthetical reference is designed to take the reader to the complete information on the works-cited page.

> Ms. Mankiller did help her people, even though she had these personal struggles. In 1985, she was appointed chief of the Cherokee Nation. She was re-elected in 1987 and 1991. While she was chief, membership in the tribe increased from 55,000 to 156,000 ("Mankiller").

Adding a Works-Cited Page

A works-cited page (also called a bibliography) lists, in alphabetical order, the books and materials you actually used in your report. Double-space the information and indent the second line of each entry one-half inch (5 spaces). Underline the titles and other words that would be italicized in print. (See page 206. Also see <thewritesource.com> for more information.)

Avoiding Plagiarism

Plagiarism is using another writer's ideas or words as if they were your own, without giving credit. You should give credit in your paper for the following kinds of information: material copied directly from another source and information written in your own words that contains key ideas or words from another source.

A Works-Cited Page or Bibliography

A **works-cited page** lists your sources. Alphabetize your sources by the author's last name (if given) or by the title.

BOOKS: Author or editor (last name first). Title (underlined). City where the book was published: Publisher, copyright date.

> **Ashby, Ruth, and Deborah Gore Ohrn, eds. Herstory: Women Who Changed the World. New York: Penguin, 1995.**

MAGAZINES: Author (last name first). "Article title" (in quotation marks). Title of the magazine (underlined) Date (day month year): Page numbers of the article.

> **Markham, Lois. "A Gallery of Great Native Americans." Kids Discover Aug.-Sep. 1996: 6-7.**

ENCYCLOPEDIAS: Author (if available). "Article title" (in quotation marks). Title of the encyclopedia (underlined). Edition or version. Type other than book (CD-ROM, Diskette, etc.). Date published.

> **"Wilma Mankiller." The 1996 Grolier Multimedia Encyclopedia. Version 8.0.3. CD-ROM. 1996.**

INTERNET: Author (if available). "Article title" (in quotation marks). Source title (under-lined). Date published. Date found <URL> (address).

> **"Wilma Mankiller." Women's History Biographies. 1997. 2 Jan. 1997 <www.thomson.com/gale/mankill.html>**

INTERVIEWS: Person interviewed. Type of interview. Date (day month year).

> **Wieland, Carl. Personal interview. 5 Jan. 1997.**

Sample Works-Cited Page

Here is the start of Hannah's works-cited page:

Works Cited

Ashby, Ruth, and Deborah Gore Ohrn, eds. Herstory:

Women Who Changed the World. New York:

Penguin, 1995.

Markham, Lois. "A Gallery of Great Native

Americans." Kids Discover Aug.-Sep. 1996: 6-7.

Checklist for Writing Reports

✓ **PREWRITING: Choosing a Subject**

____ Make a web diagram for a general subject.

____ Put a star next to your favorite question (or idea).

____ Research this question to find a specific subject.

✓ **Gathering Details**

____ List questions about your specific subject.

____ Find good sources of information.

____ Use a gathering grid to answer the questions. (See page 200.)

____ Use a note card if you need more room for an answer.

____ Add new questions and ideas that come to mind.

____ Double-check your information.

✓ **WRITING and REVISING**

____ Begin with an interesting idea.

____ Organize your main points and details in the best order.

____ Use quotations and brief stories.

____ Write a strong ending.

____ Prepare a works-cited page (if assigned).

✓ **EDITING and PROOFREADING**

____ Check for clear and complete sentences.

____ Make sure all the words are spelled correctly.

____ Use correct punctuation and capitalization.

____ List all the sources you used on your works-cited page.

____ Follow the correct form for your final copy.

Workplace
Writing

Writing in the Workplace

Writing Business Letters

Writing E-Mail and Proposals

Writing in the Workplace

People in the workplace write for many different reasons. They write letters to apply for jobs, place orders, and discuss problems. They write reports to propose new projects and communicate by e-mail to set up meetings and make inquiries.

In today's workplace, you will need good thinking and writing skills to get your job done. Writing is also a key to using new technology effectively.

Many forms of **workplace writing** can help you in school, too. You may write business letters to request information or communicate with your teacher by e-mail to ask questions or get help. You may also write a proposal to inform your teacher about your plan for completing a research paper.

Here are other workplace forms you may use as a student:

memos	**brochures**	**bulletins**
newsletters	**ads**	**minutes**

What's Ahead

The traits of good writing are listed on the next page. A handbook writing sample that demonstrates each trait is also identified.

● **Traits of Good Workplace Writing**

Traits of Good Workplace Writing

Workplace writing needs to be clear and complete. In other words, it must show the traits found in all good writing. Six traits of good writing are listed below, along with examples of how student writers used these qualities in their own writing. (Also see pages 17-22.)

Ideas (details and focus)

- In his *request letter* on page 215, Carlos Avila focuses on three questions he would like answered about a career.

Organization (strong opening and clear divisions)

- To clarify his project, the student divides his *project proposal* on page 221 into four sections.

Voice (tone, style, and awareness of audience)

- In an *e-mail message* on page 219, the student uses a friendly, informal voice to ask a teacher about references for a report.

Word Choice (appropriate language and phrasing)

- To present her Internet *editorial* on page 166 in the best way, Valerie Keller uses the appropriate technical terms and refers to specific organizations.

Sentence Style (rhythm and readability)

- In her *report* on pages 196-197, Hannah Graff uses linking words and phrases to keep her sentences smooth reading. She also uses a variety of sentence patterns to make her writing interesting to read.

Correctness (punctuation, grammar, and spelling)

- In her *summary* on page 194, Dawn Stover makes sure her subjects and verbs agree and her pronouns match their antecedents. Her summary is free of other errors, too.

3337 Orangewood Drive
Boca Beach, FL 33433
April 8, 1997

Mr. Gregory Christopher
Executive Director
Society of Professional Journalists
16 South Jackson Street
Greencastle, IN 46135

Dear Mr. Christopher:

I am a student at Cooper School in Boca
Beach, and I am writing a report about
careers in journalism. I want to become a
journalist when I graduate from school.

Please send me information about this
career. I need to know these things:
1. Which colleges are the best for
   journalists?
2. What kinds of jobs are available?
3. How much money do journalists make?

Please send me any information that might
answer these questions. Thank you for your
help.

Sincerely,

Writing Business Letters

In a friendly letter, you share personal news with someone you know. In a **business letter,** you share or ask for information in order to get something done. You may need information for a report. You may also be trying to solve a problem or to state your feelings about an important subject. All of these can be done in a business letter.

When you write a business letter, you should state your ideas clearly, without going on and on about your subject. In addition, you should follow the correct form for a business letter. People will be more likely to take your letter seriously if it is written correctly.

What's Ahead

On the next page, you will learn about three main types of business letters. Then you will find writing guidelines, an explanation of the parts of a business letter, and more.

- **Types of Business Letters**
- **Writing Guidelines**
- **Parts of a Business Letter**
- **Sample Business Letter**
- **Sending the Letter**

Types of Business Letters

Letter of Request

Write a letter of request when you need information. (The sample letter on page 215 is a letter of request.)

- **Explain why you are writing.**
- **Ask questions if you have them.**
- **State what you would like to receive (and when).**
- **Thank the person for helping you.**

Letter of Complaint

Write a letter of complaint when you have a problem and want the reader to do something about it. (*To complain* means "to state your unhappiness about something.")

- **Explain the problem and possible causes.**
  (You may have a product that doesn't work right.)
- **State what you would like the reader (or company) to do about the problem.**
- **Be honest, respectful, and courteous.**
  (Let someone know that you have a problem, but don't be rude about it.)

Letter of Opinion

Write a letter of opinion when you want to share your feelings about something. You could write to your school or local newspaper or to a public official.

- **Explain the situation you are writing about.**
- **State your opinions or feelings about this situation.**
- **Support your opinion with facts and examples.**
- **End by asking that the situation be changed.**

Writing Guidelines: Business Letter

PREWRITING Choosing a Subject

- Consider why you need to write a business letter. (See page 212.)
- Decide who should receive the letter.

Gathering Details

- Gather all the facts and information you will need.
- Organize your facts and ideas. Use an outline or other graphic organizer to put your facts and ideas in order.

WRITING Writing the First Draft

- Put your facts and ideas into sentences.
- Use simple, clear words.
- Write short paragraphs.

REVISING Improving Your Writing

- Review your draft to make sure that you have included all the needed facts and information.
- Make sure everything is in the best possible order and is easy to understand.

EDITING Checking for Errors

- Make sure your letter has all the needed parts. (See page 214.)
- Check your letter for errors (spelling, grammar, etc.). Make sure that the name of the person you are writing to is spelled correctly and that the address is correct.
- Be as neat as possible, especially if your letter is handwritten.

Parts of a Business Letter

1 The **heading** includes your address (if you are the one sending the letter) and the date. Write the heading at least one inch from the top of the page at the left-hand margin.

2 The **inside address** includes the name and address of the person or organization you are writing to.

- If the person has a title, make sure to include it. (If the title is short, write it on the same line as the name, separated by a comma. If the title is long, write it on the next line.)
- If you are writing to an organization or a business, but not to a specific person, begin the inside address with the name of the organization or business.

3 The **salutation** is the greeting. Always put a colon after the salutation.

- If you know the person's name, use it in your greeting.

   Dear Mr. Christopher:

- If you don't know the name of the person who will read your letter, use a salutation like one of these:

   Dear Store Owner: (the person's title)
   Dear Sir or Madam:
   Dear Madison Soccer Club:
   Dear Society:

4 The **body** is the main part of the letter. Do not indent your paragraphs, but skip a line between paragraphs.

5 The **closing** is placed after the body. Use **Yours truly,** or **Sincerely,** to close a business letter. Capitalize only the first word of the closing, and put a comma after the closing.

6 The **signature** ends the letter. If you are using a computer, leave four spaces after the closing; then type your name. Write your signature between the closing and the typed name.

Sample Business Letter

(1) 3337 Orangewood Drive
Boca Beach, FL 33433
April 8, 2003

— Four to Seven Spaces

(2) Mr. Gregory Christopher
Executive Director
Society of Professional Journalists
16 South Jackson Street
Greencastle, IN 46135

— Double Space

(3) Dear Mr. Christopher:

— Double Space

(4) I am a student at Cooper School in Boca Beach, and I am writing a report about careers in journalism. I want to become a journalist when I graduate from school.

Please send me information about this career. I need to know these things:
1. Which colleges are the best for journalists?
2. What kinds of jobs are available?
3. How much money do journalists make?

Please send me any information that might answer these questions. Thank you for your help.

— Double Space

(5) Sincerely,

— Four Spaces

(6) *Carlos Avila*

Carlos Avila

Sending the Letter

Addressing the Envelope

Most business letters are mailed in a standard-sized (4-1/8" × 9-1/2") business envelope.

- Begin the name and address of the person you are writing to about halfway down the envelope, and a little to the left of the middle.
- Write your name and address in the upper left-hand corner of the envelope.
- Put a stamp in the upper right-hand corner.

MR CARLOS AVILA
3337 ORANGEWOOD DR
BOCA BEACH FL 33433

MR GREGORY CHRISTOPHER
EXECUTIVE DIRECTOR
SOCIETY OF PROFESSIONAL JOURNALISTS
16 S JACKSON ST
GREENCASTLE IN 46135

The United States Postal Service asks that you use all capital letters, no punctuation, and postal abbreviations. (See page 370 for these abbreviations.)

Folding Your Letter

After you have addressed the envelope, fold your letter in thirds so it will fit neatly inside the envelope.

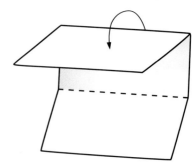

Writing E-Mail and Proposals

You know how easy it is to share your thoughts and feelings with family and friends. They care about what is happening in your life and want to encourage you and give you advice. With the use of e-mail, you can discuss your assignments and ask questions in the evening or on weekends. It's also easy to communicate with classmates and teachers after school.

This type of communication is important in the workplace, too. When people are able to share their ideas and concerns, a business will operate more efficiently. Think of open communication as an important part of life for everyone—in school, at home, and on the job.

What's Ahead

This chapter contains guidelines and samples for writing e-mail messages and proposals to teachers.

- Writing Guidelines: E-mail
- Sample E-Mail Message
- Writing Guidelines: Proposals
- Sample Proposal

Writing Guidelines: E-Mail

E-mail is a written message sent through a computer network to a reader (or many readers). It is a fast and simple way to write, send, reply to, and store messages.

PREWRITING Choosing a Subject

- Write down the purpose for your writing.
- Gather all the details you need to include.

WRITING Writing the First Draft

- Enter an address on your e-mail form.
- Type a subject line to tell your reader the topic of your message.
- Greet your reader and explain your reason for writing.
- Provide all the details your reader needs in a logical order.
- If follow-up action is needed, state it clearly. End politely.

REVISING Improving Your Writing

- Is my message clear?
- Is it written in short, well-organized paragraphs?
- Is my message accurate? Are all addresses, dates, actions, and details correct?
- Is my message complete? Is all the needed information included?
- Is the message short? Does it fit on one or two screens?

EDITING Checking for Errors

- Is the message correct—have the spelling, punctuation, and grammar been checked carefully?

Sample E-Mail Message

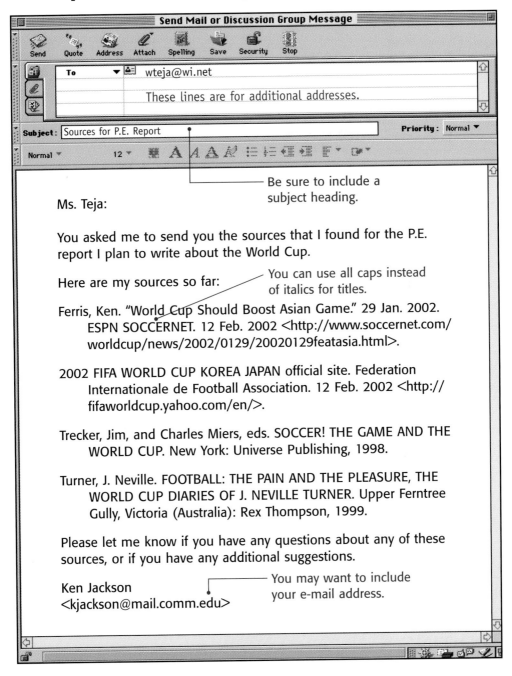

Send Mail or Discussion Group Message

Send Quote Address Attach Spelling Save Security Stop

To ▼ wteja@wi.net

These lines are for additional addresses.

Subject: Sources for P.E. Report   Priority: Normal ▼

Normal ▼   12 ▼

Be sure to include a
subject heading.

Ms. Teja:

You asked me to send you the sources that I found for the P.E.
report I plan to write about the World Cup.

Here are my sources so far: You can use all caps instead
                                of italics for titles.

Ferris, Ken. "World Cup Should Boost Asian Game." 29 Jan. 2002.
    ESPN SOCCERNET. 12 Feb. 2002 <http://www.soccernet.com/
    worldcup/news/2002/0129/20020129featasia.html>.

2002 FIFA WORLD CUP KOREA JAPAN official site. Federation
    Internationale de Football Association. 12 Feb. 2002 <http://
    fifaworldcup.yahoo.com/en/>.

Trecker, Jim, and Charles Miers, eds. SOCCER! THE GAME AND THE
    WORLD CUP. New York: Universe Publishing, 1998.

Turner, J. Neville. FOOTBALL: THE PAIN AND THE PLEASURE, THE
    WORLD CUP DIARIES OF J. NEVILLE TURNER. Upper Ferntree
    Gully, Victoria (Australia): Rex Thompson, 1999.

Please let me know if you have any questions about any of these
sources, or if you have any additional suggestions.

Ken Jackson   You may want to include
<kjackson@mail.comm.edu> your e-mail address.

Writing Guidelines: Proposals

Have you been asked to do a major project or report for one of your classes? Do you see a problem that needs fixing in your community? Do you or your school need something to be added or changed? Then write it down in a proposal—a detailed plan for doing a project, solving a problem, or meeting a need.

PREWRITING Choosing a Subject

- Think about and study the problem, project, subject, or need. Explain its background, divide it into parts, and describe what you hope to accomplish.
- Research your idea. Think about whether it will work.
- Consider ways to make your idea sound good to your reader.

WRITING Writing the First Draft

- Introduce the idea, need, or problem. Describe what you are proposing.
- Provide details to support your proposal.
  1. List equipment, materials, or other resources needed.
  2. Outline steps to take and a schedule for completing them.
  3. Explain the expected results.

REVISING Improving Your Writing

- Make sure your proposal includes enough specific details and that your details are accurate.
- Are your points organized effectively?
- Do you show that you care about this project?
- Have you used headings, lists, and white space?

EDITING Checking for Errors

- Have you checked your spelling, punctuation, and usage?

Sample Proposal

Date: February 5, 2002
To: Mr. Sawyer
From: Gloria Leon
Subject: Speech Topic

BEGINNING

**Introduce
your project.**

Project Description: For my speech, I plan to tell
   about my sister's Quinceanera.

Research Plans:
1. Write my memories of the day.
2. Review photo albums and family videos.
3. Interview family and friends.
4. Find books, magazine and newspaper
   articles, and Internet sites.
5. Look for movies, TV programs, or videos
   on the subject.
6. Read about Quinceaneras for boys.
7. Research celebrations in other countries.

MIDDLE

**Explain in
detail how the
project will be
completed.**

Deadlines:
1. February 8   Have topic approved.
2. February 9-14 Complete research.
3. February 15   Turn in speech outline.
4. February 18   Prepare note cards and
                       visual aids for speech.
5. February 19   Practice giving the speech.
6. February 20   Speeches in class begin.

**Present
your project
schedule.**

ENDING

**Focus on
results and
ask for
approval.**

Outcome: My 3-minute speech will explain the
   tradition of Quinceaneras.

Does this topic fit the assignment? Do you have
any suggestions?

Searching
to
Learn

Types of Information

Using the Internet

Using the Library

Types of Information

You've just been assigned a research report about dieting. You decide to investigate the advantages of a vegetarian diet. How would you get started? You might look for a book at home or in the library for background information on the subject. Or you might start by searching the Internet for information. You could also explore cookbooks or talk to the owner of a health-food store or a dietitian about a vegetarian diet.

As you search for information, one source often leads you to another. In this age of information, you may actually find more material than you need.

What's Ahead

There are two general sources of information—primary and secondary. This chapter explains which is which, with special attention given to primary sources. You will also learn how to judge the quality of the information you find.

- **Primary vs. Secondary Sources**
- **Types of Primary Sources**
- **Evaluating Sources of Information**

Primary vs. Secondary Sources

Primary sources are original sources. They give you firsthand information through talking about, observing, or participating in an activity. Primary sources create the information that they share. You're working with a primary source when you . . .

- **make a visit to get firsthand information,**
- **ask people (experts) questions about your subject,**
- **study a diary or journal, or**
- **conduct an experiment.**

Secondary sources contain information that has been collected from primary sources. Most nonfiction books, newspapers, magazines, and encyclopedias are secondary sources of information. They include information that has been gathered and summarized from primary and other secondary sources. You're working with secondary sources when you . . .

- **read an article about your subject,**
- **check out a reference book,**
- **visit a Web site, or**
- **watch a CD for information.**

Primary Sources	Secondary Sources
1	**1**
Talk to a vegetarian	Article on vegetarian diet
2	**2**
Visit a health-food store	Encyclopedia entry about vegetarians
3	**3**
Interview a dietitian	TV documentary about vegetarians
4	**4**
Attend a workshop on vegetarian diets	Web site reviewing a vegetarian cookbook

Types of Primary Sources

Primary sources are able to provide you with firsthand details. This section discusses five types of primary sources.

Observation and Participation   Observing people, places, and situations is a common method of gathering information. Taking part in an event also supplies firsthand details. For example, if you are researching vegetarian diets, you could try a particular diet yourself.

Surveys and Forms   A survey or questionnaire can be a helpful form of primary research. First list your questions or make up an easy-to-fill-in form. Then give it to the people who will be able to supply the information you need. Collect the finished forms and study the responses to your questions. You can also do surveys over the phone, through the mail, or on a Web site.

Interviews   In an interview, you can talk with someone who is an expert on your subject. You can conduct an interview in person, over the phone, by e-mail, or through the mail. (For tips on interviewing, see page 164.)

Presentations   Attending lectures or workshops, viewing museum displays, and visiting exhibits can provide you with firsthand information about different topics. You can also listen to certain radio interviews, TV forums, or other live events. Be sure to take notes on the important details.

Diaries, Journals, and Letters   Reading personal writing is an interesting way to gather information. You may find this sort of information in personal collections, bookstores, and historical museums.

"If two or three sources of information all say the same thing, the information is probably trustworthy."

Evaluating Sources of Information

There is a lot of information available to you. Before you use any information, you have to decide if it is trustworthy. Ask yourself the following questions to help you judge the value of your sources:

Is the source primary or secondary?

Firsthand facts are often more trustworthy than secondhand facts. However, most well-respected secondary sources will be just as trustworthy as primary sources.

Is the source an expert?

An expert is an authority on a certain subject. You may need to ask a teacher, parent, or librarian for help when deciding how well-respected a source is on a particular subject.

Is the information accurate?

Sources that are well-respected are more likely to be accurate. For example, a large-city daily newspaper is more likely to be reliable than a supermarket tabloid.

Is the information complete?

Judge whether information is complete by looking at the subject from all sides. If a source provides certain facts about a subject, but you still have questions, keep looking for more information.

Is the information current?

Be sure you have the most up-to-date information on a subject. Check for copyright and posting dates in books, articles, and on-line information.

Is the source biased?

A "bias" means literally a tilt toward one side. Politicians, infomercials on TV, and businesses often have something to gain by using facts and emotions that make them sound really good, often too good to be true. Avoid such one-sided sources.

Using the Internet

The information superhighway connects computers to one another and sends information all around the world. It makes all types of information available to all types of people. Students and teachers, mothers and fathers, business people and retirees are all traveling in this new way.

You may already know how to use this superhighway, or you may be ready to try it for the first time. Either way, this chapter will give you important facts about using electronic sources on the Internet.

What's Ahead

First you will learn about the Internet, the worldwide computer network that is a great source of information. Then you will learn about another valuable source of information—CD-ROM's. The final two pages include tips for using electronic sources and a glossary of Internet terms.

- **Understanding the Internet**
- **Using CD-ROM's**
- **Using Electronic Sources**
- **Internet Terms**

Understanding the Internet

A **computer network** is a group of computers that can "talk" to one another. Many businesses and schools have their own computer networks.

The **Internet** is a huge worldwide computer network. (*Internet* is short for "interconnected networks." People often call it "the Net.") When you get on the Internet, you can search for information on computers all over the world. You can also send messages to people all over the world. The World Wide Web, e-mail, and Usenet News are three important parts of the Internet.

The World Wide Web

The **World Wide Web** is a special kind of technology that makes the Internet easier and more fun to use. The Web allows you to see pictures and hear sounds on the Internet. Information is arranged to look like pages in a book or magazine. There are millions of Web pages (also called Web sites). Many businesses have their own Web pages. Some classrooms even have their own Web pages!

Points to Remember . . .

- **There are special pages on the Web that help you search for information.** These pages work a little like a computer catalog in a library. You type in a keyword, and the computer finds Web pages that fit the keyword.

- **Web pages are all linked together.** This allows you to jump from one page to another page that has more information about the same topic. Let's say you are interested in African elephants. You can select the name of a country where they live. The computer will show you a Web page about that country.

- **Each Web site has an address.** If you know the address for the site you want to visit, just key in the address. Here is the address for a Web site about the Arctic:

http://www.lib.uconn.edu/ArcticCircle

Usenet News

Usenet News is another part of the Internet. It is like e-mail, except you exchange messages with a whole group of people.

Usenet News is made up of thousands of **newsgroups.** A newsgroup is a group of people who share an interest and "talk" about it on-line. For example, there are newsgroups of people interested in the stars. Some of the interested people are astronomers. (*Astronomy* is the study of matter in outer space.) Some are students like you. Others just like to learn about stars.

Points to Remember . . .

- **Get to know the group.** When you try out a new group, find out what the group is all about before you send any messages.
- **Read the FAQ's.** FAQ stands for "frequently asked questions." Many newsgroups have FAQ's—and answers—to help new people get acquainted.
- **Don't believe everything you read.** People sometimes get their facts wrong. Always check information to make sure it is correct.

Netiquette

Netiquette is a word that was created by Internet users. It is a combination of "net" and "etiquette." (*Etiquette* means "good manners." *Netiquette* means "using good manners on the Net.")

Here are a few basic rules of netiquette:

1. **Don't use the Internet to waste people's time.** Don't send silly e-mail messages that clutter up people's mailboxes.

2. **Use your time on the Internet wisely.** There may be other students waiting to use the computer. And there are almost always a lot of people trying to get on the Internet. Remember that the Internet is a highway: Don't hold up traffic!

3. **Respect the law.** Some of the material on the Internet is covered by laws that limit how you may use the material. Make sure you know what the rules are, and follow them.

Using CD-ROM's

CD-ROM's are different from the other electronic sources covered in this chapter. To use a CD-ROM, you don't have to network with other computers. You just slide a CD into your own computer.

CD-ROM's pack thousands of pages of information onto one disk. The information on a CD-ROM is sometimes called a *database*. Your classroom or library may have some or all of the following on CD-ROM:

- encyclopedias
- atlases
- national and international telephone directories
- guides to magazine and newspaper articles

Points to Remember . . .

- **Make sure you have the right CD.** Finding out the contents of a CD-ROM is not as easy as finding out the contents of a book.

- **Each CD-ROM has its own rules for finding information.** Make sure you know how to search the CD-ROM you are using. Ask for help if you need it. Many CD-ROM's ask you to use keywords to search for information. Think of the best keywords for your topic. Use *and, or,* and *not* to narrow your search.

Topic:	**Keywords:**
African elephants	Elephants *and* African
	Elephants *not* Asian

- **Know the time covered on the CD-ROM.** Find out how far back the information goes. If a CD-ROM lists magazine articles for the past year, you won't find an article that was published two years ago. Also find out how up-to-date the CD-ROM is.

- **If you need the latest information, a CD-ROM is probably not your best source.** Search for information on the Internet instead.

Using Electronic Sources

Traveling on the information superhighway takes skill. Here are some tips to help you get the most out of every trip:

Work carefully. Finding the information you need may take time. Try different keywords. If you have trouble, ask someone for ideas.

Be patient. Sometimes there are traffic jams on the information superhighway. You may have to wait while your computer searches for information. Or you may need to try again at another time.

Keep learning. Listen to people you know who are computer experts. Ask them questions.

Write down important information. Write down the e-mail addresses of people you know and the addresses of Web pages you want to visit.

Where to Learn More

These Web sites will help you learn about electronic sources. (Availability of information on the Internet changes from time to time. When a Web site changes, there will be a link from the old address to the new one.)

1 **http://osiris.sund.ac.uk/misc/www_begin.html**
A Beginner's Guide to the World Wide Web: This site helps you get started on the Web.

2 **http://www.screen.com/start/guide**
Life on the Internet: This Web site helps you find information and tells about other good sites for beginners.

3 **http://www.onlinesupport.com/**
Online Support Center: At this site, you can get answers to your questions about the Net and the Web.

Internet Terms

Browser A computer program for reading information on the World Wide Web.

Bulletin board A service that permits users to leave, store, or receive messages by computer modem.

Domain The last part (letters) of an Internet or e-mail address.

E-mail (electronic mail) Mail that is exchanged by computer.

Home page The part of the World Wide Web that your computer automatically goes to when you get on the Web.

HTML (hypertext markup language) The computer language used to create World Wide Web documents.

HTTP (hypertext transfer protocol) The technology that allows a user to move from one document to another on the Internet.

Internet A worldwide collection of computer networks; short for "interconnected networks."

ISP (Internet service provider) A company that provides a computer user with access to the Internet.

Log on To connect your computer to an Internet service provider.

Netiquette The term for using good manners on the Internet.

Network A group of computers (or other devices) connected together electronically.

Telecommunications The technology that allows computers to communicate with one another over phone lines, satellites, etc.

URL (universal resource locator) The address of a page on the World Wide Web.

Usenet news Part of the Internet made up of many newsgroups; allows you to exchange messages with groups of people.

Web site A page on the World Wide Web. Businesses often have Web sites.

World Wide Web All of the files contained on Internet information servers that may be navigated using hypertext links.

Using the Library

The **library** is a good place to find answers to all your questions. If you have questions about writing subjects, questions about famous people or favorite things, questions about anything at all, go to the library. You will find answers there.

However, libraries contain many, many books and other materials—including CD's, magazines, and newspapers. As a result, you must know how to search for information in the library before you will find what you need.

What's Ahead

This chapter will help you begin your search. You will learn how to use the card or computer catalog in the library. You will also learn how to find books on the library's shelves. Finally, you will learn about reference books and the *Readers' Guide,* which are both helpful when you are doing classroom reports.

- **Searching for Information**
- **Using a Computer Catalog**
- **Using a Card Catalog**
- **Finding Books**
- **Using Reference Books**
- **Using the *Readers' Guide***

Searching for Information

In every library there is a computer catalog or a card catalog. A **computer catalog** lists all of the books the library contains. A **card catalog** lists all of the same information, but it is written on paper cards that are filed in drawers. Either catalog is the place to go to begin your search for information.

Catalog Entries

Whether on cards or on a computer, a library catalog contains three kinds of entries:

1. **Title entries** begin with the book's title. When a title begins with *An, A,* or *The,* the entry is filed under the next word in the title.

> ### Worst Day I Ever Had, The

2. **Author entries** begin with the name of the book's author. The author's last name is listed first.

> ### McMane, Fred

3. **Subject entries** begin with the subject of the book.

> ### SPORTS

Using a Computer Catalog

With a computer catalog, you can find information on the same book in three ways:

1 If you know the book's **title,** enter the title.

2 If you know the book's **author,** enter the author's name. (When the library has more than one book by the same author, there will be more than one entry.)

3 Finally, if you know only the **subject** you want to learn about, enter the subject or a keyword. (A *keyword* is a word that is related to the subject.)

If your subject is . . .	your keywords might be . . .
mammals that live in the ocean,	marine mammals, whales, or porpoises.

✳ Every computer catalog is a little different. The first time you use a particular computer catalog, either check the instructions for using it or ask a librarian for help.

Sample Computer Catalog Entry

```
Author:      Minnis, Whitney
Title:       How to get an athletic
             scholarship: a student-athlete's
             guide to collegiate athletics
Published:   ASI, 1995
             104 pp.
Subjects:    Sports
             Scholarships

STATUS:                   CALL NUMBER:
Not checked out           378.30973

LOCATION:
General collection
```

Using a Card Catalog

With a card catalog, you can also find information on the same book in three ways:

1. If you know the book's **title,** look up the title card.

2. If you know the book's **author,** look up the author card. (When the library has more than one book by the same author, there will be more than one card with that author's name at the top.)

3. Finally, if you know only the **subject** you want to learn about, look up the subject card.

Sample Catalog Cards

Title Card

How to Get an Athletic Scholarship ——————— **Title heading**

———————— **Call number**

378.30973 Minnis, Whitney
How to get an athletic scholarship:
a student-athlete's guide to collegiate athletics

ASI Pub. (c1995) 104-pp. illus.

Author Card

378.30973 Minnis, Whitney ——————————— **Author's name**
How to get an athletic scholarship: ————— **Title**
a student-athlete's guide to collegiate athletics

ASI Pub. (c1995) 104-pp. illus.

Everything high school students need to know to
qualify and apply for athletic scholarships for

Subject Card

SPORTS —————————————————— **Subject heading**
378.30973 Minnis, Whitney
How to get an athletic scholarship:
a student-athlete's guide to collegiate athletics

ASI Pub. (c1995) 104-pp. illus.
——————————————— **Publisher and copyright date**

Everything high school students need to know to
qualify and apply for athletic scholarships for
college.

1 Sports 2 Scholarships

Each kind of card is filed separately in alphabetical order. When you find the card you are looking for, write down the book's call number, title, and author.

Finding Books

Nonfiction Books Every nonfiction book in the library has its own **call number.** Nonfiction books are arranged on the shelves according to these numbers.

■ **Some call numbers contain decimals.**
The number 973.19 is a smaller number than 973.2. That's because 973.2 is actually 973.20, but the zero isn't written. The number 973.19 will be on the shelf before 973.2.

■ **Some call numbers include letters.**
The number 973.19D will be on the shelf before 973.19E.

Call numbers are usually based on the **Dewey decimal classification system.** In this system, all information is divided into ten main classes.

The Ten Classes of the Dewey Decimal System

000 General Topics	500 Pure Science
100 Philosophy	600 Technology (Applied Science)
200 Religion	700 Literature
300 The Social Sciences	800 The Arts, Recreation
400 Language	900 Geography and History

Biographies Every biography is arranged in alphabetical order according to the last name of the person the book is written about. These books are shelved under the call number 921. This number and the last name of the book's subject appear on the book's spine.

Fiction Books Every fiction book is arranged alphabetically according to the first three letters of the author's last name. These books are located in a separate section in the library.

Using Reference Books

Reference books are a special kind of nonfiction book. You use these books to find specific facts and information. The reference section in a library contains encyclopedias and many other types of reference books, including dictionaries and thesauruses.

Using Encyclopedias

An **encyclopedia** is a set of books (or a CD) with articles on every topic you can imagine. The topics are arranged alphabetically. Each article gives basic information about the topic.

Tips for Using Encyclopedias

- **At the end of an article, you may find a list of related topics.** Look them up to learn more about your topic.

- **The index can help you find out more about your topic.** The index is usually in the back of the last volume in the set of encyclopedias. It lists all the places in the encyclopedia where you will find more information about your topic. (See below.)

- **Most libraries have more than one set of encyclopedias.** Each encyclopedia includes different information. You can learn more by looking up your topic in different sets of encyclopedias.

Sample Encyclopedia Index

Here are some index entries for *Citizenship* from the *World Book Encyclopedia Index.*

Encyclopedia volume ⟶

Citizenship Ci:568 *with pictures*

    Colonial Life in America (Voting Requirements) Ci:793

    Constitution of the United States (Amendment 14) Ci:1013

    Indian, American (The United States) I:181-182

    Law (Ancient Roman Law) L:**133-134** ⟶ Page numbers

    Naturalization N:66

Related topics ⟶ **Citizenship Act** [1977]

    Citizenship (Canadian Citizenship) Ci:571

Citizenship Day [custom] Ci:572

Other Reference Books

Here are just a few of the other reference books that you will find in many libraries.

Bartlett's Familiar Quotations ■ contains over 20,000 quotations. (A *quotation* is something a person said or wrote.) Quotations can make your writing more interesting. Here is a quotation from writer Jorge Luis Borges:

> *"I have always imagined that Paradise will be a kind of library."*

Current Biography ■ contains short biographies of famous people. Each biography includes a photo, the person's birth date, address, and other useful information. A new edition comes out every month. Use the newest edition to find up-to-date information.

The Eye Witness Atlas of the World ■ contains maps of the countries of the world, illustrations, color photographs, and information about each country.

Facts About the Presidents ■ contains important facts about all the presidents of the United States, from George Washington to the current president.

Kane's Famous First Facts ■ lists "firsts" of all kinds, such as the first person to walk on the moon.

Webster's New Geographical Dictionary ■ contains much information about well-known places. It explains the history and geography of each place.

The World Almanac and Book of Facts ■ contains facts and figures about history, politics, business, sports, entertainment, and more. It is published each year. Always use the newest edition to find up-to-date information.

Understanding the Parts of Nonfiction Books

Here are explanations of the parts found in many nonfiction books, listed from the front of the book to the back.

- The **title page** is usually the first page with printing on it. It tells the title of the book, the author's name, the publisher's name, and the city where the book was published.

- The **copyright page** comes next. It tells the year the book was published. This can be important. Some of the information in an old book may no longer be correct.

- A **preface, foreword, introduction,** or **acknowledgement** may follow the copyright page. (A book may have more than one of these, or none of these!) These parts usually tell what the book is about and why it was written.

- The **table of contents** shows how the book is organized. It gives the names and page numbers of the sections and chapters.

- The **body** is the main part of the book.

- The **appendix** has "extra" information, such as maps, tables, lists, etc. (There may be more than one appendix, or none.)

- The **glossary,** if there is one, explains special words used in the book. It's like a mini-dictionary.

- The **bibliography,** if there is one, lists books, articles, etc., that the author used while writing the book. To learn more about the topic, read the materials listed in the bibliography.

- The **index** is an alphabetical list of all the topics in the book. It gives the page numbers where each topic is covered. An index helps when you're looking for information on a specific topic.

Using the *Readers' Guide*

The ***Readers' Guide to Periodical Literature*** will help you find information in magazine articles. Each new printing or issue of the *Readers' Guide* lists all the magazine articles that were published in one month. Here is how to use the *Readers' Guide:*

1 **Find the correct edition.** If you want the latest information, find the newest issue. If you want information about something that happened last May, find the issues that list articles published last May and June.

2 **Look up your subject.** Subjects are listed alphabetically.

3 **Write down information about articles you want to read.** Write down the name of the magazine, the date it was published, the name of the article, and the page number of the article.

4 **Check the cross-references.** Cross-references are notes in the *Readers' Guide* telling you about other articles on your topic.

5 **Find the magazine.** The librarian may have to get it for you.

More About the *Readers' Guide*

- If you can't find any articles about your topic, try looking under a different word. For example, if there is no listing for "Flu," look under "Influenza" or "Viruses." (*Influenza* is the medical name for *flu,* and it is caused by a *virus.*)

- Articles are listed under the author's name, too. If you know the name of an author who wrote about your topic, look up the name. You will find all the articles by that author.

- At the end of each year, all the monthly issues are published together in one book.

- Your library may also have the CD-ROM version of the *Readers' Guide* on computer. Ask your librarian for help.

 The *Readers' Guide* is especially useful if you need the latest information for reports and other projects. Magazines are published much more frequently than books are.

Thinking
to
Learn

Thinking and Writing

Thinking Clearly

Thinking Creatively

Thinking and Writing

You probably don't spend a lot of your time thinking about thinking. Yet thinking is one of the most important things you do. You can't read, write, or even speak without thinking. The better you are at thinking, the better you'll be at everything else you do.

Believe it or not, thinking can be compared to math. Just as there are different kinds of math (addition, subtraction, division, etc.), there are different kinds of thinking. And just as you need the right kind of math to solve a problem, you need the right kind of thinking to complete each of your assignments.

What's Ahead

This chapter tells you about six kinds of thinking that you often use in school. They are listed below. Soon, you may know them as well as you know addition, subtraction, multiplication, and division.

- **Recalling Information**
- **Understanding Information**
- **Applying Information**
- **Analyzing Information**
- **Synthesizing Information**
- **Evaluating Information**

Recalling

When you **recall,** you remember information.

You recall when you . . .

- write down facts, terms, and definitions, and
- study the information until you know it very well.

These test questions ask you to recall.

Directions: Fill in the blanks below with the correct numbers.

1. Americans throw away __195 million__ tons of trash a year.

2. Almost ___55 million___ tons of the total is packaging materials.

Directions: Define each term by completing the sentence.

1. A *midden* is __what scientists call a pit where Stone Age people threw their trash__ .

2. The three R's of trash reduction are __reduce,__ __reuse,__ and __recycle__ .

Tips for Recalling

- Listen carefully in class, and read your assignments carefully, too.
- Take careful notes when you listen and read. (See pages 313-318 for help with your note taking.)
- Use graphic organizers, pictures, or other devices to help you remember things.

Understanding

When you **understand** information, you know what it means.

You understand when you . . .

- explain something,
- tell how something works, or
- restate important details.

This test question asks you to show understanding.

Directions: Explain the three R's of trash reduction.

The three R's of trash reduction are reduce, reuse, and recycle. Reduce means reducing the amount of trash you make. (This is sometimes called precycling.) Reuse means reusing things instead of throwing them away. Recycle means using paper, glass, aluminum, and other things to make new products, instead of throwing them away. Using the three R's is a good way to help the environment because all three help reduce the amount of trash we make.

Tips for Understanding

- Talk about the information with a friend or family member.
- Rewrite the information in your own words.
- Show the information in a drawing, graphic organizer, chart, or map.

Applying

When you **apply** information, you use it.

You apply when you . . .

- use information to solve problems in school, and
- solve problems in your daily life.

This assignment asks you to apply information to your own life.

Assignment: Make a trash-reduction plan for your family.

Family Trash-Reduction Plan

We can reduce trash by . . .
- not using paper plates or Styrofoam cups.
- shopping for products that don't have a lot of packaging.

We can reuse by . . .
- taking grocery bags back to the store to use again.
- saving boxes and wrapping paper to use again.

We can recycle by . . .
- taking our newspapers, plastic, glass jars, and soft-drink cans to the recycling center.

Tips for Applying

- Write about the information in your journal. Think about its usefulness to you as you write.

- Find answers to any questions you have about the information. In order to apply something, you need to understand it completely.

Analyzing

When you **analyze** information, you break the information down into parts. There are many different ways to do this.

You analyze when you . . .

- tell how things are alike or different,
- tell which parts are most important,
- divide things into different groups, or
- give reasons for something.

This assignment asks you to analyze what you know.

Assignment: In a paragraph, tell how a dump and a landfill are different.

A landfill is better for the environment than a dump. A dump is just a place where trash is put. Garbage is left out in the open, and it attracts animals that may get sick and spread disease. Chemicals in trash (such as paint and insect killer) can leak into the ground and pollute the water. Landfills were invented to prevent these problems. In a landfill, trash is covered with dirt right away to keep animals away. Landfills are also lined with clay and plastic to keep chemicals from leaking into the water supply.

Tips for Analyzing

■ **Think about the different parts that make up the whole.**

■ **Consider how the parts are related to one another. (See page 267 for a helpful graphic organizer.)**

Synthesizing

When you **synthesize,** you create something new using information you have already learned about.

You synthesize when you . . .

- add some new ideas to the information,
- use the information to make up a story or some other creative piece of writing, or
- predict what may happen in the future because of this information.

RECYCLE

This assignment asks you to synthesize what you know.

Assignment: Write a title-down report about waste in America. Use the letters in the word "garbage" to begin each sentence.

Garbage is food waste; trash is all other waste.
Americans make 195 million tons of trash a year.
Reducing, reusing, and recycling can cut down
    on trash.
Buying products with very little packaging is one
    good way to reduce trash.
All the packaging we throw away adds up to 55
    million tons a year.
Garbage and trash take up a lot of room.
Everything we throw away adds to a mountain
    of trash somewhere.

Tip for Synthesizing

■ **Use your imagination! Think of creative ways to restate the information. (See pages 257-259 for ideas.)**

Evaluating

When you **evaluate,** you tell the value of something. You tell how good or bad something is.

You evaluate when you . . .

- tell your opinion about something, or
- tell the good points and bad points about something.

This assignment asks you to evaluate something.

Assignment: Explain the good points and the bad points about landfills.

Landfills are much better than dumps. They keep chemicals from polluting the water. And, when a landfill is full, the land can be used. Two big airports, JFK in New York and Newark in New Jersey, are built on landfills. But landfills are not perfect. They take up a lot of space that is needed for homes, schools, and other things. And even though everybody needs a place to put their trash, people never want a landfill in their neighborhood. They would rather have a park or a shopping mall. So we are running out of places to put landfills.

Tip for Evaluating

■ Before you can evaluate something, you must know a lot about it. You must be able to recall facts and understand what they mean. Then you can form your opinion.

Guidelines for Thinking and Writing

This chart reviews the important types of thinking you will use in school assignments and tests.

Recalling means remembering information. Use recalling when you are asked to . . .

- fill in the blanks
- define terms
- list facts or words
- label parts of something

Understanding means knowing what information means. Use understanding when you are asked to . . .

- explain something
- choose the best answer
- tell how something works
- tell if something is true or false
- summarize something

Applying means using information. Use applying when you are asked to . . .

- use information in your own life
- solve a problem

Analyzing means breaking information down into parts. Use analyzing when you are asked to . . .

- compare things
- contrast things
- put things in order
- divide things into groups
- give reasons for something
- tell why something is the way it is

Synthesizing means using information to create something new. Use synthesizing when you are asked to . . .

- create something
- imagine something
- combine things
- predict something

Evaluating means using information to tell the value of something. Use evaluating when you are asked to . . .

- judge something
- rate something
- tell your opinion of something

Thinking Clearly

Thinking clearly can help you in many ways. For example, it can help you form strong arguments and complete your writing assignments. It can also help you make good decisions and solve problems.

Clear thinking is especially important when you must plan a major assignment like a speech, an essay, or a report. Whenever you have such an assignment, follow these basic steps:

1. **Know** the purpose of your assignment.
2. **Gather** the information you need.
3. **Work** to understand this information.
4. **Focus** on one main point to prove or explain.
5. **Complete** your work.

What's Ahead

This chapter offers guidelines and examples to help you think and write clearly. You will learn the difference between facts and opinions, how to avoid unclear thinking, and more.

- **Making Good Decisions**
- **Using Facts and Opinions**
- **Avoiding Unclear Thinking**
- **Solving Problems**

Making Good Decisions

Deciding what flavor of ice cream you want is usually easy. For one thing, you know what you like. For another thing, if you decide to try a new flavor and don't like it, it's not a big deal. But some decisions are more important . . . and harder to make. Sometimes you're not sure what to do.

Here's how to think clearly when you have a hard decision to make.

1. **Write down what you have to decide.**

2. **Write down your choices.** Under each choice, write down facts you know, feelings you have, and any questions.

3. **Find the answers to your questions.** Ask for help from someone who knows about this particular matter.

4. **Make your decision.** Put a ✔ next to each good thing and an ✗ next to each bad thing. You *could* decide to do the thing with the most ✔'s. You may also find that one checked point is more important to you than anything else.

Should I go to summer school, or not?

	Summer School	No Summer School
facts	✔ School will be easier for me next year.	✗ Next year will be really hard.
feelings	✗ It will feel like having no vacation.	✔ It would be great to have 3 months off.
questions	When does summer school start and end?	Would I be able to get a summer job?

Using Facts and Opinions

Knowing the difference between facts and opinions is important. A **fact** is a detail about something that exists or about something that really happened. (*Exists* means "to be real.") An **opinion** is a feeling or belief about something. Facts are true, but opinions are neither true nor false.

Facts	Opinions
"It is 66 degrees in the classroom." "Carlos came to school today."	"It is cold in the classroom." "Carlos should not have come to school today."

Facts Support Opinions

It is fine to share your opinions when you speak and write. But listeners and readers also expect you to give the facts that will support your opinions.

Opinions

"Carlos should not have come to school today."

Facts That Support the Opinion

"He has a sore throat and a fever. The school nurse said people with those symptoms are sick and need to stay home."

Avoiding Unclear Thinking

When you write, you must think clearly. Unclear thinking leads to writing that confuses your readers.

Don't make statements that jump to conclusions.

> *"Because oil spills kill animals, oil is bad."*
>
> This statement jumps to a conclusion—the wrong conclusion. When oil spills into the ocean and kills animals, it is a tragic event. But that doesn't mean that oil itself is bad. Oil is good when it is in the right place, like a car's engine. Oil is bad only when it is in the wrong place.

Don't make statements that make things seem better or worse than they are.

> *"Oil spills aren't so bad, because when they happen, people come together to work hard and clean up the oil."*
>
> This statement almost makes an oil spill sound like a good thing. People have a nice get-together, the oil gets cleaned up, and nothing too bad happens. But facts show that when oil spills, the damage to the environment begins immediately.

Don't make statements that are half-truths.

> *"When an oil spill happens, thousands of animals die."*
>
> This statement makes it sound like all oil spills kill thousands of animals. The biggest oil spills do kill that many animals. But many smaller oil spills cause less damage.

Don't make statements just because most people agree with them.

> *"Pollution in the oceans is not a serious problem because most of my classmates don't think it is."*
>
> This statement is based on the idea that if most people believe something, it must be true. But "most people" can be wrong. They may not have all the facts about ocean pollution and how it affects the world.

Don't make statements that compare things that aren't really like each other.

> *"An oil-polluted ocean is like a dirty fish tank."*
>
> This statement compares ocean pollution to something that is much less harmful. A dirty tank may make your pet fish sick; but a polluted ocean can harm plants and animals and the people who need them for food.

Don't make statements based on feelings instead of on facts.

> *"Oil tankers should be outlawed because they spill oil in the oceans."*
>
> This statement is based on feelings. Although some oil tankers do spill oil, most tankers do not. Plus, most oil that ends up in the ocean is spilled on land, not from tankers. Although it is bad when oil gets into the oceans, outlawing tankers would not solve the problem.

 Knowing the difference between facts and opinions is very important for persuasive writing assignments. To write persuasively, you must be able to form a strong opinion and have many facts to support it.

Solving Problems

Does your life sometimes seem like one problem after another? Guess what? That means you're normal. Here's how to use clear thinking to solve problems.

1 **Name the problem.** Figure out exactly what the problem is. Although problems make you feel upset or unhappy, your feelings are not the problem. The problem is the thing that causes your feelings.

2 **Think of everything you know about the problem.** What caused the problem? Has this problem happened before? If so, when? Has this problem happened to anyone else you know?

3 **Consider different ways to solve the problem.** Think of as many different solutions as you can.

Don't expect quick, easy solutions to every problem. Clear thinking often takes a lot of time . . . and planning.

4 **Predict what may happen if you try each solution.** If the solution will cause more trouble than the problem itself, forget it! Think about whether you can use two solutions together. Also think about what will happen if you do nothing. Sometimes that's the best solution.

5 **Choose the best solution and try it.** There may be more than one good solution. Try the easiest one first.

6 **Evaluate the solution.** How did things work out? If this problem happens again, what will you do?

Thinking Creatively

Leonardo da Vinci was a very creative person. He painted the famous portrait called the Mona Lisa. He also imagined airplanes, helicopters, submarines, and movable bridges, long before they were actually made. We know this because Leonardo drew detailed pictures of these inventions.

Leonardo found new ways to do just about everything. When he wrote in his journal, he wrote everything backward! (This is called mirror writing, because you read it by looking at it in a mirror.) He was an artist, a scientist, an inventor—a creative thinker in many different ways.

What's Ahead

Thinking creatively means thinking of completely new ideas, as well as thinking about old ideas in new ways. It is the type of thinking that can make everything more interesting, from writing a report to cleaning your room. On the next two pages, you'll find information that will help you think creatively.

- **Becoming a Creative Thinker**
- **Asking "What If?" Questions**

Becoming a Creative Thinker

To think creatively, you may have to change the way you do certain things. The ideas on this page will help you get started.

Find things to think about. Read good books, watch good movies, listen to good music, and look at good art. All these things will fill your mind with interesting things to think about.

Spend time with creative people. You probably know some very creative thinkers—people who have their own way of dressing, their own way of talking. They see things differently than other people do. Watch them. Listen to them.

Look at something in a new way. Stand on your head and take a look around your room. If you don't like that idea, close your eyes and "see" your room with your hands.

Look at something through someone else's eyes. Look at your house through your dog's eyes by crawling around on your hands and knees for awhile. Look at an assignment through someone else's eyes. Ask yourself, "If *(fill in any name)* had this assignment, what would he or she do?"

Find a new way to do something. Maybe you always leave a note when you go out, to let your family know where you are. Try doing this in a different way—draw a picture, leave a recorded message, or so on.

Begin. You may have a project to do, but you don't know how to begin. Just write whatever comes to your mind, no matter how silly it seems. You will probably write down some ideas that surprise you.

Do things in a different order. Try writing the last sentence of a paragraph first, and then going back to the beginning.

Write in a journal. It's the perfect place to write down all of the creative thoughts you've been thinking. (See pages 125-128 for more ideas about journals.)

Asking "What If?" Questions

Ask yourself "what if?" questions to help you see things in new ways. Here are some examples:

- **What if** two interesting people who never knew each other *had* been friends? (What if Benjamin Franklin could have talked about his inventions with Leonardo da Vinci, Thomas Edison, or Bill Gates?)

- **What if** someone from the past could visit the present? (What if Leonardo da Vinci visited a school in today's world?)

- **What if** certain objects were made of different materials? (Plastic clothes? Cardboard cars? Rubber highways?)

- **What if** a certain person had never been born, or a certain invention had never been invented? How would the world be different? (Without telephones? Without cement? Without glass?)

- **What if** animals and objects could talk? (A tree? A door? The animals at the zoo?)

- **What if** there were no paper money and no coins? What would we use for money?

※ If you're trying to think creatively, but you're stuck, stop for awhile. Think about something else. When you go back to your project, you may have some new ideas.

Reading
to
Learn

Study-Reading Skills

Reading Symbols and Charts

Improving Your Vocabulary

Understanding Literature

Study-Reading Skills

Study-reading is very different from reading for enjoyment. You read popular novels because you enjoy a good story. You read magazines and newspapers to get the latest news and sports scores. But you study-read textbooks to learn new information and prepare for class. Your textbooks are nonfiction. By study-reading, you can find out . . .

who has made important discoveries,

what natural and social changes have occurred,

why certain events are important, and

how different things work.

What's Ahead

This chapter will help you improve your study-reading skills. You will learn about common patterns of nonfiction used in textbooks, such as description and comparison. You will also learn about two important study-reading strategies.

- **Patterns of Nonfiction**
- **Study-Reading Strategies**
- **Study-Reading Checklist**

Patterns of Nonfiction

Knowing the common patterns of nonfiction makes it easier to understand your assigned reading. Six patterns are reviewed in this chapter: *description, main idea / supporting details, comparison / contrast, process, cause and effect,* and *chronological order.*

Description

This encyclopedia article is about blue whales and follows the **description pattern.** It tells what this whale looks like, what it eats, how it breathes, and so on.

Previewing

Whales   999

Kinds of baleen whales

Baleen whales have no teeth. Instead, they have hundreds of thin plates in the mouth. A whale uses these plates to strain out food from the water. The plates are called *baleen* or *whalebone* and consist of the same material as human fingernails. The baleen hangs from the whale's upper jaw.

There are 10 kinds of baleen whales. Scientists divide them into three groups: (1) right whales; (2) gray whales; and (3) rorquals.

Right whales have a thick, solid body and an unusually large head. The head of most right whales makes up about a third of the total body length. Right whales swim slowly, averaging about 3 miles per hour. They feed by swimming into a mass of plankton with their mouths open. Water flows through the baleen, and the plankton becomes entangled in the baleen fibers. There are three main kind of right whales: (1) bowhead whales; (2) black right whales; and (3) pygmy right whales.

Bowhead whales, also called *Greenland whales,* have the longest baleen of all baleen whales. They have a highly arched mouth suited to the huge baleen, which may grow as long as 13 feet. Bowhead whales are black with white areas on the tail and the tip of the lower jaw. They measure up to 60 feet long and live only in the Arctic Ocean.

Black right whales usually are called simply *right whales.* Compared with bowhead whales, they have shorter...

Rorquals are baleen whales that have long grooves on the throat and chest. These grooves may number from 10 to 100 and are 1 to 2 inches deep. They enable a rorqual to open its mouth extremely wide and gulp enormous quantities of food and water. As the whale closes its mouth, its tongue forces the water out of the mouth through the baleen. The food becomes trapped inside the baleen and is swallowed by the whale. All rorquals have a *dorsal,* or back, fin, and so they are sometimes called *finback whales.* Most of them have a long, streamlined shape and can swim faster than other whales.

There are six kinds of rorquals. They are (1) blue whales; (2) Bryde's whales; (3) fin whales; (4) humpback whales; (5) minke whales; and (6) sei whales.

Blue whales live in all the oceans but are rare. They are sometimes called *sulfur-bottom* whales because some of them have growths of tiny yellowish, or sulfur-colored plants, called *diatoms* on the belly.

Blue whales are the largest animals that have ever lived. They grow up to 100 feet long and can weigh more than 150 tons. They have speckled blu... ...e skin, small, thin ...hey can live in

...rom the water ...s called baleen, ...h. The whale ...mal. It lunges ...ns of water and ...quirts the water ...krill inside. ...eeper than ...ive at shallow ...ce three to six ...for several ...y sharply ...ducing a loud

...cal and sub- ...ith a white ... Unlike other ...nall fish and

Study-Reading

Blue whales are the largest animals that ever lived. The blue whale reaches up to 100 feet (30 meters) long and can weigh over 150 tons. It has speckled blue-gray and white skin, small, thin flippers, and a large, strong tail. It can live in any ocean.

The blue whale strains food from the water using 260 to 400 thin, fringed plates called baleen, hanging from each side of its mouth. The whale eats primarily **krill,** a shrimplike animal. It lunges through masses of krill, taking in tons of water and food. It then closes its mouth and squirts the water out through the baleen, trapping the krill inside.

Blue whales usually dive no deeper than about 300 feet (90 meters) because krill tend to live at shallow depths. The whales surface to breathe three to six times in rapid succession, then dive for several minutes. When surfacing, they exhale sharply through their blowholes (nostrils), producing a loud sound.

Note Taking

WEB: The important information in a description can be easily organized in a web.

Blue Whales

First, name the subject in the middle of the web.

Then, list the important details around it.

largest animal

must surface to breathe

up to 100 feet long

eats krill (shrimplike animal)

Blue Whales

Can weigh over 150 tons

Can live in any ocean

Speckled blue-gray and white, small flippers

Main Idea/Supporting Details

This information from a social studies book follows the **main idea/supporting details pattern.** The heading at the top of the page tells you the main idea. The rest of the page gives details that support this idea. Reading material that explains or introduces a subject usually follows this pattern.

Previewing

What Are ZIP Codes?

What does ZIP stand for? Zone Improvement Program. ZIP codes weren't around when Benjamin Franklin was the first postmaster general. The five-digit numbers that tell the post office where your house is began under JFK's postmaster general, J. Edward Day. "The U.S. Post Office was handling more than half the world's mail in 1963," said Day. "Anybody could see that a machine could comprehend the meaning of 70631 easier than it could locate and direct a letter to Anaktuvuk Pass, Alaska." To get people to start using the codes, the singer Ethel Merman recorded a special version of the song "Zip-A-Dee Doo Dah" from the movie *Pinocchio.* It seems to have worked.

Study-Reading

What does ZIP stand for? Zone Improvement Program. ZIP codes weren't around when Benjamin Franklin was the first postmaster general. The five-digit numbers that tell the post office where your house is began under JFK's postmaster general, J. Edward Day. "The U.S. Post Office was handling more than half the world's mail in 1963," said Day. "Anybody could see that a machine could comprehend the meaning of 70631 easier than it could locate and direct a letter to Anaktuvuk Pass, Alaska." To get people to start using the codes, the singer Ethel Merman recorded a special version of the song "Zip-A-Dee Doo Dah" from the movie *Pinocchio.* It seems to have worked.

TABLE ORGANIZER: Important information that follows the main idea/supporting details pattern can be arranged in a simple table organizer.

Note Taking

What Are ZIP Codes?

The tabletop names the main idea.

ZIP Codes

| ZIP stands for Zone Improvement Program | five-digit numbers | started in early 1960's | help machines sort mail |

The legs of the table list supporting details.

Comparison/Contrast

Comparison/contrast is another important pattern of nonfiction. The information below, from a science book, compares and contrasts red and white blood cells. The first part of the text describes red blood cells. The second part contrasts them to white blood cells. A few comparisons are made at the end of the article.

Study-Reading

1　**RED BLOOD CELLS**　**Red blood cells** transport oxygen throughout your body. They are the most numerous cells in your blood. Healthy red blood cells look like tiny saucers, as shown in the photograph at right. Their red color comes from **hemoglobin** *[HEE muh gloh bun]*, an iron-rich protein that attaches to oxygen very easily.

　　A red blood cell lives about 120 days. Every day of your life, your body must produce new red blood cells to replace those that die. As explained in Chapter 13, "Bones and Muscles," red blood cells are produced by red bone marrow in spongy bone.

2　**WHITE BLOOD CELLS**　**White blood cells** protect your body against infections. They are larger than red blood cells, but there are usually fewer of them. Unlike red blood cells and platelets, which can only float along with the blood flow, white blood cells can move by themselves.

　　When bacteria, viruses, or other disease-causing organisms enter your body, white blood cells move through the walls of capillaries and into body tissue to attack the invaders.

3　　Unlike red blood cells, most white blood cells live only a few days. During an infection, some may live only a few hours. Like red blood cells, though, new white blood cells must always be produced to replace ones that die. Some white blood cells are produced by red bone marrow. Others are formed in the lymphatic system.

VENN DIAGRAM: Important information that compares two things can be organized in a Venn diagram.

Note Taking

Red and White Blood Cells

Areas 1 and 2 list details showing how the two subjects are different.

1.

2.

Red Blood Cells

3.

White Blood Cells

- transport oxygen
- small, saucer shaped
- live 120 days

- needed for life
- produced by red bone marrow

- protect your body from infection
- larger
- move by themselves
- live only a few days

Area 3 lists details common to both subjects.

Process

This information from a health textbook follows the **process pattern.** It describes what happens over time when a person stops using tobacco. Phrases like "During the first 24 hours" and "Within a few days" help readers follow the process.

Previewing

Study-Reading

HEALTH BENEFITS When someone stops using tobacco, the body immediately begins to clean itself. During the first 24 hours, the levels of nicotine and carbon monoxide in the bloodstream rapidly drop. Without repeated doses of nicotine, the heart rate decreases, blood vessels no longer constrict unnaturally, and blood pressure is lowered. Without carbon monoxide, the amount of oxygen in the bloodstream increases.

Within a few days, a smoker's chronic cough begins to clear up, although coughing may continue for a few weeks. With the source of irritation from smoke removed, cilia in the air passages begin to recover. The lungs slowly clear, and breathing is easier—even for someone with permanent damage from emphysema. Colds and lung infections occur less often.

In time, much of the damage caused by tobacco is reversed, even in heavy users. Long-term studies of smokers who quit show a steady decline in their risk of heart disease, chronic lung disease, lung cancer, oral cancer, and other types of cancers. Within two years, the ex-smoker's risks of heart and lung disease are about the same as those of someone who never smoked.

LIST: **Important information that follows the process pattern can be arranged in a list.**

Note Taking

When Someone Stops
Using Tobacco

during first day, nicotine and
carbon monoxide levels drop

↓

This list shows the steps or stages in the order that they are given in the reading.

heart rate and blood pressure
are lowered

↓

within a few days,
cough clears up

↓

easier breathing as lungs clear

↓

in time, lower risk of
lung and heart disease
and cancer

Cause and Effect

This information from a magazine follows the **cause and effect pattern.** It shows how different needs or interests caused the Spanish to move north (the effect) into land that is now the southwestern part of the United States. Reading material that follows this pattern helps you better understand complicated subjects.

Previewing

The Move North

For many reasons, the people of the Middle Americas were urged to move to the north. Besides Mexico, the Spanish claimed a giant territory that included the present-day states of California, Nevada, Utah, Colorado, New Mexico, Arizona, and Texas. In 1821, Mexico declared its freedom from Spain, so the Mexican flag flew over this area. However, the Mexicans began to lose their land in the 1840's. In less than 50 years, the land that is now the southwestern part of the United States had changed hands three times. This all began when the Spanish moved north.

Some Spaniards wanted more land, some wa
spread C
moved no
food in t
already
north.

Study-Reading

For many reasons, the people of the Middle Americas were urged to move to the north. Besides Mexico, the Spanish claimed a giant territory that included the present-day states of California, Nevada, Utah, Colorado, New Mexico, Arizona, and Texas. Some Spaniards moved north because they wanted more land, others wanted gold, and some wanted to spread Christianity. The Spanish also ventured north because there was not much food in the south. However, there were already people living in the area of the north.

In less than 50 years, the land that is now the southwestern part of the United States had changed hands three times. This all began when the Spanish moved north.

CAUSE/ EFFECT ORGANIZER: Important information that shows cause and effect can be organized in the following way.

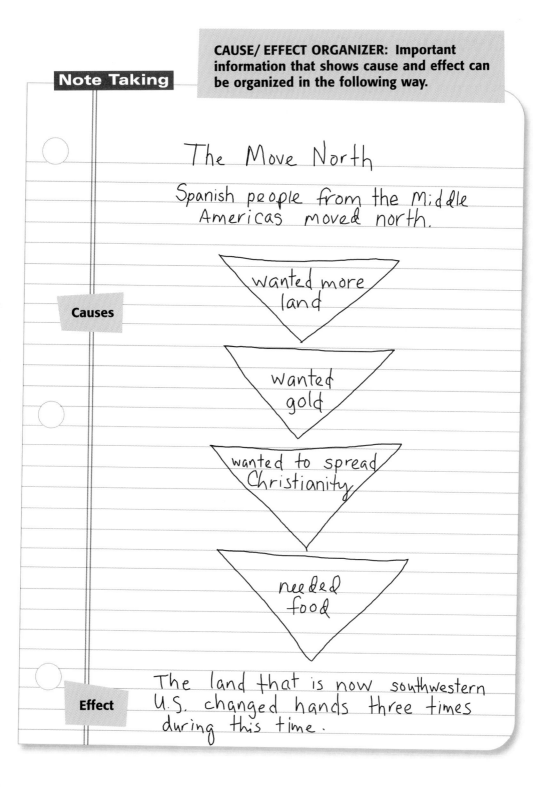

The Move North

Spanish people from the Middle Americas moved north.

Causes

wanted more land

wanted gold

wanted to spread Christianity

needed food

Effect

The land that is now southwestern U.S. changed hands three times during this time.

Chronological Order

This article taken from the Internet follows the **chronological pattern** of organization. (*Chronological* means "according to time.") The article gives important events that happened during different years of the Civil War.

Previewing

— AMERICA'S CIVIL WAR —

In 1860, Abraham Lincoln was elected president of the United States. Because Lincoln was against the spread of slavery, the pro-slavery South seceded from the U.S. Eleven southern states formed their own country, the Confederate States of America. The Confederate army attacked Fort Sumter, South Carolina, in April 1861. The Civil War had begun.

Study-Reading

— AMERICA'S CIVIL WAR —

In 1860, Abraham Lincoln was elected president of the United States. Because Lincoln was against the spread of slavery, the pro-slavery South seceded from the U.S. Eleven southern states formed their own country, the Confederate States of America. The Confederate army attacked Fort Sumter, South Carolina, in April 1861. The Civil War had begun. The Confederates won battles at Bull Run in 1861 and Richmond in 1862. Even though the South was winning, Lincoln issued the Emancipation Proclamation in 1862. It said that all slaves were free, including those in Confederate states. In 1863, a great Confederate general, Stonewall Jackson, was killed. That same year, the Confederates lost important battles at Gettysburg and Vicksburg. In 1865, the Union army took over the southern cities of Atlanta and Richmond, which was the Confederate capital. Confederate General Robert E. Lee surrendered at Richmond on April 4, 1865. The war was over, and so was slavery in America.

TIME LINE: Information about important events can be arranged chronologically on a time line.

America's Civil War

1860 — Lincoln elected; South secedes

1861 — South attacks Fort Sumter and wins at Bull Run.

1862 — South wins at Richmond. Emancipation Proclamation given.

1863 — Stonewall Jackson killed. South loses at Gettysburg.

1864

1865 — Union takes Atlanta and Richmond. Lee surrenders.

Study-Reading Strategies

There are many strategies that good readers use to help them better understand reading material. (A *strategy* is a plan or way of doing something.) The next two pages show you two of them.

SQ3R

SQ3R stands for the five steps in the following study-reading process: *Survey, Question, Read, Recite, Review.* Here is how this strategy works.

Survey　Look over, or survey, your reading text. Look briefly at each page. Look at the headings, subheadings, chapter titles, pictures, and boldfaced type. Also skim the first and last paragraphs.

Question　Ask yourself questions that you want to have answered as you read. You can turn the headings and subheadings into questions. For example, the heading *Clues That a Person Is a Smoker* can be turned into the question *What are the clues that a person is a smoker?*

Read　Read the assignment carefully. See if it follows one of the basic patterns of nonfiction. Reread any confusing parts. Use context clues or a dictionary to figure out words or ideas that you don't know or understand.

Recite　Repeat to yourself what you learned from your reading. (Do it in any language.) Stop at the end of each section, page, or chapter and answer the questions that you asked in step 2.

Review　Review the material using a graphic organizer, pictures, or an outline that shows the important information from the text. Also answer any review questions that may have been assigned.

KWL

KWL is a good study-reading strategy to use when you already know something about the topic. KWL stands for what I *Know*, what I *Want* to know, and what I *Learned*.

How to Use a KWL Chart

1. Write the topic of your reading at the top of a sheet of paper. Then divide the sheet into three columns and put a **K,** a **W,** and an **L** above the columns.

2. List what you already **know** in the "K" column.

3. Fill in the "W" column with questions you **want** to explore.

4. When you finish reading, fill in the "L" column with things you **learned.**

Dolphins		
K (What do I Know?)	**W** (What do I Want to know?)	**L** (What I Learned)
1. Dolphins are smart. 2. Dolphins can swim fast.	1. How does a dolphin breathe? 2. How do dolphins "talk"? 3. How do dolphins sleep?	1. A dolphin surfaces and breathes through a hole in the top of its head. 2. Dolphins "talk" by making high, sharp whistles. 3.

Study-Reading Checklist

Use this checklist as a guide whenever you have study-reading assignments to complete.

✔ Before you read . . .

_____ Know exactly what the reading assignment is, when it is due, and what you have to do to complete it.

_____ Gather all the materials you may need to complete your work (notebook, handouts, dictionary, etc.).

_____ Decide how much time you will need to complete the assignment and when and where (library, study hall, home) you will do it.

✔ As you read . . .

_____ Know your textbooks and what they contain; use the table of contents, index, and so on.

_____ Use a specific strategy for your study-reading.

_____ If questions are part of the assignment, look them over before you begin reading.

_____ Use titles and headings to help you ask yourself questions about what may be coming up next.

_____ Notice words or phrases that are in **boldface** or _italics_.

_____ Study maps, charts, graphs, and other illustrations to help you understand and remember information.

_____ Determine the pattern of nonfiction that the reading follows. (See pages 262-273.)

_____ Take good notes. (See pages 313-318.)

✔ After you read . . .

_____ Reread difficult parts; then ask someone for help if necessary.

_____ List things you want to check on or ask about.

_____ Make note cards or flash cards to study later.

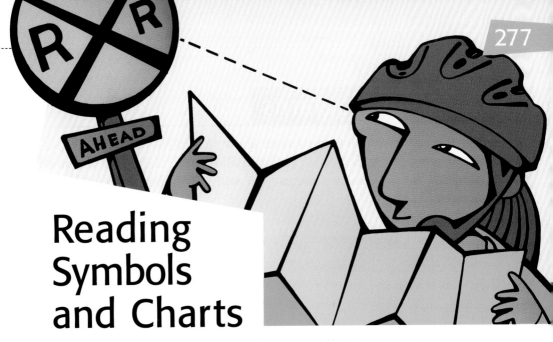

Reading Symbols and Charts

There's more to reading than just words. Words do a great job of giving basic information. But symbols and charts give information, too—through pictures, graphic organizers, numbers, shapes, and so on.

A **symbol** is a simple picture that stands for something. The letters of the alphabet are symbols that stand for sounds. In math, = is a symbol that stands for "equals." Some symbols, like these three examples, are used all over the world.

What's Ahead

The pages that follow in this chapter will help you read three important types of charts: diagrams, graphs, and tables. The final page gives helpful tips for reading charts.

- **Reading Diagrams**
- **Reading Graphs**
- **Reading Tables**
- **Checklist for Reading a Chart**

Reading Diagrams

Diagrams are drawings that show the parts of something. A diagram may leave out some parts to show only the parts you need to learn. On the next two pages, you will learn about three types of diagrams.

Picture Diagrams

Picture diagrams show how something is put together.

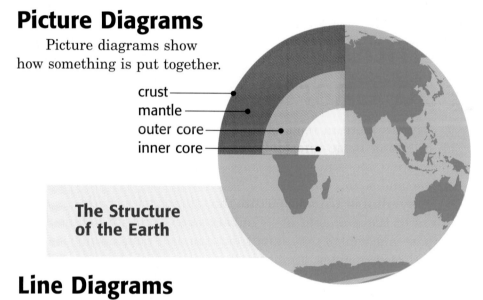

crust
mantle
outer core
inner core

The Structure of the Earth

Line Diagrams

Line diagrams are like picture diagrams: They show how something is put together. But there is one difference. Line diagrams show something you can't really see. Instead of objects, line diagrams show ideas and relationships.

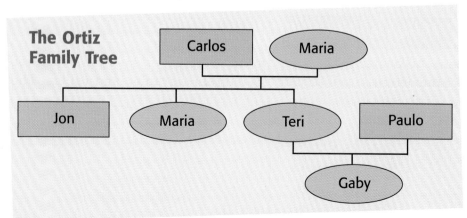

The Ortiz Family Tree

Carlos — Maria

Jon   Maria   Teri   Paulo

Gaby

Flow Diagrams

Flow diagrams show a process or a cycle. They show how something happens. The words used on diagrams are called *labels*.

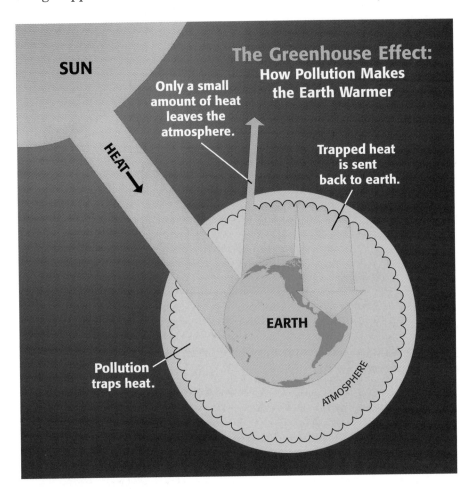

SUN

The Greenhouse Effect: How Pollution Makes the Earth Warmer

Only a small amount of heat leaves the atmosphere.

HEAT

Trapped heat is sent back to earth.

Pollution traps heat.

EARTH

ATMOSPHERE

A Closer Look at Diagramming

Some diagrams show time going by. Time may be shown moving from top to bottom. In the line diagram on the previous page, the people listed at the top of the diagram were born before the people listed at the bottom.

A diagram may also show time moving from left to right. Look at the flow diagram above. As it shows heat moving from the sun to the earth, time moves from left to right across the page.

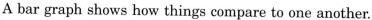

Reading Graphs

Graphs are pictures of information. Different types of graphs show different types of information. The next three pages show you three common graphs.

Bar Graphs

A bar graph shows how things compare to one another.

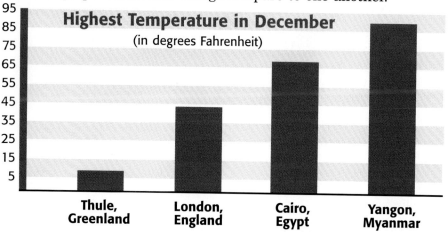

The bars on a bar graph may be vertical or horizontal. (*Vertical* means "up and down." *Horizontal* means "from side to side.") Sometimes the bars on graphs are called *columns*. The part that shows numbers is called the *scale*.

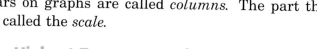

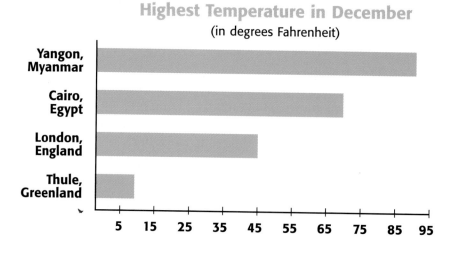

Line Graphs

A line graph shows how something changes as time goes by. A line graph always begins with an L-shaped grid. One line of the grid shows passing time; the other line shows numbers.

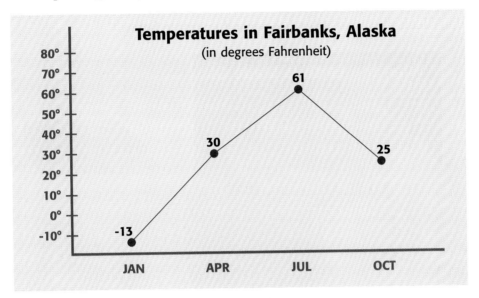

A line graph may have more than one line. Each line shows a different subject.

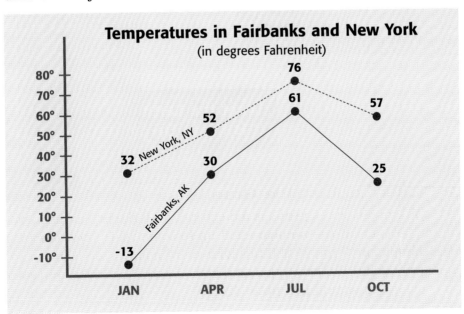

Pie Graphs

A pie graph shows how all the parts of something add up to make the whole. A pie graph often shows percentages. (A *percentage* is the part of a whole stated in hundredths: 35% = 35/100.) It's called a pie graph because it is usually a circle. But some pie graphs don't look like pies. (See the second example below.)

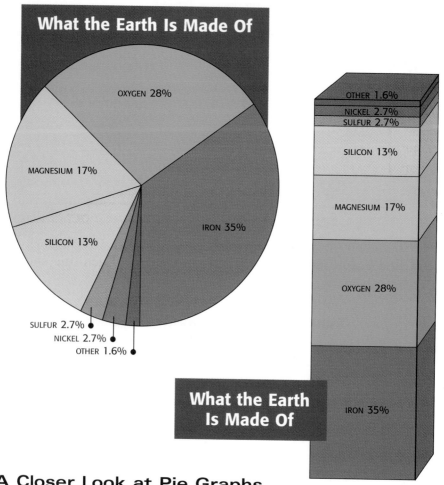

A Closer Look at Pie Graphs

You can tell that a graph is a pie graph if all the percentages add up to 100%, or all the numbers add up to some other total amount. For example, if you have $20 to spend every month, you could make a pie graph showing how you spend your money. All the numbers in your pie graph should add up to $20.

Reading Tables

Tables have two parts: rows and columns. *Rows* go across and show one kind of information or data. *Columns* go up and down and show a different kind of data. The table makes it easy to see how the two types of data fit together.

To read a table that has two columns, read across each row.

Richter Scale	
Magnitude of Earthquake	Effects of Earthquake
0-2	not felt by people
2-3	felt by people nearby
3-4	felt by people in a bigger area; hanging items such as light fixtures sway
4-5	dishes, windows break; walls crack
5-6	furniture moves; weak buildings damaged
6-7	walls and buildings collapse
7-8	buildings destroyed; pipes break; cracks in ground
8 and higher	bridges destroyed; large cracks in ground; waves

To read a table that has more than two columns, find where a row and a column meet. In the table below, if the wind speed is 15 and the air temperature is 20, the windchill factor is -5.

The Windchill Factor

Wind speed (mph)	Thermometer reading (degrees Fahrenheit)										
	35	30	25	20	15	10	5	0	-5	-10	-15
5	33	27	21	19	12	7	0	-5	-10	-15	-21
10	22	16	10	3	-3	-9	-15	-22	-27	-34	-40
15	16	9	2	-5	-11	-18	-25	-31	-38	-45	-51
20	12	4	-3	-10	-17	-24	-31	-39	-46	-53	-60
25	8	1	-7	-15	-22	-29	-36	-44	-51	-59	-66
30	6	-2	-10	-18	-25	-33	-41	-49	-56	-64	-71

NOTE: This chart gives equivalent temperatures for combinations of wind speed and temperatures. For example, the combination of a temperature of 10° Fahrenheit and a wind blowing at 10 mph has a cooling power equal to -9° F. Wind speeds of higher than 45 mph have little additional cooling effect.

Checklist for Reading a Chart

Whether you are reading a textbook or a magazine, charts can help you understand the information. Here's how to use a chart and words together to understand what you are reading.

First, look over both the words and the chart.

____ Read the titles, the subtitles, the first sentence of each paragraph, and the summary, if there is one.

____ Determine what the text is about.

____ Look at the titles of the chart. Be sure about the subject of the chart. Notice the type of chart (bar graph, diagram, pie graph, etc.).

Next, read the text and the chart.

Finally, ask yourself these questions:

____ What does the chart tell me?

____ What part of the text does the chart relate to? (Each chart probably gives more information about one part of the text.)

____ What information in the chart is also given in the text? (Sometimes a chart and the text tell the same thing, but in different ways.)

____ What information in the chart is not given in the text? (Sometimes a chart gives information that is not in the text. That's why it's important to read charts.)

Improving Your Vocabulary

Your vocabulary is all the words you know and use. As you improve your vocabulary, you also improve your ability to learn and to communicate.

One of the best ways to improve your vocabulary is to read. Books, magazines, newspapers, and even the Internet are filled with all kinds of new words and ideas. Many words and ideas centered around a particular topic are related. That makes them easier to learn, understand, and remember.

What's Ahead

As you read and write, there are many strategies that you can use to improve your vocabulary. In this chapter you will learn about the strategies listed below. Try some of them as you work on future assignments.

- **Using Context**
- **Using a Thesaurus**
- **Using a Dictionary**
- **Using a Bilingual Dictionary**
- **Keeping a Personal Dictionary**
- **Studying New Words**
- **Prefixes, Suffixes, and Roots**

Using Context

When you are reading, you may come across a word you don't know. You can use **context** (the words and ideas surrounding the unknown word) to figure it out.

Hints for Using Context
When you come to a word you don't know . . .

- Look for a **synonym**—a word or words that have the same meaning as the unknown word.

  > Raja and Harris often get into **skirmishes**, but they don't let these little arguments stop their friendship.

  (*Skirmishes* are little arguments.)

- Look for an **antonym**—a word or words that have the opposite meaning of the unknown word.

  > Alex tried to **conceal** his feelings, but his frown showed us that he was very sad.

  (*Conceal* is the opposite of *show.*)

- Look for words that give a **definition** of the unknown word.

  > Paula is a **graphologist**, a person who studies people's handwriting to learn about their personalities.

  (A *graphologist* studies handwriting.)

- Look for words that appear in a **series** to give a definition of the unknown word.

  > The **dulcimer**, the banjo, and the fiddle are popular musical instruments in the southeastern United States.

  (A *dulcimer*, like a banjo and a fiddle, is a musical instrument.)

Using a Thesaurus

A **thesaurus** is a reference book that gives synonyms and antonyms for words. A thesaurus helps you in two different ways:

1. It helps you find just the right word for a specific sentence.

2. It keeps you from using the same words again and again.

If a thesaurus is organized alphabetically, look up the word as you would in a regular dictionary. If you have a traditional thesaurus, you must first look your word up in the index in the back of the book.

Finding the Best Word A thesaurus would be helpful if you need a word that means *very cold.*

> Because of the _____ weather, none of the cars in our neighborhood would start.

Sample Thesaurus Entry

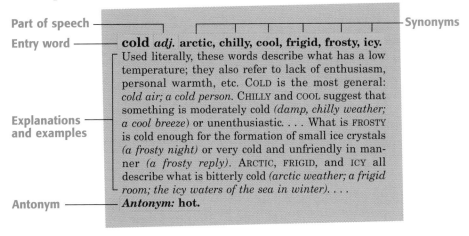

Part of speech — Synonyms

Entry word — **cold** *adj.* **arctic, chilly, cool, frigid, frosty, icy.** Used literally, these words describe what has a low temperature; they also refer to lack of enthusiasm, personal warmth, etc. COLD is the most general: *cold air; a cold person.* CHILLY and COOL suggest that something is moderately cold *(damp, chilly weather; a cool breeze)* or unenthusiastic. . . . What is FROSTY is cold enough for the formation of small ice crystals *(a frosty night)* or very cold and unfriendly in manner *(a frosty reply)*. ARCTIC, FRIGID, and ICY all describe what is bitterly cold *(arctic weather; a frigid room; the icy waters of the sea in winter)*. . . .

Explanations and examples

Antonym — ***Antonym:* hot.**

After reading the list of synonyms, you decide on *arctic* because it describes very cold weather.

> Because of the __arctic__ weather, none of the cars in our neighborhood would start.

Using a Dictionary

When context clues don't help you figure out an unknown word, you can look it up in a **dictionary.** Remember that a word may have more than one meaning, so read them all. In addition to helping you understand the meanings of words, here are some other things that a dictionary can help you with.

Guide words are words located at the top of every page. They list the first and last entry words on a page, and they help you know which words fall in alphabetical order between the entry words.

Entry words are the bold words that are defined on the dictionary page. Entry words are listed in alphabetical order.

Syllable divisions show where you can divide a word into syllables. Some dictionaries use heavy black dots to divide the syllables. Other dictionaries put extra space between them.

Usage labels tell you how a word is used (*slang, informal, nonstandard,* etc.).

Spelling and capital letters are given for every entry word. If an entry is capitalized, capitalize it in your writing, too.

Parts of speech labels tell you the different ways a word can be used. For example, the word *crawl* can be used as a verb (as in *A baby* crawls *before he or she learns to walk*), or it can be used as a noun (as in *The baby did a slow* crawl *across the bedroom floor*).

Synonyms are words with similar meanings. Antonyms (words with opposite meanings) may be listed last.

Accent marks show which syllable or syllables should be stressed when you say a word.

Pronunciation key and phonetic respellings give symbols and words to help you figure out how to pronounce words.

Sample Dictionary Page

Entry word —— **Bron·të** (brŏn'tē). Family of British novelists and poets, including **Charlotte** (1816-55), known for *Jane Eyre* (1847), **Emily** (1818-48), known for *Wuthering Heights* (1847), and **Anne** (1820-49), known for *Agnes Gray* (1847).

Syllable divisions —— **bron·to·saur** (brŏn'tə-sôr') or **bron·to·sau·rus** (brŏn'tə-sôr'əs) n. A large herbivorous dinosaur of the genus *Apatosaurus* (or *Brontosaurus*) of the Jurassic Period. [NLat. *Brontosaurus,* genus name : Gk. *brontē,* thunder + Gk. *sauros,* lizard.]

Bronx (brŏngks). A borough of New York City in SE NY on the mainland N of Manhattan. Pop. 1,203,789.

Usage label —— **Bronx cheer** n. *Slang.* A loud sound expressing disapproval; a raspberry. [After the BRONX.]

bronze (brŏnz) n. **1.a.** Any of various alloys of copper and tin, sometimes with traces of other metals. **b.** Any of various alloys of copper, with or without tin, and antimony, phosphorus, or other components. **2.** A work of art made of one of these alloys. **3.a.** *Color.* A moderate yellowish to olive brown. **b.** A pigment of this color. – *adj.* **1.** Made of or consisting of bronze. **2.** *Color.* Of the color bronze – *tr.v.* **bronzed, bronz·ing, bronz·es.** To give the color or appearance of bronze to. [Fr. < Ital. *bronzo.*] – **bronz'er** n. – **bronz'y** *adj.*

Spelling and capital letters —— **Bronze Age** (brŏnz) n. A period of human culture between the Stone Age and the Iron Age, characterized by weapons and implements made of bronze.

brooch (brōch, brōōch) also **broach** (brōch) n. A relatively large decorative pin or clasp. [ME *broche,* pointed tool, brooch, pin. See BROACH[1].]

Parts of speech —— **brood** (brōōd) n. **1.** The young of certain animals, esp. a group of young birds or fowl. **2.** The children in one family. – *v.* **brood·ed, brood·ing, broods.** – *tr.* **1.** To sit on or hatch (eggs). **2.** To protect (young) by or as if by covering with the wings. – *intr.* **1.** To sit on or hatch eggs. **2.** To hover envelopingly; loom. **3.a.** To be deep in thought; meditate. **b.** To focus the attention on a subject persistently and moodily; worry. **c.** To be depressed. – *adj.* Kept for breeding: *a brood hen.* [ME < OE *brōd.* See **bhreu-*.**] – **brood'ing·ly** *adv.*

Synonyms —— **Syns:** *brood, dwell, fret, mope, stew, worry.* The central meaning shared by these verbs is "to turn over in the mind moodily and at length": *brooding about life; dwelled on defeat; fretting over the job; moping about illness; stewing over her; worrying about bills.*

Accent mark —— **brood·er** (brōō'dər) n. **1.** One that broods. **2.** A heated enclosure in which fowls are raised.

brontosaur

Pronunciation key

ă	pat	oi	boy
ā	pay	ou	out
âr	care	ŏŏ	took
ä	father	ōō	boot
ĕ	pet	u	cut
ē	be	ûr	urge
ĭ	pit	th	thin
ī	pie	*th*	this
îr	pier	hw	which
ŏ	pot	zh	vision
ō	toe	ə	about,
ô	paw		item

Stress marks:
' (primary);
' (secondary), as in
dictionary (dĭk'shə-nĕr'ē)

Using a Bilingual Dictionary

A **bilingual dictionary** includes words in two languages. Bilingual dictionaries are useful when you know a word in one language *(Spanish),* and you want to learn it in another language *(English).* The sample entries come from the two different parts in a Spanish/English, English/Spanish bilingual dictionary.

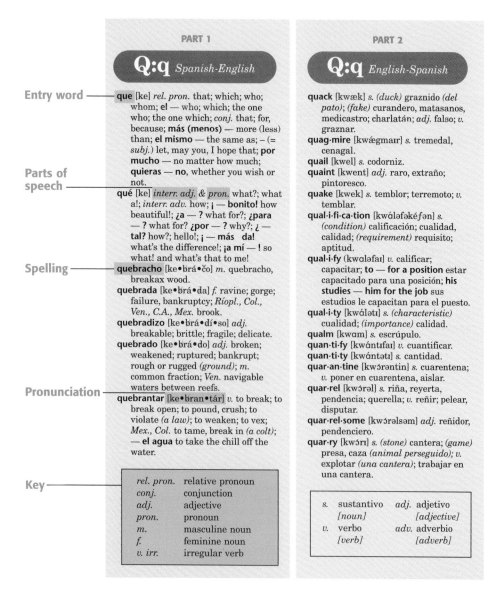

PART 1

Q:q *Spanish-English*

Entry word ——— **que** [ke] *rel. pron.* that; which; who; whom; **el —** who; which; the one who; the one which; *conj.* that; for, because; **más (menos) —** more (less) than; **el mismo —** the same as; **– (=** *subj.)* let, may you, I hope that; **por mucho —** no matter how much; **quieras — no,** whether you wish or not.

Parts of speech ——— **qué** [ke] *interr. adj. & pron.* what?; what a!; *interr. adv.* how; **¡ — bonito!** how beautiful!; **¿a — ?** what for?; **¿para — ?** what for? **¿por — ?** why?; **¿ — tal?** how?; hello!; **¡ — más da!** what's the difference!; **¡a mí — !** so what! and what's that to me!

Spelling ——— **quebracho** [ke•brá•čo] *m.* quebracho, breakax wood.

quebrada [ke•brá•da] *f.* ravine; gorge; failure, bankruptcy; *Ríopl., Col., Ven., C.A., Mex.* brook.

quebradizo [ke•brá•dí•so] *adj.* breakable; brittle; fragile; delicate.

quebrado [ke•brá•do] *adj.* broken; weakened; ruptured; bankrupt; rough or rugged *(ground); m.* common fraction; *Ven.* navigable waters between reefs.

Pronunciation ——— **quebrantar** [ke•bran•tár] *v.* to break; to break open; to pound, crush; to violate *(a law);* to weaken; to vex; *Mex., Col.* to tame, break in *(a colt);* **— el agua** to take the chill off the water.

Key ———

rel. pron.	relative pronoun
conj.	conjunction
adj.	adjective
pron.	pronoun
m.	masculine noun
f.	feminine noun
v. irr.	irregular verb

PART 2

Q:q *English-Spanish*

quack [kwæk] *s. (duck)* graznido *(del pato); (fake)* curandero, matasanos, medicastro; charlatán; *adj.* falso; *v.* graznar.

quag·mire [kwǽgmaɪr] *s.* tremedal, cenagal.

quail [kwel] *s.* codorniz.

quaint [kwent] *adj.* raro, extraño; pintoresco.

quake [kwek] *s.* temblor; terremoto; *v.* temblar.

qual·i·fi·ca·tion [kwáləfəkéfən] *s. (condition)* calificación; cualidad, calidad; *(requirement)* requisito; aptitud.

qual·i·fy (kwɑləfaɪ] *v.* calificar; capacitar; **to — for a position** estar capacitado para una posición; **his studies — him for the job** sus estudios le capacitan para el puesto.

qual·i·ty [kwáləti] *s. (characteristic)* cualidad; *(importance)* calidad.

qualm [kwɑm] *s.* escrúpulo.

quan·ti·fy [kwántɪfaɪ] *v.* cuantificar.

quan·ti·ty [kwántətɪ] *s.* cantidad.

quar·an·tine [kwɔ́rəntin] *s.* cuarentena; *v.* poner en cuarentena, aislar.

quar·rel [kwɔrəl] *s.* riña, reyerta, pendencia; querella; *v.* reñir; pelear, disputar.

quar·rel·some [kwɔ́rəlsəm] *adj.* reñidor, pendenciero.

quar·ry [kwɔ́rɪ] *s. (stone)* cantera; *(game)* presa, caza *(animal perseguido); v.* explotar *(una cantera);* trabajar en una cantera.

s.	sustantivo [noun]	*adj.*	adjetivo [adjective]
v.	verbo [verb]	*adv.*	adverbio [adverb]

Keeping a Personal Dictionary

You can improve your vocabulary by keeping a personal dictionary. It's best to put each new word on a note card or on a half sheet of paper. (Make sure to keep your words in a safe place.)

Sample Note Cards

Here are two ways to set up personal dictionary note cards. Feel free, however, to use any way that works best for you.

shiver
(shĭv'ər)
shiver means "to shake" (verb)

Some people shiver when they are cold or afraid.

Synonyms:
quake, quiver, shake, shudder, tremble

shiv·er
(shĭv'ər)

1. to shake, to tremble
2. to quiver, to vibrate

I shiver when I get cold.

synonyms: quake, shake, shudder

Studying New Words

Word Parts You can figure out the meanings of new words by using the three word parts:

- **prefixes** (common word beginnings)
- **suffixes** (common word endings)
- **roots** (common word bases)

For example, if you know that the prefix *non-* means "not," you can figure out the meaning of the word *nonsense:* "something that does not make sense." And if you know that the suffix *-less* means "without," you can figure out the meaning of the word *hopeless:* "without hope." Before you can use word parts well, however, you must learn the meanings of some of the most common prefixes, suffixes, and roots.

On the next eight pages, you will find a list of the most common prefixes, suffixes, and roots in the English language. Learn as many as you can . . . a few at a time.

Word Families You can also use word families to help you figure out new words. For example, suppose you know that the word *trust* means "to believe in someone or something." If you were to see the words *trustful* or *trustworthy,* you would be able to figure out that they are all part of the same word family, and that they all have to do with believing in someone or something.

Prefixes, Suffixes, and Roots

On the next several pages, you will find many of the common prefixes, suffixes, and roots in the English language.

Prefixes

A **prefix** is a word part that is added before a word. (*Pre-* means "before.") A prefix changes the meaning of the word it is added to. For example, the prefix *un-* added to the word *fair (unfair)* changes the word's meaning to "not fair."

ambi- *[both]*
ambidextrous (skilled with both hands)

anti- *[against]*
antifreeze (a liquid that works against freezing)
antiwar (against wars and fighting)

astro- *[star]*
astronaut (person who travels among the stars)
astronomy (study of the stars)

auto- *[self]*
autobiography (writing that is about yourself)

bi- *[two]*
bilingual (using or speaking two languages)
biped (having two feet)

circum- *[in a circle, around]*
circumference (the line or distance around a circle)
circumnavigate (to sail around)

co- *[together, with]*
cooperate (to work together)
coordinate (to put things together)

ex- *[out]*
exhale (to breathe out)
exit (the act of going out)

fore- *[before, in front of]*
foremost (in the first place, before everyone or everything else)
foretell (to tell or show beforehand)

hemi- *[half]*
hemisphere (half of a sphere or globe)

hyper- *[over]*
hyperactive (overactive)

im- *[not, opposite of]*
impatient (not patient)
impossible (not possible)

in- *[not, opposite of]*
inactive (not active)
incomplete (not complete)

inter- *[between, among]*
international (between or among nations)
interplanetary (taking place between the planets)

macro- *[large]*
macrocosm (the entire universe)

mal- *[bad, poor]*
malnutrition (poor nutrition)

micro- *[small]*
microscope (an instrument used to see very small things)

mono- *[one]*
monolingual (using or speaking only one language)

non- *[not, opposite of]*
nonfat (without the normal fat content)
nonfiction (based on facts; not made-up)

over- *[too much, extra]*
overeat (to eat too much)
overtime (extra time; time beyond regular hours)

poly- *[many]*
polygon (a figure or shape with three or more sides)
polysyllable (a word with more than three syllables)

post- *[after]*
postscript (a note added at the end of a letter, after the signature)
postwar (after a war)

pre- *[before]*
pregame (activities that occur before a game)
preheat (to heat before using)

re- *[again, back]*
repay (to pay back)
rewrite (to write again or revise)

semi- *[half, partly]*
semicircle (half a circle)
semiconscious (half conscious; not fully conscious)

sub- *[under, below]*
submarine (a boat that can operate underwater)
submerge (to put underwater)

trans- *[across, over; change]*
transcontinental (across a continent)
transform (to change from one form to another)

tri- *[three]*
triangle (a figure that has three sides and three angles)
tricycle (a three-wheeled vehicle)

un- *[not]*
uncomfortable (not comfortable)
unhappy (not happy; sad)

under- *[below, beneath]*
underage (below or less than the usual or required age)
undersea (beneath the surface of the sea)

uni- *[one]*
unicycle (a one-wheeled vehicle)
unisex (a single style that is worn by both males and females)

Numerical Prefixes

deci- *[tenth part]*
decimal system (a number system based on units of 10)

centi- *[hundredth part]*
centimeter (a unit of length equal to 1/100 meter)

milli- *[thousandth part]*
millimeter (a unit of length equal to 1/1000 meter)

micro- *[millionth part]*
micrometer (one-millionth of a meter)

deca- or **dec-** *[ten]*
decade (a period of 10 years)

hecto- or **hect-** *[one hundred]*
hectare (a metric unit of land equal to 100 ares)

kilo- *[one thousand]*
kilogram (a unit of mass equal to 1,000 grams)

mega- *[one million]*
megabit (one million bits)

Suffixes

A **suffix** is a word part that is added after a word. Sometimes a suffix will tell you what part of speech a word is. For example, many adverbs end in the suffix *-ly*.

-able *[able, can do]*
  agreeable (able or willing to agree)
  doable (can be done)

-al *[of, like]*
  magical (like magic)
  optical (of the eye)

-ed *[past tense]*
  called (past tense of "call")
  learned (past tense of "learn")

-ess *[female]*
  lioness (a female lion)

-ful *[full of]*
  helpful (giving help; full of help)

-ic *[like, having to do with]*
  symbolic (having to do with symbols)

-ily *[in some manner]*
  happily (in a happy manner)

-ish *[somewhat like or near]*
  childish (somewhat like a child)

-ism *[characteristic of]*
  heroism (characteristic of a hero)

-less *[without]*
  careless (without care)

-ly *[in some manner]*
  calmly (in a calm manner)

-ology *[study, science]*
  biology (the study of living things)

-s *[more than one, plural noun]*
  books (more than one book)

-ward *[in the direction of]*
  westward (in the direction of west)

-y *[containing, full of]*
  salty (containing salt)

Comparative Suffixes

-er *[comparing two things]*
  faster, later, neater, stronger

-est *[comparing more than two]*
  fastest, latest, neatest, strongest

Noun-Forming Suffixes

-er *[one who]*
  painter (one who paints)

-ing *[the result of]*
  painting (the result of a painter's work)

-ion *[act of, state of]*
  perfection (the state of being perfect)

-ist *[one who]*
  violinist (one who plays the violin)

-ment *[act of, result of]*
  amendment (the result of amending, or changing)
  improvement (the result of improving)

-ness *[state of]*
  goodness (the state of being good)

-or *[one who]*
  actor (one who acts)

Roots

A **root** is a word or word base from which other words are made by adding a prefix or a suffix. Knowing the important roots can help you figure out the meaning of difficult words.

ali, alter [*other*]
  alias (a person's other name)
  alternative (another choice)

am, amor [*love, like*]
  amiable (friendly)
  amorous (loving)

anni, annu, enni [*year*]
  anniversary (happening at the same time every year)
  annually (happening once a year)
  centennial (happening once every 100 years)

anthrop [*human being*]
  anthropoid (like or of a human being)
  anthropology (the study of humankind)

aster [*star*]
  aster (star flower)
  asterisk (starlike symbol [*])

aud [*hear, listen*]
  audible (can be heard)
  auditorium (a place to listen to speeches and performances)

bibl [*book*]
  Bible (sacred book of Christianity)
  bibliography (list of books)

bio [*life*]
  biography (book about a person's life)
  biology (the study of life)

chrome [*color*]
  monochrome (having one color)
  polychrome (having many colors)

chron [*time*]
  chronological (in time order)
  synchronize (to make happen at the same time)

cide [*the killing of; killer*]
  homicide (the killing of one person by another person)
  pesticide (pest [bug] killer)

cise [*cut*]
  incision (a thin, clean cut)
  incisors (the teeth that cut or tear food)
  precise (cut exactly right)

cord, cor [*heart*]
  cordial (heartfelt)
  coronary (relating to the heart)

corp [*body*]
  corporation (a legal body; business)
  corpse (a dead human body)

cosm [*universe, world*]
  cosmos (the universe or world)
  microcosm (a small world)

cred [*believe*]
  credible (capable of being believed)
  incredible (unbelievable)

cycl, cyclo [*wheel, circular*]
  bicycle (a vehicle with two wheels)
  cyclone (a very strong circular wind)

dem [*people*]
  democracy (ruled by the people)
  epidemic (affecting many people at the same time)

dent, dont *[tooth]*
dentures (false teeth)
orthodontist (dentist who straightens teeth)

derm *[skin]*
dermatology (the study of skin)
epidermis (outer layer of skin)

dic, dict *[say, speak]*
dictionary (a book of words that people use or say)
predict (to tell about something in advance)

dynam *[power]*
dynamite (powerful explosive)
dynamo (power producer)

equi *[equal]*
equinox (day and night of equal length)
equivalent (the same or equal to)

fac, fact *[do, make]*
factory (a place where people make things)
manufacture (make by hand or machine)

fide *[faith, trust]*
confident (having faith or trust in oneself)
fidelity (faithfulness to a person or cause)

fin *[end]*
final (the last of something)
infinite (having no end)

flex *[bend]*
flexible (able to bend)
reflex (bending or springing back)

flu *[flowing]*
fluent (flowing smoothly or easily)
fluid (waterlike, flowing substance)

forc, fort *[strong]*
force (strength or power)
fortify (to make strong)

fract, frag *[break]*
fracture (to break)
fragment (a piece broken from the whole)

gen *[birth, produce]*
congenital (existing at birth)
genetics (the study of inborn traits)

geo *[of the earth]*
geography (the study of places on the earth)
geology (the study of the earth's physical features)

grad *[step, go]*
gradual (step-by-step)
graduation (taking the next step)

graph *[write]*
autograph (writing one's name)
graphology (the study of hand-writing)

greg *[herd, group]*
congregation (a group that functions together)
segregate (to group apart)

hab, habit *[live]*
habitat (the place in which one lives)
inhabit (to live in)

hetero *[different]*
heterogeneous (different in birth or kind)
heterosexual (having interest in the opposite sex)

homo *[same]*
homogeneous (of the same birth or kind)
homogenize (to blend into a uniform mixture)

hum *[earth]*
exhume (to take out of the earth)
humus (earth; dirt)

hydr *[water]*
dehydrate (to take the water out of)
hydrophobia (the fear of water)

Roots *(continued)*

ject *[throw]*
  eject (to throw out)
  project (to throw forward)

leg *[law]*
  legal (related to the law)
  legislators (people who make laws)

log, logo *[word, thought, speech]*
  dialog (speech between two people)
  logic (thinking or reasoning)

luc, lum *[light]*
  illuminate (to light up)
  translucent (letting light come through)

magn *[great]*
  magnificent (great)
  magnify (to make bigger or greater)

man *[hand]*
  manicure (to fix the hands)
  manual (done by hand)

mania *[insanity]*
  kleptomania (abnormal desire to steal)
  maniac (an insane person)

mar *[sea, pool]*
  marine (of or found in the sea)
  mariner (sailor)

medi *[middle, between]*
  mediocre (between good and bad; average)
  medium (in the middle)

mega *[large]*
  megalith (large statue)
  megaphone (large horn used to make voices louder)

mem *[remember]*
  memo (a note or reminder)
  memorial (a reminder of a person or an event)

meter *[measure]*
  meter (unit of measure)
  voltameter (device to measure volts)

migra *[wander]*
  immigrant (person who moves to another country)
  migrant (person who moves from place to place)

mit, miss *[send]*
  emit (send out; give off)
  transmission (sending over)

mob, mot *[move]*
  mobile (movable)
  promotion (being moved ahead in rank or performance)

mon *[warn, remind]*
  admonish (to warn or remind)
  monument (a structure used as a reminder of a person or an event)

mort *[death]*
  immortal (something that never dies)
  mortal (subject to death; causing death)

multi *[many, much]*
  multicultural (of or including many cultures)
  multiped (an animal with many feet)

nat *[to be born]*
  innate (inborn)
  nativity (birth)

neur *[nerve, nervous system]*
  neurologist (a doctor who treats the nervous system)
  neurosurgery (surgery on part of the nervous system)

nov *[new]*
  innovation (a new idea)
  renovate (to make like new again)

numer *[number]*
  innumerable (too many to count)
  numerous (large in number)

omni [all, completely]
omnipresent (present everywhere at the same time)
omnivorous (eating all kinds of food)

onym [name]
anonymous (without a name)
pseudonym (false name)

pac [peace]
pacific (peaceful)
pacifist (person who is against war)

path, pathy [feeling, suffering]
empathy (feeling for another)
telepathy (feeling from a distance)

patr [father]
patriarch (the father of the family)
patron (father figure)

ped [foot]
pedal (lever worked by the foot)
pedestrian (one who travels by foot)

pend [hang, weigh]
pendant (a hanging object)
pendulum (a hanging weight that swings back and forth)

phil [love]
Philadelphia ("city of brotherly love")
philosophy (the love of wisdom)

phobia [fear]
acrophobia (a fear of high places)
agoraphobia (a fear of public, open places)

phon [sound]
phonics (related to sounds)
symphony (sounds made together)

photo [light]
photo-essay (a story told mainly with photographs)
photograph (picture made using light rays)

pop [people]
population (the number of people in an area)
populous (full of people)

port [carry]
export (carry out)
portable (able to be carried)

proto [first]
protagonist (the main character in a story)
prototype (the first model made)

psych [mind, soul]
psychiatry (the study of the mind)
psychology (the science of mind and behavior)

rupt [break]
interrupt (to break into)
rupture (to break)

sci [know]
conscious (being aware)
omniscient (knowing everything)

scope [instrument for viewing]
kaleidoscope (instrument for viewing patterns and shapes)
periscope (instrument used to see above the water)

scrib, script [write]
manuscript (something written by hand)
scribble (write quickly)

sen [old]
senile (showing old age)
senior (an older person)

sequ, secu [follow]
sequence (one thing following another)

Roots (continued)

spec [look]
inspect (look at carefully)
specimen (an example to look at)

sphere [ball]
hemisphere (half of a sphere; one of the halves of the earth)

spir [breath]
expire (breathe out; die)
inspire (breathe into; give life to)

strict [tighten]
boa constrictor (a large snake that coils around its prey and squeezes it to death)
constrict (draw tightly together)

tact, tag [touch]
contact (touch)
contagious (spreading disease by touching)

tele [over a long distance; far]
telephone (machine used to speak to people over a distance)
telescope (machine used to see things that are very far away)

tempo [time]
contemporary (from the current time period)
temporary (lasting for a short time)

tend, tens [stretch, strain]
extend (to stretch and make longer)
tension (the act of stretching something tight)

terra [earth]
terrain (the earth or ground)
terrestrial (relating to the earth)

therm [heat]
thermal (related to heat)
thermostat (a device for controlling heat)

tom [cut]
anatomy (the science of cutting apart plants and animals for study)
atom (a particle that cannot be cut or divided)

tox [poison]
intoxicated (poisoned inside; drunk)
toxic (poisonous)

tract [draw, pull]
traction (the act of pulling)
tractor (a machine for pulling)

typ [print]
prototype (the first printing or model)
typo (a printing error)

vac [empty]
vacant (empty)
vacuum (an empty space)

val [strength, worth]
equivalent (of equal worth)
evaluate (to find out the worth of)

ver, vers [turn]
divert (to turn aside)
reverse (to turn back)

vid, vis [see]
supervise (to oversee or watch over)
videotape (record on tape for viewing)

viv [alive, life]
revive (to bring back to life)
vivacious (full of life)

voc [call]
vocalize (to speak, sing, or call)
vocation (the way a person earns a living; a person's calling)

vor [eat]
carnivorous (flesh-eating)
herbivorous (plant-eating)

zoo [animal or animals]
zoo (a place where animals are kept)
zoology (the study of animal life)

Understanding Literature

Each subject you study has its own special vocabulary. When you study geography, you may learn words like *canyon, mesa,* or *delta.* When you study math, you may learn words like *percent, ratio,* and *parallel.*

Literature, too, has its own vocabulary. (*Literature* is the fiction, drama, poetry, and some of the nonfiction that you read.) Knowing the "language of literature" helps you to understand the different stories, poems, and plays. It also helps you to put into words your thoughts and feelings about different forms of literature.

What's Ahead

This chapter includes two lists of terms related to the study of literature. "Types of Literature" lists the different forms of fiction and nonfiction you may be assigned to read. "Elements of Literature" lists terms used to describe the different parts of literature. (See pages 113-123 for more literary terms.)

- **Types of Literature**
- **Elements of Literature**

Types of Literature

There are two main types of literature. **Fiction** is literature that is made-up. It comes from a writer's imagination. **Nonfiction** is literature about real people, places, things, or ideas. Fiction and nonfiction are broken into many different types, too. Below, you will find brief descriptions of some of the most common types of literature. If you need more information, see the index in your handbook.

Autobiography A type of nonfiction in which a person tells the story of his or her own life.

Biography A type of nonfiction in which a person tells the story of someone else's life.

Comedy Fiction or nonfiction that deals with life in a light, humorous way.

Drama A type of literature that uses a lot of dialogue and is meant to be performed in front of an audience; also called a play.

Essay A short piece of nonfiction written about a single subject. An essay often expresses a person's point of view or gives information about a subject.

Fable A short story that ends with a moral (lesson) and often uses talking animals as the main characters.

Fantasy A story that takes place in an imaginary world in which the characters often have supernatural powers or abilities.

Folktale A story that was originally passed from generation to generation by word of mouth. Folktale characters are usually all good or all bad and end up getting the reward or punishment they deserve.

Historical Fiction A made-up story based on actual historical times, places, and facts.

Myth A traditional story that tries to explain some mystery of nature or a religious or cultural belief. The gods and goddesses in myths have supernatural powers, but the humans usually do not.

Novel A fictional work that is longer than a short story. The plot, characters, and settings are much more developed in a novel than they are in a short story.

Play (See *drama.*)

Poetry A type of literature that uses concise, colorful, and often rhythmic language to express ideas or emotions. Examples: rhyming poetry, free verse, haiku, ballad, narrative poetry.

Prose Literature that is written in an everyday form of spoken or written sentences.

Realism Writing that shows life as it really is.

Science Fiction Fiction that often takes place in the future and is based on real or imaginary scientific developments.

Short Story A fictional story that usually can be read in one sitting. Most short stories have only a few main characters and focus on one problem, or conflict.

Tall Tale A humorous, exaggerated story often based on the life of a real person. The story is exaggerated more and more until the main character can seemingly do impossible things.

Tragedy Literature in which the hero is destroyed by some tragic flaw within his or her character.

Elements of Literature

The following glossary includes many terms used to describe the elements or parts of literature. You will find this information helpful when you write or talk about short stories, novels, and other types of literature.

Action The events that happen in a story.

Antagonist The person or force that fights against the hero or protagonist in a story. (See *protagonist.*)

Character A person or an animal that performs the action in a story.

Characterization The ways in which a writer makes a character seem real. This can be done by . . .

- sharing a character's conversations, thoughts, or actions,
- describing the character's appearance, and
- showing what others think of the character.

Conflict A problem or struggle between two opposing forces in a story. There are five basic types of conflicts:

Person Against Person One character has a problem with another character or characters.

Person Against Self A character struggles with him- or herself.

Person Against Society A character has a problem with society, the school, the law, or a tradition.

Person Against Nature A character struggles against an element of nature: a blizzard, a hurricane, extreme heat, etc.

Person Against Fate (God) A character struggles with a problem that seems beyond his or her control.

Dialogue The words that characters speak to each other. Dialogue is set off with quotation marks. (See page 357.)

Foil A character who serves as a contrast or challenge to the main character.

Main Character The most important character in a story, novel, or play. A piece of literature may have more than one main character. (See *protagonist*.)

Minor Character The less important character (or characters) in a story, novel, or play.

Mood The feeling a reader gets from a story.

Moral The lesson that a story teaches. In fables, the moral is directly stated at the end.

Narrator The person or character who is telling a story.

Plot The story's action, which is a series of events called a *plot line*. A typical plot line contains five parts:

Exposition The beginning of a story, when the setting, characters, and conflict are introduced.

Rising Action The main part of a story, when the main character tries to solve his or her problem.

Climax The most exciting or important part in a story. The climax is often called the turning point.

Falling Action The part of a story that leads to the ending, or resolution.

Resolution The end part of a story, when the problem is solved.

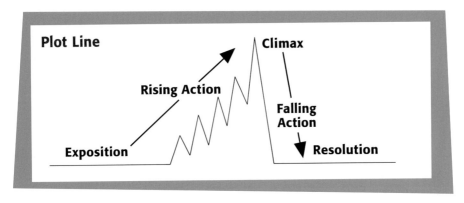

Point of View The angle from which a story is told, which depends upon who is telling it. The different types of point of view are listed here:

First Person In first-person point of view, one of the characters tells the story.

Third Person In third-person point of view, someone on the outside of the story is telling it. There are actually three third-person points of view:

- **Third-Person Omniscient (All-Knowing)** The narrator is able to tell about the thoughts and feelings of all the characters in the story.

- **Third-Person Limited Omniscient** The narrator is able to tell about the thoughts and feelings of one character only.

- **Camera (Objective) View** The narrator tells the story, but shares no thoughts or feelings of the characters.

Protagonist The main character in a story, novel, or play. The protagonist is often a good or heroic character.

Setting The time and place of a story.

Surprise Ending An unexpected event that comes at the end of a story.

Theme A message about life or human nature that the writer shares with the reader. The reader must usually figure out the theme, since it is not stated directly.

Tone The writer's attitude toward his or her subject. A writer's tone can be serious, funny, and so on.

Total Effect The overall influence that a story has on a reader.

Learning
to
Learn

Viewing Skills

Classroom Skills

Group Skills

Speaking and Listening Skills

Test Taking

Planning Skills

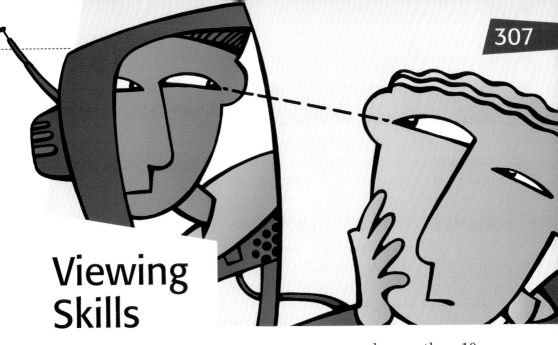

Viewing Skills

If you are an average teenager, you spend more than 10 hours a week watching television. Television affects what you know, what you think, and even what you buy. That means you need to be a smart viewer.

Compare your own TV-viewing habits to the table on this page. It shows the average amount of time teens spend watching TV each week.

Average TV Viewing for Teens (Ages 12-17)			
M-F 10 a.m to 4:30 p.m.	**M-F** 4:30 to 7:30 p.m.	**M-Sun** 7:30 to 11 p.m.	**Sat** 7 a.m. to 1 p.m.
1 hr., 43 min.	**2 hrs., 45 min.**	**5 hrs., 15 min.**	**41 min.**

What's Ahead

This chapter will help you learn about watching two types of television programs: news reports and TV specials. You will also learn about four selling methods used in commercials.

- **Watching the News**
- **Watching TV Specials**
- **Watching Commercials**

Watching the News

You watch the news to find out what is happening in your city and elsewhere. It's important to watch each news story closely to make sure the reporting is complete and fair.

Watch for Completeness

A good news story gives you the most important information. It answers the **5 W's:** *who? what? when? where?* and *why?*

The following brief news story was read by Peter Jennings on *ABC World News Tonight* on February 26, 1997. As you can see, it answers the 5 W's, giving all the basic information.

In New York this evening
where   when

at the Grammy Awards, the winner
where

is . . . Hillary Rodham Clinton.
who

The First Lady took top honors
what

in the nonmusical category

for a recorded version of her book,
why

It Takes a Village, the best-seller

about a community's roles in

child rearing. Mrs. Clinton, who

seemed pleased with herself, said

she was amazed.

Watch for Correctness

News reporters must be careful to be correct. When they are not sure what happened, they should say things like this:

- **"We are getting reports that an earthquake has struck Japan."**
- **"According to one source, several people were hurt in the accident."**

The red words tell you that the report may not be correct or complete. You must keep watching the news if you want to find out what really happened!

Watch for Point of View

Most news reports are objective. (*Objective* means "telling just the facts, not the reporter's feelings or opinions.") However, every news story is told from a certain point of view. (The *point of view* is a reporter's outlook or understanding of a story.) Here are two ways in which a reporter's point of view comes through.

 The reporter chooses which facts to include and which pictures to show.

Consider this news event: A candidate for president goes fishing. One reporter shows the candidate just sitting in the boat. Another reporter shows the candidate pulling in a big fish. The two reports show the same event, but from different points of view.

 The reporter chooses which people to interview.

If a story has two sides, the reporter almost always tells both sides. But remember that the reporter must choose someone to speak for each side. For example, a reporter may choose a sports hero to speak in favor of a new law, and a gang member to speak against it. What does this tell you about the reporter's point of view?

Watching TV Specials

Your teacher may ask you to watch a TV special or video. (A *TV special* is a program about an important subject. It may include film clips, interviews with experts, and so on.) The guidelines on these two pages will help you watch TV specials more thoughtfully and effectively.

Before you watch . . .

- **Make sure you know the subject of the program.**
  Think about what you already know about this subject.

- **Make a list of questions you have about the subject.**
  Leave plenty of room between questions, so you can take notes as you watch.

- **If your teacher gives you questions to answer, make sure you understand them.**

While you watch . . .

- **Look for completeness, correctness, and point of view.**
  (See pages 308-309.) Does the program seem fair in the way it presents the subject? Does the program tell *who? what? when? where?* and *why?* about the subject?

- **Look for the answers to your questions.**
  Write down words and phrases that will help you answer your questions later.

- **Think of more questions you have about the subject.**
  Write them down.

After you watch . . .

- **Write complete answers to your questions as soon as you can.**

- **To learn more, talk with someone else who also watched the program.** Ask questions like, "What did you think was the most interesting part?" "Did you understand the part about . . . ?"

- **Write about the program in your journal.** Something in the program may have made you happy, upset, or confused. Writing about it will help you remember important information.

- **Draw pictures about the program.** Drawing can also help you remember things.

Sample Journal Entry

March 5, 2002

Spirits of the Rain Forest

The Manu Reserve is in Peru. It is the biggest rain forest reserve in the world. People and animals live together in Manu. There are five tribes of people that live there. These people know everything about the plants and animals in the rain forest. They use many plants for medicines. They also use one plant to make poison arrows to get fish.

Giant river otters also live in Manu. The otters eat fish, including piranhas. Piranhas are dangerous fish that sometimes even eat humans. But otters have found the secret to eating piranhas. Otters eat the piranha's head first!

Watching Commercials

News programs and TV specials inform you. Commercials have a completely different purpose. They try to get you to buy something. Commercials do not tell both sides of the story. They only tell you that a certain product is great. Here are four selling methods you'll see in commercials:

Selling Methods

Slice of Life Some commercials look like home videos. The people in them seem to be real people who are having a great time because they drink Brand X cola, or wear Brand X shoes. But they are actors who are being paid to look like they are having a great time. Their acting probably has nothing to do with the quality of the product.

Famous Faces Some commercials show a famous person using a Brand X product. If you want to be like Michael Jordan or Oprah Winfrey, all you have to do is buy Brand X, too! But remember that the famous person may not really like this product. He or she is getting paid to talk about it.

Just the Facts Some commercials use facts and figures to sell the product. One commercial might say, "Nine out of ten teenagers say Brand X is the best frozen pizza." But the commercial may not tell you anything about the survey that produced these results. Since you're not sure the survey is trustworthy, it's difficult to believe the commercial.

Problem-Solution Other commercials show someone with a problem. Then they show Brand X solving the problem. For example, a commercial might show a lonely boy. Then the boy buys a Brand X video game. Now everybody wants to be his friend, so his problem is solved. But in the real world, people aren't really friends if they only like you because you own something.

Selling Brand X

Classroom Skills

When you are in school, your main job is to learn. You learn by listening to your teachers, reading your textbooks, talking about ideas, and doing your homework. This is why having good classroom skills will help you.

Taking good notes and writing in a learning log are two important classroom skills. Taking notes helps you in three ways:

1. Taking notes helps you **pay attention.**

2. Taking notes helps you **understand.**

3. Taking notes helps you **remember.**

Writing in a learning log helps you in this way: it gives you a chance to think carefully about the subjects you are studying.

What's Ahead

In this chapter you will learn how to practice note taking and writing in a learning log. *Remember:* Using good classroom skills will help you do your best work now . . . and for years to come.

- Setting Up Your Notes
- Taking Lecture Notes
- Taking Reading Notes
- Reviewing Your Notes
- Keeping a Learning Log

Setting Up Your Notes

Use a notebook or a three-ring binder for your notes, and write on only one side of each page. (A three-ring binder allows you to add and remove pages when you need to.)

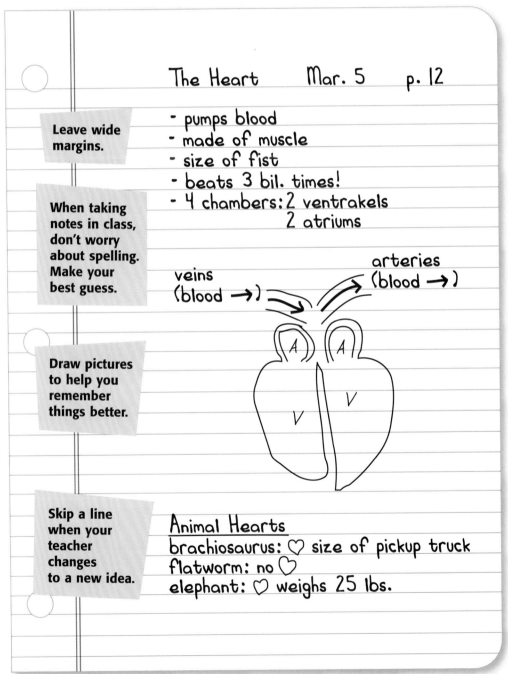

Leave wide margins.

When taking notes in class, don't worry about spelling. Make your best guess.

Draw pictures to help you remember things better.

Skip a line when your teacher changes to a new idea.

The Heart   Mar. 5   p. 12

- pumps blood
- made of muscle
- size of fist
- beats 3 bil. times!
- 4 chambers: 2 ventrakels
                    2 atriums

veins
(blood →)

arteries
(blood →)

Animal Hearts
brachiosaurus: ♡ size of pickup truck
flatworm: no ♡
elephant: ♡ weighs 25 lbs.

Taking Lecture Notes

The following tips will help you take lecture notes. (A *lecture* is a talk that teaches you something.) Your teacher may present a lecture when he or she introduces a new unit or reviews important information for a test. Your ability to remember and understand a lecture increases greatly if you take good notes.

- **Write the topic and the date at the top of each page.** You may also want to number each page of notes. Then, if a page gets out of order, you'll know exactly where it belongs.

- **Listen carefully when the teacher introduces the topic.** You may hear important clues. Your teacher may say, "I'm going to explain the three branches of the federal government." Then you can listen for the three subtopics.

- **Write your notes in your own words.** Don't try to write down everything the teacher says.

- **When you hear a word that is new to you, write it down.** Don't worry about spelling. Just make your best guess.

- **Listen for key words such as *first, second, last, most important,* and so on.**

- **Copy what the teacher writes on the board or overhead projector.**

The real secret to taking good notes is listening. Don't get so busy writing that you forget to listen. If you listen carefully, you will hear details that you can add to your notes later.

Taking Reading Notes

Taking notes while you are reading is much easier than taking lecture notes. As you read, you can stop anytime to write a note. Here are some tips for taking reading notes:

1 **Preview the assignment.** Read the title, introduction, section headings or subtitles, and summary. Look at any pictures, charts, and maps. This will tell you what the reading is about.

2 **Read the whole assignment once** before you take any notes. Don't stop every time you come to a new word or idea.

3 **Take notes** as you read over the material again; read more slowly this time.

- **Write down only the important information and ideas.**

- **Try to write your notes in your own words.** Don't just copy from the book.

- **You may write down each heading or subtopic,** and then write the most important facts under each heading.

- **Remember to take notes about any important pictures, charts, or maps.** You may also make drawings.

- **Use graphic organizers.**

- **Make a list of new words.** Also write down the page number where you found each word. Look up each word in a glossary or dictionary. Choose the meaning that fits the way the word is used. Write that meaning in your notes.

- **Write down any questions you have for your teacher.**

Turn to "Study-Reading Skills," beginning on page 261, for more ways to take notes when you read.

Reviewing Your Notes

Read over your notes each day. Circle the words and phrases that you don't understand. Look up these words in a dictionary or the glossary of your textbook. Then write each word (spelled correctly) and its meaning in the margin of your notes.

- **Write any questions you may have in the margins of your notes.** Talk over your questions with a classmate or your teacher. Make sure to write down what you learn.
- **Use a highlighter to mark important parts of your notes.**
- **Rewrite your notes if they are sloppy, or if you want to reorganize them.**
- **Review your notes again before the next class.**

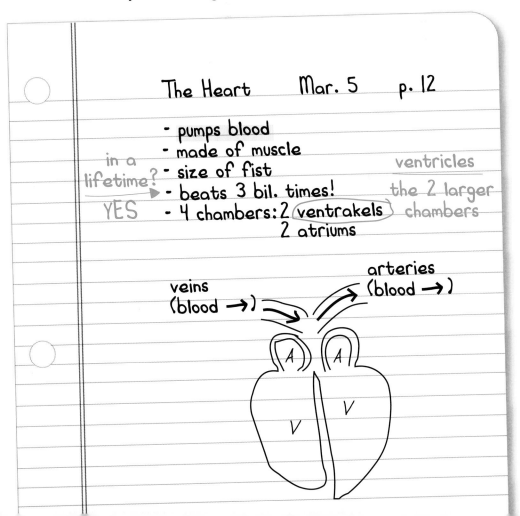

Keeping a Learning Log

A learning log is a place to write down your thoughts, feelings, and questions about what you are studying. Learning-log notes are different from lecture and reading notes. Here are some tips:

- **Keep a learning log for any subject,** but especially for one that is hard for you. This will help you learn the subject better.

- **For your learning log,** you may use a separate part of the same notebook you use to take class notes.

- **Use graphic organizers and drawings,** if you want to.

- **Write freely.** Don't worry about getting every word correct.

- **Write about any of the following ideas:**
  - the most important thing you learned from a reading assignment or lecture
  - your thoughts about a group project
  - what you learned from an experiment
  - a list of key words that come to mind after a lesson
  - your feelings about something you learned
  - your feelings about how you are doing in the subject

Mar. 7

Key words: heart (oczygen)   oxygen = an
pump   odorless gas in
blood   the air
life

Without blood pumping through our bodies, we would die. All of our organs need whatever is in blood to live. Oczygen, for one thing. Mr. Chavez always calls good citizens the lifeblood of a country. Now I know what he means.

Group Skills

You may associate the word "teamwork" with being part of an athletic team. The idea of working together, however, is an important part of life in general. You have probably worked on class projects as a team. Today, more than ever, people are expected to work in groups, bringing a variety of skills to any job.

To work well in a group, you need good communication skills. If you develop your listening, observing, cooperating, responding, and clarifying skills, you will be a valuable addition to any team or group. These skills will help you succeed at school, at home, and later on the job.

What's Ahead

This chapter will help you improve your group skills. You will find many ways to apply this information wherever and whenever you work with people.

- Skills for Listening
- Skills for Observing, Cooperating, Clarifying
- Skills for Responding

Skills for Listening

Even if you are not a good listener, you can learn to become one. You may hear perfectly well, but listening means you are paying attention to what you hear. You need to remember what you hear and then use it as you work in a group.

Show you are listening.

Show the person who is speaking that you are listening. Make eye contact, nod your head, and stay attentive. Another way to show that you are listening is to ask good questions and make helpful comments.

Think about what you are hearing.

Hearing means you are taking in sounds with your ears. Listening means you are using your mind to think about what the sounds mean. Take notes to help you remember details or questions. Remember to let the speaker finish a thought before you offer your own ideas.

Know when—and how—to interrupt.

Usually it is not polite to interrupt a speaker. If you feel that you must interrupt the discussion, say, "Excuse me. When you finish, I have something to add." Good listeners often have important things to say. You may need to jot down a note to help you remember your thought until you have a chance to share it.

Sometimes a speaker gets off the subject. You may need to interrupt politely, by saying, "Excuse me. I think we need to get back to what we are discussing."

Learn how to respond to being interrupted.

If you are interrupted by a group member, you can say, "I was not finished making my point" or "Could you please wait until I am finished?" Remember to be polite. (You can avoid being interrupted by keeping what you say short and to the point.)

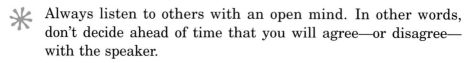 Always listen to others with an open mind. In other words, don't decide ahead of time that you will agree—or disagree—with the speaker.

Skills for Observing

Being a careful observer is an important group skill. You can learn a lot about what someone is really saying by being alert to his or her body language and tone of voice.

Reading Body Language ■ People communicate their true feelings with their voices, facial expressions, hand gestures, and their body positions. For example, leaning forward shows interest, while crossed arms may show boredom or disagreement.

Using Encouragement ■ Groups work better if the members trust one another. You can help group members feel accepted and valued by saying kind words.

Skills for Cooperating

Offering Compliments ■ One way to encourage group members is to compliment them. Simply say, "I really like your suggestion" or "That's a great idea." When group members treat one another well, they help build a strong, productive group.

Avoiding Put-Downs ■ If members of a group put one another down, they disrupt the group and eventually destroy the members' willingness to work together.

Skills for Clarifying

Clarifying means "making something clear." When you clarify an idea, you make it easy for others to understand.

Offering to Explain ■ If you are not sure that others understand you, ask, "Are there any questions?" If you know that your ideas are complicated, check often to see if anyone has questions.

Summarizing Ideas ■ You can help the whole group by summarizing what you have heard and then asking, "Is that what you were saying?" Every group needs someone to fill this important role.

Skills for Responding

When you work in a group, nearly everything you say and do is a response to what someone else has said or done. First, you hear what others have to say, or you observe their behavior and tone of voice. Then after thinking about the ways you could respond, you speak.

Thinking Before Responding

Someone may make a statement like *"The Revenge of the Squash was a dumb movie."* Without group skills, you might say, "Well, I think you're dumb." But if you respond in this way, you will probably have an argument instead of a discussion.

You can avoid an argument by saying, "You have a right to your own opinion." You can ask for more information: "Why do you feel the movie was dumb?" Or you can ask for clarification: "What do you mean by 'dumb'?"

Learning to Disagree

Never say, "I disagree *with you.*" Say instead, "I disagree. I think *The Revenge of the Squash* was a great movie." This is disagreeing with *an idea*, not with *the speaker*. You can offer other reasons for disagreeing, or you can ask the speaker more questions. In the process, the speaker may change his or her mind—or you may change yours.

Communicating with Respect

Whenever you work with a group, use respect and common courtesy.

1 **Respect yourself by**
- believing that your own thoughts and feelings have value,
- sharing your ideas clearly and politely, and
- taking responsibility for what you say.

2 **Respect others by**
- encouraging everyone to participate,
- listening openly to what others have to say, and
- using compliments whenever you can.

Speaking and Listening Skills

You could say that there are two kinds of people in the world: people who love to give speeches, and people who don't! For some people, speaking in front of a large group is exciting. They like being "on stage" and often become actors, politicians, or lawyers. For other people, though, this kind of speaking is scary.

Of course, the purpose behind *all* speaking is the same. You speak to share information or to share your feelings. Giving a speech simply takes more planning than other types of talking.

What's Ahead

Whether or not you enjoy giving speeches, this chapter will help you plan and present effective speeches. You'll also find tips to help you become a good listener, which is just as important as learning to speak well. For a multimedia version of Gloria's speech, visit **<thewritesource.com/mm.htm>**.

- ● **Planning Your Speech**
- ● **Writing Your Speech**
- ● **Practicing Your Speech**
- ● **Giving Your Speech**
- ● **Becoming a Good Listener**

Planning Your Speech

Giving a good speech takes a lot of planning. Here's a step-by-step plan for you to follow:

1 **Decide which kind of speech you will give.**

- An *informational speech* gives facts and details about a subject.
- A *persuasive speech* tries to convince listeners to agree with you about something.
- A *demonstration speech* shows how to do something.

2 **Pick your topic.**

- Choose a topic you know well.
- Choose a topic that interests you.
- Choose a topic that will interest your listeners.

Possible topics:

- Something you like to do
- A place you have been
- A special person you know
- An experience you have had
- A strong feeling or belief you want to share

Gloria León decided to give an informational speech about a special experience: her sister's *Quinceañera*. She knew all about it, and she thought her classmates would be interested in this part of her culture.

3 Gather ideas and details.

You can find information in many different places. Here are some possible sources of information:

- Gather ideas from your own memories.
- Look at photos, journals, scrapbooks, etc.
- Talk to people who know about your topic (family members, friends, neighbors, and so on).
- Read books, magazines, and newspapers.
- Watch videos, TV programs, movies, and use the Internet.

Collect as much information as you can, and make sure to take notes. (See pages 313-318 for help.) Later, you can decide which facts and details to include in your speech. Also collect photographs or other interesting items to show during your speech.

> **Gloria wrote down information from family members and from her own memories. She also picked out some photos of the event she planned to speak about.**

4 Think of an interesting beginning.

Here are some good ways to begin a speech:

- Ask a question.
- Tell a surprising fact.
- Make a bold or powerful statement.
- Share an interesting or a surprising story.
- Repeat a famous quotation.

Gloria decided to do two things to begin her speech. She shared a little story and asked a question:

> **April second was a very special day for my sister Teresita. She wore a beautiful white dress to a special church ceremony. Then she was the guest of honor at a big party with dancing, food, and gifts.**
> **Do you think my sister got married? She didn't.**

5 Put your ideas in order.

After you write your beginning, you should decide what you will say in the rest of your speech. Write your ideas and details on index cards. This makes it easy to move parts of your speech around until you get everything in the best order. The following tips will help you write your note cards: (Also see the samples on the next page.)

- Write the beginning of your speech, word for word, on index cards.
- Put each new piece of information on a separate index card. (You do not have to state this information word for word. Just include the important words or details.)
- Lay the cards out. This will help you decide what information to include in your final speech.
- Take away the cards that contain information you won't be using.
- Move the remaining cards around until all the information is in the best order.
- If you need more information, do more research and write more index cards.
- Write your ending, word for word, on an index card. (See the example below.)

6 Think of a good ending.

Don't just say "That's it" or "There's nothing more to say." Tell why this topic is important to you, or to other people. You may also repeat the main ideas of your speech.

In her ending, Gloria gave an important fact about her topic, and then told why the topic is important to her:

> **In some families, boys have a Quinceanero when they turn 15. But in the U.S., it is more common for girls to celebrate this event. Next year, I'll be 14, and my family and I will begin planning my Quinceanera.**

Sample Note Cards

Here are some of the note cards Gloria used to plan her speech. She wrote the beginning and ending note cards word for word. The other cards contain main ideas only.

①
BEGINNING:
April second was a very special day for my sister Teresita. She wore a beautiful white dress to a special church ceremony. Then she was the guest of honor at a big party with dancing, food, and gifts.

③
"Corte de Honor" (honor court)
14 couples (one for each year of life)

④
Teresita and her boyfriend stand for the 15th year.

⑥
At party, father replaced her shoes with white high heels.

⑦
ENDING:
In some families, boys have a Quinceanero when they turn 15. But in the U.S., it is more common for girls to celebrate this event. Next year, I'll be 14, and my family and I will begin planning my Quinceanera.

Writing Your Speech

You may decide to give your speech using only your note cards. Or you may decide to write out your complete speech.

A Very Special Day

BEGINNING

April second was a very special day for my sister Teresita. She wore a beautiful white dress to a special church ceremony. Then she was the guest of honor at a big party with dancing, food, and gifts.

Do you think my sister got married? She didn't. She is only 15. The big event was Teresita's Quinceanera. In Spanish, quince means "fifteen." A Quinceanera is something like a Jewish Bat Mitzvah. It means that a girl has become an adult.

MIDDLE

On my sister's 14th birthday, my mother said it was time to start planning Teresita's Quinceanera. All year long my mother and sister worked for that one big day. First Teresita had to choose 14 couples to be her Corte de Honor. Each couple in the honor court stood for one year in her life. Then she chose her escort. That was easy because she has a boyfriend. She and her boyfriend stood for her 15th year. Of course, Teresita had to find just the right dress. Our aunts planned the food and decorations, and our cousin Alex was the DJ.

Finally the big day came. After the special Mass, the party started. Teresita was surrounded by her Corte de Honor. Then our father replaced her shoes with a pair of new white high heels. This was a symbol that Teresita had become an adult. My father danced the first dance with Teresita. Then everybody danced.

ENDING

In some families, boys have a Quinceanero when they turn 15. But in the U.S., it is more common for girls to celebrate this event. Next year, I'll be 14, and my family and I will begin planning my Quinceanera.

Practicing Your Speech

Start practicing at least two days before you give your speech. Then you will be able to practice several times.

- First, practice alone. If possible, record yourself, so you can listen and find out what you need to improve.

- Next, practice giving your speech for a family member. Ask for his or her suggestions. Also make sure that a native speaker listens to your speech. Ask if everything is understandable.

Make sure to practice pronouncing the hard words. If you have a real problem pronouncing certain words, try to replace them with words that are easier to say.

Giving Your Speech

Here are some tips to follow when it's time to give your speech:

- Stand straight and tall.

- Speak loudly and clearly.

- Look up as often as you can. You don't have to make direct eye contact if that makes you nervous. Just scan your audience when you look up. (*Scan* means "to look over quickly.")

- Take your time, and let your voice add color and interest to your topic.

- Use your hands in a planned way. At the very least, hold your note cards or written speech. But don't tap your fingers on the speaker's stand or make any nervous movements with your hands.

- Keep your feet firmly on the floor. Don't sway from side to side.

- Show interest in your topic all the way through your speech. Wait a few seconds after you are done before you sit down.

Becoming a Good Listener

Listening is a very important skill. Listening carefully can help you become a successful student, worker, friend, family member, and more. Listening is much more than just hearing. To hear, you need only your ears. But to listen, you need your ears and your mind. Listening means thinking about what you hear. Here are some tips to help you become a good listener:

Pay attention. If you *want* to listen, you will.

Look at the speaker. The speaker's expressions and hand gestures often add meaning to whatever he or she is saying. *Remember:* Where your eyes go, your mind will follow.

Take notes. This is especially important if you need to recall the information you are listening to. See pages 313-318 for tips on how to take good notes.

Be aware of the speaker's tone of voice. The tone tells you how the speaker feels about the subject.

Note key words. Words and phrases such as "first," "second," "next," and "most important" help you to follow the main ideas and details.

Write down new words. If a speaker uses a word that you don't know, try to write it down. Later you can find out what it means.

Ask questions. When the speaker is finished, ask questions about things you don't understand. (You may also ask a classmate to explain things for you.)

Summarize the talk. Write a few sentences that show what you learned from the talk. This writing will help you remember information.

Test Taking

You go to school to learn information, and your teachers need to be sure that you have learned it. They need to see what you know, and what you don't know, so that they can do a better job of instructing you.

Writing reports, doing projects, and conferencing are ways to show what you know about a subject. (*Conferencing* means "talking with others about a subject.") Taking tests is another important way of showing your knowledge about a subject.

What's Ahead

To do well on a test, you need to do two things. First, you need to pay attention in class and do your daily work. This is the way you learn the material you are being tested on. Second, you need to know how to be a good test taker. This chapter gives you tips for reviewing and remembering material, and tips about the different kinds of tests.

- **Preparing for a Test**
- **Taking the Test**
- **Taking Objective Tests**
- **Taking Essay Tests**

Preparing for a Test

1 Ask questions.

- What material will be on the test? For example, will you be tested on the chapter you just read, or on all the chapters you've read this year?

- What should you study? Will the test cover only information in the book, or also the information in your class notes and other materials?

- What kinds of questions will be on the test: true/false? multiple choice? essay?

2 Review the material.

- Start reviewing a few days before the test.

- Review all the material once. Then make a list of the information that is difficult for you, or material you need to memorize for the test. Study these items especially well.

- Study for the test two or three times, not just once.

3 Study the difficult material carefully.

- Say the material out loud. First you may read aloud from your book or notes. Then put the material in your own words.

- Rewrite the information. Make lists, flash cards, or graphic organizers. Write the information from memory; then check to see if you remembered it correctly.

- Picture the material in your mind. Close your eyes and think of a list, chart, map, or time line containing the material you need to know. Then look at your book or notes to see if your picture was correct.

- Explain the material to someone else.

- Make up test questions and answer them.

Taking the Test

1 Before the test, listen carefully to what your teacher says. That way you'll be sure to hear important comments like these:

"You have 20 minutes to finish the test."

"The last question is for extra credit."

2 Put your name on the test.

3 Look over the whole test quickly. Notice what kinds of questions the test contains and how many there are.

4 Begin the test. Read the directions carefully and do exactly what they tell you to do. If you are told to answer with a ✔, don't make an ✘.

5 Read each question carefully and completely before you answer.

 Answer the questions you are sure of first. If you come to a question you don't know, go on to the next one. You can come back if you have time.

6 If you come to more directions, read them carefully. The next part probably contains a different type of question, and you will need to know this to answer correctly.

7 When you finish, use any time that is left to check your test. Make sure you answered all the questions. If you skipped some hard questions, try to answer them now.

Taking Objective Tests

There are four common kinds of objective tests. (*Objective* means "based on facts.") They are called objective tests because there is only one correct answer for each question. Here are some tips to help you do well on each kind of objective test.

True/False Test

A true/false test is a list of sentences or statements. You decide if each statement is true or false.

 ● Read the whole statement carefully. If any part of the statement is false, the answer is false.

> *false*   **Tom Sawyer, Becky Thatcher, and David Copperfield are characters in the novel *The Adventures of Tom Sawyer.***

● Be careful when you see words such as *always, all, never,* and *no.* Very few things are *always* true or *never* true.

● Watch for words that mean "not." These words include *no, not, nothing, don't, doesn't, didn't, isn't, wasn't,* and *weren't.* Make sure you understand what the statement means.

> *true*   **Tom is not happy when his aunt makes him paint the fence.**

Matching Test

A matching test has two lists. You match a word in one list to a word or phrase that goes with it in another list.

[tips] ● Read both lists before you begin answering.

● Read the directions carefully. Will you use each answer once . . . more than once . . . or not at all? If each answer is used only once, mark it off after using it. This makes it easy to see which answers you have left.

1. _____ Sid   A. was lost in the cave with Tom
2. _____ Huck   B. never took part in Tom's schemes
3. _____ Becky   C. was Tom's best friend

Multiple-Choice Test

A multiple-choice test gives several answers for each question. You decide which answer is correct, and mark it.

 • Read the directions. On most multiple-choice tests, you mark only one answer for each question (or statement). But the directions may tell you to mark all answers that are correct.

• You may be asked to mark the best answer, or the most correct answer. This means that there may be more than one correct answer, but there is only one best answer.

Which of the following people are Tom's friends?
   A. Huck Finn   **C. Willie Mufferson**
   B. Becky Thatcher   **D. Both A and B**

• Read the question carefully. One word can change the meaning of the whole question.

Tom's adventures take him to every imaginable scary place except
   A. a graveyard   **C. a pirate ship**
   B. a cave   **D. a haunted house**

• Read all the answers before you mark the one you think is correct.

Fill-in-the-Blanks Test

A fill-in-the-blanks test is made up of sentences or paragraphs with some words left out. You fill in the missing words.

 • Each blank probably stands for one word. If there are three blanks in a row, you need to write in three words.

Tom finds twelve thousand dollars' worth of
_____ _____ _____ in the cave.

• If the word just before the blank is "an," the word that fills in the blank probably begins with *a, e, i, o,* or *u.*

Tom has an _____ named Polly and a _____ named Sid.

Taking Essay Tests

Most students say that essay tests are the hardest kind. When you take an essay test, you do several things. You read the question, (or writing prompt), you think about what you know, you plan your answer, and—finally!—you write your answer. It's a big job. But you can write a good essay answer if you take it one step at a time.

 Understand the question.

- Read the question carefully. Read it at least two times.
- Find the key word or key words that tell you exactly what to do. Here are some key words you will often find in essay questions.

Compare means "tell how these things are alike."

Contrast means "tell how these things are different." *Note:* Some essay questions ask you to compare *and* contrast.

Describe means "tell how this looks, sounds, and feels." You may even describe how something smells and tastes!

Evaluate means "give your opinion about this." Write about good points and bad points. It is very important to tell why you have this opinion, and to give facts and details that support your opinion.

Explain means "tell what this means" or "tell how this works."

Identify means "answer *who? what? when? where?* and *why?* about a subject."

List means "include a specific number of examples, reasons, or causes."

Outline means "organize your answer into main points and specific examples." In some cases, you will use an actual outline. (See page 96.)

Prove means "present facts and details that show something is true."

Review means "give an overall picture of the main points about a subject."

Summarize means "tell the important information about this."

2 Plan your answer.

- On a piece of scrap paper, write the key word from the question. You may also write what the key word means.

- Then write down facts you know that fit the key word. You may use a graphic organizer, or just make a list. *Remember:* It's not necessary to write down everything you know about the subject. Instead, focus specifically on what the question is asking and write down the information that answers the question.

Social Studies Test. Chapter 23

1. Summarize how the Central Pacific Railroad was built.

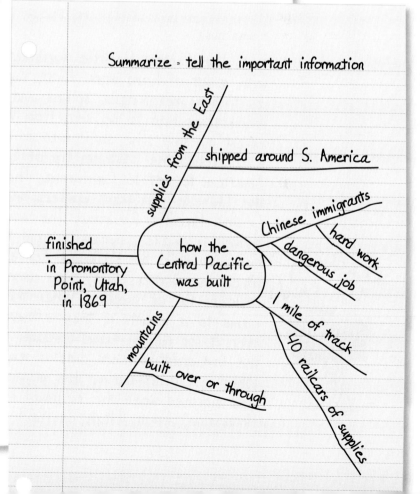

3 **Write your answer.**

- Use your notes as you write a topic sentence for your answer. Your topic sentence should repeat some words from the question.
- Decide what order to put things in. Number your notes. Put a 1 next to the fact that will come first and so on.
- Now write about each fact in your answer. You may have more than one paragraph.
- Finally, write a closing sentence.
- When you have finished, read your essay answer over. Does it include all the important information?

Social Studies Test. Chapter 23

1. Summarize how the Central Pacific Railroad was built.

The Central Pacific Railroad was built with a lot of hard work. First, supplies such as timber, metal rails, spikes and even locomotives had to be sent from the East Coast by ship. The ships had to sail all the way around the southern tip of South America to get to California. That's where the Chinese immigrant workers began the Central Pacific Railroad. The workers used shovels, pickaxes, dynamite, and their bare hands to build the railroad. For each mile of track the workers laid, they used 40 railcars full of supplies. When the workers came to a mountain, they either laid track over it, or dug a tunnel through it. Many of the immigrant workers died in explosions or other accidents during this project. The work was finished when the railroad reached Promontory Point, Utah, in 1869.

Reaching the end

PROMONTORY Point, Utah

Planning Skills

Ellen Ochoa is a good example of how planning can change a person's life. She had a big goal and didn't stop working until she achieved it. Here's her story:

Ellen always wanted to be an astronaut. In the beginning, she was not sure she could reach that goal. But she decided to try anyway. She started by setting smaller goals that would take her to her big goal. First she graduated from high school. Then she got a college degree in engineering. Next she learned to fly airplanes and became a licensed pilot. She also went back to college for a graduate degree. Finally, Ms. Ochoa was qualified. She applied for the job. In 1990, Ellen Ochoa became the first Hispanic woman astronaut in the United States.

What's Ahead

This chapter tells you how to set goals, and reach them. You will also learn about managing your time and completing assignments.

- **Setting Goals**
- **Managing Your Time**
- **Completing Assignments**

Setting Goals

Everybody has goals. You may want to save enough money to buy something important to you. You may want to play on a school sports team. Both of these are good short-term goals. But it's also important to have long-term goals. Long-term goals can take you where you want to go in life.

Set your goals.

What do you want your life to be like when you are an adult? Do you want to be a doctor, a teacher, an artist, or an athlete? These are big goals!

Learn how to reach your goals.

Ellen Ochoa learned that an astronaut needs a college degree and a pilot's license. Find out what you need to reach your goals. Improving your ability to read and write in the English language, for example, will surely help you reach other goals.

Set small goals that will take you closer to your big goals.

If, every day, you read a few pages in a book and write a few sentences in your journal, you will gradually improve your reading and writing skills. If you do today's homework, you will be ready to do tomorrow's homework. After you finish middle school, you will be ready for high school . . . and so on.

Keep trying.

Everybody fails sometimes. Albert Einstein, a genius when it came to math and physics, had difficulty learning English. Abraham Lincoln, one of the United States' most famous leaders, lost eight different elections before becoming president. So keep trying to reach your goals.

If you didn't do any extra reading, or forgot to write in your journal for a day or two, **start again today.** If you must change your goals along the way, that's okay, too. Just keep planning . . . and reaching.

Managing Your Time

Using your time wisely will help you reach your goals. But you have to get organized. Practice setting short-term goals, making out a schedule, and then working at each goal. This kind of planning will help you divide big jobs into smaller, manageable jobs.

Example I

Goal: Finish your library book by Friday morning. It is Monday morning.

Plan: Divide the number of pages you have to read (46) by the number of days (4). Make a schedule, and read each day.

READING SCHEDULE

Monday	Tuesday	Wednesday	Thursday
12 pages	12 pages	12 pages	10 pages

Example II

Goal: Finish your Saturday chores by 11:00 a.m. It is 9:00 a.m.

Plan: Decide how much time you need for each chore. Make a schedule. Get to work!

CHORE SCHEDULE

9:00 - 9:30	9:30 - 10:00	10:00 - 10:15	10:15 - 11:00
wash dishes and sweep kitchen floor	practice saxophone	rest	clean my room

Planning Sheets

The example charts below show you two ways to plan your work during the school week.

Daily Planner A daily planner lists the assignments you receive in each subject. If a certain assignment is due sometime other than tomorrow, make a note of it.

■ MONDAY, _____ *(date)* _____

English
Read pages 102–105.
Write a topic sentence.

Math
Do workbook pages 16–17.

Social Studies
Answer question sheet by Wed.

Science
Find five different leaves and bring to class.

■ TUESDAY, _____ *(date)* _____

English
Write a paragraph using my topic sentence.

Math
Look over chapter 3 for test tomorrow.

Social Studies
Finish question sheet by tomorrow.

Science
Paste leaves on paper. Write the plants' scientific names.

Weekly Planner A weekly planner is a general schedule of what you think you'll be doing all week. Usually, you write down only the most important things.

Day	Before School	School	After School	Evening
Mon.	Write note for Dad	Talk to Dave about sleepover	soccer practice	Homework (5:30–7) TV at 7
Tues.	Feed Mr. Sanchez' parrot	Big science test	Homework (3–5:30)	Shopping with Aunt Ella

Completing Assignments

The following ideas will help you reach the goal of getting your homework assignments done the right way . . . and on time.

Homework Hot Lines

Hot lines are for important messages; they are not for chatting. Get the phone numbers of one or two good students in each of your classes. Ask if you can call them when you miss school or have a question about your homework.

Overnight Folders

Use an overnight folder for all the things you have to take to and from school. When you have to take something that won't fit in the folder, put in a note to remind yourself to take it.

Special Study Spots

Put everything you need to do your homework in your special study spot: pens, pencils, paper, a ruler, and so on.

Getting It Done

1 Go over any directions your teacher has given you for each assignment.

2 As you work, you may have questions. Use your homework hot line, ask a parent for help, or keep a list of questions to ask your teacher at school.

3 Don't just quit when something is hard. If you keep thinking, you will probably figure it out.

4 If you need to take a break, make it a short one—maybe 5 or 10 minutes. (Play with your pet, look at a magazine, stretch, eat a healthful snack, etc. But avoid TV.)

5 Put completed assignment papers in your overnight folder.

Proofreader's
Guide

Marking Punctuation

Editing for Mechanics

Improving Your Spelling

Commonly Misused Words

Understanding Idioms

Understanding Sentences

The Parts of Speech

Marking Punctuation

Period

A **period** is used to end a sentence. It is also used after initials, after abbreviations, and as a decimal point.

To End a Sentence	Use a period to end a sentence that is a statement, a command, or a request. **Computers are getting smaller.** (statement) **Get your pocket computer.** (command) **Please remember extra batteries.** (request)
After an Initial	Use a period after an initial. (An *initial* is the first letter of a name.) **B. B. King** (blues musician) **Octavia E. Butler** (writer)
As a Decimal	Use a period as a decimal point and to separate dollars and cents. **Food prices have risen 48.2 percent.** **Ice-cream cones now cost $1.20.**
After Abbreviations	Place a period after each part of an abbreviation—unless the abbreviation is an acronym. (An *acronym* is a word that is formed from the first letters of words in a phrase.) Abbreviations **Mr. Mrs. Jr. Dr. U.S.A.** Acronyms **UNICEF NATO laser modem** ✳ When an abbreviation is the last word in a sentence, use one period at the end of the sentence. **Supercomputers will be able to predict rain, snow, earthquakes, etc.**

Question Mark

A **question mark** is used at the end of an interrogative sentence. (An *interrogative sentence* asks a question.)

Direct Question	A question mark is used at the end of a direct question (an interrogative sentence). **Will computers help make cars safer?**
Indirect Question	No question mark is used after an indirect question. (In an *indirect question,* you tell about the question you asked.) **I asked if cars will change a lot.**
Tag Question	A question mark is used when you add a short question to the end of a statement. (This type of statement is called a *tag question.*) **In the next century no one will carry around money, will they?** **People will miss the sound of coins, don't you think?**

Exclamation Point

An **exclamation point** is used to express strong feeling. It may be placed after a word, a phrase, or an exclamatory sentence.

Excellent!

Wow! That's great!

That new program is awesome!

Note: Never write more than one exclamation point in school writing assignments or in business letters.

I can't wait to surf the Internet!!!

(too many exclamation points)

I can't wait to surf the Internet!

(correct punctuation)

Comma

Commas keep words and ideas from running together. They make writing easier to read.

Items in a Series	Commas are used between words or phrases in a series. (A *series* contains at least three words or phrases in a row.)

In the future, robots will cook, clean, and iron.
(words in a series)

Robots will take out the trash, return phone calls, and open the front door.
(phrases in a series)

Important: A *phrase* is a group of related words like "will take out the trash." A phrase does not express a complete thought.

To Keep Numbers Clear	Commas are used in numbers of four digits or more to keep the numbers clear.

More than 700,000 immigrants come into the United States each year.

✳ When a number refers to a year, street address, or ZIP code, no comma is used. Also, write numbers in the millions and billions this way: 7.5 million, 16 billion.

Brazil, a country of 170 million people, is the largest country in South America.

In Dates and Addresses	Commas are used to set off the different parts in addresses and dates.

My family's address is 2463 Bell Street, Kansas City, Missouri 64111.

✳ Do not use a comma to separate the state from the ZIP code.

I will be 27 years old on January 2, 2015.

✳ Do not use a comma if only the month and year are written (January 2015).

Comma

To Set Off Dialogue

Use a comma to set off the words of the speaker from the rest of the sentence.

> **Writer H. G. Wells once said, "The house of 2000 will have self-cleaning windows."**

✴ If you are telling what someone has said but are not using the person's exact words, do not use commas or quotation marks.

> **Writer H. G. Wells once said that the house of 2000 would have self-cleaning windows.**

To Set Off Interruptions

Commas are used to set off a word or phrase that interrupts the main thought of a sentence. (*Interrupt* means "to break into" or "to stop.")

> **Computers can, for example, teach people how to play the trumpet or drive a car.**

WORDS: Here is a list of words and phrases you can use to interrupt main thoughts.

EXAMPLE INTERRUPTING WORDS

for example

however

moreover

to be sure

as a matter of fact

in fact

TESTS: Try one of these tests to see if a word or phrase interrupts a main thought:

1. Take the word or phrase out. The meaning of the sentence should not change.

2. Move the word or phrase to another place in the sentence. The meaning should not change.

To Set Off Interjections

A comma may be used to separate an interjection from the rest of the sentence. (An *interjection* is a word or phrase showing surprise.)

No kidding, you mean computers may be worn like a wristwatch someday?

Oh my, I see everything in 3-D!

❋ If an interjection shows very strong feeling, an exclamation point (!) may be used to separate it from the rest of a sentence.

WORDS: Here are some of the words that may be used as interjections.

EXAMPLE INTERJECTIONS	
Hello	Hey
Oh my	No kidding
Really	Wow

In Direct Address

Commas are used to separate a noun of direct address from the rest of the sentence. (A *noun of direct address* names the person being spoken to.)

Yuri, computers in the future will not need keyboards.

I know that, Maria. Computers will work with voice commands.

To Set Off Titles or Initials

Commas are used to set off titles or initials that follow a person's last name.

Gita Punwani, M.D., and Charles K. Robinson, Ph.D., are learning Spanish.
(titles following names)

But Kwon, B. J., and Rodriguez, T. C., are learning French. (initials following names)

❋ If an initial comes at the end of a statement, use only one period.

Comma

In Compound Sentences

A comma may be used before the connecting word in a compound sentence. (A *compound sentence* is made up of two or more independent clauses connected by words like *and, but, so, nor,* and *yet.*)

Computer technology will help you learn other languages, and it will translate information for you as well.

Important: An *independent clause* expresses a complete thought and can stand alone as a simple sentence.

Avoid Comma Splices! When two independent clauses are joined with only a comma and no connecting word, it is called a **comma splice**. A comma splice is a sentence error. (See page 68.)

To Separate Introductory Phrases and Clauses

A comma should be used to separate a longer phrase or a clause that comes *before* the main part of the sentence.

For the first time in recorded history, hunger could be ended everywhere on earth. (phrase)

If governments would work together, food could be distributed to everyone suffering from hunger. (clause)

❋ You usually do not need a comma when the phrase or the clause comes *after* the main part of the sentence.

Hunger could be ended everywhere on earth for the first time in recorded history.

❋ You usually do not need a comma after a brief opening phrase:

In time soybeans and sea vegetables will be used to feed the world.

(No comma is needed after *In time.*)

| **To Separate Adjectives** | Commas are used to separate two or more adjectives that modify a noun in an equal way. (*Equal* means "at the same level" or "of the same type.") |

There are plenty of nutritious, edible plants in the world.
(*Nutritious* and *edible* are separated by a comma because they equally modify *plants*.)

We may eat many unusual plants in the years to come.
(*Many* and *unusual* do not modify *plants* equally. No comma is needed between these two modifiers.)

TESTS: Use one of these tests to help you decide if adjectives modify equally:

1. Switch the order of the adjectives. If the sentence is still clear, the adjectives modify equally.

2. Put the word *and* between the adjectives. If the sentence sounds clear, the adjectives modify equally.

Remember: Do not use a comma to set off the last adjective from the noun.

Will these unusual plants help solve the terrible, tragic problem of world hunger?
(no comma needed)

| **To Set Off Explanatory Phrases** | Commas are used to set off an explanatory phrase from the rest of the sentence. (*Explanatory* means "helping to explain.") |

Sonja, back from a visit to Florida, told us about new sources of energy.

Our class, eager to hear her report, listened very carefully.

Sonja's information, almost all about solar power, was very interesting.

Comma

To Set Off Appositive Phrases

Commas are used to set off an appositive phrase from the rest of the sentence. (An *appositive phrase* renames the noun or pronoun before it.)

Mrs. Chinn, our science teacher, says that the sun is an important source of energy.
("Our science teacher" is an appositive phrase.)

Solar power and wind power, two very clean sources of energy, should be used more.
("Two very clean sources of energy" is an appositive phrase.)

EXAMPLE APPOSITIVE PHRASES

Sammy Sosa, *a star baseball player*, . . .
Henry, *our new calico cat*, . . .
Winter, *our longest season*, . . .
Blue jeans, *my favorite clothing*, . . .

To Separate Nonrestrictive Phrases and Clauses

Commas are used to set off nonrestrictive phrases and clauses from the rest of the sentence. (*Nonrestrictive* means "not necessary.")

Our usable water supply, which comes from surface water or groundwater, makes up only one percent of the total water available on earth.
(The clause "which comes from surface water or groundwater" is nonrestrictive, or not necessary to understand the basic sentence.)

 No commas are needed before or after a restrictive phrase or clause. (*Restrictive* means "limiting" or "necessary.")

Groundwater that is free from harmful chemicals is hard to find.
(The clause "that is free from harmful chemicals" is restrictive, or needed to complete the meaning of the sentence.)

Semicolon

A **semicolon** is sometimes used in the same way that a comma is used. However, a semicolon usually means a stronger pause, closer to a full stop.

To Join Two Independent Clauses

A semicolon can be used to join two independent clauses when there is no connecting word like *and* or *but*. (*Independent clauses* are simple sentences that can stand alone.)

Some cities may rest on the ocean floor; other cities may float like islands.

With Conjunctive Adverbs

A semicolon is used when two independent clauses are joined by a conjunctive adverb. The semicolon comes before the adverb, and a comma comes after it.

Living in a floating city sounds interesting; however, living in a city on the ocean floor sounds impossible.

EXAMPLE CONJUNCTIVE ADVERBS

also	meanwhile
as a result	moreover
besides	nevertheless
for example	similarly
however	then
in addition	therefore
instead	thus

To Separate Groups of Words That Contain Commas

A semicolon is used to set off groups of words in a series if part of the series already contains commas.

People in the future may live in spacious, comfortable domes; in orbiting space stations; or in underground tunnel cities.

Colon

A **colon** may be used to introduce a quotation or a list. Colons are also used in business letters and between the numbers expressing time.

To Introduce a Quotation

A colon may be used to introduce a quotation. (A *quotation* is someone else's exact words that you repeat in your writing.)

President Lincoln made this announcement in his Emancipation Proclamation: "On the 1st day of January, C.E. 1863, all persons held as slaves . . . shall be then, thenceforward, and forever free."

To Introduce a List

A colon is used to introduce a list.

The following materials can be used to build houses: plants, shells, sod, and sand.

When introducing a list, the colon often comes after summary words like *the following* or *these things*.

Computers in the home will do these things: control the lighting, regulate the heating, and provide security.

✳ It is incorrect to use a colon after a verb or a preposition.

Most houses today are made of: brick, wood, stone, or plaster. (The colon is incorrectly used after the preposition *of*.)

In a Business Letter

A colon is used after the salutation or greeting in a business letter.

Dear Ms. Kununga: Dear Sir:

Between Numbers in Time

A colon is used between the parts of a number that show time.

7:30 a.m.   1:00 p.m.   12:00 noon

Hyphen

A **hyphen** is used to divide a word at the end of a line. It is also used to form compound words and to write fractions. In addition, a hyphen is used to join the words in compound numbers from twenty-one to ninety-nine, to join letters and words, and so on.

To Divide a Word

A hyphen is used to divide a word when you run out of room at the end of a line. A word may be divided only between syllables (*ex-plor-er*). Here are some additional guidelines. Always refer to a dictionary if you're not sure how to divide a word.

- Never divide a one-syllable word: *would, large,* etc.
- Try not to divide a word of five or fewer letters: *older, habit,* etc.
- Never divide a one-letter syllable from the rest of the word: *apart-ment* not *a-partment*.
- Never divide abbreviations or contractions: *Mrs., Dr., don't, haven't,* etc.

In a Compound Word

A hyphen is used to make some compound words.

on-line file search
14-year-old computer programmer
high-speed modem

Between Numbers in a Fraction

A hyphen is used between the numbers in a fraction that is written as a word.

one-half (1/2)   five-tenths (5/10)

To Join Letters and Words

A hyphen is often used to join a letter to a word.

T-shirt   X-ray
e-mail   U-turn

Hyphen

With *Self, Ex, All, Great*	A hyphen is used to form new words beginning with the prefixes *all*, *self*, *ex*, *great*, etc. A hyphen is also used with suffixes such as *elect* and *free*.

all-around student
all-knowing teacher
self-respect
self-cleaning oven
ex-hero
great-grandmother
president-elect
smoke-free

To Form an Adjective	Use a hyphen to join two or more words that work together to form a single adjective.

voice-recognition software
on-screen directions

Dash

A **dash** is used to show a break in a sentence or to emphasize a word or a group of words.

To Show a Sudden Break in a Sentence	A dash can show a sudden break in a sentence.

Because of computers, our world—and the way we describe it—has changed greatly.

For Emphasis	A dash may be used to emphasize a word, a series of words, a phrase, or a clause.

You can learn about many subjects—customs, careers, sports, weather—on the Internet.

Quotation Marks

Quotation marks are used for each of the following reasons:

- To set off the exact words of a speaker from the rest of the sentence.
- To show the exact words a writer has quoted from a book or magazine.
- To set off certain titles.
- To note words used in a special way.

To Set Off the Exact Words of a Speaker

Quotation marks are used to set off a speaker's words in dialogue.

Martha asked, "Who can show me how to find information about Mexico?"

To Set Off Quoted Material

Quotation marks are placed before and after the exact words you quote from magazines and books.

One computer expert said, "In one day the Internet grew by 770 new sites or channels of information."

To Punctuate Titles

Quotation marks are used to punctuate titles of songs, poems, short stories, book chapters, and articles in encyclopedias, newspapers, or magazines.

"Take Me Out to the Ballgame" [song]
"Casey at the Bat" [poem]
"The Dixon Cornbelt League" [short story]
"Throwing a Curveball" [chapter in a book]
"Winning Isn't Everything" [newspaper article]

✱ When you punctuate a title, capitalize the first word, the last word, and every word in between except for articles (*a, an, the*), short prepositions (*of, for, with,* etc.), and coordinating conjunctions (*and, or, but,* etc.).

Quotation Marks

For Long Quotations

If a quotation in a report is two or more paragraphs long; place quotation marks before each paragraph and at the end of the last paragraph.

```
        "_____
_____ .
        "_____
_____ ."
```

Quotations that are more than four lines in length are set off from the rest of the paper. Usually the lines are indented 10 spaces from the left, and no quotation marks are used.

ten spaces

```
_____
    _____
    _____
    _____
    _____
    _____ .
_____
```

Placement of Punctuation

Periods and commas are always placed inside quotation marks.

> **"You are right," said David.**
> **David said, "You are right."**

Place an exclamation point or a question mark inside the quotation marks when it punctuates the quotation.

> **Alfredo asked, "Does anyone want to go for a balloon ride?"** (inside)

Place an exclamation point or a question mark outside the quotation marks when it punctuates the main sentence.

> **Did Alfredo really say, "Balloon rides are better than airplane rides"?** (outside)

Special Words

Use quotation marks around words used in a special way:

> **I like to "chill out" with my friends.**

Apostrophe

An **apostrophe** is used to form contractions, to form plurals, or to show possession. (*Possession* means "owning something.")

To Form Contractions

An apostrophe is used in a contraction to show that one or more letters have been left out.

I'm (I am)   you'd (you would)

COMMON CONTRACTIONS

couldn't (could not)	haven't (have not)	I've (I have)
didn't (did not)	he's (he is)	they're (they are)
doesn't (does not)	I'll (I will)	won't (will not)
don't (do not)	isn't (is not)	wouldn't (would not)
hasn't (has not)	it's (it is)	you'd (you would)

To Form Plurals

An apostrophe and *s* are used to form the plural of a letter or a numeral.

A's   B's   3's   10's

To Form Singular Possessives

Form the possessive of most singular nouns by adding an apostrophe and *s*.

Lia's report is on global warming.

It is one of the world's most serious problems.

Mr. Garcia's opinion is different.

✳ When a singular noun ends with an *s* or a *z* sound, the possessive may be formed by adding just an apostrophe

Carlos' weather chart is very detailed.

✳ But when the singular noun is a one-syllable word, form the possessive by adding both an apostrophe and *s*.

Chris's lab report is incomplete.

Apostrophe

| **To Form Plural Possessives** | In most cases, form the possessive of plural nouns ending in *s* by adding just an apostrophe. |

The visitors' ideas were helpful.

The lawmakers' debate dealt with immigration.

The immigrants' first view of the U.S. was the Statue of Liberty.

For plural nouns not ending in *s,* an apostrophe and *s* must be added.

Women's health is often discussed.

The children's team practices today.

The men's league starts this weekend.

Remember: The word before the apostrophe is the owner.

Justin's CD
(The CD belongs to Justin.)

the girls' uniforms
(The uniforms belong to the girls.)

| **In Compound Nouns** | The possessive of a compound noun is formed by placing the possessive ending after the last word. |

his best man's tuxedo

his sister-in-law's baby

| **With Indefinite Pronouns** | Form the possessive of an indefinite pronoun (*each, everyone, no one, anyone,* etc.) by adding an apostrophe and *s.* |

everyone's idea   **nobody's fault**

| **To Show Shared Possession** | Add an apostrophe and *s* to the last noun when possession is shared. |

Sasha and Olga's new science project deals with electricity.

Italics and Underlining

Italics is a style of type that is slightly slanted. In this sentence the word *girl* is printed in italics. In handwritten or typed material, each word or letter that should be in italics is underlined.

> In *Zlata's Diary* a young girl describes her daily life in Bosnia. (printed)
>
> In Zlata's Diary a young girl describes her daily life in Bosnia. (handwritten or typed)

In Titles

Underline (or use italics for) the titles of books, plays, very long poems, magazines, movies, record albums, cassettes, CD's, the names of ships and aircraft, and newspapers.

> The Giver [book]
> National Geographic [magazine]
> Babe [movie]
> Save the World [album]
> Andrea Doria [ship]
> Discovery [spacecraft]
> Los Angeles Times [newspaper]

Foreign Words

Underline (or use italics for) non-English words that are not commonly used in everyday English. Also underline scientific names.

> Semper fidelis means "always faithful." It is the motto of the U.S. Marine Corps.

Parentheses

Parentheses are used around words that add extra information to a sentence.

> You'll pay more for a portable computer (usually called a notebook) than you will for a desktop model.

Editing for Mechanics

Capitalization

Capitalize all proper nouns and all proper adjectives. A proper noun names a specific person, place, thing, or idea. A proper adjective is an adjective formed from a proper noun.

Common Nouns	person	country	continent
Proper Nouns	Ben Franklin	India	Africa
Proper Adjectives	Franklin stove	Indian food	African history

Names of People

Carlos

Sarah

Shaun

Capitalize the names of people and also the initials or abbreviations that stand for those names.

Michael Jordan	Sigrid Undset
Le Duc Anh	Sally Ride
Corazón C. Aquino	Benito Juárez

✳ If a woman uses both her maiden name and married name, the maiden name is listed first, and both are capitalized.

Coretta Scott King	Sandra Day O'Connor
Martha Ulforts Meyer	Kimberly Yashiki Smith

✳ Women who use two last names, often hyphenate them.

Kathleen Aguilera-Pérez
Margaret Bourke-White

Historical Names

Capitalize the names of historical documents, events, and periods of time.

Trojan War	World War II
Magna Carta	Bronze Age
the Declaration of Independence	

Abbreviations 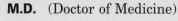	Capitalize abbreviations of organizations and titles.
	M.D. (Doctor of Medicine)
	Dr. (Doctor)
	M.A. (Master of Arts)
	Ph.D. (Doctor of Philosophy)
	Mr. (Courtesy title before the last name or full name of a man)
	Mrs. (Courtesy title before the last name or full name of a married woman)
	Ms. (Courtesy title before the last name or full name of a woman or a girl)
	U.S.A. (United States of America)
Organizations	Capitalize the name of a team, an organization, or an association.
	Houston Rockets Salvation Army International Olympic Committee
Titles Used with Names	Capitalize titles used with names of persons and the abbreviations standing for those titles.
	President Bush Mayor Martin J. Chavez Dr. Amy Lin Governor Richards
Titles	Capitalize the first word of a title, the last word, and every word in between except articles (*a, an, the*), short prepositions (*of, at, to*, etc.), and coordinating conjunctions (*and, but, or*, etc.). Follow this rule for titles of books, newspapers, magazines, poems, plays, songs, articles, movies, works of art, stories, and essays.
	The Hero and the Crown [book]
	the ***Kansas City Star*** [newspaper]
	Sports Illustrated [magazine]
	"This Land Is Your Land" [song]
	"Kid in the Park" [poem]
	You're a Good Man, Charlie Brown [play]
	Star Wars [movie]

Capitalization

First Words

Capitalize the first word of every sentence and the first word in a direct quotation. Do not capitalize the first word in an indirect quotation.

Writer James Berry was born in Jamaica. (sentence)

He explained, "It's the function of writers and poets to bring in the left-out side of the human family." (direct quotation)

Berry said he writes his stories in Jamaican dialect because it is important to tell these stories in the words of ordinary Jamaicans. (indirect quotation)

Geographic Names

Planets and
heavenly bodies. . . . . **Earth, Mars, Sirius**

Continents . . . . **Africa, Antarctica, Asia, Australia, Europe, South America**

Countries. . . . . **South Korea, Cuba, Rwanda, Poland, Colombia**

States . . . . **Florida, New Jersey, Texas, Illinois, California**

Provinces. . . . . . . **Alberta, British Columbia, Ontario**

Counties . . . . **Cook County, Dade County, Los Angeles County**

Cities . . . . **San Salvador, Nairobi, Tokyo**

Bodies of water . . . . **Yangtze (Chang) River, Lake Michigan, Bay of Bengal, Persian Gulf, Sewanee Creek**

Landforms . . . . **Cape of Good Hope, Mt. Fuji, Mojave Desert, Great Barrier Reef**

Public areas . . . . **Vietnam Memorial, Golden Gate Bridge**

Roads and highways . . . . . . **Eisenhower Expressway, Lake Shore Drive, Route 66, Highway 1, Interstate 90**

Buildings. . . . . **Taj Mahal, Mosque of Omar, the White House**

Particular Sections of the Country	Capitalize words that indicate particular sections of the country.
	A large part of the U.S. population lives on the East Coast.
	("East Coast" is a section of the country.)

Do not capitalize words that simply indicate direction.

If you keep driving west, you will end up in the Pacific Ocean. (direction)

* Capitalize proper adjectives formed from the names of specific sections of a country.

Eastern schools
Southern cooking

* Do not capitalize adjectives formed from words that simply indicate direction.

the northern part of Michigan
driving into western Brazil

Names of Languages, Religions, Nationalities, Races	Capitalize the names of languages, religions, nationalities, and races, as well as the proper adjectives formed from them.
	Spanish, Urdu, Serbian [languages]
	Islam, Christianity, Buddhism [religions]
	Chinese, Italian, Polish [nationalities]
	Asian, African, European [races]
	Japanese twig tea
	Ecuadoran coffee

Capitalize	Do Not Capitalize
American	anti-American
June, October	summer, fall
Senn High School	a high school in Chicago
Governor Christine Todd Whitman	Christine Todd Whitman, our governor
President George W. Bush	George Bush, our president
Honda Civic LS	a Honda car
We live on planet **Earth.**	The earth we live on is good.
I'm taking **Introduction to Algebra.**	It is a pre-algebra class.

Capitalization

Words Used as Names

Capitalize words such as *mother, father, aunt,* and *uncle* when these words are used as names.

> **This summer Aunt Natasha is taking night classes in English at the high school.**
> ("Aunt Natasha" is the name of a person.)

> **Then Aunt will teach Grandfather to speak English.**
> ("Aunt" and "Grandfather" are used as names.)

> **Father and Mother decided to take the class, too.**
> ("Father" and "Mother" are used as names.)

> **I asked, "Father, have you done your homework?"** ("Father" is used as a name.)

✳ Words such as *dad, uncle, mother, grandma,* etc., are not usually capitalized if they come after a possessive pronoun (*my, his, our*).

> **My father nodded. He and my mother are the best students in the class.** ("My father" and "my mother" are not used as names.)

Days of the Week

Capitalize the names of days of the week, months of the year, and special holidays.

> **Monday   June   New Year's Day   Easter**

Do not capitalize the names of seasons.

> **winter   spring   summer   fall** (or autumn)

Official Names

Capitalize the names of businesses and the official names of their products. (These are called trade names.) Do not, however, capitalize a general, descriptive word like *tissues* when it follows the product name.

> **Duracell** batteries   **Timex** watches
> **McDonald's** cookies   **Taco Bell** restaurants
> **Home Depot** stores   **Kleenex** tissues

Plurals

The **plurals** of most nouns are formed by adding *s* to the singular.

bicycle — **bicycles**   chair   — **chairs**

The plural form of nouns ending in *sh, ch, x, s,* and *z* is made by adding *es* to the singular.

brush — **brushes**   dish   — **dishes**
mess — **messes**   buzz   — **buzzes**
fox   — **foxes**   ax   — **axes**

Plurals That Do Not Change

A few words in English can be the same in the singular and in the plural.

Singular: That **sheep** always wanders away.
Plural: The other six **sheep** follow it.
Singular: I caught one **trout**.
Plural: Dad caught three **trout**.

Singular: The **deer** disappeared into the woods.
Plural: Five **deer** remained in the cornfield.

Words Ending in *o*

The plurals of words ending in *o* (with a vowel letter just before the *o*) are formed by adding *s*.

radio — **radios**   video — **videos**

The plurals of words ending in *o* (with a consonant letter before the *o*) are mostly formed by adding *es*.

echo — **echoes**   potato — **potatoes**

Exception: Musical terms and words borrowed from Spanish form plurals by adding *s*; consult a dictionary for other words of this type.

alto — **altos**   taco   — **tacos**
solo — **solos**   burro   — **burros**
banjo — **banjos**   burrito — **burritos**

Other exceptions include the following:

photo — **photos**   yo-yo — **yo-yos**

Plurals

Nouns Ending in *ful*

The plurals of nouns that end with *ful* are formed by adding an *s* at the end of the word.

two spoonfuls   **three** tankfuls
four bowlfuls   **five** cupfuls

Nouns Ending in *f* or *fe*

The plurals of nouns that end in *f* or *fe* are formed in one of two ways: If the final *f* sound is still heard in the plural form of the word, simply add *s*; if the final sound is a *v* sound, change the *f* to *v* and add *es*.

belief — **beliefs**   roof — **roofs**
cuff   —   **cuffs**   reef — **reefs**
(plural ends with *f* sound)

life   —   **lives**   knife — **knives**
wolf   —   **wolves**   leaf — **leaves**
(plural ends with *v* sound)

Nouns Ending in *y*

The plurals of common nouns that end in *y* (with a consonant letter just before the *y*) are formed by changing the *y* to *i* and adding *es*.

story — **stories**   sky — **skies**
candy — **candies**   fly — **flies**

The plurals of proper nouns ending in *y* are formed by adding *s*.

Two Penny Candys are opening in our city.

The plurals of common nouns that end in *y* (with a vowel letter just before the *y*) are formed by adding *s*.

key   —   **keys**   day — **days**
buoy — **buoys**   toy — **toys**

Compound Nouns

The plurals of compound nouns are usually formed by adding *s* or *es* to the important word in the compound.

life jackets   secretaries **of state**
sisters-in-law   houses **of assembly**

Adding an 's	The plurals of symbols, letters, numerals, and words discussed as words are formed by adding an *apostrophe* and an *s*. **two ?'s and two !'s five 7's** **x's and y's hello's and goodbye's**
Irregular Spelling	Some words take on an irregular spelling to form a plural; others words are now acceptable with the commonly used *s* or *es* ending. child — **children** goose — **geese** man — **men** woman — **women** foot — **feet** tooth — **teeth** ox — **oxen** datum — **data** cactus — **cacti** or **cactuses**

Abbreviations

	Abbreviations are shortened forms of words. You can use the following abbreviations in all your writing: **Mr. Mrs. Miss Ms. Dr. B.C.E. C.E. M.D.** **a.m. p.m. (A.M., P.M.)**
Acronyms	An acronym is a word formed from the first (or first few) letters of words in a phrase. **ROM** (read-only memory) **WHO** (World Health Organization) **MADD** (Mothers Against Drunk Driving)
Initialisms	An initialism is similar to an acronym. However, the initials used to form this type of abbreviation cannot be pronounced as a word. Initialisms are not usually followed by periods. **FBI** — Federal Bureau of Investigation **PTA** — Parent-Teacher Association **PSA** — Public Service Announcement **IRS** — Internal Revenue Service

State Abbreviations

	Standard	Postal		Standard	Postal		Standard	Postal
Alabama	Ala.	AL	Kentucky	Ky.	KY	North Dakota	N.D.	ND
Alaska	Alas.	AK	Louisiana	La.	LA	Ohio	Ohio	OH
Arizona	Ariz.	AZ	Maine	Maine	ME	Oklahoma	Okla.	OK
Arkansas	Ark.	AR	Maryland	Md.	MD	Oregon	Ore.	OR
California	Calif.	CA	Massachusetts	Mass.	MA	Pennsylvania	Pa.	PA
Colorado	Colo.	CO	Michigan	Mich.	MI	Rhode Island	R.I.	RI
Connecticut	Conn.	CT	Minnesota	Minn.	MN	South Carolina	S.C.	SC
Delaware	Del.	DE	Mississippi	Miss.	MS	South Dakota	S.D.	SD
District			Missouri	Mo.	MO	Tennessee	Tenn.	TN
of Columbia	D.C.	DC	Montana	Mont.	MT	Texas	Tex.	TX
Florida	Fla.	FL	Nebraska	Neb.	NE	Utah	Utah	UT
Georgia	Ga.	GA	Nevada	Nev.	NV	Vermont	Vt.	VT
Hawaii	Hawaii	HI	New			Virginia	Va.	VA
Idaho	Idaho	ID	Hampshire	N.H.	NH	Washington	Wash.	WA
Illinois	Ill.	IL	New Jersey	N.J.	NJ	West Virginia	W. Va.	WV
Indiana	Ind.	IN	New Mexico	N.M.	NM	Wisconsin	Wis.	WI
Iowa	Iowa	IA	New York	N.Y.	NY	Wyoming	Wyo.	WY
Kansas	Kan.	KS	North Carolina	N.C.	NC			

Address Abbreviations

	Standard	Postal		Standard	Postal		Standard	Postal
Avenue	Ave.	AVE	Lake	L.	LK	Rural	R.	R
Boulevard	Blvd.	BLVD	Lane	Ln.	LN	South	S.	S
Court	Ct.	CT	North	N.	N	Square	Sq.	SQ
Drive	Dr.	DR	Park	Pk.	PK	Station	Sta.	STA
East	E.	E	Parkway	Pky.	PKY	Street	St.	ST
Expressway	Expy.	EXPY	Place	Pl.	PL	Terrace	Ter.	TER
Heights	Hts.	HTS	Plaza	Plaza	PLZ	Turnpike	Tpke.	TPKE
Highway	Hwy.	HWY	Road	Rd.	RD	West	W.	W

Common Abbreviations

AC alternating current
a.m. ante meridiem
ASAP as soon as possible
C.O.D. cash on delivery
D.A. district attorney
DC direct current

etc. and so forth
FM frequency modulation
kg kilogram
km kilometer
kw kilowatt
lb pound
M.D. Doctor of Medicine

mpg miles per gallon
mph miles per hour
oz. ounce
pd. paid
pg. page (or p.)
p.m. post meridiem
qt. quart
R.S.V.P. please reply
vs. versus

Numbers

Numbers from one to nine are usually written as words. All numbers 10 and over are usually written as numerals.

one, five, nine, 10, 36, 152

✳ If you're comparing the numbers in a sentence, write them both as numerals or as words.

Students from 9 to 13 years old attend the school.

Students from nine to thirteen years old attend the school.

Very Large Numbers

When writing sentences, you may use a combination of numerals and words for very large numbers.

The world's population is expected to be about 7.9 billion by 2020.

You may spell out large numbers that can be written as two words.

two million   nine thousand

If you need more than two words to spell out a number, write it as a numeral.

2,220,100   9,641

Sentence Beginnings

Use words, not numerals, to begin a sentence.

Thirteen states signed the Declaration of Independence.

Numerals Only

Use numerals for any numbers in the following forms:

money	**$5.10**	decimals	**99.5**
dates	**May 10, 2002**	statistics	**65 mph**
addresses	**756 Dodge Ave.**	ZIP codes	**60202**
identification numbers	**Highway 45**	percentages	**50%**
phone numbers	**328-8641**	pages	**pages 15-17**

Improving Your Spelling

1. **Be patient.** Becoming a good speller takes time.

2. **Learn the basic spelling rules.** (See page 378.)

3. **Check your spelling** by using a dictionary or list of commonly misspelled words.

4. **Check a dictionary** for the correct pronunciation of each word you are trying to spell. Knowing how to pronounce a word will help you remember how to spell it.

5. **Look up the meaning of each word.** Knowing how to spell a word is of little use if you don't know what it means.

6. **Practice seeing the word in your mind's eye.** Look away from the dictionary page and write the word on a piece of paper. Check the spelling in the dictionary. Repeat this process until you can spell the word correctly.

7. **Make a spelling dictionary.** Include any words you frequently misspell in a special notebook.

A

	across	aisle	angel
	actual	alarm	anger
abbreviate	adapt	alcohol	angle
aboard	addition	alike	angry
about	address	alive	animal
above	adequate	alley	anniversary
absence	adjust	allowance	announce
absent	admire	all right	annoyance
absolute	adventure	almost	annual
accident	advertise	already	anonymous
accidental	advertising	although	another
accompany	afraid	altogether	answer
accomplish	after	aluminum	antarctic
according	afternoon	always	anticipate
account	afterward	ambulance	anxiety
accurate	again	amendment	anxious
accustom	against	among	anybody
ache	agreeable	amount	anyhow
achieve	agreement	analyze	anyone
acre	aid	ancient	anything

anyway
anywhere
apartment
apiece
apologize
apparent
appeal
appearance
appetite
appliance
application
appointment
appreciate
approach
appropriate
approval
approximate
architect
arctic
aren't
argument
arithmetic
around
arouse
arrange
arrival
article
artificial
asleep
assign
assistance
associate
association
assume
athlete
athletic
attach
attack
attempt
attendance
attention
attitude
attorney

attractive
audience
August
author
authority
automobile
autumn
available
avenue
average
awful
awkward

B

baggage
baking
balance
balloon
ballot
banana
bandage
barber
bargain
barrel
basement
basis
basket
battery
beautiful
beauty
because
become
becoming
before
began
beginning
behave
behavior
being
belief
believe
belong

beneath
benefit
between
bicycle
biscuit
blackboard
blanket
blizzard
bother
bottle
bottom
bough
bought
bounce
boundary
breakfast
breast
breath
breathe
breeze
bridge
brief
bright
brilliant
brother
brought
bruise
bubble
bucket
buckle
budget
building
burglar
bury
business
busy
button

C

cabbage
cafeteria
calendar

campaign
canal
cancel
candidate
candle
cannon
cannot
canoe
can't
canyon
capacity
captain
cardboard
career
careful
careless
carpenter
carriage
carrot
casualty
catalog
catastrophe
catcher
caterpillar
catsup
ceiling
celebration
cemetery
census
century
certain
certificate
challenge
champion
change
character
chief
children
chimney
chocolate
choice
chorus
circumstance

citizen
civilization
classmates
classroom
climate
climb
closet
clothing
coach
cocoa
cocoon
coffee
collar
college
color
column
comedy
coming
commercial
commission
commit
commitment
committed
committee
communicate
community
company
comparison
competition
competitive
complain
complete
complexion
compromise
conceive
concerning
concert
concrete
condemn
condition
conductor
conference
confidence

congratulate
connect
conscience
conscious
conservative
constitution
continue
continuous
control
convenience
convince
coolly
cooperate
corporation
correspond
cough
couldn't
counter
country
county
courage
courageous
court
courteous
courtesy
cousin
coverage
cozy
cracker
cranky
crawl
creditor
cried
criticize
cruel
crumb
crumble
cupboard
curiosity
curious
current
custom
customer

daily
dairy
damage
danger
daughter
dealt
decided
decision
decorate
defense
definite
definition
delicious
dependent
describe
description
desert
deserve
design
desirable
despair
dessert
determine
develop
device
devise
diamond
diary
dictionary
difference
different
difficulty
dining
diploma
director
disagreeable
disappear
disappoint
disapprove
discipline
discover

discuss
discussion
disease
dissatisfied
distinguish
distribute
divide
divine
division
doctor
doesn't
dollar
doubt
dough
dual
duplicate

E

eager
economy
edge
edition
eight
eighth
either
electricity
elephant
embarrass
emergency
emphasize
employee
employment
enclose
encourage
engineer
enormous
enough
entertain
enthusiastic
entirely
entrance
envelope

environment
equipment
equipped
escape
especially
establish
every
evidence
exaggerate
exceed
excellent
except
exceptional
excite
exercise
exhaust
exhibition
existence
expect
expensive
experience
explain
explanation
expression
extinct
extraordinary
extreme

F

facilities
familiar
family
famous
fascinate
fashion
faucet
favorite
feature
February
federal
fertile
field

fierce
fifty
finally
financial
foreign
formal
former
forth
fortunate
forty
forward
fountain
fourth
freight
friend
frighten
fulfill
further
furthermore

G

gadget
gauge
generally
generous
genius
gentle
genuine
geography
ghetto
ghost
gnaw
government
governor
graduation
grammar
grateful
grease
grief
grocery
grudge
guarantee

guard
guardian
guess
guidance
guide
guilty
gymnasium

H

hammer
handkerchief
handle
handsome
happen
happiness
hastily
having
hazardous
headache
height
hesitate
history
hoarse
holiday
honor
hoping
hopping
horrible
hospital
humorous
hurriedly
hygiene
hymn

I

icicle
identical
illiterate
illustrate
imaginary
imagine

imitation
immediate
immense
immigrant
impatient
importance
impossible
improvement
incredible
indefinitely
independent
individual
industrial
inferior
infinite
initial
innocent
instance
instead
insurance
intelligence
intention
interested
interesting
interfere
interpret
interrupt
interview
investigate
invitation
irrigate
island
issue

J

jealous
jewelry
journal
journey
judgment
juicy

K

kitchen
knew
knife
knives
knock
knowledge

L

label
laboratory
ladies
language
laugh
laundry
lawyer
league
lecture
legal
legible
legislature
leisure
length
liable
library
license
lightning
likely
liquid
literature
living
loneliness
losing
lovable
lovely

M

machinery
magazine
magnificent

maintain
majority
making
manual
manufacture
marriage
material
mathematics
maximum
mayor
meant
measure
medicine
medium
message
mileage
miniature
minimum
minute
mirror
miserable
missile
misspell
moisture
molecule
monument
mortgage
mountain
muscle
musician
mysterious

N

naive
natural
necessary
negotiate
neighbor
neither
nickel
niece
nineteen

nineteenth
ninety
noisy
noticeable
nuclear
nuisance

O

obedience
obey
occasion
occasional
occur
occurred
offense
official
often
omitted
operate
opinion
opponent
opportunity
opposite
ordinarily
original

P

package
paid
pamphlet
paradise
paragraph
parallel
paralyze
parentheses
participant
participate
particular
pasture
patience
peculiar

people
perhaps
permanent
perpendicular
persistent
personal
perspiration
persuade
phase
physician
piece
pitcher
planned
plateau
pleasant
pleasure
pneumonia
politician
possess
possible
practical
prairie
precede
precious
precise
precision
prejudice
preparation
previous
primitive
principal
principle
prisoner
privilege
probably
procedure
proceed
professor
pronounce
pronunciation
protein
psychology
pumpkin

Q

quarter
questionnaire
quiet
quite

R

raise
realize
really
receipt
receive
received
recipe
recognize
recommend
reign
relieve
remember
repetition
representative
resistance
respectfully
responsibility
restaurant
review
rhyme
rhythm
ridiculous
route

S

safety
salad
salary
sandwich
satisfactory
Saturday
scene
scenery

schedule
science
scissors
scream
screen
season
secretary
seize
sensible
sentence
separate
several
shining
similar
since
sincere
skiing
sleigh
soldier
spaghetti
specific
sphere
sprinkle
squeeze
statue
statute
stomach
stopped
straight
strength
stretched
studying
subtle
succeed
success
sufficient
summarize
suppose
surely
surprise
syllable
sympathy
symptom

T

table
teacher
technique
temperature
temporary
terrible
territory
thankful
theater
their
there
therefore
thief
thorough
though
throughout
tired
together
tomorrow
tongue
touch
tournament
toward
tragedy
treasurer
tried
tries
truly
Tuesday
typical

U

unfortunate
unique
unnecessary
until
usable
useful
using
usual

V

vacation
vacuum
valuable
variety
various
vegetable
very
view
violence
visible
visitor
voice
volume
voluntary
volunteer

W

wander
weather
Wednesday
weigh
weird
welcome
welfare
whale
where
whether
which
whole
whose
width
women
worthwhile
writing
written

Y

yellow
yesterday

Spelling Rules

i* before *e	Write *i* before *e* except after *c*, or when sounded like *a* as in *neighbor* and *weigh*. ***Exceptions*** to the "*i* before *e*" rule include the following:

either	**heir**	**sheik**
financier	**leisure**	**species**
foreign	**neither**	**their**
height	**seize**	**weird**

Silent *e*	If a word ends with a silent *e*, drop the *e* before adding a suffix that begins with a vowel. judge – **judging** create – **creative** – **creation** relate – **relating** – **relative**
Words Ending in *y*	When *y* is the last letter in a word (and a consonant letter is just before the *y*), change the *y* to *i* before adding any suffix, except those that begin with *i*. busy – **business** try – **tries** – **trying** lady – **ladies** cry – **cried** – **crying** When forming the plural of a word that ends in *y* (with a vowel letter just before the *y*), add *s*. boy – **boys** key – **keys**
Words Ending in a Consonant	When a one-syllable word (*beg*) ends in a consonant (be**g**) preceded by one vowel (b**e**g), double the final consonant before adding a suffix that begins with a vowel (be**gg**ing). When a multisyllable word (*admit*) ends in a consonant (admi**t**) preceded by one vowel (adm**i**t), the accent is on the last syllable (ad**mit**), and the suffix begins with a vowel (**i**ng)—the same rule holds true: double the final consonant (admi**tt**ing).

Commonly Misused Words

This chapter lists words that are commonly confused and used incorrectly. First, look over all of the words listed on the next 16 pages. Then, whenever you have a question about which word is the *right* one to use, turn here for help. (If this chapter doesn't answer your question, refer to a dictionary.)

a, an	The Sears Tower in Chicago is **a** skyscraper.
	    (***A*** is used before words that begin with a consonant sound.)
	We rode **an** elevator to the 90th floor!
	    (***An*** is used before words that begin with a vowel sound.)

accept, except	Everyone decided to **accept** a ride in the race car.
	    (***Accept*** means "to receive.")
	We all enjoyed the ride, **except** for Grandma.
	    (***Except*** means "other than.")

affect, effect	Hurricane Hugo will **affect** people for years.
	    (***Affect*** is a verb meaning "to influence.")
	One **effect** of the storm was the loss of many trees.
	    (***Effect*** is a noun meaning "the result.")

allowed, aloud	We are **allowed** to read any book we choose.
	    (***Allowed*** means "permitted.")
	We cannot read **aloud** in the library, however.
	    (***Aloud*** means "in a speaking voice.")

a lot	**A lot** of my friends wear hats just for fun. (***A lot*** is always two words.)

already, all ready	I **already** finished my math assignment.
	    (***Already*** is an adverb telling when.)
	So, I'm **all ready** to go skateboarding.
	    (***All ready*** is a phrase meaning "completely ready.")

alright, all right	**Alright** is the incorrect spelling of *all right*. It is **all right** if Mariko misses the bus, because she can ride her bike to school. (***All right*** is a phrase meaning "satisfactory or okay.")

altogether, all together	The strong wind finally stopped **altogether**.
	     (**Altogether** is an adverb meaning "completely.")
	 We were **all together** in the warm house.
	     (**All together** describes people or things gathered in one place at one time.)

amount, number	Brad ate a huge **amount** of food at the game.
	     (**Amount** refers to things you can measure, but not count.)
	 A small **number** of fans sat in the rain.
	     (**Number** is used when you can count things.)

annual, biannual	The school held its **annual** fall festival.
	     (**Annual** means "once a year.")
	 The city has a **biannual** budget meeting.
	     (**Biannual** means "twice a year.")

ant, aunt	An **ant** is an insect. An **aunt** is a sister of your mother or father.

anyone, any one	**Anyone** who signs up may go on the trip.
	     (**Anyone** is a pronoun meaning "any person at all.")
	 Any one of the guides could tell about the cave.
	     (**Any one** refers to a choice of one.)

assent, ascent	The pilot nodded his **assent**.
	     (**Assent** means "agreement.")
	 The control tower signaled the plane to begin its **ascent**.
	     (**Ascent** is the "act of rising.")

ate, eight	She **ate** an orange.
	     (**Ate** means "to have eaten.")
	 He picked **eight** oranges off the tree.
	     (**Eight** is a number.)

bare, bear	She dug her **bare** feet into the cool sand.
	     (**Bare** means "without covering.")
	 We saw a **bear** crossing the stream.
	     (A **bear** is a large, furry animal.)
	 Joachim couldn't **bear** listening to his baby sister cry.
	     (The verb **bear** means "to tolerate" or "to carry.")

base, bass	The **base** of the lamp was carved out of stone. 　　(**Base** [bās] is the foundation or lower part of something.) The singer's **bass** voice rumbled like thunder. 　　(A **bass** [bās] voice has a deep, low sound.) Jim never caught **bass** at the south end of the lake. 　　(A **bass** [băs] is a type of fish.)
be, bee	Mansi wants to **be** a teacher. 　　(**Be** is a verb.) A **bee** is a flying insect that makes honey.
beside, **besides**	Derrick placed the spoon **beside** the knife. 　　(**Beside** means "by the side of.") **Besides** the plate and cup, he needed a fork and spoon. 　　(**Besides** means "in addition to.")
blew, blue	The wind **blew** the fog away. 　　(**Blew** is the past tense of the verb *blow*.) The sun shone in the clear **blue** sky. 　　(**Blue** is a color.)
board, **bored**	The school **board** posted their ideas on a bulletin **board**. 　　(A **board** is a group of people in charge; a **board** is also a 　　piece of wood or cork.) When Tom got **bored**, he **bored** holes in the wood. 　　(**Bored** means "tired of something" or "to have drilled into 　　something.")
brake, **break**	I have a bad **brake** on my bicycle. 　　(A **brake** is used to slow or stop something.) If it fails, I could **break** a leg. 　　(**Break** means "to split or crack.")
bring, take	Please **bring** me my helmet. 　　(**Bring** means "to move toward the speaker.") **Take** plenty of water when you go biking. 　　(**Take** means "to carry along.")
by, buy	Have you walked **by** the pet store lately? 　　(**By** is a preposition meaning "near.") The sign on the puppy cage says, "**Buy** me, please." 　　(**Buy** is a verb meaning "to purchase.")

can, may	**Can** I get a job? 　　(**Can** asks if I am able to do something.) **May** I get an after-school job? 　　(**May** asks for permission to do something.)
capital, capitol	The **capital** of Idaho is Boise. 　　(The noun **capital** refers to a city or to money.) Both *Idaho* and *Boise* begin with **capital** letters. The mayor's opinion is of **capital** importance. 　　(The adjective **capital** means 　　"major or influential.") My father works in the **capitol**. 　　(A **capitol** is a building in which 　　government jobs are carried out.)
cell, sell	Plants and animals are made up of **cells**. Prisoners live in jail **cells**. 　　(A **cell** is a small unit of life or a small room.) Camille hopes to **sell** her bicycle. 　　(**Sell** is a verb meaning "to give up for a price.")
cent, scent, sent	The flowers cost 75 **cents** each. 　　(A **cent** is a coin, also called a penny.) The **scent** of flowers filled the air. 　　(**Scent** is an odor.) Zoe **sent** her mom a bouquet of roses. 　　(**Sent** is the past tense of the verb *send*.)
choose, chose	**Choose** a story about a favorite jungle animal. 　　(**Choose** [chüz] is a verb meaning "to select or pick.") Ling **chose** to tell a myth about a tiger. 　　(**Chose** [chōz] is the past tense of the verb *choose*.)
clothes, close	Melody put the wet **clothes** in the dryer. 　　(**Clothes** are items you wear.) She had to **close** the door before the machine would start. 　　(**Close** means "to shut.")
coarse, course	The **coarse** fabric made good curtains for the stage. 　　(**Coarse** means "rough or crude.") We made them in our sewing **course**. 　　(A **course** is a class; a **course** is also a path or direction 　　taken.)

council, counsel	The student **council** listened to the students' opinions.
	    (***Council*** refers to a group that advises.)
	It also heard the **counsel** of the administrators.
	    (***Counsel*** is a noun that means "advice"; ***counsel*** is also a
	    verb that means "to advise.")

creak, creek	Old houses **creak** in a strong wind.
	    (A ***creak*** is a squeaking sound.)
	The **creek** dries up in the summer.
	    (A ***creek*** is a stream of water, a tiny river.)

dear, deer	**Dear** is a greeting used at the beginning of a letter.
	    (***Dear*** means "loved or valued.")
	Most **deer** live in the country; some live in the suburbs.
	    (***Deer*** are animals.)

desert, dessert	A barrel cactus grows in the **desert**.
	    (***Desert*** [dé-zert] is barren wilderness.)
	The bird would not **desert** her nest.
	    (The verb ***desert*** [di-zért] means
	    "to leave or abandon.")
	You could eat pear-cactus fruit for **dessert**.
	    (***Dessert*** [di-zért] is a sweet served at the end of a meal.)

dew, do, due	The morning **dew** on the grass dampened my shoes.
	    (***Dew*** is moisture.)
	I want to **do** my report today.
	    (***Do*** is a verb meaning "to make or carry out.")
	It's not **due** until next week.
	    (***Due*** means "owed.")

die, dye	Some plants **die** if they get too much water.
	    (***Die*** means "to stop living.")
	Saffron could be used to **dye** cloth a yellow color.
	    (***Dye*** means "to change the color of something.")

doesn't, don't	Louisa **doesn't** have her driver's license.
	    (***doesn't*** = does not)
	Jake and Cody **don't** have theirs either.
	    (***don't*** = do not)

farther, further	Ka Lae, Hawaii, is **farther** south than Key West, Florida.
	  (***Farther*** refers to distance.)
	For **further** information, see an almanac.
	  (***Further*** does not refer to distance, but it does mean "more or additional.")

fewer, less	Each year Manuel counts **fewer** trees in the old orchard.
	  (***Fewer*** refers to something you can count.)
	Each year he harvests **less** fruit.
	  (***Less*** refers to a general amount that you cannot count.)

find, fined	Chintan could not **find** his bike lock.
	  (***Find*** means "to locate or discover.")
	He got **fined** for riding his bike in the bus lane.
	  (***Fined*** refers to being charged a penalty.)

flower, flour	A tulip is a spring **flower**.
	  (As a noun, ***flower*** refers to a blossoming plant. As a verb, ***flower*** refers to the act of blossoming.)
	Flour is the main ingredient in pita bread.
	  (***Flour*** is finely ground grain.)

for, four	The crowd cheered **for** the soccer players.
	  (***For*** is a preposition meaning "because of" or "directed to.")
	The home team won the game by **four** goals.
	  (***Four*** is a number.)

good, well	Yolanda plays on a **good** team!
	  (***Good*** is an adjective describing the noun *team*.)
	The other two teams did not do **well**.
	  (***Well*** is an adverb modifying the verb *do*.)

hare, hair	A **hare** is an animal similar to a rabbit. Samantha wears her **hair** in a long braid.

heal, heel	The sore took a long time to **heal**.
	  (***Heal*** means "to return to health.")
	It was on his foot just above his **heel**.
	  (The ***heel*** is the back of the foot, below the ankle.)

hear, here	I could **hear** him barking from a mile away!
	    (**Hear** means "to listen.")
	I stayed **here**, and he went over there.
	    (**Here** means "in this place.")

heard, herd	I **heard** a man calling his dog.
	    (**Heard** is the past tense of the verb *hear*.)
	The dog was moving a **herd** of sheep.
	    (**Herd** refers to a large group of animals.)

heir, air	An **heir** is a person who inherits or has the right to something. **Air** is what we breathe.

hi, high	Every morning I say **hi** to the woman at the newsstand.
	    (**Hi** is a brief greeting.)
	How **high** is the world's tallest mountain?
	    (**High** is an adjective meaning "tall.")

hole, whole	The workers made a **hole** in the main water pipe.
	    (**Hole** refers to an opening.)
	The **whole** city was without water for 24 hours.
	    (**Whole** means "entire or complete.")

hour, our	My favorite **hour** of the day is at sunset.
	    (**Hour** refers to 60 minutes.)
	We have a view of the sunset from **our** house.
	    (**Our** is a pronoun showing possession.)

immigrate, emigrate	Vladimir **immigrated** to this country from Russia.
	    (**Immigrate** means "to come into a new country or area.")
	He was 12 years old when he **emigrated**.
	    (**Emigrate** means "to leave your country for another place.")

its, it's	My computer, with **its** limited memory, is not very useful.
	    (**Its** shows possession.)
	It's an old model.
	    (**It's** is the contraction for "it is.")

knew, new	I **knew** my family planned to move.
	    (**Knew** is the past tense of the verb *know*.)
	I would be going to a **new** school.
	    (**New** means "recent or different.")

knight, night	A **knight** guarded the castle gates.
	    (***Knight*** refers to an old military rank.)
	One **night** he fell asleep on duty.
	    (***Night*** refers to the time between sunset and sunrise.)

knot, not	I had a **knot** in my shoelaces.
	    (***Knot*** refers to a lump of intertwined material.)
	It was **not** easy to undo it.
	    (***Not*** means "negative.")

know, no	Do you **know** sign language?
	    (***Know*** means "to understand.")
	No, but Sasha learned it because her sister is deaf.
	    (***No*** means "the opposite of yes.")

knows, nose	Felicia **knows** she is allergic to tree pollen.
	    (***Knows*** means "understands.")
	Every spring her **nose** itches.
	    (A ***nose*** is part of the face through which one breathes.)

lay, lie	Please **lay** the books down on the table.
	I **laid** them down yesterday. I have **laid** them down before.
	    (***Lay*** means "to place." ***Lay*** is a transitive verb; it needs a word to complete the meaning. *Books* and *them* complete the meaning by answering the question "what.")
	
	Byron **lies** on the floor to study.
	He **lay** on the floor last night. He has **lain** there before.
	    (***Lie*** means "to recline." ***Lie*** is an intransitive verb; it does not need a word to complete the meaning.)

lead, led	Mr. Warren **leads** us through the science experiments.
	    (***Lead*** [lēd] is a present tense verb meaning "to guide.")
	He **led** a research team when he was in college.
	    (***Led*** [lĕd] is the past tense of *lead*.)
	The team studied how **lead** blocks out radiation.
	    (***Lead*** [lĕd] refers to a metal or to graphite in a pencil.)

learn, teach	When did you **learn** how to knit?
	    (***Learn*** means "to get information.")
	Could you **teach** someone else how to do it?
	    (***Teach*** means "to give information.")

leave, let	Dana wanted to **leave** her application with the manager.
	    (*Leave* means "to allow something to remain behind.")
	 Her parents were not ready to **let** her get a job.
	    (*Let* means "to permit.")

like, as	John's laugh sounds **like** his father's laugh.
	    (*Like* is a preposition meaning "similar to." It usually
	    introduces a phrase.)
	 He laughs **as** he reads a book of jokes.
	    (*As* is a conjunction meaning "while or when." It usually
	    introduces a clause.)

loose,
 lose, loss
	Three tarantulas got **loose** over the weekend.
	    (*Loose* [lüs] means "free or untied.")
	 We did **lose** the smallest one.
	    (*Lose* [lüz] means to "misplace
	    or fail to win.")
	 The **loss** ruined our experiment.
	    (*Loss* means "something lost.")

made,
 maid
	Marisa always **made** her bed at home.
	    (*Made* is the past tense of the verb *make.*)
	 She liked the hotel where the **maid** did it for her.
	    (A *maid* is a female servant.)

mail,
 male
	Leave voice **mail** at this number.
	    (*Mail* refers to messages that are sent.)
	 Men are **male**; women are female.
	    (*Male* refers to the masculine sex.)

main,
 Maine,
 mane
	Rosario's **main** interest is writing poems.
	    (*Main* means "the most important.")
	 The state of **Maine** is known for lobsters.
	    (*Maine* is a state in the northeast United States.)
	 Zebras and horses have similar **manes**.
	    (*Mane* refers to the long hair on an animal's neck.)

meat,
 meet
	They served ostrich **meat** at the banquet.
	    (*Meat* is food or flesh.)
	 I asked if I could **meet** the cook.
	    (*Meet* means "to come together.")

metal, medal	Nickel coins are made mostly of copper **metal**.
	(***Metal*** is an element like iron or gold.)
	An Olympic **medal** is gold, silver, or bronze.
	(A ***medal*** is an award.)
miner, minor	A **miner** dug for diamonds in Arkansas.
	(A ***miner*** takes valuable materials from the earth.)
	A **minor** is an individual who is not legally an adult.
moral, morale	People learn **moral** behavior.
	(***Moral*** [mór-al] refers to what is right or wrong.)
	My **morale** was low when my best friend moved away.
	(***Morale*** [mo-rál] refers to someone's emotional condition.)
morning, mourning	The sad news came in a letter this **morning**.
	(***Morning*** refers to the half of the day before noon.)
	Elena is **mourning** the death of her aunt.
	(***Mourning*** means "showing sorrow.")
oar, or, ore	You need an **oar** to row a boat.
	(An ***oar*** is a stick with a wide end.)
	Would you rather ride in a sailboat **or** in a canoe?
	(***Or*** is a connecting word showing a choice.)
	The ships carried iron **ore**.
	(***Ore*** refers to a mineral made of up several materials.)
of, have	I **have** my ticket, so I could **have** gone sooner.
	(***Have*** is a main verb or a helping verb.)
	I could **of** gone sooner.
	(***Of*** is used incorrectly.)
	I lost one **of** my tickets.
	(***Of*** is used correctly as a preposition.)
one, won	Only **one** runner goes to the finals.
	(***One*** is a number.)
	Ramel **won** the final race by half a second.
	(***Won*** refers to victory.)
pain, pane	Marta's broken ankle caused a lot of **pain**.
	(***Pain*** is the feeling of being hurt.)
	A **pane** of glass broke when the door slammed shut.
	(A ***pane*** is a part or section of something.)

pair, pare, pear	A **pair** of shoes was left out in the rain. 　(***Pair*** refers to a couple, or two 　of something.) We had to **pare** the apples for the pies. 　(***Pare*** means "to peel.") The hard, green **pears** were not ready to eat. 　(A ***pear*** is a fruit.)
past, passed	Damien didn't like his **past**. *(noun)* He wanted to avoid **past** failures. *(adjective)* He walked right **past** his old gang. *(preposition)* 　(***Past*** can be a noun, an adjective, or a preposition.) The truck **passed** the slow-moving tractor. 　(***Passed*** is the past tense of the verb *pass,* meaning "to move 　away or beyond.")
peace, piece	Countries at **peace** are good places to live. 　(***Peace*** means "free from war.") The quilt maker cut the old sheet into square **pieces**. 　(A ***piece*** is a part of something.)
personal, personnel	The wrong person could read a **personal** e-mail message. 　(***Personal*** [pér-sŏn-al] means "private.") **Personnel** in one department must work well together. 　(***Personnel*** [per-son-él] are people working at a job.)
plain, plane	The Serengeti **Plain** is a large area of land in Tanzania. 　(***Plain*** means "level area", "undecorated", or "clearly seen.") The carpenter used a **plane** to finish the tabletop. 　(***Plane*** means "flat and even" or "the tool used to smooth 　wood." It may also be a short form of the word "airplane.")
pore, pour, poor	You sweat through your **pores**. 　(A ***pore*** is an opening in the skin.) If you get too hot, **pour** a glass of lemonade to drink. 　(***Pour*** means "to cause to flow.") My **poor** grades got me in hot water (trouble). 　(***Poor*** means "low or needy quality.")

principal, principle	Our **principal** came to this country from Haiti. (The noun **principal** is a school administrator or a sum of money.) Sugarcane is one of Haiti's **principal** crops. (The adjective **principal** means "most important.") A good **principle** is "respect others if you want respect." (A **principle** is an idea or a belief.)
quiet, quit, quite	Libraries are **quiet** places for people to read. (**Quiet** is the opposite of *noisy*.) Everyone must agree to **quit** talking. (**Quit** means "to stop.") It is **quite** strange to hear only whispers. (**Quite** means "completely or rather.")
raise, rays, raze	Anna would **raise** her hand in class. (**Raise** means "to lift or elevate.") Sun **rays** streamed through the window. (**Rays** are thin lines or beams.) The school board voted to **raze** the old building. (**Raze** means "to tear down completely.")
read, red	I **read** bedtime stories to my younger sister. (**Read** [rĕd] is the past tense of the verb *read* [rēd].) The folktale was about a **red** fox and a black bear. (**Red** is a color.)
right, write, rite	The man wrote his son's name on the **right** line. (**Right** means "correct or proper.") Then he had to **write** his birthplace. (**Write** means "to record in print.") The child was ready for the **rite** of christening. (A **rite** is a ritual or ceremony.)
road, rode, rowed	The **road** crossed Tampa Bay. (A **road** is a highway.) I **rode** across the bay on Skyway Bridge. (**Rode** is the past tense of the verb *ride*.) Some fishermen **rowed** their boats under the bridge. (**Rowed** means "to move a boat with oars.")

scene,
seen
	Yellow ribbons marked the **scene** of the accident.
	    (***Scene*** refers to the place something happens.)
	Graham had **seen** the two trucks collide.
	    (***Seen*** is part of the verb *see*.)

sea, see	A **sea** has salty water.
	    (A ***sea*** is a body of saltwater, smaller than an ocean.)
	I would like to **see** the Blue Nile and the Yellow Sea.
	    (***See*** means "to detect with the eye or to understand.")

seam,
seem
	The **seam** next to the zipper is ripped.
	    (A ***seam*** is a line made by joining two pieces of material.)
	Now my coat does not **seem** as warm.
	    (***Seem*** means "to appear to exist.")

sew, so,
sow
	I had to **sew** a button on my shirt.
	    (***Sew*** is a verb meaning "to stitch.")
	The weather was warm, **so** I worked in the garden.
	    (***So*** is a connecting word.)
	I wanted to **sow** flower and vegetable seeds.
	    (***Sow*** means "to plant.")

sight,
cite,
site
	Jose lost her **sight** in one eye.
	    (***Sight*** is the ability to see.)
	A filmmaker wanted to **cite** Jose's
	story in a documentary.
	    (***Cite*** means "to quote or refer to.")
	Jose visited the filming **site**.
	    (***Site*** means "location or position.")

sit, set	Some people on the subway get to **sit** down.
	    (***Sit*** means "to put the body in a seated position.")
	Others can't even **set** their briefcases down.
	    (***Set*** means "to place.")

some, sum	We needed **some** groceries.
	    (***Some*** means "an uncertain number or part.")
	The **sum** total at the checkout was $35.78.
	    (***Sum*** means "the whole amount.")

son, sun	My **son** studies the solar system. 　(A **son** is a male child.) He is fascinated by the dark spots on the **sun**. 　(The **sun** is the center of the earth's solar system.)
sore, soar	Julia's arms were **sore** after a day of hang gliding. 　(**Sore** means "painful.") What a thrill to **soar** over the sand dunes. 　(**Soar** means "to fly or rise high into the air.")
stationery, stationary	I write letters on purple **stationery**. 　(**Stationery** is paper and envelopes for letters.) A **stationary** bike lets you pedal fast but go nowhere. 　(**Stationary** means "not movable.")
steal, steel	To **steal** something from a store is called shoplifting. 　(**Steal** means "to take something without permission.") **Steel** beams form the skeletons of tall buildings. 　(**Steel** is a very strong metal.)
tail, tale	The kangaroo uses its **tail** for balance. 　(**Tail** refers to the rear part.) A tall **tale** is an exaggerated story. 　(**Tale** refers to a story.)
than, then	I'm two months older **than** you are. 　(**Than** is used in a comparison.) **Then** we'll both be 13. 　(**Then** tells when.)
their, they're, there	**Their** passports were packed in the carry-on bags. 　(**Their** shows ownership.) **They're** showing the passports to some officials. 　(**They're** is a contraction for "they are.") **There** is the line for checking through customs. 　(**There** tells where.)
threw, through	Jakub **threw** his coat in his locker. 　(**Threw** is the past tense of the verb *throw.*) He rushed **through** the door as the bell rang. 　(**Through** means "passing from one side to the other.")

to, too, two	Patrice tossed the ball **to** Guerdy.
	    (**To** is a preposition that can mean "in the direction of.")
	Marisa was **too** tired to guard Guerdy.
	    (**Too** is an adverb meaning "very." It can mean "also.")
	Guerdy easily scored **two** points.
	    (**Two** is a number.)

vain, vane, vein	You may be **vain** if you are always looking in a mirror.
	    (**Vain** means "thinking too highly of one's self." It can also
	    mean "worthless.")
	The weather **vane** was shaped like a horse.
	    (A **vane** is a flat piece of material set up to show which way
	    the wind is blowing.)
	A blood clot in the **vein** of his leg caused great pain.
	    (**Vein** refers to a blood vessel. It can also refer to a mineral
	    deposit.)

very, vary	Yvenson's story of what happened was the **very** opposite of
	Mackendy's. *(adjective)*
	It was **very** funny. *(adverb)*
	    (**Very** can be an adjective meaning "complete" or an adverb
	    meaning "extremely.")
	The details would **vary** each time they told their stories.
	    (**Vary** is a verb meaning "to change.")

waist, waste	My dad has a 36-inch **waist**.
	    (A **waist** is the part of the body just above the hips.)
	He thinks I look like I am going to **waste** away.
	    (The verb **waste** means "to shrink"; the noun **waste** refers to
	    useless material.)

wait, weight	I have to **wait** for my dad.
	    (**Wait** means "to stay somewhere expecting something.")
	Then we'll lift **weights** at the health center.
	    (A **weight** is a heavy object.
	    Weight is also a measure
	    of heaviness.)

weak, week	Max was still feeling **weak**.
	    (**Weak** means "not strong.")
	He had the flu for a **week**.
	    (A **week** is a period of seven days.)

wear, where	Sports teams **wear** uniforms.
	(**Wear** means "to have on or to carry on one's body.")
	Then players can see **where** their teammates are.
	(**Where** asks the question "in what place or situation?")
weather, whether	Heather likes cool, rainy **weather**.
	(**Weather** refers to the condition of the atmosphere.)
	Whether it's sunny or rainy, hot or cold, I enjoy the day.
	(**Whether** refers to a possibility.)
which, witch	**Which** book should I read next?
	(**Which** means "what one or ones out of a group.")
	You'd like *The Lion, the **Witch**, and the Wardrobe*.
	(A **witch** is someone using supernatural powers.)
who, which, that	The woman **who** called was a telemarketer.
	(**Who** refers to people.)
	The product, **which** was a credit card, was for my mom.
	(**Which** refers to nonliving objects or animals.)
	The phone call **that** I was waiting for came later.
	(**That** may refer to animals, people, or nonliving objects.)
who, whom	**Who** ordered this pizza?
	(**Who** is used as the subject in a sentence.)
	The pizza was ordered by **whom**?
	(**Whom** is used as the object of a preposition or as a direct object.)
who's, whose	**Who's** going hiking?
	(**Who's** is the contraction for "who is.")
	Whose backpack is this?
	(**Whose** shows or asks about possession.)
wood, would	Some baseball bats are made of **wood**.
	(**Wood** is the material that trees are made of.)
	Would you like to play baseball on Saturday?
	(**Would** is part of the verb *will*.)
your, you're	Sefton, you may pick up **your** first draft after class.
	(**Your** shows possession.)
	You're writing a very funny essay!
	(**You're** is the contraction for "you are.")

Understanding Idioms

Idioms are phrases that are used in a special way. An idiom can't be understood just by knowing the meaning of each word in the phrase. It must be learned as a whole. For example, the idiom *to bury the hatchet* means "to settle an argument," even though the individual words in the phrase mean something much different. This chapter will help you learn about some of the common idioms in American English.

a bad apple	One troublemaker on a team may be called **a bad apple**. *(a bad influence)*
an axe to grind	Mom has **an axe to grind** with the owners of the dog that dug up her flower garden. *(a problem to settle)*
apple of his eye	Daniel said that Moni is the **apple of his eye**. *(someone he likes very much)*
as plain as day	It was **as plain as day** that you didn't want to talk to me. *(very clear)*
as the crow flies	She lives only two miles from here **as the crow flies**. *(in a straight line)*
at a snail's pace	Rush-hour traffic moves **at a snail's pace**. *(very, very slowly)*
beat around the bush	Dad said, "Where were you? Don't **beat around the bush**." *(avoid getting to the point)*
benefit of the doubt	Ms. Hy gave Henri the **benefit of the doubt** when he explained why he fell asleep in class. *(another chance)*
beyond the shadow of a doubt	Salvatore won the 50-yard dash **beyond the shadow of a doubt**. *(for certain)*
blew my top	When my money got stolen, I **blew my top**. *(showed great anger)*

bone to pick	Nick had a **bone to pick** with Adrian when he learned they both liked the same girl. *(problem to settle)*
break the ice	Shanta was the first to **break the ice** in the room full of new students. *(start a conversation)*
burn the midnight oil	Carmen had to **burn the midnight oil** the day before the big test. *(work late into the night)*
bury the hatchet	Yung and Vu were told to **bury the hatchet** and start cooperating. *(settle an argument)*
champing at the bit	Dwayne was **champing at the bit** when it was his turn to bat. *(eager, excited)*
chicken feed	This plastic watch is **chicken feed** compared to my gold one. *(not worth much money)*
chip off the old block	Denise laughs like her dad. She is a **chip off the old block**. *(just like someone else)*
clean as a whistle	The kitchen was **clean as a whistle** before I made pancakes. *(very clean)*
cold shoulder	Alicia always gives me the **cold shoulder** after our disagreements. *(ignores me)*
crack of dawn	We got up at the **crack of dawn** to go fishing. *(first light of day, early morning)*
cry wolf	If you **cry wolf** too often, no one will come when you really need help. *(say you are in trouble when you aren't)*
dead of night	Jon woke up in the **dead of night** when the fire alarm went off. *(middle of the night)*
dirt cheap	This jacket was **dirt cheap** at the flea market. *(inexpensive, costing very little money)*
doesn't hold a candle to	This story **doesn't hold a candle to** the story that won the prize. *(is not as good as)*
drop in the bucket	My donation was a **drop in the bucket**. *(a small amount compared to what's needed)*

everything from A to Z	The folk festival had **everything from A to Z**. *(a lot of different things)*
face the music	José had to **face the music** when he got caught cheating on the test. *(deal with the punishment)*
fish out of water	Kendra felt like a **fish out of water** when she got off the plane in New York City. *(someone in an unfamiliar place)*
fit for a king	The food at the wedding reception was **fit for a king**. *(very special)*
flew off the handle	Tramayne **flew off the handle** when he saw his little brother playing with matches. *(became very angry)*
floating on air	Teresa was **floating on air** when she read the letter. *(feeling very happy)*
food for thought	The coach gave us some **food for thought** when she said that winning isn't everything. *(something to think about)*
get down to business	In five minutes you need to **get down to business** on this assignment. *(start working)*
get the upper hand	The other team will **get the upper hand** if we don't play better in the second half. *(win)*
give their all	The baseball players will **give their all** in the game. *(work as hard as they can)*
go fly a kite	Kendashia told her little brothers to **go fly a kite** when her friend came over. *(go away)*
have a green thumb	Mr. Nelson must **have a green thumb** because his garden looks so good. *(be good at growing plants)*
hit the ceiling	Rosa **hit the ceiling** when she saw her sister painting the television. *(was very angry)*

hit the hay	Patrice **hit the hay** early because she was tired. *(went to bed)*
in a nutshell	**In a nutshell**, Coach Roby told us to play our best. *(to summarize)*
in one ear and out the other	When Ms. Trent was talking, Jason let her directions go **in one ear and out the other**. *(without really listening)*
in the nick of time	Zong grabbed his little brother's hand **in the nick of time** before he touched the hot pan. *(just in time)*
in the same boat	My friend and I are **in the same boat** when it comes to doing Saturday chores. *(have the same problem)*
iron out	Jamil and his brother were told to **iron out** their differences about cleaning their room. *(solve, work out)*
it goes without saying	**It goes without saying** that if you study, you should be able to pass the test. *(it is clear)*
it stands to reason	**It stands to reason** that if you keep lifting weights, you will get stronger. *(it makes sense)*
keep a stiff upper lip	Remember to **keep a stiff upper lip** when you are sent to the principal's office. *(be brave)*
keep it under your hat	Mario said, "**Keep it under your hat** about Andrea's surprise party." *(don't tell anyone)*
knock on wood	Maha **knocked on wood** after saying that the test was easy. *(did something for good luck)*
knuckle down	Grandpa told me to **knuckle down** at school if I want to be a doctor. *(work hard)*
learn the ropes	Being new in school, I knew it would take some time to **learn the ropes**. *(get to know how things are done)*

leave no stone unturned	Ahmad said he would **leave no stone unturned** in looking for his ring. *(check everything)*
let's face it	"**Let's face it!**" said Mr. Sills. "You're a better long-distance runner than a sprinter." *(let's admit it)*
let the cat out of the bag	Tia **let the cat out of the bag** and got her sister in trouble. *(told a secret)*
look high and low	Grandmother told me to **look high and low** for her lost scissors. *(look everywhere)*
lose face	If I strike out again, I will **lose face**. *(be embarrassed)*
needle in a haystack	Looking for a contact lens in the grass is like trying to find a **needle in a haystack**. *(something impossible to find)*
nose to the grindstone	If I keep my **nose to the grindstone**, I will finish my homework in one hour. *(working hard)*
on cloud nine	Walking home from the party, I was **on cloud nine**. *(feeling very happy)*
on pins and needles	I was **on pins and needles** as I waited to see the doctor. *(feeling nervous)*
over and above	**Over and above** the assigned reading, I read two library books. *(in addition to)*
pain in the neck	My talkative little brother is a **pain in the neck** when I'm trying to study. *(very annoying)*
pull your leg	Don't believe everything Adnan tells you; he loves to **pull your leg**. *(tell someone a little lie as a joke)*
put his foot in his mouth	Chivas **put his foot in his mouth** when he called his teacher by the wrong name. *(said something embarrassing)*

put the cart before the horse	Sasha **put the cart before the horse** when she mailed the letter before putting on a stamp. *(did something in the wrong order)*
put your best foot forward	Grandpa said that whenever you do something, you should **put your best foot forward**. *(do the best that you can do)*
red-letter day	Amanda had a **red-letter day** because she made a new friend. *(an especially good day)*
rock the boat	The coach said, "Don't **rock the boat** if you want to stay on this team." *(cause trouble)*
rude awakening	I had a **rude awakening** when I saw the letter *F* at the top of my Spanish quiz. *(sudden, unpleasant surprise)*
save face	Grant tried to **save face** when he said he was sorry for making fun of me in class. *(fix an embarrassing situation)*
see eye to eye	My sister and I finally **see eye to eye** about who gets to use the phone first after school. *(are in agreement)*
shake a leg	I told Marisa to **shake a leg** or we would be late for dance lessons. *(hurry)*
shift into high gear	Eric had to **shift into high gear** to finish his assignment before class. *(speed up, hurry)*
sight unseen	Grandma bought the television **sight unseen**. *(without seeing it first)*
sink or swim	I will either **sink or swim** on the math test. *(fail or succeed)*
spring chicken	My aunt said that I was a **spring chicken** compared to her. *(a young person)*
stick to your guns	The principal said, "**Stick to your guns!** If you know it's wrong, don't do it." *(don't change your mind)*

sweet tooth	Dad says Grandma has a **sweet tooth**. *(has a love for sweets, likes candy and cake)*
take a dim view	My brother will **take a dim view** if I don't help him at the store. *(disapprove)*
take it with a grain of salt	If my sister tells you she has no homework, **take it with a grain of salt**. *(don't believe everything you're told)*
take the bull by the horns	This team needs to **take the bull by the horns** to win the game. *(take control)*
through thick and thin	Max and I will be friends **through thick and thin**. *(in good times and in bad times)*
time flies	When you are having fun, **time flies**. *(time passes quickly)*
time to kill	We had **time to kill** before the ballpark gates would open. *(extra time)*
to go overboard	The teacher told us not **to go overboard** with fancy lettering on our posters. *(to do too much)*
toe the line	The coach said that if we didn't **toe the line**, she would ask us to leave. *(follow the rules)*
turn over a new leaf	Starting at a new school may seem scary, but it can be a chance to **turn over a new leaf**. *(make a new start)*
two peas in a pod	My twin sister and I are like **two peas in a pod**. *(very much alike)*
under the weather	I was feeling **under the weather**, so I didn't go to school. *(sick)*
word of mouth	We found out who the new teacher was by **word of mouth**. *(talking to other people)*

Understanding Sentences

A **sentence** is made up of one or more words that express a complete thought. A sentence begins with a capital letter. It ends with a period, a question mark, or an exclamation point.

> **Greece held the first Olympics.**
> **What was the first event?**
> **It was a simple footrace!**

 For more information, turn to "Writing Basic Sentences" in your handbook, pages 65-72.

PARTS OF A SENTENCE

Subject and Predicate	A sentence must have a subject and predicate (verb) in order to express a complete thought. The subject, the predicate, or both may be unstated, but they must be clearly understood.

I want more information.
(In this sentence, *I* is the subject, and *want* is the verb.)

Listen to this!
(This sentence is missing a subject. *You* is the understood subject.)

Who likes the Olympics? Everyone.
(In the second sentence, *everyone* is the subject, but there is no predicate. *Does* is the understood predicate.)

What does everyone like about the Olympics? The action.
(In the second sentence, both the subject and the predicate are missing. *Everyone* is the understood subject, and *likes* is the understood predicate.)

Other Parts	A sentence may also contain other parts, including modifying words, phrases, and clauses. You can learn about these parts, starting on page 404.

Subject

	A **subject** is the part of a sentence that does something or is talked about. **Salt Lake City** hosted the 2002 Winter Olympics.
Simple Subject	The simple subject is the subject without the words that describe or modify it. The first women's bobsled **races** were held.
Complete Subject	The complete subject is the simple subject and all the words that describe it. **The first women's bobsled races** were held.
Compound Subject	A compound subject has two or more simple subjects. **Sarah Hughes** and **Michelle Kwan** won medals in ice skating in 2002.

Predicate

	A **predicate** (verb) is the part of the sentence that says something about the subject. All Olympic athletes **practice.**
Simple Predicate	The simple predicate is the predicate (verb) without the words that modify or complete it. The first stadium **held** 40,000 people.
Complete Predicate	The complete predicate is the simple predicate with all the words that modify or complete it. The first stadium **held 40,000 people.**
Compound Predicate	A compound predicate has two or more simple predicates, or verbs. Only men **ran** and **jumped** in the Olympics.

Modifiers

A **modifier** is a word or a group of words that describes another word.

> **The early Olympics held chariot races.**
> (*The* and *early* modify *Olympics,* and *chariot* modifies *races.*)

> **People slowly added more events.**
> (*Slowly* modifies *added,* and *more* modifies *events.*)

Clauses

A **clause** is a group of words that has a subject and a predicate.

> **the Greeks included wrestling as an Olympic sport** (*Greeks* is the subject and *included* is the predicate in this clause.)

> **before they added boxing** (*They* is the subject and *added* is the predicate in this clause.)

Independent Clauses

An independent clause expresses a complete thought and can stand alone as a sentence.

> **The Greeks included wrestling as an Olympic sport.**

Dependent Clauses

A dependent clause does *not* express a complete thought and cannot stand alone as a sentence. Dependent clauses usually begin with a subordinating conjunction like *before.* (See page 433.)

> **before they added boxing**

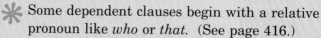 Some dependent clauses begin with a relative pronoun like *who* or *that.* (See page 416.)

A **dependent clause** plus an **independent clause** forms a complex sentence:

> **The Greeks included wrestling as an Olympic sport before they added boxing.**

Phrases

A **phrase** is a group of related words that, unlike a clause, does not have a subject and a predicate. Phrases do not express complete thoughts, so they are not sentences.

the Olympics (This is a noun phrase.)

began in Greece (This is a verb phrase.)

about 3,000 years ago (This is a prepositional phrase. See page 432.)

* If you put these phrases together, they would form a complete sentence:

The Olympics began in Greece about 3,000 years ago.

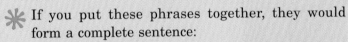

BASIC PHRASES

Phrases are named by how they are used in a sentence.

Noun Phrase:	the Olympics
Verb Phrase:	began in Greece
Prepositional Phrase:	about 3,000 years ago

Special Verbal Phrases

A **verbal phrase** is a group of words introduced by a *verbal* (a verb used as another part of speech). There are three types of verbals: *gerunds, participles,* and *infinitives.* (See page 425.)

Running long distances has always been a part of the Olympics.
(*Running long distances* is a gerund phrase, and it serves as the subject of the sentence.)

Starting as a national festival, the Olympics has grown into a huge international event.
(*Starting as a national festival* is a participial phrase modifying the noun *Olympics.*)

The festival was held to honor Zeus.
(*To honor Zeus* is an infinitive phrase, and it serves as an adverb modifying *was held.*)

TYPES OF SENTENCES

Simple Sentences

A simple sentence includes only one independent clause (and states only one complete thought). The subject may be simple or compound. The predicate may also be simple or compound.

> **The ancient Olympics had many heroes.**
> (simple subject, simple predicate)

> **A wrestling champion caught a bull and carried it around the stadium.**
> (simple subject, compound predicate)

> **Boxing and wrestling were combined in one event.** (compound subject, simple predicate)

Compound Sentences

A compound sentence is made up of two or more simple sentences (also called independent clauses). The two sentences are joined by a coordinating conjunction, punctuation, or both. (Coordinating conjunctions include words like *and, but,* and *or.* See page 433.)

> **The Olympics stopped in 394 C.E., and they did not start again for more than 1,500 years.**
> (The conjunction *and* connects two independent clauses.)

> **The first modern Olympics were held in 1896, but women didn't compete until 1900.**
> (The conjunction *but* connects two independent clauses.)

Complex Sentences

A complex sentence contains one independent clause (in boldface) and one or more dependent clauses (in red). Dependent clauses begin with a subordinating conjunction like *when* or a relative pronoun like *who* or *that.*

> **There were no Olympic Games** when World Wars I and II were fought.

KINDS OF SENTENCES

Declarative Sentences	Declarative sentences make statements. They tell something about a person, a place, a thing, or an idea. **The Winter Games include many sports.** **Figure skating is my favorite event.**
Interrogative Sentences	Interrogative sentences ask questions. **Is hockey a sport in the Winter Games?**
Tag Questions	Tag questions are questions that are tagged, or added, to the end of statements. The main verb in the statement is either positive *(was)* or negative *(wasn't)*. The verb in the "tag" is always the opposite of the main verb.

Tag question: **That was a great hockey game, wasn't it?**

Answer: **Yes, it was.**
(or) **No, it wasn't.**

Tag question: **That last goal didn't count, did it?**

Answer: **Yes, it did.**
(or) **No, it didn't.**

Imperative Sentences	Imperative sentences give commands. They often contain an understood subject *(you)*. **Think about all of the Olympic athletes in history.** **Check out this list of champions.**
Exclamatory Sentences	Exclamatory sentences communicate strong emotion or surprise. **It would be awesome to be in the Olympics!** **I would love to win a gold medal!**

The Parts of Speech

In the English language there are eight parts of speech. They help you understand words and how to use them in sentences. Every word in every sentence is a part of speech—a noun, a verb, an adjective, etc. The chart below lists the eight parts of speech.

Nouns	Words that name people, places, things, or ideas **Christina Sung Somalia basket bravery**
Pronouns	Words used in place of nouns **he she it they you anyone several**
Verbs	Words that show action or link a subject to another word in the sentence **shout throw collect is are**
Adjectives	Words that describe nouns or pronouns **rainy green smooth twelve wonderful**
Adverbs	Words that describe verbs, adjectives, and other adverbs **slowly yesterday now bravely louder**
Interjections	Words (set off by commas or exclamation points) that show strong emotions **Stop! Hey,** how are you? **For goodness sakes,** let's get going!
Prepositions	Words that show position or direction and introduce prepositional phrases **about up inside upon between to**
Conjunctions	Words that connect other words or groups of words **and but or so because when**

NOUNS

A **noun** is a word that names a person, a place, a thing, or an idea.

PERSON:	Jackie Robinson	ballplayer
PLACE:	Pakistan	country
THING:	*Hatchet*	book
IDEA:	Labor Day	holiday

Sometimes an article—*a, an,* or *the*—comes before a noun.

a book   an orange   the class

A possessive pronoun can also come before a noun.

his question   her answer

Kinds of Nouns

Common Nouns

A common noun is any noun that does not name a specific person, place, thing, or idea. Common nouns are not capitalized.

girl   city   game   school

Proper Nouns

A proper noun names a specific person, place, thing, or idea. Proper nouns are capitalized.

Jose   Seoul   Nintendo   Cooper School

Concrete Nouns

A concrete noun names a thing that can be seen or touched. Concrete nouns are either common or proper.

water	**team**	**monument**
Red Sea	**Chicago Bulls**	**Statue of Liberty**

Abstract Nouns

An abstract noun names something that you can think about but cannot see or touch. Abstract nouns can be either common or proper.

faith	**sadness**	**democracy**
Islam	**Buddhism**	**Christianity**

Number of Nouns

Singular or Plural	The **number** of a noun tells you whether the noun refers to one thing *(singular)* or more than one thing *(plural)*.
Singular Nouns	A singular noun names one person, place, thing, or idea. **baby gym orange child**
Plural Nouns	A plural noun names more than one person, place, thing, or idea. **babies gyms oranges children** ✳ (See page 369 for spelling of irregular plurals like *children*.)

Special Types of Nouns

Compound Nouns	A compound noun is made up of two or more words. **busboy** (written as one word) **blue jeans** (written as two words) **two-wheeler** (written as a hyphenated word)
Collective Nouns	A collective noun names a collection of persons, animals, places, or things. **PERSONS** **class team clan group family** **ANIMALS** **herd flock litter pack colony** **PLACES** **United States Andes Mountains** **THINGS** **collection bunch batch**
Specific Nouns	Specific nouns make your writing come alive. ✳ See page 110 in "The Art of Writing."

Count and Noncount Nouns

Count Nouns	Count nouns are nouns that can have *a, an,* or *one* in front of them.

SINGULAR

a shoe an example one nurse

To make the plural of most count nouns, add *s* or *es* to the noun.

PLURAL

two shoes a few examples some nurses

Noncount Nouns	Noncount nouns can have neither *a, an,* or *one* nor a number word (*one, two, three,* etc.) in front of them. They have no plural form.

sugar furniture luck happiness

* Some nouns can be count or noncount.

hair light paper chicken

Noncount Weather Nouns	Many weather terms are noncount nouns.

sleet drizzle thunder
snow dew lightning

Noncount Abstract Nouns	Many abstract nouns are noncount nouns. (Abstract nouns name ideas rather than people, places, or things.

education health fun coverage

Incorrect: I have a lot of funs.
Correct: I have a lot of fun.

Noncount Collective Nouns	The name of a whole category or group may be a noncount noun. But the parts of the category may be count nouns.

CATEGORY	PARTS	
homework	assignment	report
furniture	bed table	chair
money	quarter	dollar

Gender of Nouns

Nouns have **gender.** They are feminine (*female*), masculine (*male*), neuter (*neither male nor female*), or indefinite (*male or female*).

<u>FEMININE</u> (female)

cow   hen   mother   hostess   women

<u>MASCULINE</u> (male)

bull   rooster   uncle   brother   men

<u>NEUTER</u> (neither male nor female)

tree   cobweb   closet

<u>INDEFINITE</u> (male or female)

child   pilot   dentist   parent

Uses of Nouns

Subject Nouns

A noun may be the subject of a sentence. The subject is the part of the sentence that does something or is being talked about.

Puerto Rico has beautiful weather.

Predicate Nouns (Nominatives)

A predicate noun follows a form of the *be* verb (*is, are, was, were,* etc.) and renames the subject.

Puerto Ricans are U.S. citizens.
(*Citizens* is a predicate noun because it renames *Puerto Ricans.*)

Possessive Nouns

A possessive noun shows ownership. An apostrophe is used with possessive nouns.

Puerto Rico's main language is Spanish.

Object Nouns

An object noun is used as a direct object, an indirect object, or the object of a preposition.

Puerto Rico means "rich port" in Spanish.
("*Rich port*" is the direct object. *Spanish* is the object of the preposition *in.*)

PRONOUNS

A **pronoun** is a word that is used in place of a noun.

Thomas Jefferson lived on his family farm.
(The pronoun *his* is used in place of the noun *Thomas Jefferson's.*)

Antecedents

An antecedent is the noun that a pronoun refers to or replaces. All pronouns have antecedents.

Thomas Jefferson was the third U.S. president. *He* wrote the Declaration of Independence. (*Thomas Jefferson* is the antecedent of the pronoun *he.*)

✳ Pronouns must agree with their antecedents in number and person.

Personal Pronouns

Personal pronouns are the most common pronouns. Here are some common personal pronouns: (See page 414 for a complete list.)

I   you   he   she   it   we   they   me   him   her

Number of Pronouns

Singular or Plural

Pronouns can be either singular or plural.

SINGULAR

I know where Jefferson was born.

I   me   you   he   she   him   her   it

PLURAL

Mr. Nelson told us in social studies class.

we   us   you   they   them

✳ The pronouns *you, your,* and *yours* may be singular or plural.

Person of Pronouns

First Person	A first-person pronoun is used in place of the name of the speaker. **I learned about Thomas Jefferson in school.** **We studied him in social studies.**
Second Person	A second-person pronoun is used to name the person or thing spoken to. **Tarik, did you read about Jefferson?** **Do you know about Jefferson's schooling?**
Third Person	A third-person pronoun is used to name the person or thing spoken about. **He learned Latin, Greek, and French.** **It was hard to learn a new alphabet.** **A Scottish minister taught him.**

Personal Pronouns

SINGULAR PRONOUNS

	Subject Pronouns	Possessive Pronouns	Object Pronouns
First Person	I	my, mine	me
Second Person	you	your, yours	you
Third Person	he, she, it	his, her, hers, its	him, her, it

PLURAL PRONOUNS

	Subject Pronouns	Possessive Pronouns	Object Pronouns
First Person	we	our, ours	us
Second Person	you	your, yours	you
Third Person	they	their, theirs	them

 My, your, our, its, and *their* always come before nouns and function as possessive adjectives. Other pronouns such as *his* or *her* may or may not come before nouns.

Uses of Pronouns

Subject Pronouns

A subject pronoun is used as the subject of a sentence.

> **Jefferson went to college in Virginia.**
> **He was only 16 at the time.**
>
> (The pronoun *he* is the subject of this sentence.)

A subject pronoun is also used after a form of the *be* verb (*am, is, are, was, were,* etc.). A subject pronoun in this position is called a predicate nominative.

> **Todd is one who loves to read about Jefferson.**
>
> (The pronoun *one* is a predicate nominative in this sentence.)

Possessive Pronouns

A possessive pronoun shows ownership. (See page 414.) An apostrophe is not used with a possessive pronoun.

> **Jefferson helped the colonies gain their independence.**
>
> **His powerful writing helped express the colonists' feelings.**
>
> **In its final form, the Declaration of Independence was a strong argument for freedom of the colonies.**

Object Pronouns

An object pronoun is used after an action verb or in a prepositional phrase.

> **Fighting in the Revolutionary War did not interest him.** (The pronoun *him* is a direct object.)
>
> **Jefferson felt some sympathy for the slaves, but he gave little help to them.** (The pronoun *them* is the object of the preposition *to.*)
>
> **Helping the citizens of Virginia gave him great pleasure.** (*Him* is an indirect object because it names the person *to whom* pleasure was given.)

Other Types of Pronouns

Reflexive Pronouns	A reflexive pronoun refers back to the subject of a sentence. **Thomas Jefferson and Benjamin Franklin devoted themselves to their country.**
Relative Pronouns	A relative pronoun connects a dependent clause to the independent clause. (See page 404.) **Thomas Jefferson, who was our third president, served two terms.**
Interrogative Pronouns	An interrogative pronoun asks a question. **Who knows the name of Jefferson's home?**
Indefinite Pronouns	An indefinite pronoun refers to people or things that are not named or known. **Someone should know the answer.**
Demonstrative Pronouns	A demonstrative pronoun points out a noun without naming the noun. **That is a hard question.**

TYPES OF PRONOUNS

Relative
who, whose, which, what, that, whoever, whatever, whichever

Reflexive
myself, himself, herself, itself, yourself, themselves, ourselves

Interrogative
who, whose, whom, which, what

Demonstrative
this, that, these, those

Indefinite Pronouns

all	both	everything	nobody	several
another	each	few	none	some
any	each one	many	no one	somebody
anybody	either	most	nothing	someone
anyone	everybody	much	one	something
anything	everyone	neither	other	such

VERBS

A **verb** shows action or links the subject to another word in the sentence. The verb is the main word in the predicate part of the sentence.

> **Harriet Tubman escaped from slavery.**
> (*Escaped* is an action verb.)
> **She was an African American.**
> (*Was* is a linking verb.)

Types of Verbs

Action Verbs	An action verb tells what the subject is doing. **Tubman lived in Maryland as a child.**
Linking Verbs	A linking verb links a subject to a noun or an adjective in the predicate part of the sentence. **Tubman became famous.** (The verb *became* links the adjective *famous* to the subject *Tubman*.) **LINKING VERBS** **is are was were am been being smell look taste feel appear seem become**
Helping Verbs	Helping verbs (also called auxiliary verbs) include *has, had,* and *have; do* and *did;* and forms of the verb "be" (*is, are, was, were,* etc.). See the chart below. **Tubman had married before she escaped.** (The verb *had* helps state a past action: *had married.*)

"BE" VERBS

Present		Past		Future	
singular	**plural**	**singular**	**plural**	**singular**	**plural**
I am	we are	I was	we were	I will be	we will be
you are	you are	you were	you were	you will be	you will be
he, she, it is	they are	he, she, it was	they were	he, she, it will be	they will be

Modal Verbs	Modal verbs help the main verb express meaning. (See the chart below.)
	Harriet Tubman could live in the woods. (The modal *could* helps express the meaning of the main verb *live*.)
	✳ Modals are sometimes grouped with helping or auxiliary verbs.

COMMON MODAL VERBS

Modal	Expresses	Sample Sentence
can	ability	I *can* program a VCR.
could	ability possibility	I *could* baby-sit Tuesday. He *could* be sick.
might	possibility	I *might* be early.
may	possibility request	I *may* sleep late Saturday. *May* I be excused?
must	strong need	I *must* study more.
have to	strong need	I *have to* (have got to) exercise.
ought to	feeling of duty	I *ought to* (should) help Dad.
shall	polite offer	*Shall* I stay longer?
will	intent	I *will* visit my grandma soon.
would	desire	I *would* like to travel by train.
would + you	polite request	*Would* you help me?
could + you	polite request	*Could* you type this letter?
will + you	polite request	*Will* you give me a ride?
can + you	polite request	*Can* you make supper tonight?

Tenses of Verbs

The time of a verb is called its **tense.** Tense is shown by endings *(talked)*, by helping verbs *(did talk)*, or by both *(have talked)*.

Present Tense	The present tense of a verb states an action that *is happening now* or that *happens regularly*. **Today, we honor Tubman's work.** **She serves as an inspiration for all of us.**
Past Tense	The past tense of a verb states an action that *happened at a specific time in the past.* **Ms. Tubman made 19 rescue trips.** **She even rescued her parents.**
Future Tense	The future tense of a verb states an action that *will take place.* **I will remember her story forever.**

Perfect Tenses

Present Perfect Tense	The present perfect tense states an action that *is still going on.* Add *has* or *have* before the past participle form of the main verb. **Stories about slavery have always interested me.**
Past Perfect Tense	The past perfect tense states an action that *began and was completed in the past.* Add *had* before the past participle form of the main verb. **She had served in the Civil War.**
Future Perfect Tense	The future perfect tense states an action that *will begin in the future and end at a specific time in the future.* Add *will have* before the past participle form of the main verb. **I will have studied for three hours.**

Continuous Tenses

Present Continuous Tense

The present continuous tense states an action that *is not finished at the time of stating it.* Here's how you form this tense:

the helping verb + the *ing* form
am, is, or *are* of the main verb

am **learning**

I am learning about the treatment of slaves.

Past Continuous Tense

The past continuous tense states an action that *was happening at a certain time in the past.* It can also refer to an event that *took place for a limited time.* Here's how you form this tense:

the helping verb + the *ing* form
was or *were* of the main verb

was **living**

Harriet Tubman was living in Maryland before she was freed.

Future Continuous Tense

The future continuous tense states an action that *will take place at a specific time in the future.* Here's how you form this tense:

will + the helping verb + the *ing* form
be of the main verb

will **be** **studying**

Next week, I will be studying more about slavery.

OR

phrase noting + the helping verb + the *ing* form
the future *be* of the main verb

am going to **be** **learning**

I am going to be learning about the beginnings of slavery.

Forms of Verbs

Singular and Plural Verbs	A singular verb is used when the subject in a sentence is singular.
	Tubman's life still interests many people. (The subject *life* and the verb *interests* are both singular.)
	A plural verb is used when the subject is plural.
	All people want their freedom. (The subject *people* and the verb *want* are both plural.)
Active and Passive Voice	A verb is active if the subject is doing the action.
	Tubman made many rescue trips. (The verb *made* is active because the subject *Tubman* is doing the action.)
	A verb is passive if the subject is not doing the action.
	Many rescue trips were made by Tubman. (The verb *were made* is passive because the subject *trips* is not doing the action.)
Regular Verbs	Most verbs in the English language are regular. You add *ed* to regular verbs when you state a past action or use *has, have,* or *had* with the verb.
	REGULAR VERBS
	I listen. Earlier I listened. I have listened.
	He talks. Earlier he talked. He has talked.
Irregular Verbs	Some verbs in the English language are irregular. Usually you do not add *ed* to an irregular verb when you state a past action or use *has, have,* or *had* with the verb. Instead of adding *ed*, the word changes. (See the chart on pages 422-423.)
	IRREGULAR VERBS
	I speak. Earlier I spoke. I have spoken.
	She runs. Earlier she ran. She has run.

COMMON IRREGULAR VERBS

The **principal parts** of the common irregular verbs are listed below. The part used with the helping verbs *has, have,* or *had* is called the **past participle.**

PRESENT TENSE	I write.
PAST TENSE	Earlier I wrote.
PAST PARTICIPLE	I have written.
PRESENT TENSE	She hides.
PAST TENSE	Earlier she hid.
PAST PARTICIPLE	She has hidden.

Present Tense	Past Tense	Past Participle	Present Tense	Past Tense	Past Participle
be (am, is, are)	was, were	been	drink	drank	drunk
begin	began	begun	drive	drove	driven
bite	bit	bitten	eat	ate	eaten
blow	blew	blown	fall	fell	fallen
break	broke	broken	feel	felt	felt
bring	brought	brought	fight	fought	fought
build	built	built	find	found	found
burst	burst	burst	fly	flew	flown
buy	bought	bought	freeze	froze	frozen
catch	caught	caught	get	got	got, gotten
choose	chose	chosen	give	gave	given
come	came	come	go	went	gone
cost	cost	cost	grow	grew	grown
cut	cut	cut	hang (suspend)	hung	hung
dive	dove, dived	dived	hide	hid	hidden
do	did	done	hit	hit	hit
draw	drew	drawn	hold	held	held

COMMON IRREGULAR VERBS

Present Tense	Past Tense	Past Participle	Present Tense	Past Tense	Past Participle
hurt	hurt	hurt	shrink	shrank	shrunk
keep	kept	kept	sing	sang	sung
know	knew	known	sink	sank	sunk
lay (place)	laid	laid	sit	sat	sat
lead	led	led	speak	spoke	spoken
leave	left	left	spend	spent	spent
lend	lent	lent	spin	spun	spun
let	let	let	spread	spread	spread
lie (recline)	lay	lain	spring	sprang	sprung
lose	lost	lost	stand	stood	stood
make	made	made	steal	stole	stolen
meet	met	met	swear	swore	sworn
pay	paid	paid	swim	swam	swum
put	put	put	swing	swung	swung
read	read	read	take	took	taken
ride	rode	ridden	teach	taught	taught
ring	rang	rung	tear	tore	torn
rise	rose	risen	tell	told	told
run	ran	run	think	thought	thought
say	said	said	throw	threw	thrown
see	saw	seen	wake	woke waked	woken waked
sell	sold	sold			
send	sent	sent	wear	wore	worn
set	set	set	weave	wove	woven
shake	shook	shaken	win	won	won
shine (light)	shone	shone	write	wrote	written

Uses of Action Verbs

Transitive Verbs	A verb is transitive if it is followed by an object *(noun or pronoun)*. The object makes the meaning of the verb complete. **After the Civil War, Harriet Tubman raised money for schools.** (Without the object *money,* the meaning of the transitive verb *raised* would be incomplete.) **She also started a home for elderly blacks.** (Without the object *home,* the meaning of the transitive verb *started* would be incomplete.)
Followed by a Direct Object	A direct object receives the action of a transitive verb. The direct object answers the question *what?* or *whom?* after the verb. **Tubman helped many poor people.** (The noun *people* is a direct object. It answers the question *helped whom?*) **In 1869, Sarah Bradford wrote a book about Harriet Tubman** (The noun *book* is a direct object. It answers the question *wrote what?*)
Followed by an Indirect Object	An indirect object receives the action of a transitive verb, indirectly. An indirect object names the person *to whom* or *for whom* something is done. In order for a sentence to have an indirect object, it must have a direct object. **Tubman offered many African Americans a new life.** (*African Americans* is an indirect object because it names the people *to whom* a new life was offered. *Life* is the direct object in the sentence.) **She gave runaways shelter.** (*Runaways* is an indirect object because it names the people *to whom* shelter was given. *Shelter* is the direct object in the sentence.)

More Uses of Action Verbs

Intransitive Verbs	An intransitive verb does not need an object to make its meaning complete. **Tubman died in 1913.** (*Died* is intransitive because there is no direct object following it. The date *1913* is the object of the preposition *in*.)
Special Verbs	Some verbs can be transitive or intransitive. **We read *Harriet Tubman* (a book title) by Earl Conrad.** (The direct object *Harriet Tubman* receives the action of the transitive verb *read*.) **We read in class.** (There is no direct object in this sentence, so the verb *read* is intransitive.)

Verbals

	Verbals are words that are made from verbs but are used as other parts of speech.
Gerund	A gerund is a verb form that ends in *ing* and is used as a noun. **Sleeping is fun.** (The gerund *sleeping* serves as the subject in this sentence.)
Participle	A participle is a verb form that ends in *ing* or *ed*. A participle is used as an adjective. **The sleeping student didn't hear the assignment.** (The participle *sleeping* modifies the noun *student*.)
Infinitive	An infinitive is a verb form introduced by the word *to*. It is used as a noun, an adjective, or an adverb. **She likes to sleep.** (The infinitive *to sleep*, a noun, serves as a direct object.)

COMMON TWO-WORD VERBS

This chart lists verbs in which two words work together to express a specific action.

break down . . . . to take apart or fall apart
call off . . . . cancel
call up . . . . make a phone call
clear out . . . . leave a place quickly
cross out . . . . draw a line through
do over . . . . repeat
figure out . . . . find a solution
fill in/out . . . . complete a form or an application
fill up . . . . fill a container or tank
find out . . . . discover
get in . . . . enter a vehicle
get out of . . . . leave a car, a house, or a situation
get over . . . . recover from a sickness or a problem
give back . . . . return something
give in/up . . . . surrender or quit
hand in . . . . give homework to a teacher
hand out . . . . give someone something
hang up . . . . put down a phone receiver
leave out . . . . omit or don't use
let in/out . . . . allow someone or something to enter or go out
look up . . . . find information
mix up . . . . confuse
pay back . . . . return money or a favor
pick out . . . . choose
point out . . . . call attention to
put away . . . . return something to its proper place
put down . . . . place something on a table, the floor, etc.
put off . . . . delay doing something
shut off . . . . turn off a machine or light
take part . . . . participate
talk over . . . . discuss
think over . . . . consider carefully
try on . . . . put on clothing to see if it fits
turn down . . . . lower the volume
turn up . . . . raise the volume
write down . . . . write on a piece of paper

✱ Don't divide a two-word verb in a sentence. For example, write "I *handed out* the papers," not "I *handed* the papers *out*."

ADJECTIVES

Adjectives are words that modify (describe) nouns or pronouns.

> **beautiful sky   new moon**

- Adjectives tell what kind, how many, or which one.

> **amazing universe   nine planets   that one**

- In English, adjectives usually come *before* the words they describe.

> **black holes   unsolved mysteries**

- In English, adjectives are never plural—even when the nouns they describe are plural.

> **red giants   old stars   distant galaxies**

Articles

The words *a, an,* and *the* are special adjectives called articles. The article *the* can come before any singular or plural word.

> **the sun   the meteors   the living earth**

The article *a* comes before singular words that begin with consonant sounds or before singular words that begin with the long *u* sound.

> **a yellow sunset   a shooting star
> a unique constellation**

The article *an* comes before singular words that begin with all vowel sounds except for long *u*.

> **an orbit   an unusual atmosphere**

Proper Adjectives

Proper adjectives are formed from proper nouns. Proper adjectives are always capitalized.

> **In 1610, an Italian scientist named Galileo studied the sun using a telescope.**

Common Adjectives

Common adjectives are any adjectives that are not proper. They are never capitalized.

> **Galileo was the first person to see dark spots on the sun.**

Special Kinds of Adjectives

Compound Adjectives	Compound adjectives are made up of more than one word. Some compound adjectives are spelled as one word; others are hyphenated. **Galileo saw new stars with his low-powered telescope. Galileo gained worldwide fame.**
Demonstrative Adjectives	Demonstrative adjectives point out specific nouns. For example, *this* and *these* point out nouns that are nearby, and *that* and *those* point out nouns that are distant. **This planet is closer to the sun than that planet.** **Those stars are farther away than these stars.** ✳ When *this, that, these,* and *those* do not come before nouns, they are pronouns, *not* adjectives.
Indefinite Adjectives	Indefinite adjectives tell *approximately* (not exactly) how many or how much. **Most stars live for many millions of years.** **Some stars are trillions of miles from Earth.** **Few people can imagine a distance that far.**
Predicate Adjectives	Predicate adjectives follow linking verbs and describe subjects. **The Milky Way galaxy is huge.** (*Huge* describes the subject *galaxy.* *Huge* follows the linking verb *is.*) **The Milky Way looks oval in the sky.** (*Oval* describes the subject *Milky Way.* *Oval* follows the linking verb *looks.*) **Part of the Milky Way appears far-off and milky looking.** (*Far-off* and *milky looking* describe the subject *Milky Way.* These two adjectives follow the linking verb *appears.*)

Forms of Adjectives

Positive Adjectives	The positive (base) form of an adjective describes a noun without comparing it to another noun. **The planet Uranus is large.** **The planet Uranus is interesting.**
Comparative Adjectives	The comparative form of an adjective compares two people, places, things, or ideas. **Saturn is larger than Uranus.** (The ending *er* is added to one-syllable adjectives.) **Saturn is more interesting than Uranus.** (The word *more* is usually added before adjectives with two or more syllables.)
Superlative Adjectives	The superlative form of an adjective compares three or more people, places, things, or ideas. **Jupiter is the largest planet of all.** (The ending *est* is added to one-syllable adjectives.) **Jupiter is the most interesting planet.** (The word *most* is usually added before adjectives with two or more syllables.)
Two-Syllable Adjectives	Some adjectives that are two syllables long show comparisons either by their *er/est* endings or by using the words *more* and *most*. **friendly friendlier friendliest** **friendly more friendly most friendly**

SPECIAL FORMS OF ADJECTIVES

Positive	Comparative	Superlative
good	better	best
bad	worse	worst
many	more	most
little	less	least

✳ Do not use *more* or *most* with forms of *good* and *bad*.

ADVERBS

Adverbs are words that modify (describe) verbs, adjectives, or other adverbs.

> **Our plane landed smoothly.**
> (*Smoothly* modifies the verb *landed.*)
> **We were extremely excited.**
> (*Extremely* modifies the adjective *excited.*)
> **We walked rather quickly.**
> (*Rather* modifies the adverb *quickly.*)

In English, adverbs can come before or after the words they modify.

> **My grandmother approached us slowly.**
> (*Slowly* modifies the verb *approached.*)
> **She softly said our names and smiled.**
> (*Softly* modifies the verb *said.*)

Types of Adverbs

Adverbs of Time	Adverbs of time tell *when, how often,* or *how long.* **We thought we would never see her again, even though we thought of her frequently.**
Adverbs of Place	Adverbs of place tell *where, to where,* or *from where.* **We walked outside to the car.** **We moved forward.**
Adverbs of Manner	Adverbs of manner tell *how* something is done. **Grandma drove slowly in the city.** **We eagerly asked her how to pronounce things in English.**
Adverbs of Degree	Adverbs of degree tell *how much* or *how little.* **We thoroughly enjoyed the day.**

Forms of Adverbs

Positive Adverbs	In the positive form, an adverb does not make a comparison. **My cousin runs fast.** **Grandmother speaks softly.**
Comparative Adverbs	The comparative is formed by adding *er* to one-syllable adverbs or the word *more* or *less* before longer adverbs. **My cousin runs faster than my brother.** **Grandmother speaks more softly than her daughter.**
Superlative Adverbs	The superlative is formed by adding *est* to one-syllable adverbs or the word *most* or *least* before longer adverbs. **My cousin runs fastest in games like soccer.** **Grandmother speaks most softly in a large group.**

SPECIAL FORMS OF ADVERBS

Positive	Comparative	Superlative
well	better	best
badly	worse	worst
quickly	more quickly	most quickly
fairly	less fairly	least fairly

Do not confuse *well* and *good*. (See page 384.)

INTERJECTIONS

Interjections are words or phrases that express strong emotions. Commas or exclamation marks are used to separate interjections from the rest of the sentence.

Hurry, you're going to miss the bus!
Ow! That's my toe you're stepping on.

PREPOSITIONS

Prepositions are words that show position or direction and introduce prepositional phrases.

The center of your brain is your body's warmest part. (The preposition *of* helps to show position and introduces the prepositional phrase *of your brain.*)

Prepositional Phrases

Prepositional phrases include a preposition, the object of the preposition (a noun or a pronoun), and any words that modify the object.

The coolest parts of your body are your fingers and toes. (*Of* is a preposition; *body* is the object of the preposition; and *your* is a modifier.)

Prepositional phrases are used as adjectives or adverbs.

Your lungs will float in water.
(The prepositional phrase *in water* is used as an adverb modifying *will float.*)

The top of the spine supports the skull.
(The prepositional phrase *of the spine* is used as an adjective modifying *top.*)

COMMON PREPOSITIONS

aboard	below	in	through
about	beneath	inside	throughout
above	beside	into	till
across	besides	like	to
across from	between	near	toward
after	beyond	of	under
against	but	off	underneath
along	by	on	until
along with	down	onto	up
among	during	out	up to
around	except	outside	upon
at	except for	over	with
before	for	past	within
behind	from	since	without

CONJUNCTIONS

Conjunctions connect individual words or groups of words. (See the chart below.)

Plants and animals are living things.

Are there more insects in deserts or in rain forests?

Kinds of Conjunctions

Coordinating Conjunctions	A coordinating conjunction connects equal parts: two or more words, phrases, or clauses. **Some living things produce food, and other living things consume food.** (The conjunction *and* connects two independent clauses to make a compound sentence.)
Correlative Conjunctions	A correlative conjunction is used in pairs. **Neither tree frogs nor alligators live in deserts.** (*Neither* and *nor* work as a pair in this sentence to connect two words.)
Subordinating Conjunctions	A subordinating conjunction introduces the dependent clause in a complex sentence. (See page 406.) **The desert climate is considered harsh because it is so hot and dry.**

COMMON CONJUNCTIONS

Coordinating	and, but, or, nor, for, so, yet
Correlative	either/or, neither/nor, not only/but also, both/and, whether/or, as/so
Subordinating	after, although, as, as if, as long as, as though, because, before, if, in order that, since, so, so that, though, unless, until, when, where, whereas, while

 Relative pronouns can also connect clauses. (See page 416.)

Student

Almanac

Language

Science

Mathematics

Computers

Geography

Government

History

Language

The language lists in this section of your handbook should be both interesting and helpful. You can look through this section when you want to work on your handwriting or study traffic signs, or when you need to send a "signed" message across a noisy room.

Manual Alphabet (Sign Language)

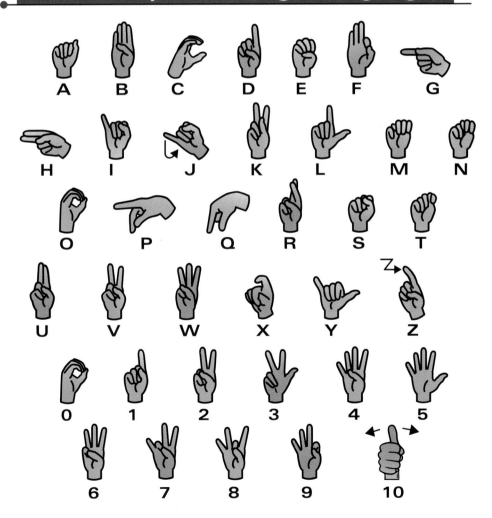

Language Families

Language families are groups of languages. Languages within a specific group are related because they all developed from the same language. English belongs to the **Indo-European** language family, as do many other languages. (See the chart below.)

The map shows all of the major language families plus the main languages in each family. (See the key on the next page.)

The Indo-European Family Today

Albanian		
Armenian		
Balto-Slavic	Bulgarian Czech Latvian Lithuanian Polish Russian Serbo-Croatian Slovenian Slovak Ukrainian	
Celtic	Breton Irish (Celtic) Scots (Celtic) Welsh	
Germanic	Dutch English German Scandinavian	Danish Icelandic Norwegian Swedish
Greek		
Indo-Iranian	Bengali Farsi Hindi Pashto Urdu	
Romance	French Italian Portuguese Romanian Spanish	

Major Language Families

	Indo-European		Malayo-Polynesian
	Sino-Tibetan		Mon-Khmer
	Afro-Asian		Niger-Kordofanian
	Uralic and Altaic		Nilo-Saharan
	Japanese and Korean		Khoisan
	Dravidian		All others

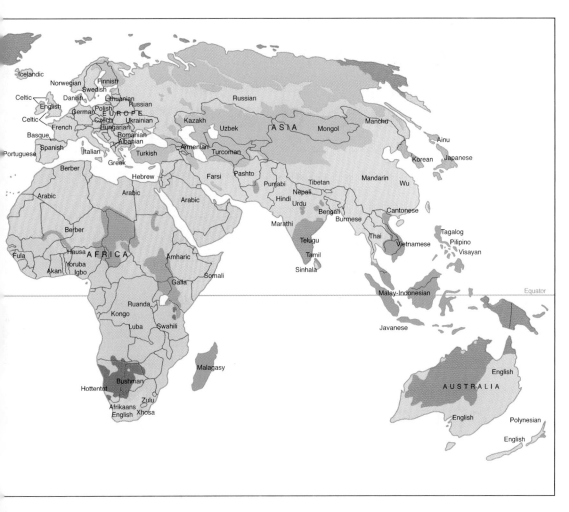

Manuscript Alphabet

A B C D E F G

H I J K L M N

O P Q R S T

U V W X Y Z

a b c d e f g

h i j k l m n

o p q r s t

u v w x y z

0 1 2 3 4 5 6 7 8 9

Cursive Alphabet

Aa Bb Cc Dd

Ee Ff Gg Hh

Ii Jj Kk Ll

Mm Nn Oo

Pp Qq Rr Ss

Tt Uu Vv

Ww Xx Yy Zz

Slanting Your Paper

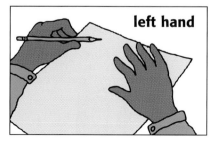

left hand

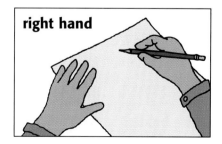

right hand

Traffic Signs

RED Regulatory Signs

These signs are red to get your attention: they tell you to do (or not do) something. The red circle and stripe tells you NO.

BLACK AND WHITE Informational Signs

Informational signs are black and white and shaped like a square or rectangle. They provide basic information for pedestrians and drivers.

YELLOW Warning Signs

Yellow in color, these signs warn of a possible danger. Many warning signs are in the shape of a diamond.

GREEN Directional or Guide Signs

These green signs give traffic directions or provide information on trail and bike routes.

BLUE Service Signs

These blue signs mean there are services nearby.

Science

The science facts that follow should be both interesting to use and helpful to have at your fingertips. "Animal Facts," "Periodic Table of the Elements," "The Metric System," and "Our Solar System" all hold useful information that may be expected of you in other classes at various times.

Animal Facts

Animal	Male	Female	Young	Group	Gestation (days)	Longevity (years)
Bear	He-bear	She-bear	Cub	Sleuth	180-240	18-20 (34)*
Cat	Tom	Queen	Kitten	Clutter/Clowder	52-65	10-17 (30)
Cattle	Bull	Cow	Calf	Drove/Herd	280	9-12 (25)
Chicken	Rooster	Hen	Chick	Brood/Flock	21	7-8 (14)
Deer	Buck	Doe	Fawn	Herd	180-250	10-15 (26)
Dog	Dog	Bitch	Pup	Pack/Kennel	55-70	10-12 (24)
Donkey	Jack	Jenny	Foal	Herd/Pace	340-385	18-20 (63)
Duck	Drake	Duck	Duckling	Brace/Herd	21-35	10 (15)
Elephant	Bull	Cow	Calf	Herd	515-760	30-60 (98)
Fox	Dog	Vixen	Cub/Kit	Skulk	51-60	8-10 (14)
Goat	Billy	Nanny	Kid	Tribe/Herd	135-163	12 (17)
Goose	Gander	Goose	Gosling	Flock/Gaggle	30	25-30
Horse	Stallion	Mare	Filly/Colt	Herd	304-419	20-30 (50+)
Lion	Lion	Lioness	Cub	Pride	105-111	10 (29)
Monkey	Male	Female	Boy/Girl	Band/Troop	149-179	12-15 (29)
Rabbit	Buck	Doe	Bunny	Nest/Warren	27-36	6-8 (15)
Sheep	Ram	Ewe	Lamb	Flock/Drove	121-180	10-15 (16)
Swan	Cob	Pen	Cygnet	Bevy/Flock	30	45-50
Swine	Boar	Sow	Piglet	Litter/Herd	101-130	10 (15)
Tiger	Tiger	Tigress	Cub		105	19
Whale	Bull	Cow	Calf	Gam/Pod/Herd	276-365	37
Wolf	Dog	Bitch	Pup	Pack	63	10-12 (16)

* ( ) Record for oldest animal of this type

Periodic Table of the Elements

Legend:
- Alkali metals
- Alkaline earth metals
- Transition metals
- Lanthanide series
- Actinide series
- Other metals
- Nonmetals
- Noble gases

Key:
- Atomic Number — 2
- Symbol — He
- Atomic Weight (or Mass Number of most stable isotope in parentheses) — 4.00260

(Of elements 110–121, some are still unknown, and some are recently claimed but unnamed. They have temporary systematic names.)

1a	2a	3b	4b	5b	6b	7b	8	8	8	1b	2b	3a	4a	5a	6a	7a	0
1 H Hydrogen 1.00797																	2 He Helium 4.00260
3 Li Lithium 6.941	4 Be Beryllium 9.0128											5 B Boron 10.811	6 C Carbon 12.01115	7 N Nitrogen 14.0067	8 O Oxygen 15.9994	9 F Fluorine 18.9984	10 Ne Neon 20.179
11 Na Sodium 22.9898	12 Mg Magnesium 24.305											13 Al Aluminum 26.9815	14 Si Silicon 28.0855	15 P Phosphorus 30.9738	16 S Sulfur 32.064	17 Cl Chlorine 35.453	18 Ar Argon 39.948
19 K Potassium 39.0983	20 Ca Calcium 40.08	21 Sc Scandium 44.9559	22 Ti Titanium 47.88	23 V Vanadium 50.94	24 Cr Chromium 51.996	25 Mn Manganese 54.9380	26 Fe Iron 55.847	27 Co Cobalt 58.9332	28 Ni Nickel 58.69	29 Cu Copper 63.546	30 Zn Zinc 65.39	31 Ga Gallium 69.72	32 Ge Germanium 72.59	33 As Arsenic 74.9216	34 Se Selenium 78.96	35 Br Bromine 79.904	36 Kr Krypton 83.80
37 Rb Rubidium 85.4678	38 Sr Strontium 87.62	39 Y Yttrium 88.905	40 Zr Zirconium 91.224	41 Nb Niobium 92.906	42 Mo Molybdenum 95.94	43 Tc Technetium (98)	44 Ru Ruthenium 101.07	45 Rh Rhodium 102.906	46 Pd Palladium 106.42	47 Ag Silver 107.868	48 Cd Cadmium 112.41	49 In Indium 114.82	50 Sn Tin 118.71	51 Sb Antimony 121.75	52 Te Tellurium 127.60	53 I Iodine 126.905	54 Xe Xenon 131.29
55 Cs Cesium 132.905	56 Ba Barium 137.33	57–71* Lanthanides	72 Hf Hafnium 178.49	73 Ta Tantalum 180.948	74 W Tungsten 183.85	75 Re Rhenium 186.207	76 Os Osmium 190.2	77 Ir Iridium 192.22	78 Pt Platinum 195.08	79 Au Gold 196.967	80 Hg Mercury 200.59	81 Tl Thallium 204.383	82 Pb Lead 207.19	83 Bi Bismuth 208.980	84 Po Polonium (209)	85 At Astatine (210)	86 Rn Radon (222)
87 Fr Francium (223)	88 Ra Radium 226.025	89–103** Actinides	104 Rf Rutherfordium (261)	105 Db Dubnium (262)	106 Sg Seaborgium (263)	107 Bh Bohrium (262)	108 Hs Hassium (265)	109 Mt Meitnerium (266)	110 (269)	111 (272)							

*Lanthanides

57 La Lanthanum 138.906	58 Ce Cerium 140.12	59 Pr Praseodymium 140.908	60 Nd Neodymium 144.24	61 Pm Promethium (145)	62 Sm Samarium 150.36	63 Eu Europium 151.96	64 Gd Gadolinium 157.25	65 Tb Terbium 158.925	66 Dy Dysprosium 162.50	67 Ho Holmium 164.950	68 Er Erbium 167.26	69 Tm Thulium 168.934	70 Yb Ytterbium 173.04	71 Lu Lutetium 174.967

**Actinides

89 Ac Actinium 227.028	90 Th Thorium 232.038	91 Pa Protactinium 231.036	92 U Uranium 238.029	93 Np Neptunium 237.048	94 Pu Plutonium (244)	95 Am Americium (243)	96 Cm Curium (247)	97 Bk Berkelium (247)	98 Cf Californium (251)	99 Es Einsteinium (252)	100 Fm Fermium (257)	101 Md Mendelevium (258)	102 No Nobelium (259)	103 Lr Lawrencium (260)

The Metric System

Even though the metric system is not the official system of measurement in the United States, it is used in science, medicine, and some other fields.

The metric system is a form of measurement based on the decimal system (units of 10), so there are no fractions. The table below lists the basic measurements in the metric system.

● LINEAR MEASURE (LENGTH OR DISTANCE)

1 centimeter	= 10 millimeters	=	0.3937 inch
1 decimeter	= 10 centimeters	=	3.937 inches
1 meter	= 10 decimeters	=	39.37 inches or 3.28 feet
1 dekameter	= 10 meters	=	393.7 inches
1 kilometer	= 1,000 meters	=	0.621 mile

● SQUARE MEASURE (AREA)

1 square centimeter	= 100 square millimeters	=	0.155 square inch
1 square decimeter	= 100 square centimeters	=	15.5 square inches
1 square meter	= 100 square decimeters	= 1,549.9 sq. inches or 1.196 sq. yards
1 square dekameter	= 100 square meters	=	119.6 square yards
1 square kilometer	= 100 square hectometers	=	0.386 square mile

● CAPACITY MEASURE

1 centiliter	= 10 milliliters	=	0.338 fluid ounce
1 deciliter	= 10 centiliters	=	3.38 fluid ounces
1 liter	= 10 deciliters	=	1.057 liquid qts. or 0.908 dry qt.
1 kiloliter	= 1,000 liters	=	264.18 gallons or 35.315 cubic feet

● LAND MEASURE

1 centare	= 1 square meter	=	1,549.9 square inches
1 hectare	= 100 ares	=	2.471 acres
1 square kilometer	= 100 hectares	=	0.386 square mile

● VOLUME MEASURE

1 cubic centimeter	= 1,000 cubic millimeters	=	0.061 cubic inch
1 cubic decimeter	= 1,000 cubic centimeters	=	61.023 cubic inches
1 cubic meter	= 1,000 cubic decimeters	=	35.314 cubic feet

● WEIGHTS

1 centigram	= 10 milligrams	=	0.1543 grain
1 decigram	= 10 centigrams	=	1.5432 grains
1 gram	= 10 decigrams	=	15.432 grains
1 dekagram	= 10 grams	=	0.3527 ounce
1 kilogram	= 1,000 grams	=	2.2046 pounds

American to Metric Table

The following table shows you what the most common U.S. measurements are in the metric system. You probably already know that 1 inch equals 2.54 centimeters. But, did you know that 1 gallon equals 3.7853 liters?

● LINEAR MEASURE (LENGTH OR DISTANCE)

1 inch		=	2.54 centimeters
1 foot	= 12 inches	=	0.3048 meter
1 yard	= 3 feet	=	0.9144 meter
1 mile	= 1,760 yards or 5,280 feet	=	1,609.3 meters

● SQUARE MEASURE (AREA)

1 square inch		=	6.452 square centimeters
1 square foot	= 144 square inches	=	929 square centimeters
1 square yard	= 9 square feet	=	0.8361 square meter
1 acre	= 4,840 sq. yards	=	0.4047 hectare
1 square mile	= 640 acres	=	.259 hectares or 2.59 sq. kilometers

● CUBIC MEASURE

1 cubic inch		=	16.387 cubic centimeters
1 cubic foot	= 1,728 cubic inches	=	0.0283 cubic meter
1 cubic yard	= 27 cubic feet	=	0.7646 cubic meter
1 cord	= 8 cord feet	=	3.625 cubic meters

● DRY MEASURE

1 pint		=	0.5505 liter
1 quart	= 2 pints	=	1.1012 liters
1 peck	= 8 quarts	=	8.8096 liters
1 bushel	= 4 pecks	=	35.2383 liters

● LIQUID MEASURE

4 fluid ounces	= 1 gill	=	0.1183 liter
1 pint	= 4 gills	=	0.4732 liter
1 quart	= 2 pints	=	0.9463 liter
1 gallon	= 4 quarts	=	3.7853 liters

Some Ways to Measure When You Don't Have a Ruler

1. A standard sheet of paper is 8-1/2 inches by 11 inches.
2. A quarter is approximately 1 inch wide.
3. A penny is approximately 3/4 inch wide.
4. U.S. paper currency is 6-1/8 inches long by 2-5/8 inches wide.

Conversion Table

To change metric measurements into American measurements, multiply by the numbers listed below. To change American to metric, divide by those numbers.

To Change	to	Multiply By
acres	square miles	0.001562
Celsius	Fahrenheit	*1.8
	*(Multiply Celsius by 1.8; then add 32.)	
cubic meters	cubic yards	1.3079
cubic yards	cubic meters	0.7646
Fahrenheit	Celsius	*0.556
	*(Multiply Fahrenheit by .556 after subtracting 32.)	
feet	meters	0.3048
feet	miles	0.0001894
feet/sec.	miles/hr.	0.6818
grams	ounces	0.0353
grams	pounds	0.002205
hours	days	0.04167
inches	centimeters	2.5400
liters	gallons (U.S.)	0.2642
liters	pints (dry)	1.8162
liters	pints (liquid)	2.1134
liters	quarts (dry)	0.9081
liters	quarts (liquid)	1.0567
meters	miles	0.0006214
meters	yards	1.0936
metric tons	tons	1.1023
miles	kilometers	1.6093
miles	feet	5,280
miles/hr.	feet/min.	88
millimeters	inches	0.0394
ounces	grams	28.3495
ounces	pounds	0.0625
pounds	kilograms	0.4536
pounds	ounces	16
quarts (dry)	liters	1.1012
square feet	square meters	0.0929
square kilometers	square miles	0.3861
square meters	square feet	10.7639
square miles	square kilometers	2.5900
square yards	square meters	0.8361
tons	metric tons	0.9072
tons	pounds	2,000
yards	meters	0.9144
yards	miles	0.0005682

Sun

Mercury

Venus

Earth

Mars

Jupiter

Saturn

Our Solar System

The nine planets in our solar system orbit around the sun.

Mercury has the shortest year. It is 88 days long.

Venus spins the slowest. It takes 243 days to spin around once.

Earth supports life for plants, animals, and people.

Mars has less gravity than Earth. A 50-pound person would weigh about 19 pounds on Mars.

Jupiter is the largest planet. It is more than 10 times bigger than Earth.

Saturn has seven rings. It also has the most moons—23.

Uranus has the most rings—15.

Neptune is three times as cold as Earth.

Pluto is the smallest planet and the farthest from the sun.

Uranus

Neptune

Pluto

	Sun	Moon	Mercury	Venus	Earth	Mars	Jupiter	Saturn	Uranus	Neptune	Pluto
Orbital Speed (in miles per second)		0.6	29.8	21.8	18.5	15.0	8.1	6.0	4.2	3.4	3.0
Rotation on Axis	24 days 16 hrs. 48 min.	27 days 7 hrs. 43 min.	59 days	243 days	23 hrs. 56 min.	24 hrs. 37 min.	9 hrs. 55 min.	10 hrs. 39 min.	17 hrs. 8 min.	16 hrs. 7 min.	6 days
Mean Surface Gravity (Earth = 1.00)		0.16	0.39	0.9	1.00	0.38	2.53	1.07	0.91	1.14	0.07
Density (times that of water)	100 (core)	3.3	5.4	5.3	5.5	3.9	1.3	0.7	1.27	1.6	2.03
Mass (times that of Earth)	333,000	0.012	0.056	0.82	6×10^{21} metric tons	0.10	318	95	14.5	17.2	0.0026
Approx. Weight of a 150-Pound Human		24	59	135	150	57	380	161	137	171	11
Number of Satellites	9 planets	0	0	0	1	2	16	23	15	8	1
Mean Distance to Sun (in millions of miles)		93.0	36.0	67.24	92.96	141.7	483.8	887.1	1,783.9	2,796.4	3,666
Revolution Around Sun		365.25 days	88.0 days	224.7 days	365.25 days	687 days	11.86 years	29.46 years	84.0 years	165 years	248 years
Approximate Surface Temperature (degrees Fahrenheit)	10,000° (surface) 27,000,000° (center)	lighted side 260° dark side -280°	-346° to 950°	850°	-126.9° to 136°	-191° to -24°	-236°	-203°	-344°	-360°	-342° to -369°
Diameter (in miles)	865,400	2,155	3,032	7,519	7,926	4,194	88,736	74,978	32,193	30,775	1,423

Additional Units of Measure

Below are some additional units of measure that you may come across in or out of school. They are used to measure everything from boards to "light." The ones at the bottom of the page are used in shipbuilding, in the military, and with horses.

Astronomical Unit (A.U.) 93,000,000 miles, the average distance of the earth from the sun (Used in astronomy).

Board Foot (bd. ft). 144 cubic inches (12 in. x 12 in. x 1 in.) (Used for lumber).

Bolt 40 yards (Used for measuring cloth).

Btu British thermal unit—amount of heat needed to increase the temperature of one pound of water by one degree Fahrenheit (252 calories).

Gross 12 dozen or 144.

Knot A rate of speed—one nautical mile per hour.

Light, Speed of 186,281.7 miles per second.

Light-year 5,878,000,000,000 miles—the distance that light travels in a year.

Pi (π) 3.14159265+—the ratio of the circumference of a circle to its diameter.

Roentgen Dosage of unit of radiation exposure produced by X rays.

Score 20 units.

Sound, Speed of Usually placed at 1,088 feet per second at 32° F at sea level.

MISCELLANEOUS MEASUREMENTS		
3 inches	=	1 palm
4 inches	=	1 hand
6 inches	=	1 span
18 inches	=	1 cubit
21.8 inches	=	1 Bible cubit
2-1/2 feet	=	1 military pace

Mathematics

This chapter is your guide to the language of mathematics. It lists and defines many of the common (and not so common) mathematical signs, symbols, shapes, and terms. The chapter also includes helpful math tables and easy-to-follow guidelines for solving word problems.

Common Math Symbols

+	plus (addition)
−	minus (subtraction)
×	multiplied by
÷	divided by
=	is equal to
>	is greater than
<	is less than
±	plus or minus
%	percent
¢	cents
$	dollars
°	degree

Advanced Math Symbols

´	minute (also foot)
´´	second (also inch)
:	is to (ratio)
π	pi
√	square root
≠	is not equal to
≥	is greater than or equal to
≤	is less than or equal to
∠	angle
⊥	is perpendicular to
‖	is parallel to
∴	therefore

A Chart of Prime Numbers Less than 500

2	3	5	7	11	13	17	19	23	29
31	37	41	43	47	53	59	61	67	71
73	79	83	89	97	101	103	107	109	113
127	131	137	139	149	151	157	163	167	173
179	181	191	193	197	199	211	223	227	229
233	239	241	251	257	263	269	271	277	281
283	293	307	311	313	317	331	337	347	349
353	359	367	373	379	383	389	397	401	409
419	421	431	433	439	443	449	457	461	463
467	479	487	491	499					

Multiplication and Division Table

X	0	1	2	3	4	5	6	7	8	9	10
0	0	0	0	0	0	0	0	0	0	0	0
1	0	1	2	3	4	5	6	7	8	9	10
2	0	2	4	6	8	10	12	14	16	18	20
3	0	3	6	9	12	15	18	21	24	27	30
4	0	4	8	12	16	20	24	28	32	36	40
5	0	5	10	15	20	25	30	35	40	45	50
6	0	6	12	18	24	30	36	42	48	54	60
7	0	7	14	21	28	35	42	49	56	63	70
8	0	8	16	24	32	40	48	56	64	72	80
9	0	9	18	27	36	45	54	63	72	81	90
10	0	10	20	30	40	50	60	70	80	90	100

Decimal Equivalents of Common Fractions

1/2	.5000	1/32	.0313	3/11	.2727	6/11	.5455
1/3	.3333	1/64	.0156	4/5	.8000	7/8	.8750
1/4	.2500	2/3	.6667	4/7	.5714	7/9	.7778
1/5	.2000	2/5	.4000	4/9	.4444	7/10	.7000
1/6	.1667	2/7	.2857	4/11	.3636	7/11	.6364
1/7	.1429	2/9	.2222	5/6	.8333	7/12	.5833
1/8	.1250	2/11	.1818	5/7	.7143	8/9	.8889
1/9	.1111	3/4	.7500	5/8	.6250	8/11	.7273
1/10	.1000	3/5	.6000	5/9	.5556	9/10	.9000
1/11	.0909	3/7	.4286	5/11	.4545	9/11	.8182
1/12	.0833	3/8	.3750	5/12	.4167	10/11	.9091
1/16	.0625	3/10	.3000	6/7	.8571	11/12	.9167

Roman Numerals

I	1	VIII	8	LX	60	$\overline{V}$	5,000
II	2	IX	9	LXX	70	$\overline{X}$	10,000
III	3	X	10	LXXX	80	$\overline{L}$	50,000
IV	4	XX	20	XC	90	$\overline{C}$	100,000
V	5	XXX	30	C	100	$\overline{D}$	500,000
VI	6	XL	40	D	500	$\overline{M}$	1,000,000
VII	7	L	50	M	1,000		

Word Problems

Solving word problems requires careful reading, thinking, and planning. If you try to take shortcuts, you will probably not solve them correctly. The guidelines below give you the important steps to follow the next time you work on word problems.

Guidelines for Solving Word Problems

1. **Read the problem carefully.** It's important that you understand all the parts. Pay special attention to the key words and phrases—such as "in all" or "how many." Read the problem again to be sure you understand it well. (Draw a picture or diagram if that helps make the problem easier to figure out.)

2. **Collect the information.** Gather the information you need to solve the problem. First of all, find all the numbers in the problem. (Remember, some numbers may be written as words.) Also study any maps, charts, or graphs that go along with the problem. They often contain important information, too.

3. **Set up the problem.** Decide whether you need to add, subtract, multiply, or divide. Do this by looking for the key words and phrases in the problem.

   ■ The following words tell you to add or multiply: *altogether, in all, in total.*

   ■ The following phrases tell you to subtract: *how many more than, how many less than, find the difference, how many are left, how much younger than.*

   ■ Each of these phrases tells you to divide: *how much . . . each (or per), how many . . . each (or per).*

4. **Solve the problem.** Once the problem is set up, with all the steps in the right order, you're ready to solve it. Show your work so you can check it later.

5. **Check your answer.** Here are several ways to check your answer: Do the problem again, do it a different way, use a calculator, or start with your answer and work backward.

Addition

Word Problem: A shirt costs $8.79, a pair of pants costs $14.99, and sweaters cost $12.99 each. What would be the total cost if someone bought all three items?

STEP 1: Read the problem.	*Discussion:* As you read the problem, you'll find two key phrases: "total cost" and "all three."
STEP 2: Collect the information.	*Discussion:* The numbers you need to solve the problem are $8.79, $14.99, and $12.99.
STEP 3: Set up the problem. $ 8.79 14.99 + 12.99 ——	*Discussion:* This is a one-step problem in which you must add three numbers. (The word "total" is a key word that tells you to add; "all three" tells you which numbers to add.) Be sure to line up the decimal points in the numbers.
STEP 4: Solve the problem. 1 2 2 $ 8.79 14.99 + 12.99 —— $36.77	*Discussion:* Bring the decimal point, which separates the dollars from the cents, down to your answer.
STEP 5: Check your answer. 1 2 2 $ 14.99 12.99 + 8.79 —— $36.77	*Discussion:* Check your answer by adding the three numbers in a different order. Make sure that you have copied the numbers correctly and that your answer makes sense.

Answer: The total cost for the three items of clothing is $36.77.

Fractions

Word Problem: One-fourth of the actors from the community play attend Park High School. One-third of the actors attend Jefferson Junior High School. What fraction of the entire cast for the spring play attend the two schools?

STEP 1: Read the problem.	*Discussion:* As you read the problem, you'll find that the key words are "what fraction."
STEP 2: Collect the information.	*Discussion:* The numbers you need to solve this problem are "one-fourth" and "one-third."
STEP 3: Set up the problem. $$\frac{1}{4} + \frac{1}{3} = ?$$	*Discussion:* To solve this problem, you will have to add the two fractions. (You might want to draw a picture that "shows" the information.)
STEP 4: Solve the problem. $$\frac{1 \times 3}{4 \times 3} = \frac{3}{12}$$ $$\frac{1 \times 4}{3 \times 4} = \frac{4}{12}$$ $$\frac{3}{12} + \frac{4}{12} = \frac{7}{12}$$	*Discussion:* To add fractions, you must have common denominators. So, you must find the least common multiple (LCM) of the numbers 3 and 4—the denominators of the two fractions. The LCM is 12.
STEP 5: Check your answer. $$\frac{7}{12}$$	*Discussion:* Check your answer to make sure it is written in its simplest terms (7/12 cannot be simplified any further). Also compare your answer to your picture. Since 7/12 and the picture are both a little more than half, the answer makes sense.

Answer: The fraction of the cast that attends the two schools is 7/12.

Math Terms

Addition (+) is combining numbers to get a total, which is called a *sum*. The sum of 3 plus 5 is 8; 3 + 5 = 8.

An **angle** is made when two rays share a common endpoint. An angle is measured in degrees. The three most common angles are *acute, obtuse,* and *right angles*.

<90°	>90° and <180°	90°	180°
acute angle	obtuse angle	right angle	straight angle

Area is the total surface within a closed figure (circle, square). The area of a rectangle is figured by multiplying the length by the width. Area is measured in square units such as square inches or feet.

12'
6' area is 72 square feet
area

The **average** is found by adding a group of numbers together and then dividing that sum by the number of separate numbers. The average of 7, 8, and 9 is 8, because 7 + 8 + 9 = 24, and 24 ÷ 3 numbers = 8. This is also called the mathematical *mean*.

A **circle** is a round, closed figure. All the points on its circumference (edge) are the same distance from the center of the figure.

Circumference is the distance around the edge of a circle. circumference

A **common denominator** is a multiple shared by the denominators of two or more fractions. For example, 6 is a common denominator of 1/2 (3/6) and 1/3 (2/6); 6 is a multiple of both 2 and 3. To add or subtract fractions, you must find a common denominator; 1/2 + 1/3 = 3/6 + 2/6 = 5/6. The lowest common denominator is also called the *least common multiple* (LCM) of the denominators.

Congruent (≅) is the term for two figures, line segments, or angles that are the same size and shape.

congruent triangles

Data is a set of numbers collected to compare.

A **decimal** is a fraction written in the decimal number system. (*Decimal* means "based on the number 10.") Decimals are written using a decimal point and place values—tenths, hundredths, thousandths, and so on. The fraction 1/2 is .5, or 5/10.

A **degree** is a unit of measurement for angles and arcs. It is written as a small circle [°]. You can write 90°, or 90 degrees. There are 360° in a circle.

The **denominator** is the bottom number of a fraction. In the fraction 1/3, the denominator is 3. It indicates the number of parts needed to make a whole unit.

A **diagonal** is a straight line from one vertex of a quadrilateral to the opposite vertex.

The **diameter** is the length of a straight line through the center of a circle.

diameter

A **dividend** is a number to be divided. In the equation 12 ÷ 2 = 6, 12 is the dividend.

Division (÷) is a basic math operation used to determine how many times one quantity is contained in another. Division also tells you how many times you have to subtract a number to reach zero. For example, 10 ÷ 5 = 2 because you subtract 5 two times to reach zero (10 − **5** = 5 − **5** = 0).

The **divisor** is the number that divides the dividend. In the statement 12 ÷ 2 = 6, 2 is the divisor.

An **equation** is a statement that says two numbers or mathematical expressions are equal to each other (2 + 10 = 12 or $x + 4 = 9$). Equations use the equal sign (=).

An **estimate** is a reasonable guess at an answer. If you add 6.24 and 5.19, you can estimate the answer will be around 11, because 6 + 5 = 11.

An **even number** is a number that can be divided by 2 without having a remainder (2, 4, 6, and so on). For example, 4 ÷ 2 = 2.

An **exponent** is the small, raised number to the right of the base number that shows how many times the number is to be multiplied by itself. In the expression 2^3, 3 is the exponent (2 is the base). So, 2^3 means you need to multiply 2 three times (2 × 2 × 2 = 8).

A **factor** is a number that is being multiplied. In 4 × 3 = 12, the factors are 4 and 3.

A **fraction** is a number that expresses a part of a whole. In the fraction 3/4, 4 is the *denominator*—the number of equal parts that make up the whole. The number 3 is the *numerator*—the number of parts being talked about.

fraction

Geometry is the study of two-dimensional shapes (circles, triangles), solids (spheres, cubes), and positions in space (points).

A **horizontal** is a line parallel to the earth's surface, or horizon, going across rather than up and down. A *vertical* is a line that is straight up and down and perpendicular to the horizon.

A **hypotenuse** of a right triangle is the side opposite the right angle.

hypotenuse intersections isosceles triangle

An **intersection** is the point where two figures in geometry cross each other.

An **isosceles triangle** is a triangle with two sides of equal length and two congruent angles. (See *triangle.*)

Length is the distance along a line from one point to another.

A **line** is all points formed by extending a line segment both directions, without end.

line

Lowest common denominator (See *common denominator.*)

Mean is another word for *average.* (See *average.*)

The **median** is the middle number when a group of numbers is arranged in order from the least to the greatest, or greatest to least. In 1, 4, 6, the median (middle number) is 4. In 1, 4, 6, 8, the median is 5, halfway between 4 and 6.

A **multiple** is a quantity into which another quantity can be divided, with zero as the remainder (both 6 and 9 are multiples of 3).

Multiplication ($\times$) is like addition because you add the same number a certain number of times ($2 \times 4 = 4 + 4$). When you multiply numbers, the answer is called the *product.* The product of 2 times 4 is 8 because $2 \times 4 = 8$. (A raised dot also means multiplication. 2×3 is the same as $2 \cdot 3$.)

The **numerator** is the top number of a fraction. In the fraction 5/6, the numerator is 5.

An **obtuse** angle is an angle greater than 90 degrees and less than 180 degrees. (See *angle.*)

An **odd number** is a number that cannot be divided evenly by 2. The numbers 1, 3, 5, 7, and so on, are odd numbers.

Opposite numbers are any two numbers whose sum is zero (−2 and +2 are opposite numbers).

Parallel refers to lines that never intersect.

parallel lines

Percent is a way of expressing a number as a fraction of 100. (Percent means "per hundred.") The percent symbol is %. So, 1/2 expressed as a percentage is 50/100, which is 50%.

The **perimeter** is the distance around the edge of a multisided figure. If a triangle has three sides, each 3 feet long, its perimeter is 9 feet (3 + 3 + 3 = 9).

3'   3'

3'
perimeter = 9'

Perpendicular refers to two lines that intersect forming right angles (90° angles.)

perpendicular lines

Pi (π) is the ratio of the circumference of a circle to its diameter. Pi is approximately 3.14.

Place value is the value of the place of a digit depending on where it is in the number.

3497 is 3—thousands, 4—hundreds, 9—tens, 7—ones

.3497 is 3—tenths, 4—hundredths, 9—thousandths, 7—ten-thousandths

A **point** is an exact location on a plane.

A **positive number** is a number greater than 0.

A **prime number** is a number that cannot be divided evenly by any number except itself and 1. The number 6 is not a prime number because it can be divided by 1, 2, 3, and 6. The number 5 is a prime number because it can only be divided evenly (without a remainder) by 1 and 5.

The **product** is the number you get when you multiply two or more numbers. For example, 8 is the product of 2 times 4, because 2 × 4 = 8.

The **quotient** is the number you get when you divide one number by another number. If 8 is divided by 4, the quotient is 2, because 8 ÷ 4 = 2.

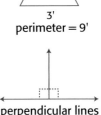

The **radius** (r) is the distance from the center of a circle to its circumference. (The radius is half the diameter.)

radius

A **ratio** is a way of comparing two numbers by dividing one by the other. The ratio of 3 to 4 is 3/4. If there are 20 boys and 5 girls in your class, the ratio of boys to girls is 20/5 (4/1 in lowest terms), or 4 : 1.

A **rectangle** is a four-sided closed figure with four right angles and with opposite sides parallel and congruent.

A **right angle** is an angle that measures 90 degrees. A right angle is formed when two perpendicular lines meet. (See *angle*.)

Rounding is a way to figure an approximate number if you don't need an exact number. If 2323 people attended a soccer game, you could say about 2000 people were there. If 2857 people attended, you could say 3000. Round up if the number is greater than half (2500 is halfway between 2000 and 3000). Round down if the number is less than half.

A **solid** is a three-dimensional figure in geometry, like a cube, a cone, a prism, or a sphere.

solid

A **square** is a rectangle that has four sides of equal length and four right angles. *Square* also refers to the product of a number multiplied by itself. The square of 4 is 16 ($4^2 = 16$; $4 \times 4 = 16$).

square

The **square root** of a number is a number that, when multiplied by itself, gives the original number as the product. The symbol for square root is $\sqrt{}$. The square root of 4 is 2, because $2 \times 2 = 4$ ($\sqrt{4} = 2$).

Subtraction (−) is the inverse (opposite) of addition. Instead of adding one number to another, you take one number away from another. When you subtract two numbers, you find the difference between them. So, $11 - 6 = 5$.

The **sum** is the number you get when you add numbers. For example, 7 is the sum of 4 plus 3, because $4 + 3 = 7$.

A **triangle** is a closed figure with three sides. The sum of the angles in every triangle is 180°. Triangles can be classified by *sides:* equilateral, scalene, or isosceles; or by *angles:* right, equiangular, acute, or obtuse.

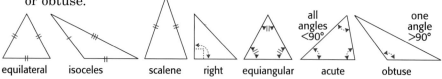

| equilateral | isoceles | scalene | right | equiangular | acute | obtuse |

all angles <90°

one angle >90°

A **vertex** is the point where two sides of a plane figure meet (corner). The plural of *vertex* is *vertices*.

Vertical (See *horizontal*.)

vertex

Computers

An Internet service provider (ISP) allows you to conduct research and communicate on-line. The provider gives you access, via a personal computer or a LAN, to the World Wide Web, e-mail, and newsgroups. (Study the chart below to see how the Net works.)

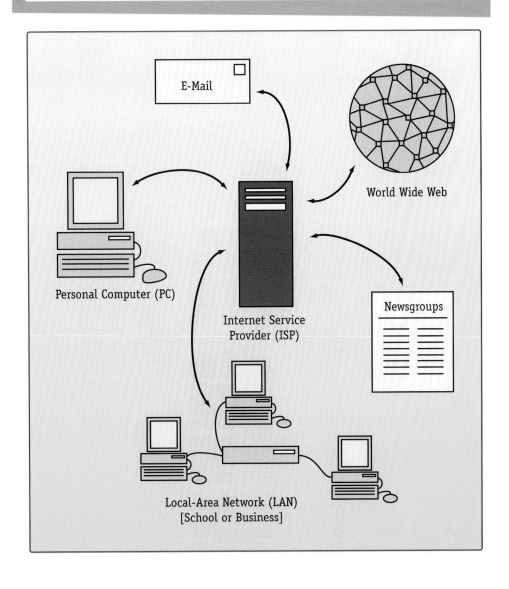

E-Mail

World Wide Web

Personal Computer (PC)

Internet Service
Provider (ISP)

Newsgroups

Local-Area Network (LAN)
[School or Business]

Computer Keyboard

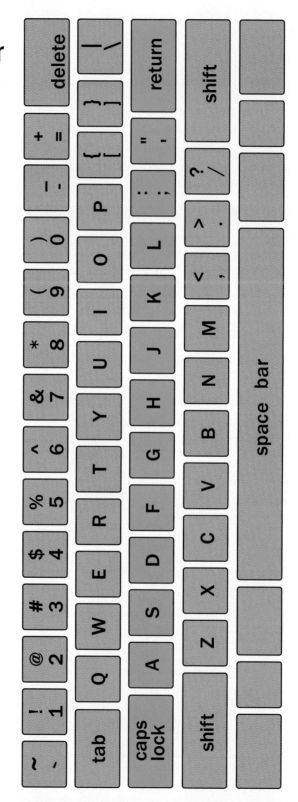

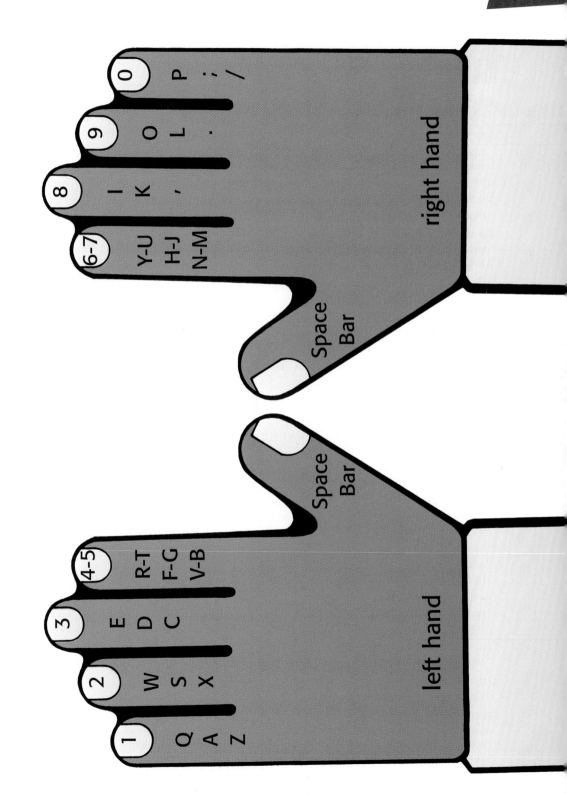

Computer Terms

Access To open and use a computer file.

ASCII (American Standard Code Information Interchange) A set of letters, numbers, and symbols that computers use to store and work with data.

Audio file A computer document of sounds.

Backup A duplicate copy of a file or program, made in case the original is lost or destroyed.

Bit A unit of computer memory.

Boot To start up a computer system by loading a program into the memory. Also called *start up*.

BPS (Bits Per Second) A measure of how fast data is transmitted over a network.

Bug An error in a program.

Byte Eight bits of information acting as a single piece of data. Computer memory is measured in bytes.

CD-ROM A compact disc that can store audio, text, and video data.

Character A letter or number used to display information on a computer screen or printer.

Chip A tiny piece of silicon with thousands of electrical elements. Also called an *integrated circuit*.

Circuit board A board inside a computer, used to hold and connect computer chips and electrical parts.

Command An instruction telling a computer to perform a certain task.

Compress To make a file smaller for easier storage or transmission.

Computer A machine that can accept data, process according to a set of stored instructions, and then output the results.

Computer program Software containing commands that tell the computer to perform certain tasks.

Configuration A computer and all devices connected to it.

CPU (Central Processing Unit) The part that performs computations and controls other parts of the computer system.

CRT (Cathode Ray Tube.) The electronic vacuum tube found in some computer monitors and TV screens.

Cursor A pointer on the monitor that shows where the next character typed on the keyboard will appear.

Cyberspace The imaginary world perceived by humans when using a computer network or a virtual reality program. (See *Virtual reality*.)

Database A program and a collection of information organized in such a way that a computer can access a certain item or group of items.

Desktop The monitor screen as it appears when the computer is on but no programs are open.

Device A piece of computer hardware that performs a certain task.

Directory The table of contents for all files on a disk.

Disk drive The device that reads and writes information on a disk.

Download To copy a program or file from another computer to your own.

Drag To move items on the screen by pressing the mouse button while sliding the mouse.

DVD (digital video disk) A CD with high-resolution audio and video.

Emoticon A set of characters that, when viewed sideways, resembles a face. Adds emotion to messages. :)

Error message A message, displayed by the computer, that tells you what type of error has occurred.

Exit To close or quit a program.

FAQ (Frequently Asked Questions) A list of common questions and answers.

File A collection of information stored under a single title.

Floppy Disk A magnetic storage device that records computer data.

Font A typeface (type style) used by a printer.

Footprint The space on a desk taken up by a computer.

Format To prepare (initialize) a blank disk for use.

Freeware Software in the public domain (can be used free of charge).

FTP (File Transfer Protocol) A system for uploading and downloading files on the Internet or on a network.

GB (Gigabyte) A measure of computer memory; 1,000 megabytes (MB).

Hard copy A printed copy.

Hard drive A device for long-term storage of files and programs.

Hardware The electronic and mechanical parts of a computer system.

Host A computer whose programs serve another computer in a computer-to-computer link.

Hypertext or **hypermedia** A system of web-like links among pages on the Internet or within a program.

Icon A picture or symbol that identifies computer folders, files, or functions.

Input Information placed into a computer from a disk drive, keyboard, mouse, or other device connected to a computer.

Interactive A computer program in which the user and computer exchange information.

Interface The hardware and software that is used to link one computer or computer device to another. Also the way a program communicates to a user.

K (Kilobyte) A measure of computer memory; 1,024 bytes (about 170 words).

Keyboard An input device used to enter information on a computer by striking keys.

Laser printer A printer that uses a laser to make high-quality printouts.

Link A connection from one hypertext page to another.

Listserve A program sending e-mail messages to a set of addresses organized around a topic, allowing its subscribers to conduct a group discussion by e-mail. Also called a *mailing list* or a *mail server*.

Load To move information from a storage device into a computer's memory.

Mainframe A large computer, with many terminals, with power enough to be used by many people at once. (See *terminal*.)

MB (Megabyte) 1,000 kilobytes (K).

Memory Chips in the computer that store data and programs.

Menu A list of program choices from which a user can select.

Modem (MOdulator DEModulator) A device that handles information or data over phone lines.

Monitor A video screen that displays computer information.

Mouse A manual input device that controls the pointer on the screen.

MUD (Multi-User Domain) An imaginary world (usually text-based) made up of "rooms" where users can interact with the setting and other users.

Multimedia A program that can combine text, graphics, video, voice, music, and animation.

Newsgroup A bulletin-board style discussion on a timely topic.

On-line To be connected to a computer network.

On-line service A business that serves as a network for its users, providing e-mail, chat rooms, and so on.

Open To load a program for use.

Operating system A software system that controls a computer (Windows, Mac OS, and DOS).

Output Information that a computer sends out to a monitor, printer, modem, or other device.

Peripheral A device connected to a computer (a printer, a monitor).

Pixel One dot on the screen. There are usually 72 pixels per inch.

Printout A hard copy; a computer document printed on paper.

Program A set of instructions that tells a computer what to do.

Programmer A person who writes or produces a computer program.

Programming language A special language used when writing a computer program.

Prompt A question or an instruction on the screen that asks users to make a choice or give information.

Quit To close a program.

RAM (Random Access Memory) The part of a computer's memory that stores programs and documents temporarily while you are using them.

Resolution The number of dots per square inch (dpi) on a computer screen. Images on the screen are made up of tiny dots. The more dots there are, the higher the resolution and the clearer the picture.

ROM (Read-Only Memory) The part of a computer's memory that has its permanent instructions. It cannot record new data.

Save To transfer a document for permanent storage.

Scanner A device used to read a printed image, picture, or text and save it as an electronic file.

Server The hosting computer of a network. (See *host*.)

Shareware Programs made as demos for a test period, then paid for.

Software The program that tells a computer how to do a certain task.

Spam Bulk (junk) e-mail that is sent to many people at once.

Spreadsheet A computer program that displays numbers and text in a worksheet form.

Surfing Exploring the Net, going from link to link.

System A collection of hardware and software working together to form a working computer.

Terminal A keyboard and monitor sharing a mainframe (computer) with other terminals.

Text file A computer document made up of ASCII characters only.

Upload To send a file from your computer to another computer.

Virtual reality A technology that immerses users in a computer-created environment.

Virus A command (bug) that is put into a computer system to cause problems.

Window A box on a computer screen in which text or graphics is displayed.

Word processor A program that allows users to write, revise, edit, save, and print text documents.

Geography

To study geography, you need maps, including *political maps* like the ones provided in this chapter. Political maps show how the world is divided into countries and states. The chapter also includes guidelines for using maps, a special time-zone map, and much more.

Using Maps

Mapmakers use special marks and symbols to show direction (north, south, east, and west). On most maps, north is at the top. But you should always check the *directional finder* (compass rose) to make sure you know where north is. If there is no symbol, you can assume that north is at the top of the page.

The Legend

Other important marks and symbols are explained in a box printed on each map. This box is called the *legend,* or *key.* It is included to help you understand and use the map. This map legend, which goes with the United States map, also includes symbols for state capitals and state boundaries.

UNITED STATES		
✪ National Capital	———	International Boundaries
Austin ◉ State Capitals	———	State Boundaries
Dallas • Cities	**TEXAS**	State Names
0 100 200 300 400 Miles		

The Map Scale

Legends also explain the map scale. The map scale shows you how far it really is between places. For example, a scale might show that one inch on the map equals 100 miles on the earth. If two cities are shown five inches apart, then they are really 500 miles apart. A ruler makes using a scale easy, but even an index card or a piece of paper will work. Here is the scale from the map of the United States.

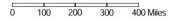

0   100   200   300   400 Miles

Latitude and Longitude

Latitude and *longitude* lines are another part of many maps and are very useful. These are imaginary lines, placed on a map by map-makers, and used to locate any point on the earth.

Latitude ● The imaginary lines that go from east to west around the earth are called lines of **latitude.** The line of latitude that goes around the earth exactly halfway between the North Pole and the South Pole is called the *equator.* Latitude is measured in degrees, with the equator being 0 degrees (0°).

Above the equator, the lines are called *north latitude* and measure from 0° to 90° north (the North Pole). Below the equator, the lines are called *south latitude* and measure from 0° to 90° south (the South Pole). On a map, latitude numbers are printed along the sides.

Longitude ● The lines on a map that run north and south from the North Pole to the South Pole are lines of **longitude.** Longitude is also measured in degrees, beginning with 0 degrees. The line of longitude located at 0° is called the *prime meridian* and passes through Greenwich, England.

Lines east of the prime meridian are called *east longitude.* Lines west of the prime meridian are called *west longitude.* On a map, longitude numbers are printed at the top and bottom.

Coordinates ● The latitude and longitude numbers of a country or other place are called its **coordinates.** In each set of coordinates, latitude is given first, then longitude. To locate a place on a map using its coordinates, find the point where the two lines cross. (On the map of the globe above, Guinea is located at 10° N, 10° W. Can you find it? Check the map on page 473 to be sure.)

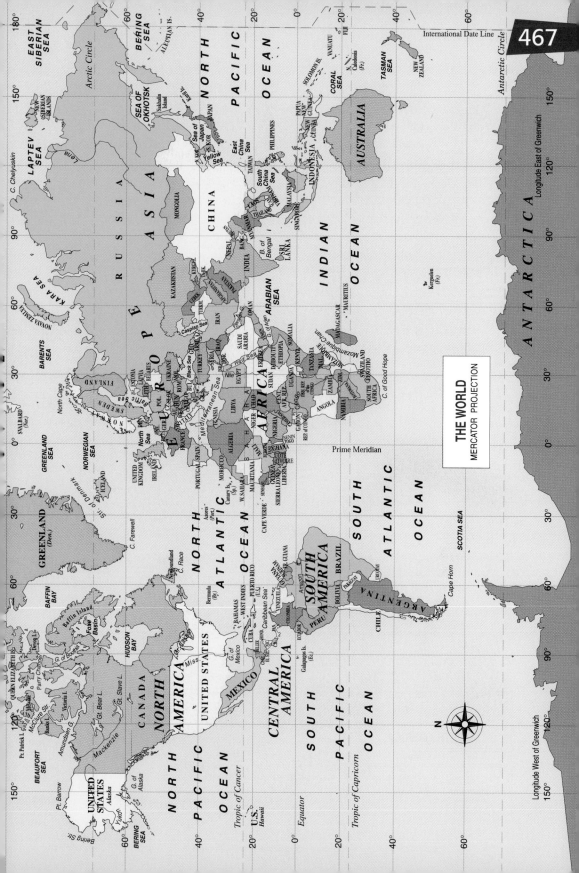

THE WORLD
MERCATOR PROJECTION

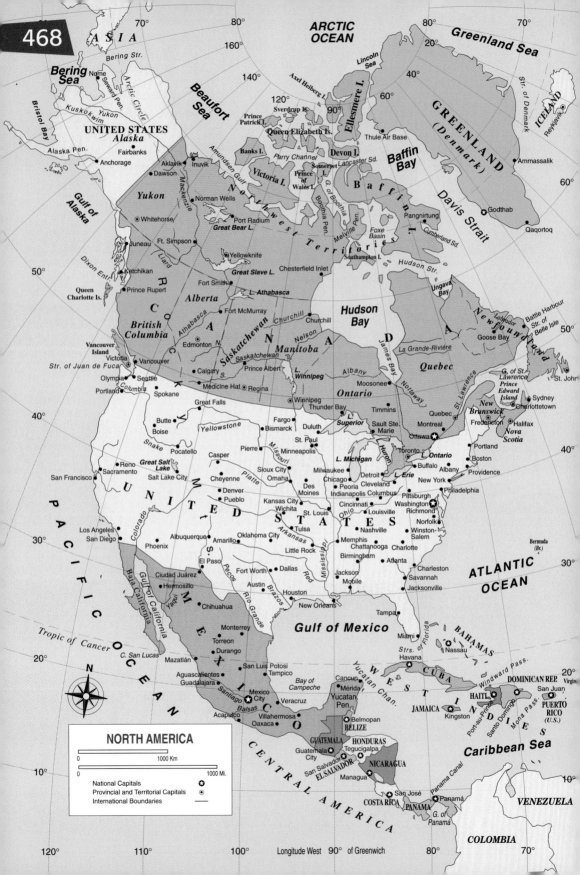

ASIA

ARCTIC OCEAN

Greenland Sea

Bering Str.

70°   80°   160°   140°   120°   90°   60°   40°   80°   70°

Bering Sea

Nome
Seward Pen.
Yukon
Kuskokwim

Arctic Circle

Beaufort Sea

Axel Heiberg I.

Lincoln Sea

20°

ICELAND

Bristol Bay

UNITED STATES
Alaska

Alaska Pen.

Fairbanks
Anchorage
Dawson

Gulf of Alaska

Yukon
Whitehorse

Juneau
Ft. Simpson

Ketchikan
Prince Rupert

Queen Charlotte Is.

Dixon Entr.

Vancouver Island
Victoria

British Columbia

Str. of Juan de Fuca
Olympia
Seattle
Portland

Reykjavík

60°

Sverdrup Is.
Prince Patrick I.
Banks I.

Queen Elizabeth Is.

Thule Air Base

GREENLAND
(Denmark)

Ammassalik

Devon I.

Baffin Bay

Davis Strait

Godthab

Qaqortoq

Parry Channel
Somerset I.
Lancaster Sd.

Victoria I.
Prince of Wales I.
G. of Boothia

Boothia Pen.

Baffin I.

Pangnirtung

Cumberland Sd.

Aklavik
Inuvik

Mackenzie

Amundsen Gulf

Norman Wells

Port Radium
Great Bear L.

Yellowknife

Great Slave L.

Fort Smith

L. Athabasca

Alberta

Fort McMurray

Edmonton

Calgary

Medicine Hat

Whitehorse

C A N A D A

Northwest Territories

Melville Pen.

Foxe Basin

Southampton I.

Chesterfield Inlet

Hudson Str.

Ungava Bay

Labrador

Battle Harbour
Str. of Belle Isle

Goose Bay

Newfoundland

Chisholm

Churchill

Hudson Bay

La Grande-Rivière

Quebec

James Bay

Saskatchewan
Saskatchewan
Prince Albert
Regina

Manitoba

L. Winnipeg

Winnipeg
Thunder Bay

Ontario

Albany

Moosonee

Nottaway

St. Lawrence

New Brunswick
Quebec
Fredericton

Prince Edward Island
Charlottetown

G. of St. Lawrence
St. John's

Sydney
Halifax
Nova Scotia

Butte
Boise

Great Falls

Fargo
Bismarck

Duluth

Timmins

Sault Ste. Marie

Superior

Montreal
Ottawa

Portland
Boston

Nova Scotia

Spokane

Yellowstone

Pierre

Minneapolis
St. Paul

Milwaukee

L. Michigan
Chicago

Detroit
Cleveland

L. Huron

L. Erie

Toronto
L. Ontario
Buffalo
Albany
Providence

New York

Snake

Pocatello

Casper

Sioux City
Omaha
Des Moines

Peoria
Indianapolis Columbus

Cincinnati

Pittsburgh
Washington
Richmond

Philadelphia

Reno
Sacramento

Great Salt Lake
Salt Lake City

Cheyenne
Denver
Pueblo

Kansas City

Wichita

St. Louis

Ohio

Louisville
Nashville

Norfolk

San Francisco

U N I T E D   S T A T E S

Colorado

Arkansas

Memphis
Chattanooga

Charlotte

Winston-Salem

Charleston

Los Angeles
San Diego

Phoenix

Albuquerque
Amarillo

Oklahoma City
Little Rock

Atlanta

Savannah

El Paso

Fort Worth
Dallas

Red

Jackson
Mobile

Jacksonville

Bermuda (Br.)

ATLANTIC OCEAN

Ciudad Juárez
Hermosillo

Chihuahua

Baja California

Gulf of California

Austin

Houston

New Orleans

Tampa

Miami

BAHAMAS
Nassau

M E X I C O

Monterrey

Torreon
Durango

Rio Grande

Strs. of Florida
Havana

CUBA

WEST

DOMINICAN REP.
San Juan
Virgin

Tropic of Cancer

C. San Lucas

Mazatlán

San Luis Potosí
Tampico

Yucatan Chan.

Cancún
Mérida
Yucatan Pen.

HAITI
Port-au-Prince
Santo Domingo

PUERTO RICO (U.S.)

Mona Pass.

PACIFIC OCEAN

Aguascalientes
Guadalajara

Santiago

Mexico City
Veracruz

Bay of Campeche

JAMAICA
Kingston

Windward Pass.

INDIES

Acapulco

Balsas

Villahermosa
Oaxaca

Belmopan
BELIZE

Caribbean Sea

GUATEMALA
Guatemala City

San Salvador
EL SALVADOR

HONDURAS
Tegucigalpa

Managua

NICARAGUA

Panama Canal

N

San José

COSTA RICA

PANAMA
Panamá

G. of Panama

VENEZUELA

C E N T R A L   A M E R I C A

COLOMBIA

120°   110°   100°   Longitude West 90° of Greenwich   80°   70°

NORTH AMERICA

0	1000 Km
0	1000 Mi.

National Capitals ⊕
Provincial and Territorial Capitals ⊙
International Boundaries ——

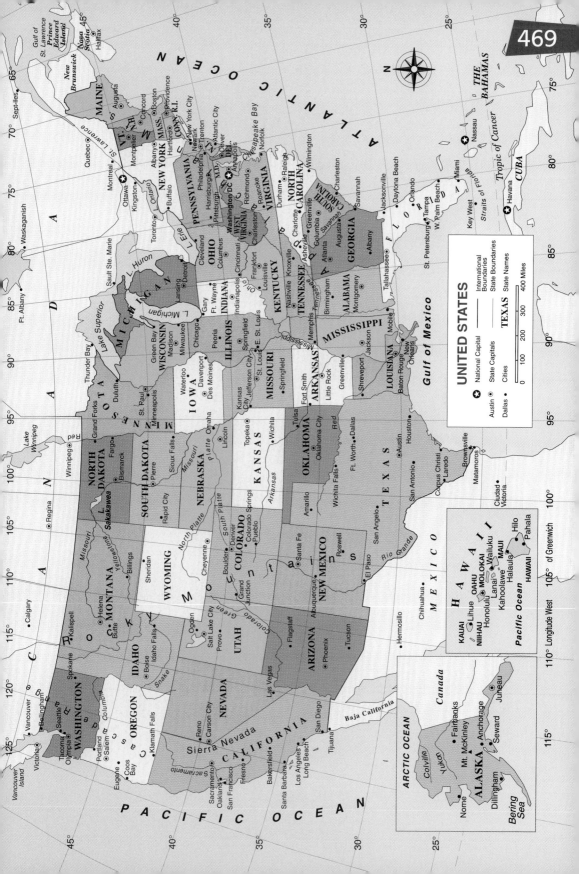

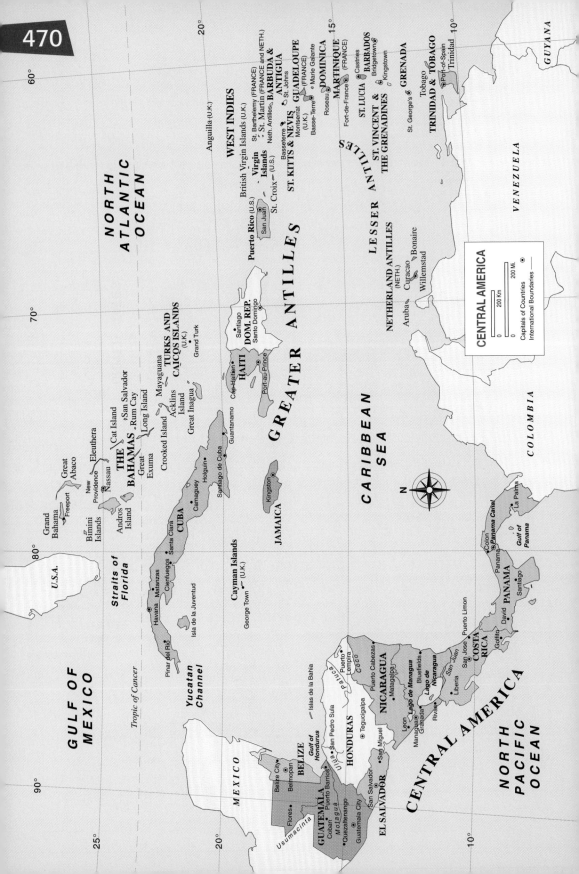

GULF OF MEXICO

NORTH ATLANTIC OCEAN

U.S.A.

Straits of Florida

Tropic of Cancer

Yucatan Channel

Grand Bahama
Freeport
Bimini Islands
Andros Island
New Providence
Nassau
Great Abaco
Eleuthera
THE BAHAMAS
Cat Island
San Salvador
Rum Cay
Long Island
Great Exuma
Mayaguana
Crooked Island
Acklins Island
Great Inagua

Anguilla (U.K.)

WEST INDIES

British Virgin Islands (U.K.)
Virgin Islands (U.K.)
St. Barthelemy (FRANCE)
St. Martin (FRANCE and NETH.)
BARBUDA &
ANTIGUA
Neth. Antilles
St. Johns
St. Kitts
St. Croix (U.S.)
Basseterre
ST. KITTS & NEVIS
Montserrat (U.K.)
GUADELOUPE (FRANCE)
Basse-Terre
Marie Galante
DOMINICA
Roseau
MARTINIQUE (FRANCE)
Fort-de-France
ST. LUCIA
Castries
ST. VINCENT &
THE GRENADINES
Kingstown
BARBADOS
Bridgetown
GRENADA
St. George's
Tobago
TRINIDAD & TOBAGO
Port-of-Spain
Trinidad

Puerto Rico (U.S.)
San Juan

LESSER ANTILLES

NETHERLAND ANTILLES (NETH.)
Aruba
Curaçao
Bonaire
Willemstad

VENEZUELA

Pinar del Rio
Havana
Matanzas
Cienfuegos
Santa Clara
CUBA
Isla de la Juventud
Camaguey
Holguin
Santiago de Cuba
Guantanamo
Cayman Islands (U.K.)
George Town

Santiago
DOM. REP.
Santo Domingo
HAITI
Cap-Haïtien
Port-au-Prince

TURKS AND CAICOS ISLANDS (U.K.)
Grand Turk

GREATER ANTILLES

Kingston
JAMAICA

CARIBBEAN SEA

N

COLOMBIA

GUYANA

MEXICO

BELIZE
Belize City
Belmopan

Gulf of Honduras

HONDURAS
San Pedro Sula
Ulua
Tegucigalpa
Islas de la Bahia
Puerto Cortes
Lempira
Coco
Puerto Cabezas

GUATEMALA
Cobán
Puerto Barrios
Motagua
Quezaltenango
Guatemala City
Flores
Usumacinta

EL SALVADOR
San Salvador
San Miguel

NICARAGUA
Matagalpa
León
Managua
Lago de Managua
Granada
Rivas
Lago de Nicaragua
Bluefields

COSTA RICA
Liberia
San Juan
San Jose
Puerto Limon

PANAMA
David
Golfito
Santiago
Panama
Colon
Panama Canal
Gulf of Panama
La Palma

CENTRAL AMERICA

NORTH PACIFIC OCEAN

CENTRAL AMERICA
200 Km
200 Mi.
Capitals of Countries
International Boundaries

Caribbean Sea

West Indies

NORTH ATLANTIC OCEAN

Pt. Gallinas
G. de Venezuela

Port of Spain
TRINIDAD & TOBAGO

Barranquilla
Maracaibo
Caracas
Cumana
Ciudad Guayana

Monteria
Cucuta
VENEZUELA
San Cristobal
Orinoco
Georgetown
Paramaribo

Medellin
GUYANA
SURINAME
FR. GUIANA
Cayenne

Buenaventura
COLOMBIA
Bogota
Boa Vista
Oyapock

Cali
Orinoco

Pasto
Negro

Quito
ECUADOR
Branco
Macapa
I. de Marajo
Equator

Guayaquil
Manaus
Belém
Abaetetuba

G. of Guayaquil
Amazon
Amazon
Santarem
Sao Luis

Sullana
Iquitos
Benjamin Constant
Xingu
Fortaleza
Teresina

Chiclayo
Maranon
Javari
Jurua
Purus
Madeira
Tapajos
Araguaia
Natal

Trujillo
Ucayali
Rio Branco
Porto Velho
Roosevelt
Tocantins
Parnaiba
Juazeiro do Norte
Recife

PERU
Guapore
B R A Z I L
Porto Nacional

Lima
Trinidad
Sao Francisco
Aracaju

Ica
Lake Titicaca
BOLIVIA
Cuiaba
Brasilia
Salvador

Arequipa
La Paz (de facto)
Cochabamba
Santa Cruz
Goiania
Ilhéus

Arica
Sucre (legal)
Paraguay
Belo Horizonte

Tocopilla
Mariscal Estigarribia
Campo Grande
Vitória

Antofagasta
PARAGUAY
Parana
Sao Paulo
Rio de Janeiro

San Salvador de Jujuy
Asuncion
Santos
Paranaguá

Copiapó
Resistencia
Encarnación
Curitiba

San Miguel de Tucuman
Uruguay
Florianópolis

La Serena
Salado
Santana do Livramento
Porto Alegre

Ovalle
Cordoba
Salto
L. dos Patos

Valparaiso
Rosario
Melo

Santiago
Mendoza
URUGUAY
Montevideo

Concepcion
Buenos Aires
La Plata
Rio de la Plata

Santa Rosa
C. San Antonio

Valdivia
Negro
Colorado
Bahia Blanca
Mar del Plata

Puerto Montt
San Carlos de Bariloche
G. San Matias

Ancud
PTO. MADRYN
Chubut

I. Grande de Chiloé
ARCHIPIELAGO de los CHONOS
Comodoro Rivadavia

G. San Jorge
C. Tres Puntas

Puerto Aisen
San Julián

Bahia Grande
FALKLAND ISLANDS
(Br. - claimed by Arg.)

Rio Gallegos
Stanley

Punta Arenas

I. Santa Inés
I. de los Estados

Cape Horn

SOUTH GEORGIA ISLAND
(U.K.)

SOUTH PACIFIC OCEAN

SOUTH ATLANTIC OCEAN

Tropic of Capricorn

A N D E S   M O U N T A I N S

C H I L E

A R G E N T I N A

SOUTH AMERICA

0   600 Km
0   600 Mi.

Capitals of Countries ⊙
International Boundaries ——

Longitude West of Greenwich

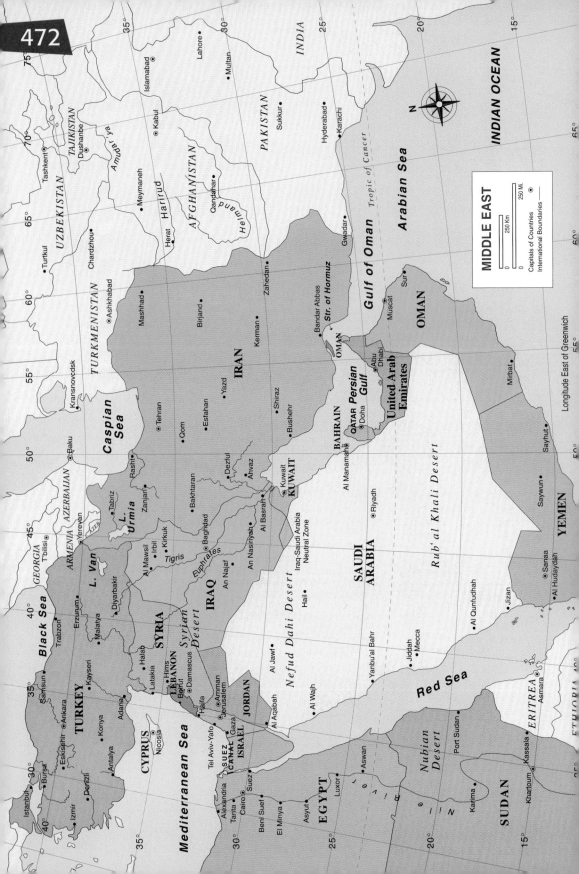

MIDDLE EAST

250 Km
0   250 Mi.
● Capitals of Countries
—— International Boundaries

INDIAN OCEAN

Arabian Sea

Gulf of Oman

Tropic of Cancer

Str. of Hormuz

Persian Gulf

Red Sea

Mediterranean Sea

Black Sea

Caspian Sea

Nubian Desert

Rub' al Khali Desert

Nefud Dahi Desert

Syrian Desert

L. Urmia

L. Van

INDIA

PAKISTAN

AFGHANISTAN

TAJIKISTAN

UZBEKISTAN

TURKMENISTAN

IRAN

IRAQ

SYRIA

TURKEY

GEORGIA

ARMENIA

AZERBAIJAN

CYPRUS

LEBANON

ISRAEL

JORDAN

EGYPT

SAUDI ARABIA

KUWAIT

BAHRAIN

QATAR

United Arab Emirates

OMAN

YEMEN

SUDAN

ERITREA

ETHIOPIA

OMAN

Lahore
Multan
Islamabad
Kabul
Sukkur
Hyderabad
Karachi
Gwadar
Qandahar
Herat
Meymaneh
Chardzhou
Dushanbe
Tashkent
Turkul
Krasnovodsk
Ashkhabad
Mashhad
Birjand
Zahedan
Kerman
Yazd
Shiraz
Bushehr
Bandar Abbas
Sur
Muscat
Mirbat
Sayhut
Saywun
Sanaa
Al Hudaydah
Jizan
Al Qunfudhah
Mecca
Jiddah
Yanbu'al Bahr
Al Wajh
Al Aqabah
Riyadh
Hail
Al Jawf
Al Manamah
Doha
Abu Dhabi
Tehran
Qom
Esfahan
Ahvaz
Dezful
Baku
Rasht
Tabriz
Zanjan
Yerevan
Tbilisi
Tahran
Bakhtaran
Baghdad
Al Basrah
An Nasiriyah
An Najaf
Kuwait
Iraq-Saudi Arabia Neutral Zone
Al Mawsil
Kirkuk
Irbil
Diyarbakir
Erzurum
Trabzon
Samsun
Ankara
Kayseri
Malatya
Eskisehir
Bursa
Istanbul
Izmir
Denizli
Antalya
Konya
Adana
Nicosia
Latakia
Halab
Hims
Beirut
Damascus
Haifa
Tel Aviv-Yafo
Jerusalem
Amman
Gaza
Alexandria
Cairo
Tanta
Beni Suef
El Minya
Asyut
Luxor
Aswan
Suez
Port Sudan
Khartoum
Kassala
Asmara
Katima

Amudar'ya
Harirud
Helmand
Tigris
Euphrates
SUEZ CANAL
NILE RIVER

Longitude East of Greenwich

35° 30° 25° 20° 15°

75° 70° 65° 60° 55° 50° 45° 40° 35° 30°

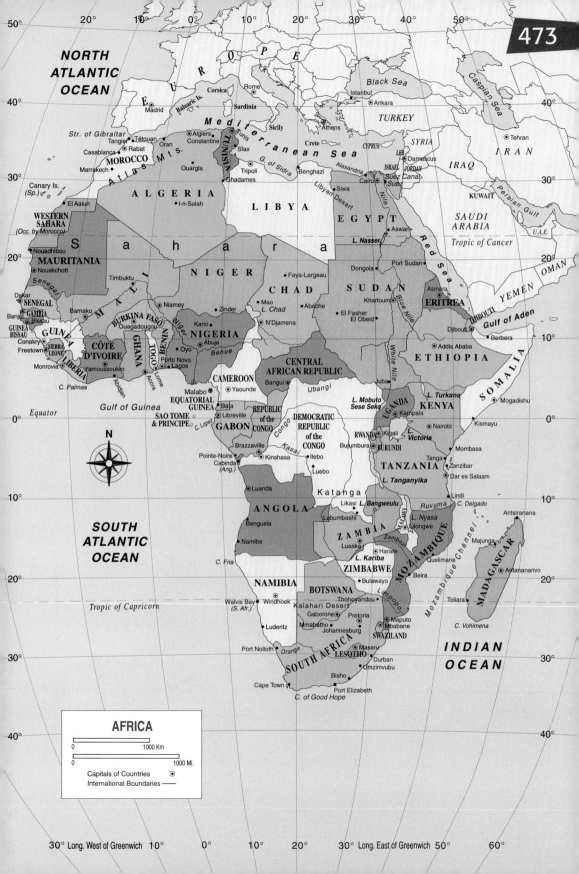

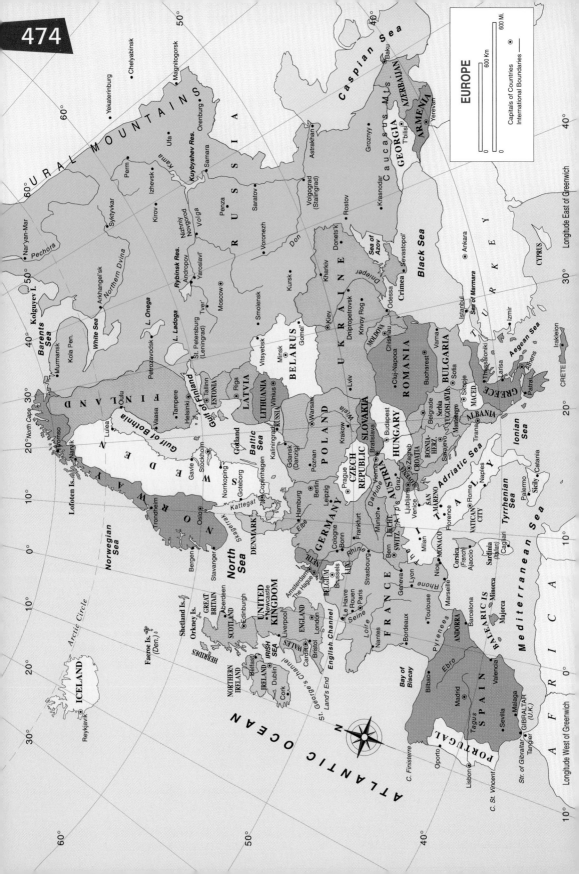

EUROPE

600 Km
600 Mi.

⊙ Capitals of Countries
— International Boundaries

ATLANTIC OCEAN

ICELAND

Reykjavík

Faeroe Is.
(Den.)

Shetland Is.

Orkney Is.

GREAT
BRITAIN

SCOTLAND

Aberdeen

Edinburgh

Newcastle

UNITED
KINGDOM

ENGLAND

Liverpool

WALES

Cardiff

Bristol

London

IRISH
SEA

NORTHERN
IRELAND

Belfast

IRELAND

Dublin

Cork

HEBRIDES

Land's End

St. George's Channel

English Channel

NORWEGIAN Sea

Norwegian
Sea

Lofoten Is.

North Cape

Tromsø

Narvik

S
W
E
D
E
N

N
O
R
W
A
Y

Trondheim

Bergen

Stavanger

Oslo

Göteborg

Norrköping

Gävle

Stockholm

Gotland

Skagerrak

Kattegat

DENMARK

Copenhagen

Baltic
Sea

North
Sea

Hamburg

Elbe

Bonn

Cologne

Frankfurt

Leipzig

Berlin

G E R M A N Y

Munich

NETH.

Amsterdam

The Hague

Rotterdam

BELGIUM

Brussels

LUX.

Le Havre

Rouen

Paris

Seine

Strasbourg

F R A N C E

Nantes

Loire

Bordeaux

Bay of
Biscay

Toulouse

Marseille

Nice

Lyon

Geneva

Bern

SWITZ.

LIECHT.

AUSTRIA

Rhine

Rhône

Pyrenees

ANDORRA

Bilbao

Barcelona

Madrid

Ebro

Tagus

Valencia

S P A I N

Sevilla

Málaga

GIBRALTAR
(U.K.)

Tangier

Str. of Gibraltar

Lisbon

Oporto

P O R T U G A L

C. St. Vincent

C. Finisterre

BALEARIC IS.

Minorca

Majorca

Corsica
(French)

Ajaccio

Sardinia
(Italian)

Cagliari

MONACO

Milan

Florence

Venice

Rome

VATICAN
CITY

SAN
MARINO

Naples

I T A L Y

Tyrrhenian
Sea

Sicily

Palermo

Catania

Mediterranean Sea

A F R I C A

A L P S

Po

SLOVENIA

Ljubljana

Zagreb

CROATIA

BOSNIA-
HERZ.

Sarajevo

Graz

Vienna

HUNGARY

Budapest

Danube

Belgrade

Serbia

Montenegro

YUGOSLAVIA

Skopje

MACED.

ALBANIA

Tirana

Adriatic Sea

Ionian
Sea

GREECE

Athens

Patrai

Larisa

Thessaloníki

Ioánnina

Aegean Sea

CRETE

Irakleion

SLOVAKIA

Bratislava

CZECH
REPUBLIC

Prague

P O L A N D

Kraków

Warsaw

Wisła

Poznań

Gdańsk (Danzig)

Kaliningrad

LITHUANIA

Vilnius

Kaunas

LATVIA

Riga

ESTONIA

Tallinn

Gulf of Finland

Helsinki

Tampere

F I N L A N D

Vaasa

Oulu

Luleå

Gulf of Bothnia

Petrozavodsk

L. Ladoga

L. Onega

St. Petersburg
(Leningrad)

Tver

Moscow

Smolensk

Minsk

BELARUS

Gomel

Vitsyebsk

Kursk

Kiev

U K R A I N E

Lviv

Krivoy Rog

Dnepr

Dnipropetrovsk

Donets'k

Kharkiv

ROMANIA

Bucharest

Cluj-Napoca

MOLDOVA

Chişinău

Odessa

BULGARIA

Sofia

Varna

Crimea

Sevastopol'

Black Sea

Sea of
Azov

Rostov

T U R K E Y

Istanbul

Sea of Marmara

İzmir

Ankara

CYPRUS

Longitude East of Greenwich

White
Sea

Barents
Sea

Kolguyev I.

Kola Pen.

Murmansk

Arkhangel'sk

Northern Dvina

Syktyvkar

Nar'yan-Mar

Pechora

U R A L   M O U N T A I N S

Yekaterinburg

Chelyabinsk

Magnitogorsk

Orenburg

Ufa

Kama

Kuybyshev Res.

Izhevsk

Perm

Kirov

Samara

Penza

Volga

Saratov

Nizhniy
Novgorod

Yaroslavl'

Andropov

Rybinsk Res.

R U S S I A

Voronezh

Don

Volgograd
(Stalingrad)

Astrakhan

Caspian Sea

Caucasus Mts.

Krasnodar

Grozny

GEORGIA

Tbilisi

ARMENIA

Yerevan

AZERBAIJAN

Baku

Arctic Circle

Longitude West of Greenwich

50°

60°

60°

50°

40°

30°

20°

10°

0°

10°

20°

30°

40°

50°

60°

North Cape

20°

30°

40°

ATLANTIC
OCEAN

GREENLAND

UNITED STATES
(Alaska)

ICELAND

BERING
SEA

ARCTIC
North Pole
OCEAN

60°   80°   60°
20°
0°
20°   180°
40°   160°
60°   140°
80° 100° 120°

ALEUTIAN IS.

BRITISH ISLES

BARENTS
SEA

NOVAYA ZEMLYA

SEVERNAYA
ZEMLYA

LAPTEV SEA

NEW
SIBERIAN IS.

EAST
SIBERIAN
SEA

Anadyr

Komandorskiye Is.

London

NORTH
SEA

Svalbard

KARA SEA

Nordvik

Srednekolymsk

Kolyma

Magadan

Petropavlovsk-
Kamchatskiy

Paris

BALTIC
SEA

Berlin

St. Petersburg

Dudinka

Arctic Circle

Lena

Yakutsk

Nikolayevsk

Sakhalin I.

SEA OF
OKHOTSK

Kamchatka Pen.

Vienna

Warsaw

Moscow

Kiev

E U R O P E

R   U   S   S   I   A

Salekhard

Khanty-Mansiysk

Tura

Komsomol'sk

Skovorodino

Khabarovsk

Hokkaido

KURIL IS.

Perm'

Yekaterinburg

Chelyabinsk

Magnitogorsk

Ob'

Tomsk

Krasnoyarsk

Kirensk

Amur

Hakodate

Vladivostok

Istanbul

BLACK SEA

Ural'sk

Omsk

Novosibirsk

Barnaul

Irkutsk

Chita

Ulan-Ude

L.
Baykal

Qiqihar

Changchun

Shenyang

N.
KOREA

Sendai

Honshu

Tokyo

SEA
OF
JAPAN

Izmir

Ankara

TURKEY

Erzurum

Karaganda

Semipalatinsk

Ulaanbaatar

Dandong

Pyongyang

Seoul

Nagoya

Adana

KAZAKHSTAN

ARAL SEA

L. Balkhash

Hovd

Uliastay

MONGOLIA

Gobi

INNER MONGOLIA

Beijing

Tianjin

S.
KOREA

Hiroshima

Shikoku

Kyushu

MED.
SEA

CYPRUS

Aleppo

SYRIA

CASPIAN SEA

Krasnovodsk

Bishkek

Alma-Ata

Urumqi

YELLOW
SEA

Nagasaki

LEBANON

Beirut

Damascus

Tabriz

UZBEK.

Tashkent

KYRGYZ.

Kokand

Aksu

SINKIANG

Yumen

Jinan

Huang

GRAND CANAL

Kaifeng

Shanghai

RYUKYU IS. (Jap.)

Jerusalem

ISRAEL

Amman

IRAQ

Baghdad

Tehran

TURKMENISTAN

Ashkhabad

TAJIK.

Shache

Jiuquan

Lanzhou

Xi'an

Nanjing

EAST
CHINA
SEA

JORDAN

Basra

Mashad

Hotan

C   H   I   N   A

Wuhan

Tropic of Cancer

KUWAIT

IRAN

Herat

Kabul

Srinagar

TIBET

Lhasa

Chongqing

Changsha

Fuzhou

Taipei

BAHRAIN

Shiraz

AFGHANISTAN

Islamabad

Himalayas

Thimphu

Chang (Yangtze)

TAIWAN

QATAR

RED
SEA

Riyadh

Bandar
Abbas

Quetta

BHUTAN

Guangzhou

HONG KONG

U.S. ARAB
EMIR.

Persian G.

Gwadar

PAKISTAN

New Delhi

NEPAL

Kathmandu

Brahmaputra

Myitkyina

PACIFIC
OCEAN

Mecca

Muscat

G. of Oman

Karachi

Kanpur

Indus

Hanoi

Luzon

SAUDI
ARABIA

OMAN

Ahmadabad

I   N   D   I   A

Calcutta

Dhaka

Mandalay

LAOS

G. of Tonkin

Hainan

Manila

PHILIPPINES

Samar

Sanaa

Daman

BANGLA-
DESH

MYANMAR

Vientiane

SOUTH
CHINA
SEA

Mindoro

Leyte

YEMEN

Aden

G. of Aden

Socotra

Bombay

Hyderabad

Yanam

Rangoon

THAILAND

Mekong

VIETNAM

Palawan

Negros

Davao

ARABIAN
SEA

Bangalore

Madras

BAY OF
BENGAL

Bangkok

CAMBODIA

Phnom Penh

Ho Chi Minh City
(Saigon)

Mindanao

Mahe

Karikal

G. of
Thailand

SABAH

Kota Kinabalu

Madurai

SRI LANKA
(CEYLON)

Kandy

BRUNEI

SARAWAK

CELEBES
SEA

Manado

Colombo

MALDIVES

Male

George Town

Str. of Malacca

MALAYA

MALAYSIA

Kuching

Banjarmasin

Celebes

BANDA
SEA

East Timor

Medan

Kuala Lumpur

SINGAPORE

Borneo

Ujung Pandang

Flores

Timor

SEYCHELLES

Equator

Sumatra

INDONESIA

Palembang

Jakarta

JAVA

Surabaya

JAVA SEA

Sumbawa

FLORES SEA

TIMOR
SEA

N

AFRICA

MADAGASCAR

SUNDA IS.

Broome

20°

INDIAN   OCEAN

40°

40°

20°

20°

40°

AUSTRALIA

Tropic of Capricorn

Perth

ASIA

0   1200 Km.

0   1200 Mi.

◉ Capitals of Countries
—— International Boundaries

60°   Longitude East of Greenwich   80°   100°   120°

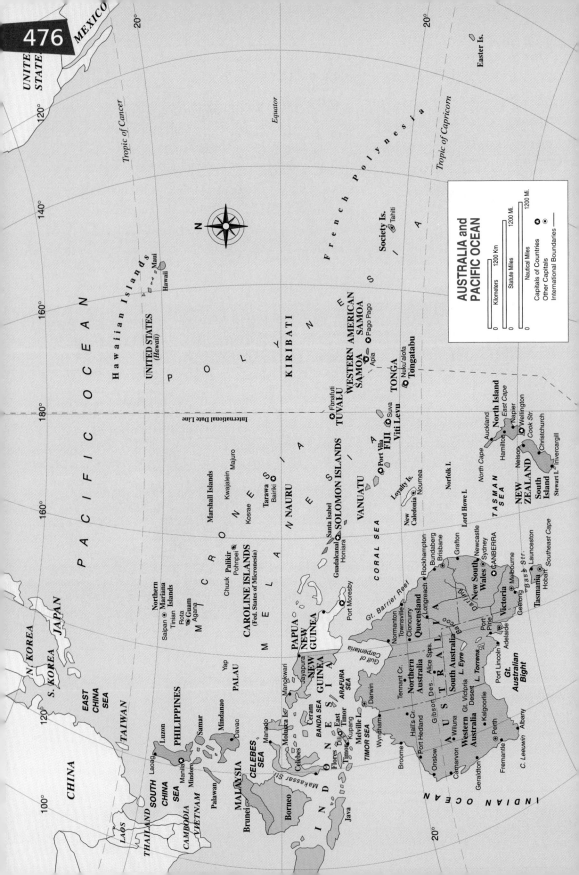

MEXICO

UNITED
STATES

Easter Is.

Tropic of Cancer

Equator

Tropic of Capricorn

AUSTRALIA and PACIFIC OCEAN

Kilometers   1200 Km
0

Statute Miles   1200 Mi.
0

Nautical Miles   1200 Mi.
0

Capitals of Countries
Other Capitals
International Boundaries

N

F r e n c h   P o l y n e s i a

Society Is.
Tahiti

P A C I F I C   O C E A N

H a w a i i a n   I s l a n d s

Maui
Hawaii

UNITED STATES
(Hawaii)

KIRIBATI

WESTERN AMERICAN
SAMOA   SAMOA
Pago Pago

Apia
TONGA   Nuku'alofa
TUVALU   Tongatabu
Funafuti

FIJI   Suva
Viti Levu

International Date Line

P O L Y N E S I A

M I C R O N E S I A

Marshall Islands
Kwajalein   Majuro

Kosrae

Tarawa
Bairiki

NAURU

Port Vila

VANUATU

N E W   G U I N E A   Noumea
New
Caledonia   Loyalty Is.
Norfolk I.

North Cape
Auckland
Hamilton   North Island   East Cape
Napier
Nelson   Wellington
South Island   Christchurch
Invercargill
Stewart I.   Cook Str.

NEW
ZEALAND

TASMAN
SEA

Lord Howe I.

Newcastle
Sydney
CANBERRA
Melbourne
Geelong   Bass Str.
Tasmania   Launceston
Hobart   Southeast Cape

CORAL SEA

Gt. Barrier Reef

SOLOMON ISLANDS
Santa Isabel
Guadalcanal   Honiara

Port Moresby

PAPUA
NEW
GUINEA

Chuuk   Palikir
Pohnpei

CAROLINE ISLANDS
(Fed. States of Micronesia)

Northern
Saipan   Mariana
Tinian   Islands
Rota
Guam
Agana

Yap
PALAU

Mangkwari
Jayapura   NEW GUINEA

ARAFURA
SEA

Molucca Is.
Ceram
BANDA SEA   East
Flores   Timor
Dili   Kupang
Timor
TIMOR SEA
Melville I.
Darwin
Wyndham

CELEBES
SEA

Manado
Celebes
MAKASSAR STR.

Borneo

Brunei

MALAYSIA

CHINA

LAOS

THAILAND
CAMBODIA
VIETNAM

SOUTH
CHINA
SEA

Palawan
Laoag
Luzon
Mindoro
Manila
PHILIPPINES
Samar
Mindanao
Davao

TAIWAN

EAST
CHINA
SEA

S. KOREA
N. KOREA

JAPAN

I N D O N E S I A

Java

Normanton
Cloncurry
Longreach

Gulf of
Carpentaria

Tennant Cr.
Northern
Australia

Alice Sprs.
Gibson Des.   L. Eyre
Gt. Victoria   L. Torrens
Desert   Adelaide
Kalgoorlie
Western   Wiluna   Gt.
Australia   Australian
Perth   Bight
Fremantle
C. Leeuwin   Albany
Geraldton

A U S T R A L I A

South Australia
Port Augusta
Port Pirie
Port Lincoln

Queensland
Rockhampton
Bundaberg
Brisbane
Grafton

New South
Wales

Victoria

Port
Hedland
Onslow
Carnarvon
Broome
Halls Cr.

Darling

Murray

Murrumbidgee

Gt. Dividing Range

INDIAN OCEAN

Index to World Maps

Country	Latitude	Longitude	Country	Latitude	Longitude
Afghanistan	33° N	65° E	Costa Rica	10° N	84° W
Albania	41° N	20° E	Côte d'Ivoire	8° N	5° W
Algeria	28° N	3° E	Croatia	45° N	16° E
Andorra	42° N	1° E	Cuba	21° N	80° W
Angola	12° S	18° E	Cyprus	35° N	33° E
Antigua and			Czech Republic	50° N	15° E
Barbuda	17° N	61° W	Denmark	56° N	10° E
Argentina	34° S	64° W	Djibouti	11° N	43° E
Armenia	41° N	45° E	Dominica	15° N	61° W
Australia	25° S	135° E	Dominican Rep.	19° N	70°
Austria	47° N	13° E	East Timor	10° S	125° E
Azerbaijan	41° N	47° E	Ecuador	2° S	77° W
Bahamas	24° N	76° W	Egypt	27° N	30° E
Bahrain	26° N	50° E	El Salvador	14° N	89° W
Bangladesh	24° N	90° E	Equatorial Guinea	2° N	9° E
Barbados	13° N	59° W	Eritrea	17° N	38° E
Belarus	54° N	25° E	Estonia	59° N	26° E
Belgium	50° N	4° E	Ethiopia	8° N	38° E
Belize	17° N	88° W	Fiji	19° S	174° E
Benin	9° N	2° E	Finland	64° N	26° E
Bhutan	27° N	90° E	France	46° N	2° E
Bolivia	17° S	65° W	Gabon	1° S	11° E
Bosnia-			The Gambia	13° N	16° W
Herzegovina	44° N	18° E	Georgia	43° N	45° E
Botswana	22° S	24° E	Germany	51° N	10° E
Brazil	10° S	55° W	Ghana	8° N	2° W
Brunei Darussalam	4° N	114° E	Greece	39° N	22° E
Bulgaria	43° N	25° E	Greenland	70° N	40° W
Burkina Faso	13° N	2° W	Grenada	12° N	61° W
Burundi	3° S	30° E	Guatemala	15° N	90° W
Cambodia	13° N	105° E	Guinea	11° N	10° W
Cameroon	6° N	12° E	Guinea-Bissau	12° N	15° W
Canada	60° N	95° W	Guyana	5° N	59° W
Cape Verde	16° N	24° W	Haiti	19° N	72° W
Central African			Honduras	15° N	86° W
Republic	7° N	21° E	Hungary	47° N	20° E
Chad	15° N	19° E	Iceland	65° N	18° W
Chile	30° S	71° W	India	20° N	77° E
China	35° N	105° E	Indonesia	5° S	120° E
Colombia	4° N	72° W	Iran	32° N	53° E
Comoros	12° S	44° E	Iraq	33° N	44° E
Congo,			Ireland	53° N	8° W
Dem. Rep. of the	4° S	25° E	Israel	31° N	35° E
Congo,			Italy	42° N	12° E
Republic of the	1° S	15° E	Jamaica	18° N	77° W

Country	Latitude	Longitude	Country	Latitude	Longitude
Japan	36° N	138° E	Oman	22° N	58° E
Jordan	31° N	36° E	Pakistan	30° N	70° E
Kazakhstan	45° N	70° E	Palau	8° N	138° E
Kenya	1° N	38° E	Panama	9° N	80° W
Kiribati	0° N	175° E	Papua New Guinea	6° S	147° E
North Korea	40° N	127° E	Paraguay	23° S	58° W
South Korea	36° N	128° E	Peru	10° S	76° W
Kuwait	29° N	47° E	The Philippines	13° N	122° E
Kyrgyzstan	42° N	75° E	Poland	52° N	19° E
Laos	18° N	105° E	Portugal	39° N	8° W
Latvia	57° N	25° E	Qatar	25° N	51° E
Lebanon	34° N	36° E	Romania	46° N	25° E
Lesotho	29° S	28° E	Russia	60° N	80° E
Liberia	6° N	10° W	Rwanda	2° S	30° E
Libya	27° N	17° E	St. Kitts & Nevis	17° N	62° W
Liechtenstein	47° N	9° E	Saint Lucia	14° N	61° W
Lithuania	56° N	24° E	Saint Vincent and		
Luxembourg	49° N	6° E	the Grenadines	13° N	61° W
Macedonia	43° N	22° E	San Marino	44° N	12° E
Madagascar	19° S	46° E	São Tomé and		
Malawi	13° S	34° E	Príncipe	1° N	7° E
Malaysia	2° N	112° E	Saudi Arabia	25° N	45° E
Maldives	2° N	70° E	Scotland	57° N	5° W
Mali	17° N	4° W	Senegal	14° N	14° W
Malta	36° N	14° E	Serbia	45° N	21° E
Marshall Islands	7° N	172° E	Seychelles	5° S	55° E
Mauritania	20° N	12° W	Sierra Leone	8° N	11° W
Mauritius	20° S	57° E	Singapore	1° N	103° E
Mexico	23° N	102° W	Slovakia	49° N	19° E
Micronesia	5° N	150° E	Slovenia	46° N	15° E
Moldova	47° N	28° E	Solomon Islands	8° S	159° E
Monaco	43° N	7° E	Somalia	10° N	49° E
Mongolia	46° N	105° E	South Africa	30° S	26° E
Montenegro	43° N	19° E	Spain	40° N	4° W
Morocco	32° N	5° W	Sri Lanka	7° N	81° E
Mozambique	18° S	35° E	Sudan	15° N	30° E
Myanmar	25° N	95° E	Suriname	4° N	56° W
Namibia	22° S	17° E	Swaziland	26° S	31° E
Nauru	1° S	166° E	Sweden	62° N	15° E
Nepal	28° N	84° E	Switzerland	47° N	8° E
The Netherlands	52° N	5° E	Syria	35° N	38° E
New Zealand	41° S	174° E	Taiwan	23° N	121° E
Nicaragua	13° N	85° W	Tajikistan	39° N	71° E
Niger	16° N	8° E	Tanzania	6° S	35° E
Nigeria	10° N	8° E	Thailand	15° N	100° E
Northern Ireland	55° N	7° W	Togo	8° N	1° E
Norway	62° N	10° E	Tonga	20° S	173° W

Country	Latitude	Longitude	Country	Latitude	Longitude
Trinidad & Tobago	11° N	61° W	Uruguay	33° S	56° W
Tunisia	34° N	9° E	Uzbekistan	40° N	68° E
Turkey	39° N	35° E	Vanuatu	17° S	170° E
Turkmenistan	40° N	55° E	Venezuela	8° N	66° W
Tuvalu	8° S	179° E	Vietnam	17° N	106° E
Uganda	1° N	32° E	Wales	53° N	3° W
Ukraine	50° N	30° E	Western Samoa	10° S	173° W
United Arab			Yemen	15° N	44° E
Emirates	24° N	54° E	Yugoslavia	44° N	19° E
United Kingdom	54° N	2° W	Zambia	15° S	30° E
United States	38° N	97° W	Zimbabwe	20° S	30° E

Geographic Facts

THE CONTINENTS

	Area (Sq Km)	Percent of Earth's Land
Asia	44,026,000	29.7
Africa	30,271,000	20.4
North America	24,258,000	16.3
South America	17,823,000	12.0
Antarctica	13,209,000	8.9
Europe	10,404,000	7.0
Australia	7,682,000	5.2

MAJOR ISLANDS

	Area (Sq Km)
Greenland	2,175,600
New Guinea	792,500
Borneo	725,500
Madagascar	587,000
Baffin	507,500
Sumatra	427,300
Honshu	227,400
Great Britain	218,100
Victoria	217,300
Ellesmere	196,200
Celebes	178,700
South (New Zealand)	151,000
Java	126,700

LONGEST RIVERS

	Length (Km)
Nile, *Africa*	6,671
Amazon, *South America*	6,437
Chang Jiang (Yangtze), *Asia*	6,380
Mississippi-Missouri, *North America*	5,971
Ob-Irtysk, *Asia*	5,410
Huang (Yellow), *Asia*	4,672
Congo, *Africa*	4,667
Amur, *Asia*	4,416
Lena, *Asia*	4,400
Mackenzie-Peace, *North America*	4,241

THE OCEANS

	Area (Sq Km)	Percent of Earth's Water Area
Pacific	166,241,000	46.0
Atlantic	86,557,000	23.9
Indian	73,427,000	20.3
Arctic	9,485,000	2.6

World Time Zones

The world's time zones start at the prime meridian and divide the world into 24 time zones. When going west, travelers must set their watches back one hour for each time zone they cross. Going east, they must set their watches forward one hour for each zone.

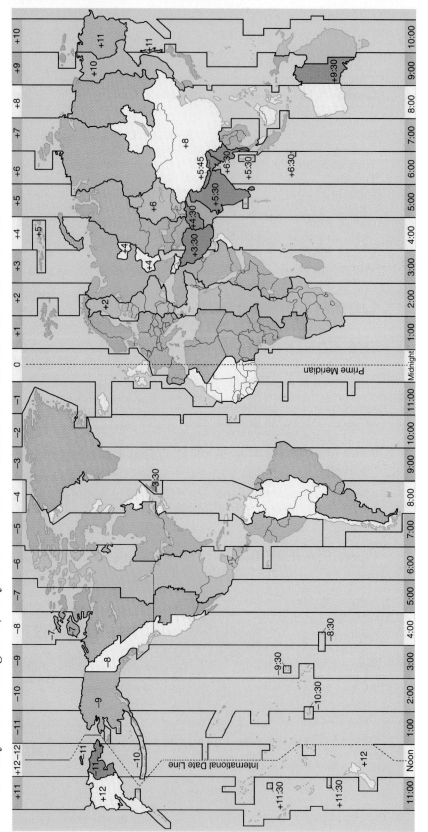

Government

Every country in the world has a government. The purpose of the government is to make and enforce laws and to protect the rights of its citizens. Every major country in the world also has a constitution, a basic set of laws by which the people are governed.

The U.S. Constitution establishes the form of the United States government and explains the rights and responsibilities of its citizens. This section of your handbook takes a closer look at those rights and responsibilities, and how the government is organized. We hope you find it interesting and useful.

Branches of Government

Legislative Branch	Executive Branch	Judicial Branch

Duties/Responsibilities

Makes Laws	Enforces Laws Makes Policy	Interprets Laws

Components

Congress		President	Supreme Court
Senate	House of Representatives	Vice President	Circuit Courts
President of the Senate	Speaker of the House	Cabinet	District Courts
			Special Courts

President's Cabinet

The Cabinet is a group of advisors appointed by the president to help set policies and make decisions. The Cabinet usually meets weekly with the president.

Department of State

Department of Health and Human Services

Department of Education

Department of Defense

Department of the Treasury

Department of Veterans Affairs

Department of Commerce

Department of the Interior

Department of Energy

Department of Housing and Urban Development

Attorney General

Department of Labor

Department of Agriculture

Department of Transportation

Individual Rights & Responsibilities

Individual Rights

Freedom of Assembly

Freedom to hold meetings. Meetings must be peaceful.

Freedom of Speech

Freedom to express ideas and opinions. No one may say untrue things about other citizens.

Freedom of Petition

Freedom to ask the government to pass laws.

Freedom of the Press

Freedom to print books, newspapers, and magazines. No one may print things that hurt American citizens.

Freedom of Religion

Freedom to practice the religion of your choice.

Freedom of Equal Justice

All persons accused of a crime must receive fair and equal treatment under the law.

Freedom and Security of Citizens

No one may search someone's home. People have the right to bear arms to protect themselves.

Duties of Citizenship
- American citizens must serve as jury members when called upon.
- American citizens must pay taxes to fund the government.
- American citizens must attend school.
- American citizens must testify in court.
- American citizens must obey the law.
- American citizens must help to defend the nation.

U.S. Presidents and Vice Presidents

#	President	Term	Vice President	#
1	George Washington	April 30, 1789 – March 3, 1797	John Adams	1
2	John Adams	March 4, 1797 – March 3, 1801	Thomas Jefferson	2
3	Thomas Jefferson	March 4, 1801 – March 3, 1805	Aaron Burr	3
	Thomas Jefferson	March 4, 1805 – March 3, 1809	George Clinton	4
4	James Madison	March 4, 1809 – March 3, 1813	George Clinton	
	James Madison	March 4, 1813 – March 3, 1817	Elbridge Gerry	5
5	James Monroe	March 4, 1817 – March 3, 1821	Daniel D. Tompkins	6
	James Monroe	March 4, 1821 – March 3, 1825		
6	John Quincy Adams	March 4, 1825 – March 3, 1829	John C. Calhoun	7
7	Andrew Jackson	March 4, 1829 – March 3, 1833	John C. Calhoun	
	Andrew Jackson	March 4, 1833 – March 3, 1837	Martin Van Buren	8
8	Martin Van Buren	March 4, 1837 – March 3, 1841	Richard M. Johnson	9
9	William Henry Harrison*	March 4, 1841 – April 4, 1841	John Tyler	10
10	John Tyler	April 6, 1841 – March 3, 1845		
11	James K. Polk	March 4, 1845 – March 3, 1849	George M. Dallas	11
12	Zachary Taylor*	March 5, 1849 – July 9, 1850	Millard Fillmore	12
13	Millard Fillmore	July 10, 1850 – March 3, 1853		
14	Franklin Pierce	March 4, 1853 – March 3, 1857	William R. King	13
15	James Buchanan	March 4, 1857 – March 3, 1861	John C. Breckinridge	14
16	Abraham Lincoln	March 4, 1861 – March 3, 1865	Hannibal Hamlin	15
	Abraham Lincoln*	March 4, 1865 – April 15, 1865	Andrew Johnson	16
17	Andrew Johnson	April 15, 1865 – March 3, 1869		
18	Ulysses S. Grant	March 4, 1869 – March 3, 1873	Schuyler Colfax	17
	Ulysses S. Grant	March 4, 1873 – March 3, 1877	Henry Wilson	18
19	Rutherford B. Hayes	March 4, 1877 – March 3, 1881	William A. Wheeler	19
20	James A. Garfield*	March 4, 1881 – Sept. 19, 1881	Chester A. Arthur	20
21	Chester A. Arthur	Sept. 20, 1881 – March 3, 1885		
22	Grover Cleveland	March 4, 1885 – March 3, 1889	Thomas A. Hendricks	21
23	Benjamin Harrison	March 4, 1889 – March 3, 1893	Levi P. Morton	22
24	Grover Cleveland	March 4, 1893 – March 3, 1897	Adlai E. Stevenson	23
25	William McKinley	March 4, 1897 – March 3, 1901	Garret A. Hobart	24
	William McKinley*	March 4, 1901 – Sept. 14, 1901	Theodore Roosevelt	25
26	Theodore Roosevelt	Sept. 14, 1901 – March 3, 1905		
	Theodore Roosevelt	March 4, 1905 – March 3, 1909	Charles W. Fairbanks	26
27	William H. Taft	March 4, 1909 – March 3, 1913	James S. Sherman	27
28	Woodrow Wilson	March 4, 1913 – March 3, 1917	Thomas R. Marshall	28
	Woodrow Wilson	March 4, 1917 – March 3, 1921		
29	Warren G. Harding*	March 4, 1921 – Aug. 2, 1923	Calvin Coolidge	29
30	Calvin Coolidge	Aug. 3, 1923 – March 3, 1925		
	Calvin Coolidge	March 4, 1925 – March 3, 1929	Charles G. Dawes	30
31	Herbert C. Hoover	March 4, 1929 – March 3, 1933	Charles Curtis	31

32 Franklin D. Roosevelt ...... March 4, 1933 – Jan. 20, 1937 .... John N. Garner 32

Franklin D. Roosevelt .... Jan. 20, 1937 – Jan. 20, 1941 .... John N. Garner

Franklin D. Roosevelt .... Jan. 20, 1941 – Jan. 20, 1945 .... Henry A. Wallace 33

Franklin D. Roosevelt* ...... Jan. 20, 1945 – April 12, 1945 .... Harry S. Truman 34

33 Harry S. Truman .... April 12, 1945 – Jan. 20, 1949

Harry S. Truman .... Jan. 20, 1949 – Jan. 20, 1953 .... Alben W. Barkley 35

34 Dwight D. Eisenhower .... Jan. 20, 1953 – Jan. 20, 1957 .... Richard M. Nixon 36

Dwight D. Eisenhower .... Jan. 20, 1957 – Jan. 20, 1961 .... Richard M. Nixon

35 John F. Kennedy* .... Jan. 20, 1961 – Nov. 22, 1963 .... Lyndon B. Johnson 37

36 Lyndon B. Johnson .... Nov. 22, 1963 – Jan. 20, 1965

Lyndon B. Johnson .... Jan. 20, 1965 – Jan. 20, 1969 ..... Hubert H. Humphrey 38

37 Richard M. Nixon .... Jan. 20, 1969 – Jan. 20, 1973 .... Spiro T. Agnew 39

Richard M. Nixon* .... Jan. 20, 1973 – Aug. 9, 1974 .... Gerald R. Ford 40

38 Gerald R. Ford .... Aug. 9, 1974 – Jan. 20, 1977 ..... Nelson A. Rockefeller 41

39 James E. Carter .... Jan. 20, 1977 – Jan. 20, 1981 .... Walter Mondale 42

40 Ronald W. Reagan .... Jan. 20, 1981 – Jan. 20, 1985 .... George H. W. Bush 43

Ronald W. Reagan .... Jan. 20, 1985 – Jan. 20, 1989 .... George H. W. Bush

41 George H. W. Bush .... Jan. 20, 1989 – Jan. 20, 1993 .... J. Danforth Quayle 44

42 William J. Clinton .... Jan. 20, 1993 – Jan. 20, 1997 .... Albert Gore, Jr. 45

William J. Clinton .... Jan. 20, 1997 – Jan. 20, 2001 .... Albert Gore, Jr.

43 George W. Bush .... Jan. 20, 2001 – .... Richard B. Cheney 46

(*Did not finish term)

Order of Presidential Succession

1. Vice president
2. Speaker of the House
3. President pro tempore of the Senate
4. Secretary of state
5. Secretary of the treasury
6. Secretary of defense
7. Attorney general
8. Secretary of the interior
9. Secretary of agriculture
10. Secretary of commerce
11. Secretary of labor
12. Secretary of health and human services
13. Secretary of housing and urban development
14. Secretary of transportation
15. Secretary of energy
16. Secretary of education
17. Secretary of veterans affairs

The U.S. Constitution

The Constitution is made up of three main parts: a **preamble,** 7 **articles,** and 27 **amendments.** The *preamble* states the purpose of the Constitution, the *articles* explain how the government works, and the 10 original *amendments* list the basic rights guaranteed to all American citizens. Together, these parts contain the laws and guidelines necessary to set up and run a successful national government.

Besides giving power to the national government, the U.S. Constitution gives some power to the states and some to the people. Remember this when you study the Constitution.

The Preamble

We the people of the United States, in order to form a more perfect Union, establish justice, insure domestic tranquility, provide for the common defense, promote the general welfare, and secure the blessings of liberty to ourselves and our posterity, do ordain and establish this Constitution for the United States of America.

The Articles of the Constitution

The articles of the Constitution explain how each branch of government works and what each can and cannot do. The articles also explain how the federal and state governments must work together, and how the Constitution can be amended or changed.

ARTICLE 1 explains the legislative branch, how laws are made, and how Congress works.

ARTICLE 2 explains the executive branch, the offices of the President and Vice President, and the powers of the executive branch.

ARTICLE 3 explains the judicial branch, the Supreme Court and other courts, and warns people about trying to overthrow the government.

ARTICLE 4 describes how the United States federal government and the individual state governments work together.

ARTICLE 5 tells how the Constitution can be amended, or changed.

ARTICLE 6 states that the United States federal government and the Constitution are the law of the land.

ARTICLE 7 outlines how the Constitution must be adopted to become official.

The Bill of Rights

To get the necessary votes to approve the Constitution, a number of changes (amendments) had to be made. These 10 original amendments are called the Bill of Rights. They guarantee all Americans some very basic rights, including the right to worship and speak freely and the right to have a jury trial.

AMENDMENT 1 People have the right to worship, to speak freely, to gather together, and to question the government.

AMENDMENT 2 People have the right to bear arms.

AMENDMENT 3 The government cannot have soldiers stay in people's houses without their permission.

AMENDMENT 4 People and their property cannot be searched without the written permission of a judge.

AMENDMENT 5 People cannot be tried for a serious crime without a jury. They cannot be tried twice for the same crime or be forced to testify against themselves. Also, they cannot have property taken away while they are on trial. Any property taken for public use must receive a fair price.

AMENDMENT 6 In criminal cases, people have a right to a trial, to be told what they are accused of, to hear witnesses against them, to get witnesses in their favor, and to have a lawyer.

AMENDMENT 7 In cases involving more than $20, people have the right to a jury trial.

AMENDMENT 8 People have a right to fair bail (money given as a promise the person will return for trial) and to fair fines and punishments.

AMENDMENT 9 People have rights that are not listed in the Constitution.

AMENDMENT 10 Powers not given to the federal government are given to the states or to the people.

The Other Amendments

The Constitution and the Bill of Rights were ratified in 1791. Since that time, more than 7,000 amendments to the Constitution have been proposed. Because three-fourths of the states must approve an amendment before it becomes law, just 27 amendments have been passed. The first 10 are listed under the Bill of Rights; the other 17 are listed below. (The date each amendment became law is given in parentheses.)

AMENDMENT 11 A person cannot sue a state in federal court. (1795)

AMENDMENT 12 President and Vice President are elected separately. (1804)

AMENDMENT 13 Slavery is abolished, done away with. (1865)

AMENDMENT 14 All persons born in the United States or those who have become citizens enjoy full citizenship rights. (1868)

AMENDMENT 15 Voting rights are given to all citizens regardless of race, creed, or color. (1870)

AMENDMENT 16 Congress has the power to collect income taxes. (1913)

AMENDMENT 17 United States Senators are elected directly by the people. (1913)

AMENDMENT 18 Making, buying, and selling alcoholic beverages is no longer allowed. (1919)

AMENDMENT 19 Women gain the right to vote. (1920)

AMENDMENT 20 The President's term begins January 20; Senators' and Representatives' terms begin January 3. (1933)

AMENDMENT 21 (Repeals Amendment 18) Alcoholic beverages can be made, bought, and sold again. (1933)

AMENDMENT 22 The President is limited to two elected terms. (1951)

AMENDMENT 23 District of Columbia residents gain the right to vote. (1961)

AMENDMENT 24 All voter poll taxes are forbidden. (1964)

AMENDMENT 25 If the Presidency is vacant, the Vice President takes over. If the Vice Presidency is vacant, the President names someone and the Congress votes on the choice. (1967)

AMENDMENT 26 Citizens 18 years old gain the right to vote. (1971)

AMENDMENT 27 No law changing the pay for members of Congress will take effect until after an election of Representatives. (1992)

History

A famous American author, Oliver Wendell Holmes, once said, "When I want to understand what is happening today or try to decide what will happen tomorrow, I look back." In other words, we can learn a lot about the world around us by looking at what has happened in the past—by studying history.

Historical Time Line

The historical time line included on the next 11 pages will help you look back. The time line covers the period from 1500 to the present. You'll notice that the time line is divided into three main parts: United States and World History, Science and Inventions, and Literature and Life. You'll discover many interesting things in the time line—when watches were invented (*1509*), where and when the first African slaves were brought to America (*Virginia in 1619*), and who developed the first pair of blue jeans (*Levi Strauss in 1850*).

But even before the first European settlers arrived in the United States, there were many Native American tribes living here. As you'll see on the map below, each tribe lived in one of five major regions. American history really begins with the Native Americans.

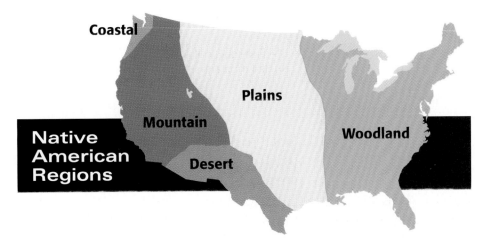

Coastal

Plains

Mountain

Woodland

Desert

Native American Regions

1500	1520	1540	1560	1580

U.S. and World History

1492
Columbus lands in the West Indies.

1519
Magellan begins three-year voyage around the world.

1513
Ponce de León explores Florida; Balboa reaches Pacific.

1519
Aztec empire dominates Mexico.

1565
Spain settles St. Augustine, Florida, the first permanent European colony.

1570
League of Iroquois Nations is formed.

1588
England defeats the Spanish Armada and rules the seas.

Science and Inventions

1507
Book on surgery is developed.

1509
Watches are invented.

1530
Bottle corks are invented.

1531
Haley's comet appears and causes panic.

1545
French painter Garamond sets first type.

1558
The magnetic compass is invented by John Dee.

1585
Dutch mathematicians introduce decimals.

1596
The thermometer is invented.

Literature and Life

1500
The game of Bingo is developed.

1507
Glass mirrors are greatly improved.

1536
The first songbook is used in Spain.

1564
The first horse-drawn coach is used in England.

1580
The first water closet is designed in Bath, England.

1599
Copper coins are first made.

U.S. POPULATION: (Native American)
approximately 1,100,000

(Spanish)
1,021

1600	1620	1640	1660	1680	1700

1607
The first English settlement is established at Jamestown, Virginia.

1673
Marquette and Joliet explore the Mississippi River for France.

1629
Massachusetts Bay Colony is established.

1619
First African slaves are brought to Virginia.

1620
Plymouth Colony is founded by Pilgrims.

1682
William Penn founds Pennsylvania.

1608
The telescope is invented.

1629
Human temperature is measured by a physician in Italy.

1682
Halley's Comet is studied by Edmund Halley and named for him.

1641
First cotton factories open in England

1671
The first calculation machine is invented.

1609
Galileo makes the first observations with a telescope.

1643
Torricelli invents the barometer.

1687
Newton describes gravity.

1600
Shakespeare's plays are performed at Globe Theatre in London.

1630
Popcorn is introduced to the Pilgrims by Native Americans.

1658
The first illustrated book for children, *World of Invisible Objects,* is written by John Comenius.

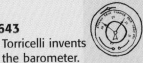

1653
The first postage stamps are used in Paris.

1685
The first drinking fountain is used in England.

1622
The year begins on January 1, instead of March 25.

1697
Charles Perrault writes *Tales of Mother Goose.*

(English)
350   **2,302**   **26,634**   **75,058**   **151,507**

1700	1710	1720	1730	1740

U.S. and World History

1700
France builds forts at Mackinac and Detroit to control fur trade.

1705
The Virginia Act establishes public education.

1733
The British Molasses Act places taxes on sugar and molasses.

1718
New Orleans is founded by France.

1707
England (English)and Scotland (Scots) become Great Britain (British).

1747
The Ohio Company is formed to settle the Ohio River Valley.

Science and Inventions

1701
Seed drill that plants seeds in a row is invented by Jethro Tull.

1728
The first dental drill is used by Pierre Fauchard.

1735
Rubber is found in South America.

1709
The pianoforte (first piano) is invented by Christofori Bartolommeo.

1742
Benjamin Franklin invents the efficient Franklin stove.

Literature and Life

1700
The Selling of Joseph by Samuel Sewall is the first book against slavery of Africans.

1718
First hot-water home heating system developed.

1726
Jonathan Swift writes *Gulliver's Travels*.

1731
Benjamin Franklin begins the first public library.

1704
The *Boston News-Letter* is the first successful newspaper in the American colonies.

1737
An earthquake in Calcutta, India, kills 300,000 people.

U.S. POPULATION: (English Colonies)

250,888	331,711	466,185	629,445	905,563

| 1750 | 1760 | 1770 | 1780 | 1790 | 1800 |

1750
Flatbed boats and Conestoga wagons begin moving settlers west.

1763
Britain wins the French and Indian War.

1775
The first battles of the Revolutionary War are fought.

1787
The U.S. Constitution is signed.

1765
The Stamp Act tax is imposed on the colonies by Britain.

1776
The Declaration of Independence is signed on July 4.

1789
George Washington becomes the first U.S. president.

1781
The British surrender October 19.

1752
Benjamin Franklin discovers that lightning is a form of electricity.

1770
The first steam carriage is invented.

1764
"Spinning jenny," a machine for spinning cotton, is invented.

1783
The first hot-air balloon is flown.

1793
Eli Whitney invents the cotton gin to remove the seeds from cotton.

1796
The smallpox vaccine is developed.

1752
The first American hospital is established in Philadelphia.

1757
Streetlights are installed in Philadelphia.

1764
Mozart writes his first symphony.

1773
Phillis Wheatley publishes a book of poetry.

1782
The American bald eagle is first used as a symbol of the United States.

1786
The first ice-cream company in America begins production.

1790
The U.S. government takes its first official census.

1791
Benjamin Bannekar surveys the new capital, Washington, D.C.

| 1,170,760 | 1,593,625 | 2,148,076 | 2,780,369 | 3,929,157 |

1800	1810	1820	1830	1840

U.S. and World History

1800
Washington, D.C., becomes the U.S. capital.

1814
U.S. defeats Britain in the War of 1812.

1836
Texans defend the Alamo.

1803
The Louisiana Purchase doubles the size of the U.S.

1819
The U.S. acquires Florida from Spain.

1838
The Cherokee Nation is forced west on the "Trail of Tears."

1830
Native Americans are forced west by the Indian Removal Act.

1804
Lewis and Clark explore the Louisiana Territory and the Northwest.

1848
Gold is discovered in California.

Science and Inventions

1800
The battery is invented by Count Volta.

1816
The stethoscope is invented.

1839
Kirkpatrick Macmillan invents the bicycle.

1816
Joseph Niépce takes the first photograph.

1836
Samuel Morse invents the telegraph.

1802
Robert Fulton builds the first steamboat.

1846
Elias Howe invents the sewing machine.

Literature and Life

1804
The first book of children's poems is published.

1828
The first Webster's Dictionary is published.

1846
Harriet Tubman conducts the Underground Railroad.

1814
Francis Scott Key writes "The Star-Spangled Banner."

1834
Louis Braille perfects a writing system for the blind.

1848
Sojourner Truth writes about being a woman.

1812
Uncle Sam becomes a symbol of the U.S.

1849
The safety pin is invented.

U.S. POPULATION:				
5,308,080	7,240,102	9,638,453	12,860,702	17,063,353

1850	1860	1870	1880	1890	1900

1860
Abraham Lincoln is elected president.

1865
The Civil War ends, and the 13th Amendment to the Constitution ends slavery.

1892
An immigration station is opened at Ellis Island, N.Y.

1869
Immigrant workers complete the coast-to-coast railroad in Utah.

1898
The U.S. defeats Spain in the Spanish-American War.

1861
The Civil War begins.

1870
The 15th Amendment gives African Americans the right to vote.

1851
Isaac Singer produces a sewing machine.

1876
Alexander Graham Bell invents the telephone.

1893
Charles and Frank Duryea build the first successful U.S. gasoline-powered automobile.

1860
Jean Lenoir builds an internal combustion engine.

1879
Thomas Edison invents the lightbulb.

1896
Marconi invents the wireless radio.

1850
Oscar Levi Strauss makes the first blue jeans.

1864
Red Cross is established

1876
The National Baseball League is established.

1892
The "Pledge of Allegiance" is written by F. Bellamy.

1869
Chewing gum is patented.

1852
Harriet Beecher Stowe's novel *Uncle Tom's Cabin* strengthens the anti-slavery movement.

1886
The Statue of Liberty is erected in New York harbor to welcome immigrants.

1896
The first movie is shown in the U.S.

23,191,876	31,443,321	38,558,371	50,189,209	62,979,766

1900	1905	1910	1915	1920

U.S. and World History

1900
Women compete in the Olympics for the first time.

1909
National Association for the Advancement of Colored People (NAACP) is founded.

1917
The United States enters World War I.

1917
Puerto Rico becomes a commonwealth of the U.S.

1904
One million immigrants arrive in the U.S., mostly from Europe.

1914
The Panama Canal opens.

1918
World War I ends in Europe.

1920
Women are given the right to vote.

Science and Inventions

1901
Walter Reed discovers yellow fever is carried by mosquitoes.

1903
Orville and Wilbur Wright fly the first successful airplane.

1904
New York City develops a subway system.

1911
Marie Curie wins the Nobel Prize in chemistry.

1912
Garrett Morgan invents automatic traffic light.

1913
Henry Ford establishes the assembly line for making automobiles.

1915
A coast-to-coast telephone system is established.

1921
The tuberculosis vaccine is discovered.

1922
The electron scanner for television is developed.

Literature and Life

1900
The hot dog is created in New York City.

1900
American Baseball League established.

1905
First nickelodeon movie theater established in Pittsburgh.

1903
The first World Series is played.

1913
Arthur Wynne invents the crossword puzzle.

1913
Boys Life magazine published by Boy Scouts.

1918
More than 20 million people die in a world-wide flu epidemic.

1920
The first radio station, KDKA, is founded in Pittsburgh.

1922
King Tut's tomb is discovered.

U.S. POPULATION:

76,212,168	92,228,496	106,021,537

1925	1930	1935	1940	1945	1950

1927
Charles Lindbergh is the first to fly solo across the Atlantic.

1929
Wall Street stock market crashes.

1933
Franklin Roosevelt becomes president and enacts the New Deal to end the Depression.

1935
Dennis Chavez becomes the first Hispanic U.S. senator.

1941
The U.S. enters World War II on Dec. 7.

1945
The United States joins the United Nations.

1945
World War II ends.

1929
Alexander Fleming develops penicillin.

1926
John Baird demonstrates his television system.

1935
Radar is invented.

1931
The Empire State Building (102 stories, 1,250 feet) is completed as the tallest in the world.

1938
Modern-type ballpoint pens are developed.

1938
The photocopy machine is produced.

1939
Dr. Charles Drew sets up first blood bank

1940
Enrico Fermi develops the nuclear reactor.

1925
Potato chips are produced in New York City.

1933
Albert Einstein immigrates to the U.S.

1947
Jackie Robinson becomes the first African American major-league baseball player.

1927
Wings wins the first Academy Award for motion pictures.

1931
"The Star-Spangled Banner" becomes the U.S. national anthem.

1936
Jesse Owens is first person to win four Olympic medals.

1938
Superman "Action Comics" are created.

1947
Anne Frank's *Diary of a Young Girl* is published.

123,202,624

132,164,569

1950	1955	1960	1965	1970

U.S. and World History

1950
The United States enters the Korean War.

1955
The Civil Rights movement begins when Rosa Parks refuses to move to the back of the bus.

1959
Alaska and Hawaii become states.

1954
The Korean War ends.

1962
Cesar Chavez starts the National Farm Workers Association.

1963
President John F. Kennedy is assassinated.

1965
U.S. troops are sent to Vietnam.

1969
Neil Armstrong and Buzz Aldrin are the first men on the moon.

Science and Inventions

1951
Fluoridated water is discovered to prevent tooth decay.

1954
Jonas Salk develops the polio vaccine.

1957
Russia launches the first satellite, *Sputnik I.*

1958
Stereo long-playing records are produced.

1960
First laser invented by Theodor Maiman.

1963
Cassette tapes are developed.

1971
The space probe *Mariner* maps the surface of Mars.

1974
The 110-story Sears Tower in Chicago is the tallest building in the U.S.

Literature and Life

1950
New York City is the world's largest city, with 8 million people.

1951
Fifteen million American homes have televisions.

1955
Disneyland opens.

1957
Elvis Presley is the most popular rock 'n' roll musician in the U.S.

1963
Martin Luther King, Jr., delivers "I Have a Dream" speech.

1964
The Beatles appear on *The Ed Sullivan Show.*

1970
The first Earth Day focuses on protecting the environment.

U.S. POPULATION:
151,325,798   179,323,175   203,302,031

| 1975 | 1980 | 1985 | 1990 | 1995 | 2000 |

1975
The Vietnam War ends.

1981
U.S. hostages are returned from Iran after 444 days.

1981
Sandra Day O'Connor becomes the first woman Supreme Court Justice.

1979
Iran seizes U.S. hostages.

1983
Sally Ride becomes the first U.S. woman in space.

1989
The Berlin Wall in Germany is torn down.

1991
The Soviet Union becomes a commonwealth of 10 independent nations.

1991
Persian Gulf War "Operation Desert Storm" begins.

1995
More than 23 million people living in the U.S. were born in other countries.

1976
The *Concorde* is the first supersonic passenger jet.

1977
Apple Computer produces first personal computer.

1984
Compact discs (CD's) are developed.

1981
Scientists identify AIDS.

1987
Dr. Ben Carson is first doctor to separate Siamese twins joined at the head.

1991
Scientists report a growing danger of a hole in the earth's ozone layer.

1993
Apple's Newton Writing Pad computer is produced.

1999
Scientists map the first chromosome.

1976
An earthquake in Tangshan, China, kills 240,000 people.

1976
The U.S. celebrates 200 years as a nation.

1979
Yellow ribbons symbolize support for return of U.S. hostages in iran

1986
Martin Luther King, Jr., Day is proclaimed a national holiday.

1987
The Whipping Boy wins the Newbery Award.

1993
In the New York City school district, more than 100 languages are spoken.

1994
Walk Two Moons wins the Newbery Award.

1994
Zlata's Diary: A Child's Life in Sarajevo, by a Bosnian teenager, is a bestseller in the U.S.

226,542,203   248,709,873

2000

U.S. and World History

2001
George W. Bush becomes first son of a president to take office since John Quincy Adams in 1825.

2001
Terrorist-flown planes destroy the World Trade Center in NYC and hit the Pentagon in Washington, D.C.

Science and Inventions

2000
The U.S. Food and Drug Administration approves a new glucose (blood sugar) monitor.

2001
President Bush allows limited funding for stem-cell research.

Literature and Life

2000
The U.S. population reaches 285 million.

2000
Wildfire burned over 7,000,000 acres of land in the western United States.

2002
Winter Olympics held at Salt Lake City, Utah.

U.S. POPULATION:
287,109,706

Credits

Page 19 Excerpt from *Hispanic, Female and Young: An Anthology,* edited by Phyllis Tashlik, copyright © 1994. Piñata Books, a division of Arte Publico Press.

Page 19 Reprinted with permission of Pocket Books, an imprint of Simon & Schuster Adult Publishing Group, from *A Crossing: A Cyclist's Journey Home* by Brian Newhouse. Copyright © 1998 by Brian Newhouse.

Page 20 Excerpt from *Anne Frank and me,* by Cherie Bennett and Jeff Gottesfeld, copyright © 2001. G.P. Putnam's Sons, a division of Penguin Putnam Inc.

Page 20 Excerpt from "One Last Time," by Gary Soto, copyright © 1985 from *Living Up the Street,* Bantam Dell Publishing. Used by permission of the author.

Page 21 Excerpt from *My Dog Skip* by Willie Morris, copyright © 1995 by Willie Morris; Illustrations copyright © 1995 by Mikhail Iventisky. Permission granted by Random House, Inc.

Page 21 Excerpt from *Wilma* by Wilma Rudolph, copyright © 1977 by Bud Greenspan. The New American Library, Inc., New York, New York.

Page 30 Excerpts from *How Writers Write* by Pamela Lloyd, copyright 1987 by Pamela Lloyd; Publisher, Thomas Nelson Australia.

Page 109 Excerpt from *The Talking Earth,* by Jean Craighead George, copyright © 1983 by Jean Craighead George. Reprinted by permission of HarperCollins Publishers.

Page 176 "Stopping By Woods On a Snowy Evening" from *The Poetry of Robert Frost* edited by Edward Connery Lathem. Copyright 1951 by Robert Frost. Copyright 1923, © 1969 by Henry Holt and Company, Inc.

Page 194 "Listening Lungs" by Dawn Stover, *Popular Science Magazine,* May 1997, Vol. 250, No. 5. Copyright © 1997 Popular Science.

Page 264 "Zipping Around," *A History of Us: All the People,* copyright © 1995 by Joy Hakim. Oxford University Press, Inc.

Page 264 Digital Stock Corporation. This photograph provided by Digital Stock Corporation, 750 Second Street, Encinatis, CA 92024, phone 800-545-4514.

Pages 266 and 268 From *Perspectives on Health,* by Leroy H. Getchell, Grover D. Pippin, and Jill W. Varnes. Copyright © 1996 by D.C. Heath and Company. All rights reserved. Reprinted by permission of McDougal Littell Inc.

Page 270 From *Kids Explore America's Hispanic Heritage* by Westridge Young Writers Workshop. Copyright © 1996. Published by John Muir Publications, Santa Fe, N.M.

Page 272 Digital Stock Corporation. These photographs provided by Digital Stock Corporation, 750 Second Street, Encinatis, CA 92024, phone 800-545-4514.

Page 287 *Roget's II Notebook Thesaurus,* copyright © 1997 by Houghton Mifflin Company. Adapted and reprinted by permission from *Roget's II Notebook Thesaurus.*

Page 289 *The American Heritage College Dictionary* copyright © 1997 by Houghton Mifflin Company.

Page 290 These excerpts are from *The University of Chicago Spanish Dictionary* edited by C. Castillo and O. Bond, revised and enlarged by D. Lincoln Canfield. © 1948, 1972, 1977, 1987 by the University of Chicago. Reprinted by permission of the University of Chicago Press.

Pages 436-437 and 480 From *The World Book Encyclopedia* © 1997 World Book, Inc. Reprinted by permission of the publisher.

Index

The **index** will help you find specific information in the handbook. Entries in italics are words from the "Commonly Misused Words" section.

A/an, 379
A lot, 379
Abbreviations, 369-370
　Acronyms, 345, 369
　Address, 370
　Capitalization of, 363
　Common, 370
　Initialisms, 369
　Punctuation of, 345
　State, 370
Abstract noun, 409, 411
Accept/except, 379
Acknowledgement, 240
Acronym, 345, 369
Acrostic poetry, 177
Action, story, 303
Action verbs, 66-67, 110, 417, 421, 424-425
Active learning, 1, 243-343
Active voice, 421
Addition, word problem, 452
Address,
　Abbreviations, 370
　Letters, 214-216
　Punctuation of, 347
Adjective, 408, 427-430
　Articles, 427
　Colorful, 111
　Common, 427
　Compound, 356, 428
　Demonstrative, 428
　Forms, 429
　Hyphenated, 356
　Indefinite, 428
　Kinds of, 428
　Predicate, 67, 428

Proper, 362, 427
　Punctuation of, 351
Adverb, 408, 430-431
　Conjunctive, 353
Advising, in groups, 57-60
Affect/effect, 379
Agreement,
　Antecedent/pronoun, 71-72
　Indefinite pronouns, 70
　Subject-verb, 69-70
　Unusual word order, 70
Air/heir, 385
All right/alright, 379
Alliteration, 175
Allowed/aloud, 379
Allusion, 114
Alphabet,
　Cursive, 439
　Manual (sign language), 435
　Manuscript, 438
Alphabet poetry, 177
Alphabetizing, library, 234, 237
Already/all ready, 379
Altogether/all together, 380
Amendments, Constitutional, 487-488
Amount/number, 380
Analogy, 117
Analyzing information, 247, 250
Anecdote, 42, 117
Animal facts, 441
Annual/biannual, 380
Ant/aunt, 380
Antagonist, 303
Antecedent, 71-72, 413
Antithesis, 114
Antonym, 286, 287
Anyone/any one, 380
Apostrophe, 359-360
Appendix, 240
Applying information, 246, 250
Appositives, punctuating, 352
Argumentation, 117
Arrangement, 117
　Of details, 48, 50, 86
　Of paragraphs, 87
Articles, 427
As/like, 387

Ascent/assent, 380
Assignments, completing, 343
Assonance, 175
Ate/eight, 380
Audience, 117
Aunt/ant, 380
Autobiography, 42, 302

Balance, 117
Bar graphs, 280
Bare/bear, 380
Base/bass, 381
Basics of life checklist, 37
"Be" verbs, 417
Be/bee, 381
Beginning, 117
    Of essay, 93, 96-97
    Paragraphs, 52, 84, 87, 93, 117, 202
    Of report, 202
    Of speech, 325
    Writing the, 52
Beside/besides, 381
Biannual/annual, 380
Bibliography, 205-206, 240
Bilingual dictionary, 290
Bill of Rights, 487
Biographical writing, 143-148
Biography, 42, 237, 302
Blew/blue, 381
Block style, letter, 438
Board/bored, 381
Body, 117
    Of a letter, 135, 138, 214
    Of a paragraph, 78, 79
    Writing the, 53
Book,
    Capitalization of titles, 363
    Parts of, 240
    Punctuation of titles, 361
Book review (report), 149-154
Brainstorming, 118
Brake/break, 381
Bring/take, 381
Browser, 232
Bulletin board (Internet), 232

Business letter, 211-216, 354
    Addressing the envelope, 216
    Guidelines, 213
    Parts of, 214-215
    Types, 212
By/buy, 381

Calendar, softcover, *inside front cover*
Call number, 237
Can/may, 382
Capital/capitol, 382
Capitalization, 362-366
    Abbreviations, 363
    Geographic names, 364-365
    Historical events, 362
Card catalog, 235, 236
Caricature, 114
Case (use), nouns, 412
Case (use), pronouns, 415
Cause and effect, 40, 48, 271
    Study-reading, 270-271
CD-ROM, 230, 462
Cell/sell, 382
Cent/sent/scent, 382
Central idea, 118
Character, 303
Characterization, 150, 303
Charts, reading, 277-284
    Five W's, 48, 132, 164
    KWL, 275
    Reading, 277-284
    Sensory, 48

Checklists,
    Basics of life, 37
    Editing and proofreading, 62
    Effective writing, 22
    Evaluating, 10
    Reading charts, 284
    Report, 207
    Response to writing, 60
    Revising, 55
    Study-reading, 276
    Writing explanation, 160

Choosing a subject, 35-42
  Topics, 8-9, 12, 35-42
  Writing process, 5, 6
Chose/choose, 382
Chronological order, 50, 86, 88
  Study-reading, 272-273
Cite/site/sight, 391
Class journal, 127
Classroom report, 195-207
  Bibliography, 205
  Model, 196-197
Classroom skills, 313-318
Clause,
  Dependent, 404
  Independent, 353, 404
  Punctuation, 350, 352-353
  Restrictive, nonrestrictive, 352
Clear thinking, 251-256
Cliche, 118
Climax, 304
Closing, 118
  Letter, 138, 214
  Paragraphs, 118
  Sentences, 78, 79, 118
Clothes/close, 382
Clustering, 36, 44, 50, 172, 198, 263, 337
Coarse/course, 382
Coherence, 118
Collecting, see *Details*
Collection sheets, 46-47
Collective noun, 410, 411
Colloquialism, 118
Colon, 354
Colorful words, using, 110-111
Colors poetry, 177
Combining sentences, 63, 73-76
Comedy, 302
Comma, 347-352
  In a series, 347
  Splice, 68, 350
Commercials, 312
Common, adjective, 427
Common, noun, 409
Commonly misused words, 379-394
Comparative form, adjectives, 429
Comparative form, adverbs, 431

Comparative suffixes, 295
Compare, 336
Comparison, arrangement by, 50, 88
Comparison organizer, 267
Complaint, letter of, 212
Complete predicate, 66, 403
Complete sentence, 66-67
Complete subject, 403
Complex sentence, 76, 406
Compound
  Adjective, 356, 428
  Noun, 360, 368, 410
  Predicate, 66, 75, 403
  Sentence, 66, 76, 350, 406
  Subject, 66, 69, 75, 403
  Verb, 66, 75, 403
  Word, 355
Computer, catalog, 235
Computers, 459-464
  Keyboard, 460-461
  Terms, 232, 462-464
  Using, 227-231
  Writing with, 23-26, 217-219
Concluding paragraph, 53, 87, 93
Concrete noun, 409
Concrete poetry, 177
Conflict, 304
Conjunction, 408, 433
Conjunctive adverb, 353
Connotation, 111
Consonance, 175
Constitution, U.S., 486
  Amendments, 487-488
Context, 286
Continuous tenses, 420
Contractions, 359
Contrast, 336
Contrast couplet, 177
Conversion table, metric, 445
Coordinates, map, 466
Coordinating conjunctions, 433
Copyright page, 240
Correcting, see *Revising; Editing*
  Preparing final copy, 15, 61-62, 84
Correction symbols, *inside back cover*
Correlative conjunctions, 433
Council/counsel, 383

Count nouns, 411
Course/coarse, 382
Creak/creek, 383
Creative thinking, 257-259
Creative writing, 169-185
Cursive alphabet, 439
Cycle diagram, 48, 269

D

Daily planner, 342
Dangling (misplaced) modifier, 72
Dash, 356
Dates, punctuation of, 347
Decimal/fraction table, 450
Decimal punctuation, 345
Decision making, 252
Declarative sentences, 407
Deer/dear, 383
Definition,
 Context clue, 286
 Guidelines for writing, 100
Demonstrative adjective, 428
Demonstrative pronoun, 416
Dependent clause, 404
Describe, 336
Description, 118
 Nonfiction reading, 262
Descriptive,
 Paragraph, 80
 Writing, see *Writing, modes of*
Desert/dessert, 353
Design, page, 24-25
Details,
 Arranging, 50
 Collecting, 8, 12, 43-50, 95, 189
 Kinds of, 85
 Personal, 85
 Sensory, 122, 189
 Strategies, 44-45
 Supporting, 122
Developing a portfolio, 27-30
Dew/do/due, 383
Dewey decimal system, 237
Diagrams,
 Cycle, 48, 269
 Flow, 279

Line, 48, 92, 278
 Picture, 278
 Venn, 48, 267
Dialogue, 118, 134, 304
 Journal, 127, 128
 Punctuation, 348, 357, 358
 Writing, 42
Diary, 127
Diction, 118
Dictionary, using, 288-300
 Bilingual, 290
 Personal, 291
 Prefixes, 293-294
 Roots, 296-300
 Sample page, 289
 Suffixes, 295
Die/dye, 383
Direct
 Address, 349
 Object, 67, 424
 Question, 346
Direct quotation, punctuation
 of, 357-358, 364
Division/multiplication table, 450
Documentation, in classroom
 report, 205-206
Doesn't/don't, 383
Domain, 232
Double negative, 72
Double subject, 71
Drama, 302
Dramatic monologue, 114
Dye/die, 383

E

Editing, 5, 7, 10, 15, 61-63
Editor, letter to, 212
Editorial, writing, 42, 166-167
Effect/affect, 379
Electronic sources, 227-232
E-mail, 42, 217-219, 232
Emigrate/immigrate, 385
Emphasis, 118, 356
Encyclopedias, 238
End rhyme, 176
Endings, writing, 53

Entry words, 287, 288-289, 290
Envelop, addressing, 216

Essay, the composition, 89-103
   Informational, 90-93
   Organizing, 87
   Outlining, 96
   Persuasive, 94-97
   Sample essays, 90, 94, 130, 135-136,
     144-145, 148, 153, 157-159
   Writing guidelines, 92-93, 95-97

Essay, literary term, 119, 302
Essay test, 336-338
Evaluate, 336
Evaluating information, 226, 249, 250
Evaluating writing, 10, 55, 60
Event, describing, 101
Evidence, using, 253
Exaggeration, 114
Except/accept, 379
Exclamation point, 346
Exclamatory sentence, 346, 407
Experiences, writing about, 41, 125-141
Explain, 40, 336
Explanation, describing, 102, 155-160
Explanatory phrase, 351
Exposition, 119, 304
Expository,
   Paragraph, 82
   Writing, see *Writing, modes of*
Extended definition, 119

Fable, 184, 302
Fact vs. opinion, 253
Falling action, 304-305
Family parables, 42
Fantasy, 302
Farther/further, 384
Feature, news, 161-165
Feminine nouns, 412
Fewer/less, 384
Fiction,
   Books, 237
   Literature, 301-305

   Science, 185
   Urban, 184
Figurative language, 119
Figure of speech, in poetry, 175
Fill-in-the-blanks test, 335
Final draft, 7, 15
Find/fined, 384
First draft, 5, 7, 9, 13, 51-56
First person, point of view, 305
First words, capitalizing, 364
Firsthand account, 161-165, 187-190
Five W's,
   Chart, 48, 132, 164
   Poetry, 178
Flashback, 114
Flow diagram, 279
Flower/flour, 384
Focus, 119
   Finding a, 49
   Lacking, 112
   Statement, 52
Foil, 304
Folktale, 302
For/four, 384
Foreign words, punctuation of, 361
Foreshadowing, 114
Foreword, 240
Form, 119
Forms of writing, 42
Fraction,
   Decimal table, 450
   Punctuation, 355
   Word problem, 453
Fragment sentence, 68
   Correction symbol, *inside back cover*
Free verse, 172-174
Freewriting, 37, 119
Friendly letter, 137-141
   Guidelines, 140-141
   Model, 139
   Parts of, 138
Future continuous tense, 420
Future perfect tense, 419
Future tense, 419

Gathering grid, 46, 199-200
Gender of nouns, 412
Generalization, 119
Geographic facts, 479
Geographic names,
    capitalization of, 364-365
Geography, 465-480
Gerund, 425
    Phrase, 405
Giving credit, 205-206
Glossary, 240
Goals, setting, 340
Good / well, 384
Government,
    Branches, 481
    Presidential succession, 485
    President's cabinet, 482
    Presidents/vice presidents, 484-485
    Rights and responsibilities, 483
Grammar, definition, 119

Graphic organizers, 48
    Cause and effect, 271
    Chronological order, 273
    Comparison/contrast, 267
    Description, 263
    KWL chart, 275
    Main idea/supporting details, 265
    Process, 269
    Senses, five, 189

Graphs,
    Bar, 280
    Line, 281
    Pie, 282
Group skills, writing, 319-322
    Advising, 57-60
Growth portfolio, 28

Guidelines,
    Biographical writing, 146-147
    Business letter, 213
    Classroom report, 198-204
    Editorial, 167
    E-mail, 218

Explanation, 156
Free-verse poetry, 172-174
Freewriting, 37
Friendly letters, 140-141
Informational essay, 92-93
Listening skills, 320, 330
News story, 163-165
Observation report, 189
Paragraphs, 84
Personal narrative, 132-133
Persuasive essay, 95-97
Preparing a speech, 324-327
Proposals, 220
Selecting a topic, 5, 6, 8, 12
Story writing, 182-183
Summary writing, 192
Thinking and writing, 250
Writing about literature, 151-152
Writing groups, 58-59

Haiku, 178
Hair / hare, 384
Hand signs, 435
Handwriting, 439
Have / of, 72, 388
Heading, letter, 138, 214
Heal / heel, 384
Hear / here, 385
Heard / herd, 385
Heir / air, 385
Helping verbs, 417
Hi / high, 385
Historical
    Fiction, 302
    Names, punctuation of, 362
    Time line, 489-500
Hole / whole, 385
Home page, 232
Homework hot lines, 343
Hour / our, 385
HTML, 232
HTTP, 232
Human interest, 163
Hyperbole, 115, 175
Hyphen, 355-356

Ideas for writing, 35-42
Identify, 336
Idiom, 119
   Understanding, 395-401
Illustration, arrangement by, 50
Immigrate/emigrate, 355
Imperative sentence, 407
Importance, arrangement by, 50, 86
Indefinite adjective, 428
Indefinite noun, 412
Indefinite pronoun, 70, 360, 416
Indenting, 78
Independent clause, 404
   Punctuation of, 353
Index, 240
Indirect
   Object, 67, 424
   Question, 346
   Quotation, 364
Infinitive, 425
   Phrase, 405
Information,
   Evaluating sources, 226
   Primary, 224-225
   Searching for, 234-241
   Secondary, 224
Informational essay, 90-93
Initialisms, 369
Initials, punctuation of, 345, 349
Inside address, 214
Interjections, 349, 408, 431
Internal rhyme, 176
International time zones, 480
Internet, 459
   E-mail, 45, 217-219, 232
   Searching for information, 45, 228-232
   Terms, 232
   World Wide Web, 228
Interrogative
   Pronoun, 416
   Sentence, 407
Interruptions, punctuation of, 348
Interviewing, 45, 164, 225
Intransitive verb, 425
Introduction, 240

Introductory clause, 350
Introductory paragraph,
   Lead paragraph, 163
   Opening paragraph, 52, 87, 93, 97
Introductory phrase, 350
Invented poetry, 177-178
Irony, 115
Irregular verb, 421-423
Issue, 120
Italics, 361
Its/it's, 385

Jargon, 120
Journal, 120
Journal writing, 38, 125-128
Juxtaposition, 120

Key, map, 465
Key words
   Combining sentences, 74
   Lecture notes, 315
   For test taking, 336
Keyboard, computer, 460-461
Keywords,
   CD-ROM, 230
   Computer catalog, 235
   For Internet search, 228
Knew/new, 385
Knight/night, 386
Knot/not, 386
Know/no, 386
Knows/nose, 386
KWL, study approach, 275

Language families, map, 436-437
Latitude and longitude, 466, 477-479
Lay/lie, 386
Lead, 163
Lead/led, 386
Learn/teach, 386
Learning log, 318
Leave/let, 387

Lecture notes, 315
Legend, map, 465
Less / fewer, 384
Letter, punctuation of plurals, 369

Letters,
   Addressing the envelope, 216
   Business letters, 211-216
   Friendly letters, 137-141
   Letter of complaint, 212
   Letter of opinion, 212
   Letter of request, 212
   Writing letters, 140-141, 213

Levels of thinking, 243-250
Library, 233-241
   Card catalog, 236
   Computer catalog, 235
   Readers' Guide, 241
   Reference section, 238-239
Life map, 39
Like / as, 387
Limerick, 178
Limiting the subject, 120
Line diagrams, 48, 92, 278
Line graphs, 281
Linking verbs, 67, 417
Linking words, 88
List, in essay tests, 336
List poetry, 178
List, punctuation of, 354
Listening, role of, 59
Listening skills, 320, 330
Listing, 37, 44, 269
Literal, 120
Literary terms, 302-305
Literature,
   Elements of, 303-305
   Response to, 149-154
   Types of, 302-303
Loaded words, 120
Local color, 115
Local news, 163
Location, arrangement by, 50, 86
Log on, 232
Logic, 120
Loose / lose / loss, 387

M

Made / maid, 387
Mail / male, 387
Main character, 304
Main ideas,
   Finding, 193
   Graphic organizer, 265
Main / mane / Maine, 387
Managing time, 341-342
Manual alphabet, 435
Manuscript alphabet, 438
Mapping to study, 261-276
Maps,
   Coordinates, 466
   Index to world maps, 477-479
   Language families, 436-437
   Latitude and longitude, 466
   Legend, 465
   Map scale, 465
   Time zones, 480
   World, 467-476
Masculine nouns, 412
Matching test, 334
Math skills, 449-458
   Addition, 452
   Decimals, 450
   Fractions, 450, 453
   Metric system, 443-444
   Multiplication/division table, 450
   Prime numbers, 449
   Roman numerals, 450
   Symbols, 449
   Tables of weights/measures, 443-445,
      448
   Terms, 454-458
   Word problems, 451-453
May / can, 382
Measures, weights, 443-445, 448
Measuring, 443-445, 448
Meat / meet, 387
Memory, details, 85
Memory writing, 129-136
Metal / medal, 388
Metaphor, 115, 175
Methods of arrangement, 50
Metric conversion table, 445

Metric system, 443-444
Middle, see *Body*
Miner / minor, 388
Minor character, 304
Misplaced modifier, 72
Modal verbs, 418
Modeling, 108-109
Modes, see *Writing, modes of*
Modifier, 111, 121, 404
Mood, 304
Moral, 304
Moral / morale, 388
Morning / mourning, 388
Multiple-choice test, 335
Multiplication/division table, 450
Mystery, 185
Myth, 42, 180-181, 302

Narrative, 40, 121
  Paragraph, 81
  Writing, see *Writing, modes of*
Narrative, personal, 121, 129-136
Narrator, 304
Netiquette, 229, 232
Neuter nouns, 412
New / knew, 385
News viewing, 308-309
News writing, 161-167
Night / knight, 386
No / know, 386
Noncount nouns, 411
Nonfiction,
  Book, parts of, 240
  Literature, 237, 302
  Patterns, 262-273
Nonrestrictive phrase/clause, 352
Nonstandard language, see *Usage*
Nose / knows, 386
Not / knot, 386
Note cards, speech, 327
Note taking, 313-318
  Learning logs, 318
  Lectures, 315
  Nonfiction, 262-273
  Reading, 316

Noun, 408, 409-412
  Abstract/concrete, 409
  Case, see *Use of* below
  Collective, 410
  Common, 409
  Compound, 360, 368, 410
  Count/noncount, 411
  Gender, 412
  Number of, 410
  Phrase, 405
  Plurals of, 367-368
  Possessives, 359-360
  Proper, 362, 409
  Specific, 110, 410
  Use of, 412

Noun-forming suffixes, 295
Novel, 302
Number,
  Of nouns, 410
  Of pronouns, 413
  Of verbs, 421
Number / amount, 380
Number, shift in, 69-71
Numbers, punctuating, 347, 354, 355
Numerals, Roman, 450
Numerals, usage, 371
Numerical prefixes, 294

Oar / or / ore, 388
Object,
  Complement, 67
  Direct, 67, 424
  Indirect, 67, 424
Object, describing an, 100
Object noun, 412
Object of preposition, 432
Object pronoun, 415
Objective, 121
Objective tests, 334-335
Objective writing, 121
Observation report, 187-190
Of / have, 72, 388
Omniscient point of view, 305
One / won, 388

Onomatopoeia, 176
Opinion,
Editorial, 42, 166-167
Essay, 94-97, 103
Letter of, 212
Supporting and writing, 253-255
Oral history, 42

Organization,
Graphic, 46-48, 50, 262-275
Ideas, 86
Methods of, 50
Paragraphs in reports, 87
Sentences in paragraphs, 86
Study-reading, 262-275

Organizers, graphic, 46-48, 262-275
Our / hour, 385
Outline, 336
Sentence, 96
Topic, 96
Overnight folders, 343
Overstatement, 115
Oxymoron, 115

Pain / pane, 388
Pair / pare / pear, 389
Paradox, 115

Paragraph, 77-88
Basic parts, 52-53, 78-79
Beginnings, 52, 78, 79
Details, 85
Development, 53
Endings, 53, 78, 79
In extended writing, 87, 89-103
Model paragraphs, 52-53, 75, 80-83
Organizing, 86-87
Topic sentence, 52, 78, 79, 123
Transition/linking words, 82, 87, 88
Types, 80-83
Well-written sentences, 63, 65-72
Writing guidelines, 84

Parallelism, 115
Parentheses, 361
Parodies, 42
Participle, 425
Phrase, 405
Parts of a book, nonfiction, 240
Parts of speech, 408-433
Dictionary labels, 288-289
Passive voice, 421
Past continuous tense, 420
Past / passed, 389
Past perfect tense, 419
Past tense, 419
Patterns,
Fiction, 185
Nonfiction, 262-273
Poetry, 177-178
Sentence, 67
Peace / piece, 389
Perfect tenses, 419
Period, 345
Periodic table of the elements, 442
Person,
First/third, point of view, 305
Of pronoun, 414
Shift in, 72
Person, describing, 98
Personal dictionary, 291
Personal narrative, 121, 129-136
Personal / personnel, 389
Personal portfolio, 28
Personal pronouns, 413, 414
Personal research, 45, 195-207
Personal writing, 125-141
Friendly letters, 137-141
Journal writing, 38, 125-128
Narratives, 129-136
Personification, 116, 175
Persuading writing guidelines, 95-97, 103
Persuasion, 121
Persuasive
Essay, 94-97, 103
Paragraph, 83
Writing, see *Writing, modes of*
Photo essays, 42

Phrase, 405
  Appositive, 352
  Combining with, 75
  Explanatory, 351
  Introductory, 350
  Noun, 405
  Prepositional, 405, 432
  Restrictive, nonrestrictive, 352
  Verb, 405
  Verbal, 405
Picture diagram, 278
Pie graphs, 282
Piece/peace, 389
Place, describing, 99
Plagiarism, 121, 205
Plain/plane, 389
Planets, 446-447
Planners,
  Daily, 342
  Weekly, 342
Planning
  Sheets, 342
  Skills, 339-343
  Speeches, 324-327
  Writing, 49
Play, 303
Plot, 150, 182, 304
Plot line, 304-305
Plurals, 359, 367-369, 410, 413, 414
Poetic devices, 116
Poetry, 169-178, 303
  Free-verse, 172-174
  Invented, 177-178
  Techniques, 175-176
  Writing, 172-174
Point of view, 121, 305
Pore/pour/poor, 389
Portfolio, developing, 27-30
Positive form,
  Adjectives, 429
  Adverbs, 431
Possessive case, 412, 415
Possessive noun, 412
Possessive pronoun, 415
Possessives, forming, 359-360
Postal abbreviations, 370
Postscript, 141

Preamble, U.S. Constitution, 486
Predicate adjective, 67, 428
Predicate noun, 67, 412
Predicate of a sentence, 66, 402, 403
Preface, 240
Prefixes, list of, 293-294
  Hyphenated, 356
  Numerical, 294
Preposition, 408, 432
Prepositional phrase, 405, 432
Present continuous tense, 420
Present perfect tense, 419
Present tense, 419
Presidents, United States, 484-485
  President's cabinet, 482
  Succession to, 485
Prewriting, 5, 6, 8, 12, 35-42, 49-50
Primary sources, 224-225
Prime numbers, 449
Principal/principle, 390
Problem solving, 256
  Word problems, 451-453
Process,
  Definition, 121
  List, 48, 269
  One writer's, 11-16
  Pattern of organization, 268
  Writing, 5-7
Profile, 42
Prompts for writing, 41

Pronoun, 408, 413-416
  Agreement, 71
  Antecedent, 413
  Case, see *Use of* below
  Indefinite, 70
  Number, 413
  Object, 415
  Person of, 414
  Personal, 413, 414
  Possessive, 360, 415
  Problems, 71
  Reference, 71
  Shift, 72
  Subject, 415
  Types, 416
  Use of, 415

Pronunciation, 288-289
Proofreading, 61-63
　Marks, *inside back cover*
Proper adjective, 362, 427
Proper noun, 362, 409
Proposals, 220-221
Prose, 121, 303
Prose and poetry, 170-171
Protagonist, 305
Prove, 336
Publishing, 5, 7, 16, 31-33
Pun, 116
Punctuation, marking, 345-361
Purpose, 121

Quest pattern, 185
Question mark, 346
Questions,
　Offbeat, 44
　Tag, 346, 407
　What if? 259
Quiet / quit / quite, 390
Quotation marks, 357-358
Quotations, punctuating, 354, 357-358

Raise / rays / raze, 390
Rambling sentence, 68
Readers' Guide, 241
Reading schedule, 341

Reading and studying, 261-276
　Context, 256
　Diagrams, 278-279
　Graphs, 280-282
　Notes, 262-273, 291, 316
　Patterns of nonfiction, 262-273
　Poetry, 176
　Prefix, suffix, root (lists), 293-300
　Previewing, 276
　Strategies, 274-275
　Symbols and charts, 277-284
　Tables, 283
　Vocabulary, 285-300

Realism, 303
Recalling information, 244, 250
Red / read, 390
Reference books, 238-241, 287-290
Reference, pronouns, 71
Reflexive pronoun, 416
Regular verbs, 421
Relative pronoun, 416
Repetition, 176

Report, the classroom, 195-207
　Bibliography, 205
　Checklist, 207
　Observation, 187-190
　Organizing, 87
　Sample note cards, 201
　Sample report, 196-197
　Summary, 154, 191-194

Request, letter of, 212
Research, personal, 45, 195-207
Researching, 45
Resolution, 304
Responding,
　Skills, 322
　To writing, 58-60
Response journal, 127
Response to literature, 149-154
Restrictive phrases/clauses, 352
Review, book, 149-154
Review, term, 336
Revising, 5, 7, 9, 14, 54-56
　Checklist, 55
Revision, 121
　Checklist, 55
Rhyme, 176
Rhythm, 176
Right / write / rite, 390
Rising action, 304
Road / rode / rowed, 390
Role, group advising,
　Of author, 58
　Of listener, 59
Roman numerals, 450
Roots, list of, 296-300
Run-on sentence, 68

S

Salutation, 138, 214, 354
Sarcasm, 116
Satire, 116
Scary story, 184
Scene / seen, 391
Schedules,
  Chores, 341
  Reading, 341
Science, 441-448
Science fiction, 185, 303
Sea / see, 391
Seam / seem, 391
Searching and shaping a subject,
  6, 8-9, 12, 36-37
Secondary sources, 224
Selecting a subject, 35-42
  Strategies, 36-37
  Topics, 8-9, 12, 35-42
  Writing process, 5, 6
Sell / cell, 382
Selling methods, 312
Semicolon, 353
Sending your letter, 216
Sensory detail, 85, 122
  Chart, 48
Sent / scent / cent, 382

Sentence, 402-407
  Agreement, 69-70
  Arrangement, 67, 106
  Beginnings, 63
  Closing, 78, 79
  Combining, 63, 73-76
  Complex, 76, 406
  Composing, 65-76
  Compound, 66, 76, 350, 406
  Errors, 68
  Fragment, 68
  Kinds, 407
  Modeling, 108-109
  Outline, 96
  Parts, 66, 402-405
  Patterns, 67
  Problems, 71-72
  Punctuation, 345-346

  Rambling, 68
  Run-on, 68
  Simple, 406
  Styling, 63, 106
  Topic, 52, 78-79, 123
  Types, 406
  Variety, 63, 105-112
  Writing, 65-72, 105-112

Series, words in a, 74, 347, 351, 353
Set / sit, 391
Setting, 150, 305
Sew / so / sow, 391
Shift in, number, 69-71
Shift in, person of pronoun, 72
Short story, 303
  Characteristics of, 179
  Model, 180-181
  Sampler, 184-185
  Writing, guidelines, 182-183
Showcase portfolio, 28
Sight / cite / site, 391
Sign language, 435
Signature, 138, 214
Signs, hand, 435
Signs, traffic, 440
Simile, 116, 175
Simple
  Predicate, 66, 403
  Sentence, 406
  Subject, 66, 403
Sit / set, 391
Site / sight / cite, 391
Slang, 122
Slice of life, selling method, 312
Solar system, 446-447
Solving problems, 256
Some / sum, 391
Son / sun, 392
Sore / soar, 392
Sources,
  Citing, 205
  Electronic, 227-232
  Evaluating, 226, 249
  Library, 233-241
  Primary, 224-225
  Secondary, 224

Speaking and listening skills, 323-330
Specific details, 26-27, 85, 106, 110-111
Speech skills,
  Delivery, 329
  Organization, 324-327
  Planning, 324-327
  Sample, 328
  Writing, 328
Spelling,
  Commonly misspelled words, 372-377
  Dictionary, 285-289
  Irregular plurals, 369
  Rules, 378
Spontaneous writing, 122
SQ3R, study approach, 274
States, abbreviations, 370
Stationary/stationery, 392
Steal/steel, 392
Story writing, 179-185
  Guidelines, 182-183
  Map, 47
  Model story, 180-181
  Patterns, 185
  Short story sampler, 184-185
Structure, 122
Student response sheet, 60
Study-reading, 261-276
  Checklist, 276
  KWL, 275
  Nonfiction, 262-273
  SQ3R, 274
  Strategies, 274-275
Study skills, 261-343
  Listening, 320, 330
  Literature, 149-154
  Managing time, 341-342
  Note taking, 313-318
  Speaking, 324-329
  Study-reading, 261-276
  Test taking, 332
  Viewing, 307-312
  Vocabulary, 285-300
Study spots, 343
Style, 122
Style, writing with, 105-112

Subject noun, 412
Subject pronoun, 415
Subject, sentence, 402-403
  Complete, 403
  Compound, 66, 69, 75, 403
  Double, 71
  Simple, 66, 403
  Understood, 407, see *Imperative sentence*
Subject-verb agreement, 69-70
Subjective, 122
Subjects, writing, 40-41
  Searching and shaping, 6, 8-9, 12
  Selecting guidelines, 35-42
Subordinating conjunctions, 433
Succession to the presidency, 485
Suffixes, list of, 295
  Comparative, 295
  Hyphenated, 356
  Noun-forming, 295
Sum/some, 391
Summarize, term, 336
Summary, 122
Summary, writing the, 191-194
  In an essay test, 337-338
  Report, 154
Sun/son, 392
Superlative form,
  Adjectives, 429
  Adverbs, 431
Supporting details, 122
Surprise ending, 305
Syllable divisions, 288, 355
Symbol, 122
  Correction, *inside back cover*
  Math, 449
  Reading, 277-284
Synonym, 286, 287, 288-289
Syntax, 122
Synthesizing information, 248, 250

T

Table of contents, 240
Table organizer, 265
Tables, reading, 283
Tag question, 346, 407

Tail / tale, 392
Take / bring, 381
Tall tales, 42, 303
Teach / learn, 386
Telecommunications, 232
Television viewing, 307-312
Commercials, 312
News, 308-309
Specials, 310-311
Tense of verbs, 419-420
Test, essay, 336-338
Test, objective, 334-335
Test-taking skills, 331-338
Than / then, 392
That / who / which, 394
Their / there / they're, 392
Theme, 123, 150, 305
Thesaurus, using, 287
Thesis statement, 123, see *Topic sentence*
Thinking clearly, 251-256
Thinking creatively, 257-259
Thinking and writing, 243-250
Third person, point of view, 305
Threw / through, 392
Time line, history, 489-500
Graphic organizer, 48, 273
Study-reading, 272-273
Time management, 341-342
Time, punctuation of, 354, 361
Time-zone map, 480
Time zones, 480
Timely news, 163
Title page, 240
Titles, 56
Capitalization of, 357, 363
Punctuation of, 357, 361
Titles of people, 363
Punctuation, 349
To / too / two, 393
Tone, 123, 305
Topic, 123
Outlines, 96
Sentence, 52, 78-79, 123
Topics, writing,
Guidelines for selecting, 35-42
Sample, 40-41

Total effect, 305
Traffic signs, 440
Tragedy, 303
Traits,
Of effective writing, 17-22
Of good workplace writing, 210
Transition, 123
Transitions, 88
Paragraph, 82, 87, 88
Transitive verb, 424
Travelogues, 42
Trite, 123
True/false test, 334
Two / to / too, 393
Two-syllable adjectives, 429

Unclear thinking, 254-255
Underlining, as italics, 361
Understanding literature, 301-305
Understanding, thinking, 244, 250
Understatement, 116
Understood subject, 407, see *Imperative sentence*
United States,
Constitution, 486-488
Government, 481-485
History, 489-500
Map, 469
Presidents and vice presidents, 484-485
Unity, 123
Universal, 123
Urban fiction, 184
URL, 232
Usage, 123
Usage and commonly misused words, 379-394
Usage labels, 288
Usenet, 229, 232
Using maps, 465-480
Using the right word, 379-394

Vain/vane/vein, 393
Variety of sentence structure, 63, 105-112
Vary/very, 393
Venn diagram, 48, 267

Verb, 408, 417-426
  Action, 67, 417, 424-425
  "Be" verbs, 417
  Compound, 66, 75
  Helping, 417
  Intransitive, 425
  Irregular, 421, 422-423
  Linking, 67, 417
  Modal, 418
  Number, 421
  Phrase, 405
  Plural, 421
  Predicate in a sentence, 66, 402, 403
  Principal parts, 422-423
  Regular, 421
  Singular, 421
  Specific, 110
  Tense, 419-420
  Transitive, 424
  Two-word, 426
  Types, 417-418
  Voice, 421

Verbals, 405, 425
Verse, 169-178
Very/vary, 393
Vice presidents, United States, 484-485
Viewing skills, 307-312
Vivid details, 110-111
Vocabulary,
  Context, 286
  Improving, 285-300
  New words, 292
  Prefixes, suffixes, roots, 293-300
Voice,
  Engaging, 18, 20
  Verb, 421

Waist/waste, 393
Wait/weight, 393
Wear/where, 394
Weather/whether, 394
Web, 36, 50, 172, 198, 263, 337
Web site, 42, 232
Week/weak, 393
Weekly planner, 342
Weights and measures, 443-445, 448
Well/good, 384
Which/witch, 394
Who/which/that, 394
Who/whom, 394
Whole/hole, 385
Who's/whose, 394
Won/one, 388
Wood/would, 394
Word
  Families, 292
  Order, unusual, 70
  Parts, 292
  Pictures, studying, 277-284
  Problems, 451-453
  Processor, 459, 460-461
  Search, on Internet, 228-232
  Using the right, 379-394
Word choice, 18
  Specific, 110-111
Wordy sentence, 71
Workplace writing, 209-221
  Business letters, 211-216
  E-mail, 217-219
  Proposals, 220-221
Works cited, 205-206
World
  Maps, 467-476
  Time zones, 480
  Wide Web, 228, 232
Write/right/rite, 390
Writer/listener roles, 58-59
Writing,
  Essays, 89-103
  Forms, 42
  Guidelines, 8-10
  Paragraphs, 77-88

Prompts, 41
Sample subjects, 40
Sentences, 65-76
Techniques, 114-116
Terms, 117-123
To learn, 4, 316, 318
With computers, 23-26, 217-219
With style, 105-112
Writing assignments, correction
symbols, *inside back cover*
Writing file of ideas, 38-39
Writing forms,
Biographical, 143-148
Business letter, 211-216
Classroom reports, 195-207
Explanations, 102, 155-160
Friendly letter, 137-141
Informational essay, 90-93
Journals, 125-128
About literature, 149-154
News, 161-167
Observation reports, 187-190
Personal narrative, 129-136
Persuasive essay, 94-97, 103
Poems, 169-178
Stories, 179-185
Summaries, 154, 191-194
Writing group guidelines, 58-60
Writing in the workplace (traits), 210

Writing, modes of

DESCRIPTIVE

Details, 8, 12, 43-50, 122
Paragraph, 80
Person, place, object, event, 98-101
see *Poetry*
Test-taking 336-338
Word choice, 110-111

EXPOSITORY

Biographical, 143-148
Book reviews, 149-154
Business letters, 211-216, 354
Classroom reports, 195-207
Comparison/contrast, 266-267
Essays, 90-93

Explanations, 102, 155-160
Interviews, 45, 225
Learning logs, 318
News stories, 161-167
Note taking, 313-318
Observation reports, 187-190
Outlining, 96, 336
Paragraph, 82
Proposals, 220-221
Research papers, 195-207
Response to literature, 149-154
Speeches, 323-330
Study-reading writing, 261-276
Summaries, 154, 191-194
Test-taking, 336-338

NARRATIVE

About an event (narrating), 101
Autobiographical, 42, 302
Journals, 38, 120, 125-128
Letters, friendly, 137-141
Paragraph, 81
Personal, 121, 129-136
Stories, 179-185

PERSUASIVE

Essays, 94-97, 103
Letter,
Complaint, 212
Opinion, 212
Request, 212
Paragraph, 83
Proposals, 220-221
Thinking and writing, 243-250

Writing process, 5-7, 11-16
Choosing a subject, 5, 6, 8-9, 12,
35-42
Collecting details, 8, 12, 43-50
Editing and proofreading, 5, 7, 10,
15, 61-63
First draft, 5, 7, 9, 13, 51-56
Revising, 5, 7, 9, 14, 54-56

Your/you're, 394